Unknowing

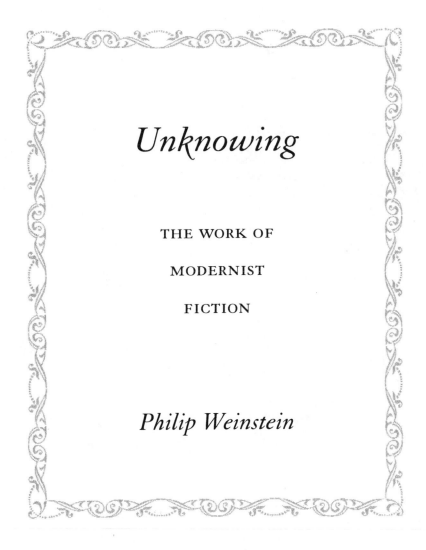

Unknowing

THE WORK OF

MODERNIST

FICTION

Philip Weinstein

CORNELL UNIVERSITY PRESS

ITHACA AND LONDON

First published 2005 by Cornell University Press
First printing, Cornell Paperbacks, 2005

Printed in the United States of America

Library of Congress Cataloging-in-Publication Data

Weinstein, Philip M.
    Unknowing : the work of modernist fiction / Philip Weinstein.
        p. cm.
    Includes bibliographical references and index.
    ISBN-13: 978-0-8014-4370-1 (cloth : alk. paper)
    ISBN-10: 0-8014-4370-9 (cloth : alk. paper)
    ISBN-13: 978-0-8014-8973-0 (pbk. : alk. paper)
    ISBN-10: 0-8014-8973-3 (pbk. : alk. paper)
    1. Fiction—20th century—History and criticism.
2. Modernism (Literature)   3. Knowledge, Theory of, in
literature.   4. Kafka, Franz, 1883–1924—Criticism and
interpretation.   5. Proust, Marcel, 1871–1922—Criticism and
interpretation.   6. Faulkner, William, 1897–1962—Criticism and
interpretation.   I. Title.
    PN3503.W393 2005
    809.3'9112'0904—dc22   2005016066

Cornell University Press strives to use environmentally responsible suppliers and materials to the fullest extent possible in the publishing of its books. Such materials include vegetable-based, low-VOC inks and acid-free papers that are recycled, totally chlorine-free, or partly composed of nonwood fibers. For further information, visit our website at www.cornellpress.cornell.edu.

Cloth printing   10 9 8 7 6 5 4 3 2 1
Paperback printing   10 9 8 7 6 5 4 3 2 1

The sense of our whole effort lies in affirming not that
the other forever escapes knowing, but that there is no meaning
in speaking here of knowledge or ignorance.

LEVINAS

. as though coinciding were the ultimate secret of communication,
and as though truth were only disclosure . . .

LEVINAS

Contents

Acknowledgments   *ix*

Introduction   1
1. Leaping: Kierkegaard's *Fear and Trembling*   11

Part One. Knowing: "Sapere Aude!"—The West Dares to Know   **21**
2. Genealogy of Realism: An Enlightenment Narrative in Five Stages   23
3. Anatomy of Realism: Coming to Know, from Defoe to Dostoevsky   49

Part Two. Unknowing: The Work of Modernist Fiction   **77**
4. Plotting Modernism: Freud   79
5. Uncanny Space: Flaubert to Beckett   95
6. Unbound Time: Proust, Kafka, Faulkner   121
7. Subject and/as Other: Kafka, Proust, Faulkner   163

**Part Three. Beyond Knowing: Postmodern and Postcolonial
Flights from Gravity**   **195**
8. Adventures in Hyperspace   197
9. Urban Nightmare and City Dreams: Rilke and Calvino   206
10. Passage and Passing: Forster and Rushdie   217
11. Arrest and Release: Faulkner, García Márquez, Morrison   231

Conclusion: Acknowledging—Modernism's Weak Messianic Power   252

Notes   *261*
Index   *303*

Acknowledgments

This book's conclusion—titled "Acknowledging"—reflects on the differences between knowing and acknowledging, and on the difficulty of making conceptual and emotional room for a range of others whom we cannot see and know, yet who may bear fundamentally on our being. In contrast, the pleasure of these acknowledgments inheres in my gratefully seeing (in my mind's eye), and knowing, a number of people and institutions whose generosity has made my work possible.

Swarthmore College has nourished my work for over three decades—in its liberal sabbatical policy and in the intensity of the educational mission to which it is dedicated. One's intellectual life is recurrently on the line at Swarthmore—in the classes and seminars one teaches—and I have learned how precious it is to be urged (challenged, sometimes cornered) to make my ideas persuasive, and to hear what is persuasive in others.' I thank, as well, the National Endowment for the Humanities; without their Fellowship in 2002–2003 this long-simmering book might never have come to a boil.

I also record my gratitude to *Etudes Faulkneriennes* and to Duke University Press, for permission to reprise work that first appeared under their auspices. Some of the commentary on Faulkner in chapter 6—"Unbound Time"—was earlier published in *Etudes Faulkneriennes* I (Rennes, 1996) and *Etudes Faulkneriennes* II (Rennes, 2000). Likewise, a version of chapter 10 first appeared in *Look Away: The U.S. South in New World Studies*, ed. Jon Smith and Deborah Cohn (Durham: Duke University Press, 2004). In addition, I acknowledge permission, granted by Random House and Chatto &

Windus, to cite extensively from the Scott Moncrieff and Kilmartin translation of Marcel Proust's *Remembrance of Things Past*, 3 volumes (1981). Likewise, I am grateful to the Israel Museum in Jerusalem and the Artists Rights Society in New York for permission to use a copy of Paul Klee's *Angelus Novus* for the cover of my book.

It has taken a long time to compress what I have come to know about modernism into the form of this book's argument. (The developing manuscript went through four earlier titles before I found my way into the final one.) A concern with locating the right venue arose once I realized there would actually *be* a book. I am grateful to Bernie Kendler of Cornell University Press for entering swiftly into the generative ideas of my project and supporting its various forms, from a six-page précis to a completed book.

A number of colleagues have provided indispensable readings of my work. Robert Roza (French scholar, friend, and former colleague) engaged the emerging book chapter by chapter, probing and speculating on its claims. David Riggs and Richard Eldridge—the one a Renaissance Literature scholar, the other an expert in modern philosophy—distanced themselves from their own fields and gave my argument the kind of hearing it rarely gets from professional neighbors. Ian Baucom and Charles Altieri supported the project during its incubation process; their own work (Baucom's on Forster and on postcolonialism, Altieri's on modernist protocols) has been instrumental for mine. Philip Fisher (with whom I first discussed the problematics of modernism when we were graduate students together) and John Matthews (fellow Faulknerian and the most demanding of sympathetic readers) read the manuscript with invaluable attention to what was achieved—and not yet achieved—in it.

I am lucky in having a further category of people to acknowledge: my family. My twin brother, Arnold, entered into the explicit and implicit investments of the book—from its earliest drafts to its final form—granting me my differences, giving me the good of his. My wife, Penny (who has read and responded to each chapter in manuscript form), is so pervasively the emotional and intellectual company I keep that—as Flaubert said in another context—she is everywhere present in this book, if nowhere visible. Finally, although my study is focused on modernism's recognition that we cannot know what tomorrow will bring, I dedicate this book to my three grandchildren who may—who knows?—one day read it: Marina, Nathaniel, and Eliza Hartnick.

Unknowing

Introduction

What is at stake when a group of major modernist writers centers their fiction on *unknowing?* Decades of reflection about Western modernism reduce to the implications of this question. Modernist and unknowing in relation to what premodernist commitment to knowing? Modernist and unknowing in relation to what postmodern and postcolonial stances toward knowing? What began as microcosmic attention to certain compelling fictional effects among a handful of twentieth-century writers escalated, to my surprise, to a speculative, macrocosmic mapping of one genre of Western imagination: a sort of metahistory of the novel.

This book redefines the project of Western modernism by arguing that the primary work of three of its central novelists—Franz Kafka, Marcel Proust, and William Faulkner—consists in strenuous acts of unknowing.[1] Their art represents human experience outside the protocols of Western knowing. Those protocols, descending from tenets and practices of Enlightenment, inform the preponderance of European realist fiction. By contrast, Kafka, Proust, and Faulkner join Sigmund Freud to make a quartet of twentieth-century explorers of unknowing. They each attend to the blind spots of this realist model of achieved knowledge and self-knowledge. Though it took the different cultural situations of Prague, Paris, and rural Mississippi to produce them, the fiction of each found its way into the same unthought of Western thinking. Each determined that inherited cultural models of maturation—of coming to know other and self—misrepresented the drama of the modern subject.[2]

I unpack *unknowing* by exploring the interrelation of three of its crucial terms: *subject*, *space*, and *time*. *Coming to know* enacts an Enlightenment premise of rational correspondence between the individual and the world. Thanks to the lawfulness of time and space, a subject learns to map the outer world accurately and, thereby, to achieve inner orientation as well. Personal identity gets confirmed by way of this arduously achieved knowledge of exterior entities. On this model, the subject who would know and the object to be known are assumed to share an implicit structural affinity—the latter destined to enter the embrace of the former. Indeed, realism cannot proceed without this assumption. Yet realism denies that it assumes anything, that the "marriage" it celebrates at the end has been secretly arranged before the beginning, that a preemptive alliance between knowing subject and knowable object, mappable space and enabling time, has already been silently set in place. Instead, realism proposes—and this is its master stroke—that the representational field of space and time and others that its protagonist moves through corresponds to the objective world itself. Its stage thus artfully configured to enable the coming resolutions, realism denies that it has stacked the deck (or pre-arranged the cards), insisting instead on its protagonist as a free-standing subject moving within a lawful and indifferent frame.

This insistence on free-standing subjectivity is precisely what modernist fiction subverts. It does so in order to reveal the human subject as situational, space/time dependent, capable of coming to know *only* if the props that enable knowing are already in place. If, however, a writer disrupts the subject's compact for negotiating objects in space and time, the subject loses its orientational grasp on others and, in so doing, loses its own coherent identity. The work of Kafka, Proust, and Faulkner dramatizes such an uncohering. In their work, the narrative props that underwrite the subject/space/time drama of coming to know are refused. In the place of knowing, there operates a dynamic of shock; in the place of developmental life-histories, there occur unmastered moments. When space becomes uncanny rather than lawful (no longer open to orientation and ownership), when time loses its negotiability (no longer linear/progressive), things become unfamiliar; the subject immersed in them becomes unfamiliar as well. The represented world itself exits from its former "liberal" condition as knowable, masterable, conducive to progress. These are flashpoints both of my novelists' work and of that larger subversion of Western cultural forms that we think of as modernism.

Although this book might open with the Enlightenment premises that my modernist writers refuse, I begin by "leaping" into arguably the first protomodern narrative of failed knowing: Søren Kierkegaard's *Fear and Trembling* (1843). Live or tell, Jean-Paul Sartre's *Nausea* declares a century later: live your life as an unknowable movement through as yet unencountered time, or tell it as a narrative already end-supplied and heading toward its goal.[3] But already in Kierkegaard the Abraham drama transforms from a comfortable, end-assured "telling" (a model of temporal development: Abraham the promised father of his people) to an intolerable "living" (Abraham the going-to-be murderer), the exposed subject undergoing an ordeal of the unresolved moment that Kierkegaard refuses to bring to resolution. It takes forever to get to, and get past, the sacrifice on Mount Moriah. No one (not Abraham, nor Kierkegaard, nor the reader) can pacify an intolerable *now* that has been sprung free from the clarifying knowledge of what is to come later.

The clarifying knowledge of what is to come later: coming to know, gradually refining one's identity within orientational space and linear time, is the bread and butter of Western fiction. No social cohesion can occur without normative scripts for how individuals are to sustain identity in space and time; as the Frankfurt School critic Theodor Adorno has claimed, "identity is the primal category of ideology."[4] Modernist "unknowing" operates, precisely, as an attack on the confidence in Western norms for securing identity and funding the career of the liberal subject. After the "leap" into Kierkegaard, part 1 attends to the emergence of Western norms of "knowing" by drawing on several representative thinkers.[5] I propose an "Enlightenment narrative" in five stages: the (Baconian) establishment of observational procedures, René Descartes's birthing of the knowing subject, Isaac Newton's articulation of a spatial/temporal "System of the World," John Locke's fashioning of the liberal/inductive plot of coming to know, and Immanuel Kant's moralizing of the narrative. The anatomy of realism that follows traces this Enlightenment narrative in realist fiction from Daniel Defoe to Fyodor Dostoevsky. I am here interested less in sustained "readings" than in catching out the unemphatic protocols of knowing (the operative subject/space/time paradigm) that regulate realist fiction. In *Crime and Punishment* the Enlightenment narrative succeeds and shatters, in equal measure. To grasp the logic of subjectivity as a scene of shattering, however, one needs an interpretive frame unavailable to Enlightenment thought.

Part 2—the center of the book—attends to "Modernist Unknowing." To analyze modernist refusal of realist protocols of knowing, I begin with an architect of modernist thinking: Freud. Freud's fundamental concepts—defenses and repression as shaping forces guaranteeing the errors of

consciousness (the subject as other); the uncanny as a spatial fault line testifying to the projectiveness of ego (its "bleeding" into space); trauma as the
wound to psyche that makes it inhabit a temporality both then and now
(the subject "bleeding" into time)—offer to the literary critic a cornucopia
of insights into the dynamic of unknowing. The work of Kafka, Proust,
and Faulkner configures these insights as *narrative forms* (even as realist
narrative configures Enlightenment convictions as narrative forms).

Analysis of Freudian reshaping of space, time, and subjectivity prepares
the way for this book's three central chapters. Attending comparatively to
the work (mainly) of Proust, Kafka, and Faulkner, these chapters focus on
uncanny space, unbound time, and the subject-as-other. Uncanny space
turns unlawful; things slip, lose their familiarity (or are hauntingly familiar
even though unknown). Unbound time forfeits linearity; progress comes to
a halt. Modernist narrative involves the discovery, not of who one is (the
drama of knowing), but that one is other. All three chapters argue that, as
the fictional subject's compact with reliable (reconfirming) space and time
founders, a poetics of knowing cedes to one of unknowing.

Kafka, Proust, and Faulkner knew Freud's work, but I do not explore
influence. Rather, they creatively share Freud's sense of the subject's self-
blindness as enacted in the experiencing of space/time. Refusing all forms
of knowing, Kafka's fiction hones in magnetically on vertigo, arrest, undoing; in Adorno's phrase, "his power is one of demolition."[6] The subject,
spawned by the social, does not own itself, cannot liberate itself, cannot
even sustain its human shape. The reader as well remains blind-sighted—
reading as a social and psycho-analysis that never delivers the enlightenment of knowing. Proust likewise reshapes the subject/space/time model.
His figures are dispossessed over time and (except for the privileged and
disembodied narrator) do not know this. Conscious memory denatures and
instrumentally revises the past. The extension of space menaces the Proustian subject (others are accessible only through the subject's falsifying lenses)
no less than the passage of time. Faulkner registers in a different way the
racial/gender fallout from a failed Enlightenment model of maturation.
The reverberating collapse of the Old South instructs him that the progress
model does not obtain. He centers his experimental fiction on moments of
collapse, redeploying time (refusing its linearity) in order to keep it from
serving as a medium that accommodates coming to know.

Part 3, "Beyond Knowing," attends to two contemporary projects for
writing past the arrest and anxiety of modernist unknowing. The first is a
genre of postmodern fiction that, rather than tell the story of subjects
undone within a social space/time that has ceased to orient, rehearses a

narrative of "vocabularies."[7] Such fiction releases narrative from the failed project of knowing. Knowing assumes a viable purchase on the exterior world; this assumption tends to be revoked in the postmodern fiction under consideration. Staging brief modernist-postmodern encounters between Faulkner and Thomas Pynchon, between Rainer Maria Rilke and Italo Calvino, and between E. M. Forster and Salman Rushdie, I show how modernist anxiety about subject orientation is replaced, in postmodern texts, by a variety of "flights"—escape from Newtonian gravity.

Finally, I consider the postcolonial genre of magic realism, by comparing Faulknerian arrest with the various modes of release that flourish in the fiction of Gabriel García Márquez and Toni Morrison. Both successor writers, though influenced by Faulkner, refuse the epistemological drive of his tragic fiction. Their postcolonial texts articulate the desire for release by reconfiguring the subject within a communal sphere no longer calibrated according to Newtonian gravity, Cartesian mastery, Lockean pursuit of a commodity-marked liberty. In a word, a communal sphere no longer knowable as Western Enlightenment has insisted for more than two centuries (in its philosophy, its economics, its colonizing, and its fiction) that the spatial/temporal globe *is* knowable—and as such, open to orientation, acquisition, and progress.[8]

The work of Emmanuel Levinas provides a valuable lens on the collapse of selfhood in modernist fiction.[9] His critique of the Western commitment to *being* (as little more, finally, than a sublime ego-logy) reveals some of the stakes of this collapse. Adorno serves as a procedural guide in the measure that he understands art objects to be—no matter how profoundly invested in the social setting in which they emerge—singular entities. One attends to them best by respecting their singularity (which is formal, not argumentative)—without sentimentalizing them, but also without immersing them (and losing their distinctiveness) within an archive of innumerable other discourses to which they are related. I draw further on both Adorno and his peer Walter Benjamin for an underlying conviction of this book: that works of art engage the social in ways all the more precious for being formally indirect; that readers engage works of art in ways not foredoomed to misrecognition. Such engagement is best understood not as knowing but as *acknowledgment*—the other not objectified and mapped, but encountered nevertheless.

Respect for the singularity of artworks operates as more than a slogan in this study; it guides its procedures. Large claims about the assumptions and procedures of Western fiction rest on a deliberately reduced number of instances and analyses. My intent is the opposite of cavalier. If I am to persuade my reader of the value of these claims—rather than just their abstract plausibility—I must show the claims at work aesthetically and extensively, emerging through the demonstrable behavior of texts themselves. To achieve this, I often have to demonstrate, and that (if done responsibly) takes up space. I therefore offer these selected instances and analyses more as ideal types—revealing tendencies—than as any statistically compelling survey of the field under consideration. In a word, I count on their resonance. In bearing down on Freud, Proust, Kafka, and Faulkner, I aim to illuminate more than their discrete modernist practices. They serve as the center for a set of claims whose circumference has taken me decades to identify and explore.

Of Freud's interpretive terms, it is *condensation,* not *displacement,* that matters in my inquiry: condensation (within the artwork itself) as an overdetermined play of meaning-effects not to be sorted out in any straight-line causality; condensation (within the interpretive act) as the con-fusing of investments (authorial, readerly, social); condensation as metaphoric in its working rather than metonymic. Rather than the god term of difference (which governs so much contemporary cultural discourse), rather than the genre of allegory (which Benjamin helped to launch into that discourse and which has fetishized the element of loss or disfigurement in our dealings with the other), I seek a form of meaning-making that Benjamin himself achieved in unparalleled fashion: symbolism (modern, not Coleridgean).[10] To see how things go together requires a strenuous undoing of how they are normally said to go together (as knowing subject and object known). This book shares Benjamin's belief that "our coming was expected," our encounter with the past and its productions can take place. "If there is hope in Kafka's work," Adorno writes, it is "in the capacity to stand up to the worst by making it into language" (*Prisms,* 254). Because of such acts of language, we engage what is not us, and the encounter that is the aim of this book is not only possible, but hopeful.

Modernism has been read throughout the past century as anything but hopeful, yet if we place it between realism and postmodernism, we can better decipher its promise. First, a hopefulness that begins by refusing the narratives of progress the West has used since the seventeenth century to characterize its own history. ("To believe in progress," Kafka writes, "is not to believe that progress has already taken place. That would be no belief.")[11] Such hopefulness is not to be confused with optimism, and its articulation occurs outside the terms of realist resolution. In modernist art, time and space do not resolve into docile conditions enabling the subject to center; the modernist narrative refuses to mimic a plot resolution it finds

missing in the real. The hopefulness of modernism is diagnostic, not predicative—providing a resonant take upon troubles rather than a fantasy
solution to them. "Progress is at home not in the continuity of the flow of
time," Benjamin writes, "but in its interferences: wherever something genuinely new makes itself felt for the first time with the sobriety of dawn."[12]
The "dawn" such works fleetingly grasp invokes a fullness of being absent
from the now-unbearable real: Faulkner's "might-have-been," Proust's
moment of the lost past suddenly reconfigured in the present, Kafka's revelation that our "own" body is imprinted by a social machine writing in a
foreign script. In these instances, the real emerges in all its deformation:
where we are yet do not wish to be.

I say "we" because the second dimension of modernist hopefulness is its
investment in its readers.[13] What is precious in this modernist literature is
the *identificatory* traffic between reader and text. The diagnostic charge
wrought into the text's experimental form is meant to release within the
reader's subjectivity. Awaken—this charge insists—from the sleep of
knowing into the strangeness of unknowing. "You must change your life,"
Rilke's torso of Apollo demands of its observer: "for here there is no place /
that does not see you."[14] If the first dimension of modernist hopefulness
reveals its difference from realist optimism, this second dimension reveals
its difference from a postmodern literature of "vocabularies." In modernism, as in Benjamin's "aura," the art object looks back. In this
encounter it connects us with what is not now, not here, not us. Such
encounters are the signature move of the modernist fiction under study
here, revealing their full value only in a postmodern climate that forswears
art's capacity to stage encounters, a climate in which all that remains of the
past are its alienated commodities, its mass-produced images, its codified
languages. Modernism is finally about the dead's capacity still to speak: not
as contemporaries (as in realism), nor as solipsistic fantasy (as in postmodernism). Instead, the dead speak a language we must learn to "unknow" if
we are to hear it. Such hearing-as-unknowing is this literature's demand,
made in the Utopian conviction that we shall not begin to recover our lives
in space and time until we grasp the extent to which we have—all
unknowing—lost them.

Modernism was for a long time in bad odor in the academy—stereotyped as highbrow, white-male, coterie-focused. To counter this reading, a
wide range of recent materialist studies of modernism has attended to its
imbrication with contemporary developments in science, technology, and
mass culture. (One undeclared aim of this recent work has been to demonstrate modernism's resemblance to a postmodernist literature that openly

declares its attachment to such phenomena.) I have learned much from this work, but my book goes another way. The protocols of the realist practice that came before modernism, and of the postmodern and postcolonial practices that come after it, allow me to bring into visibility what was most at stake in modernist experimentation. My book is enabled, then, by two final convictions: that modernist fiction attends to conditions of life that most men and women in the West experience (though few imagine in a sustained way), and that it is necessary to read this literature within an inclusive Western frame (broader than the "localism" of cultural studies) if one would see how it stages the crisis of the liberal, knowing subject. Scrutiny of this crisis permits a deeper recognition of what it means to belong to the West. I seek to show in what ways that is this literature's beauty and its burden.

Let me close on a note that is at once personal yet charged—as I have come to see—with more than personal significance. Over three decades ago, on a night I do not forget, I underwent a life-altering experience. I was a young assistant professor, struggling to sustain both my domestic and my professional identities, and—unused to drugs even though this was the late 1960s—I spent an evening smoking marijuana. This activity seemed for a while to have no results; then suddenly I experienced an internal commotion such as I had never known before. My body shook uncontrollably. I seemed to be imploding and exploding, I had to move at once. I passed the next hours walking up and down deserted neighborhood streets—my wife and a friend each holding one of my arms—trying to negotiate recurrent waves of inner disarray. My mind was not my own. Paranoid fantasy scenarios arose as though real. Space and time lost their moorings. Events replayed themselves; the streets got larger or smaller, nearer or farther, on their own. After I was finally calm enough to get into bed, I trembled until dawn. For the next two years I could not speak of this event without in a certain measure bringing it on again. A year thereafter, relocated elsewhere, I wrote the experience down. From that point on I began to gain distance from it and control over it.

This book on modernism arises primarily from my professional interests, but it grows out of that personal experience as well. Pathological though it was, that episode luridly highlighted for me the fragility of assumptions we in the West have learned to take for granted. Until then I had more or less envisaged my life as a naturally sanctioned narrative of realism. Things in the past had developed in an iterative, familiar way. By dint of luck, skill, and application, I assumed I would in time succeed, both domestically and professionally. The world I was yet to encounter was, if unknown, familiarizable. It would accommodate my eventual flourishing; it was there, so to speak, for that purpose. None of this was guaranteed, but the developmental assumptions underlying it seemed self-evident. Trauma I knew nothing about. My mind and body had always been reasonably enough under control; situations I had encountered were eventually supportive of my will. Why would a satisfying career not be in the offing?

I have had that satisfying career, but during the past thirty-five years I have become increasingly aware of the Western bias wrought into the narrative model underlying it. The figure/ground assumptions I drew on emphasized the magnitude of the figure, trivializing the role of the ground. My sense of my capacity to shape my world—to exploit its temporality, to domesticate its spatiality—was skewed. Skewed not in some personal/psychological way, but skewed culturally: I had been taught to expect what I expected. I was born, I thought, to become the creator (or at least the architect) of my scene. To be the creature within it made little sense; what sense it made was demeaning.

In time I came to recognize the larger Lockean dimensions of my figure/ground model. The right to "life, liberty, and the pursuit of happiness" was a birthright of the European Enlightenment—conceptualized in 1690, put (by the American colonies) into revolutionary practice nearly a century later. I was free to become (in the latest and most degraded version of the motto) "all that I could become," because the West had, for some three centuries, liberated itself from custom sufficiently to proclaim this emancipatory program for (a subset of) its citizens. It was as familiar as mother's milk because the immigrant European families that gave birth to my parents had, in coming to America, taught them the same program from their infancy onward. It was no less familiar in the American, British, and French novels I devoured in childhood and adolescence, the home I grew up in, the schools I attended.

Kafka, Proust, Faulkner, and Freud did not, of course, single-handedly subvert the Enlightenment project of knowledge in its two directions: knowledge of the larger world, consequent knowledge of oneself. But, among the early-twentieth-century modernists, they were—for me—the ones who most powerfully reconfigured the figure/ground model underlying the realist practice that had held the stage since the eighteenth century. Each represented the ground not only as more shaping than the figure but as licensing the possibility of the figure. Each recognized that the other comes before—and looms larger than—the self. Each understood that the creator rises out of the creature, and that the creature remains present within the creator. Each grasped that time can stand still rather than pass, that space can disorient rather than promote empowerment, that human subjects, all unaware, "bleed into" the scenes they inhabit. Each wrote narratives in which the drama of unknowing—of having to unknow, of realizing that one does not know and perhaps cannot know—takes priority over the progressive drama of coming to know oneself and one's world.

More than two centuries of Enlightenment-inspired realism prepare the coming of modernist fiction. Only against a backdrop of protocols of knowing so long established as to operate unthinkingly does an insistence on unknowing reveal its stakes. I launch this study of modernism, however, not with the emergence of the knowledge project, but rather with the menace to that project that occurs when, suddenly, one's dearest assumptions (those on which sanity depends) cease to operate: Kierkegaard's *Fear and Trembling*.

CHAPTER ONE

Leaping

Kierkegaard's *Fear and Trembling*

"HERE I AM"

This compact clause—"here I am"—appears three times in Genesis 22 (in Hebrew it is even more compact: the single word *hineni*).[1] The words not only epitomize Abraham's ordeal but serve to intimate the stakes of two other enterprises: Kierkegaard's entry into religious crisis, and modernist fiction's stance toward the subject. Here I am. To what am I exposed? To what calls on me is my annunciation of presence already a response?[2] The phrase points to the core drama on which this study is focused: the modernist subject ("I") located in an undomesticated spatial/temporal scene— "here" (nowhere else) and "now" (a moment stripped of before and after, split off from temporal project). Finally, the phrase assumes the significance of *my being in question* at a given moment. A phenomenology is already in place, in which what I do (or what happens to me) now, as I relate to what is outside, *matters*.[3]

I call this a drama, but it cannot become one until "here" and "now" become mediated by "there" and "then." (It is, until such mediation, a crisis.) Kierkegaard shares with modernist fiction the awareness that if "here" is deprived of "there," and "now" of "then"—if the subject is arrested in a moment of unmediated presence—"I" no longer functions as "I." There is no drama because drama requires a projective narrative of "I" moving through lawful space and ongoing time. If one disallows the negotiability of space and time, one disallows coherence to the (no longer moving) subject.

"I" is the "I" of "I can" (eventually, in time). Charles Dickens entitles the opening chapter of *David Copperfield* "I am born," assuring us—by looking back—that "I" began at such and such a time and place, and that "I" will continue to be, in recognizable time and space, throughout the subsequent eight hundred pages of the novel. Likewise, for Abraham to achieve coherence—father of Isaac, patriarch of Judaism—requires our extending/suturing him in space and time, our knowing that the crisis on Mount Moriah is but a temporary episode in an (eventually) exemplary career. Suppose, though, that one did not know how it came out. Suppose that, like Abraham, one was—during the unbearable moments of answering "here I am" and taking on what that might release—unknowing, in the dark.

Kierkegaard's Abraham is in the dark. So in the dark that he *becomes* dark, far from exemplary. The exemplary Abraham is the one who has come through his ordeal, been written. "We are curious about the result, about the way a book turns out," Kierkegaard writes. "We do not want to know anything about the anxiety, the distress, the paradox."[4] But if one brackets (as not yet occurred and therefore not knowable) the happy result and returns the event to the savagery of its unsecured unfolding—if one attends to the outstretched hand holding the knife—the narrative ceases to be didactic and becomes terrifying: "Anyone who looks upon this scene is paralyzed. Who strengthened Abraham's soul lest everything go black for him and he see neither Isaac nor the ram! Anyone who looks upon this scene is blinded. And yet it perhaps rarely happens that anyone is paralyzed or blinded, and still more rarely does anyone tell what happened as it deserves to be told" (22).

How does it deserve to be told? One way Kierkegaard answers this question is by focusing on the stakes of Abraham's "here I am." Abraham says these words twice to God and once to Isaac, yet how can he "be here" for both his God and his son? How can he answer them both the same, when God demands the execution of Isaac? The ordeal stretches Abraham into incoherence, which is why Kierkegaard is drawn to him at the moment of crisis: "If I were to speak about him, I would first of all describe the pain of the ordeal. . . . I would point out that the journey lasted three days and a good part of the fourth; indeed, these three and a half days could be infinitely longer than the few thousand years that separate me from Abraham" (53). Abraham's time and space are not just subjectively altered here. He becomes transformed within them; he will not exit from this scene *as himself.* Kierkegaard's second answer to the question, to which I shall return, is that, indeed, this scene cannot be told. Kierkegaard says repeatedly not only that he cannot understand Abraham but that Abraham is incomprehensible.

Let us unpack further the stakes of "here I am." It is an answer proffered before the specifics of the call ("take now thy son, thine only son Isaac . . .") have yet been heard, a response-ability in advance of the call. The call, when it comes, calls wholly into question this old man who was promised the founding of a people, who waited so many years before God granted him the son who would turn the promise into reality. On receiving such an announcement, what does one do? One trembles. We tremble when called radically into question, when immersed in a moment whose potential outcome threatens our embodied sense of who we are. The body is gripped by an anxiety for which the mind knows no domesticating frame. Something unbearable is about to happen here and now, it has already started to happen. Since nothing in the subject's cultural furnishing permits it to ward off or contain this threat to self-sustaining, the subject ceases to function. One trembles—an activity that, like crying, is primordial, deeper and older than the coping mechanisms taught and retained in the symbolic sphere where language resides.[5]

No one in the eight hundred pages of *David Copperfield* trembles thus; neither do the protagonists of Jane Austen or Stendhal or Honoré de Balzac or Leo Tolstoy or George Eliot or Henry James. They often become confused, at times even anguished, but they do not cease to function as themselves within familiar space and time.[6] The protagonists of Kafka, Proust, and Faulkner, however, encounter recurrently that which does more than thwart them; its assault undoes their identity, making them no longer recognizable to themselves. Rooms turn strange and unmanageable for K. and Marcel and Joe Christmas. Others suddenly become unknowable; their own bodies undergo eruptions, even transformations. They rarely figure out why; the disturbance lodges deeper than consciousness can fathom or social norms explain. They all become, one way or another, self-confounded, undone by events or arrangements that do not resolve into the transparent form of knowledge but register (unresolved) in the opaque form of symptoms.[7] The conceptual company these protagonists keep is that of a thinker contemporaneous with them, one whose career was devoted to plumbing disturbances opaque to the mind yet deforming the body—disturbances that left their mark yet refused to leave, rendering obscure the very track of the subject through time and space. This thinker, the fourth modernist in my study, is Freud.[8]

"THE CONTINUAL LEAP IN EXISTENCE"

Every movement of infinity is carried out through passion, and no reflection can produce a movement. This is the continual leap in existence that explains the

movement, whereas mediation is a chimera, which in Hegel is supposed to explain
everything and which is also the only thing he never has tried to explain. . . .
What our generation lacks is not reflection but passion . . . our age is actually
too tenacious of life to die, for dying is one of the most remarkable leaps . . .
(42; emphasis in the original)

Kierkegaard proposes the subject's movement through time and space as
radically unmediated, uninsured. No Hegelian dialectic can explain how
one is to move through a moment of crisis. For this reason we miss Abraham if we read him backward in time, his crisis pacified by our knowledge
of how it resolves. "If the one who is to act wants to judge himself by the
result, he will never begin" (63). The beginning (the crisis returned to its
own crisis time) is what matters—what takes courage—and Kierkegaard
calls the subject's move at this point a passionate leap, even unto death
itself, for death is the supreme move we make into nonidentity, not-self.
And at times we do make this move: Abraham makes it in raising the
knife, transforming himself into the murderer that only the angel's ultimate words keep from actualization. He makes this movement freely,
uncoerced, for "if one believes that cold, barren necessity must necessarily
be present [for the leap of spirit], then one is declaring that no one can
experience death before one actually dies, which to me seems to be crass
materialism" (46).

I shall have more to say, later, about modernist fiction's awareness that
death is not (as the Victorians thought) life's majestic other, sumptuously
arriving only when life departs, but rather life's intimate companion, its
daily secret sharer. Joseph K., Gregor, Marcel, Quentin, Darl: each of these
figures dies his death before dying, each finds himself suddenly and irre-
versibly other, his previous identity shattered, the subject-compact out of
date. ("Breathing is a sight-draft dated yesterday," Faulkner writes in *The
Hamlet;* it can be collected at any moment.)[9] For now, I address only the
examples Kierkegaard himself provided. Attending not to the result but to
"the continual leap" of self-risk, he lets us glimpse the unimaginable
change taking place within those who respond to an all-compelling call.
The annunciatory angel said nothing to others, "went only to Mary, and no
one could understand her. Has any woman been as infringed upon as was
Mary, and is it not true here also that the one whom God blesses he curses
in the same breath?" (65). If Mary's inner leap is stunning, that of Christ
and his disciples is even more so. Knowing how it comes out, we like to
imagine "Christ walking about in the promised land. We forget the anxiety, the distress, the paradox. Was it such a simple matter not to make a

mistake? Was it not terrifying that this man walking around among the others was God? Was it not terrifying to sit down to eat with him?" (66).

"Was it such a simple matter not to make a mistake?" The leap of spirit lacks, utterly, the temporal revisability of Hegelian mediation. Suppose one heard the voice wrong? Suppose one heard the wrong voice? As though hypnotized by this topic, Kafka will later imagine one Abraham after another, revealing the tragicomic risk involved in leaping:

> But another Abraham. One who wants to sacrifice altogether in the right way, and who has the right mood in general for the whole thing, but who cannot believe that he is the one meant, he, the repulsive old man and his child, the dirty boy. The true faith is not lacking to him, he has this faith, he would sacrifice in the right frame of mind if he could only believe that he is the one meant. He fears, he will ride out as Abraham with his son, but on the way he will metamorphose into Don Quixote. The world would have been horrified at Abraham if it could have seen him, he however fears that the world will laugh itself to death at the sight of him. But, it is not ridiculousness as such that he fears—of course, he fears that too, and above all his laughing along with them—but mainly he fears that this ridiculousness will make him even older and uglier, his son even dirtier, more unworthy really to be summoned. An Abraham who comes unsummoned! (Kafka, letter to Klopstock, quoted in Robbins, 93)

The seamy humor of Kafka's Abraham may seem removed from Kierkegaardian anguish, but Kierkegaard's notes for *Fear and Trembling* reveal a kindred penchant for morbid comedy. In these notes Kierkegaard has Abraham draw the knife "—and thrust it into Isaac! The very same moment Jehovah stands visible beside Abraham and says: what have you done, you poor old man! That was not required of you at all. . . . I merely wanted to test your faith! And I also shouted to you in the last moment . . . Abraham, Abraham, stop!" To which Kierkegaard has Abraham reply: "O Lord, I did not hear it; yet now that you speak of it, it seems to me that I did hear such a voice . . . [but] one is somewhat overstrained at such a moment. . . . When you command me to sacrifice my child—and at the critical moment a voice is heard that says, 'Stop,' I am obliged to think it is the tempter's voice that wants to keep me from carrying out your will" (267). One may be "somewhat overstrained at such a moment," even as poor metamorphosed Gregor is momentarily "overstrained," unable to move swiftly and efficiently from bedroom to office.[10] Virtually a gallows humor operates in the savage gap between superhuman demand and merely human capacity.

"THIS IS NOT THE SYSTEM"

"This is not the system; it has not the least thing to do with the system," Johannes de Silentio insists (8). Nothing of Abraham's journey to Mount Moriah is premappable by Kantian categorical imperative or Hegelian dialectic. "System" provides reflective formulae for domesticating time into repeatable pattern, assuring in advance how one is to move through the present into the future, intact, even progressive. "System" removes the vicissitudes of temporal unknowing from one's deciding how to act, erases the necessity of leaping. Although "system" may indeed apply to how it all will look from a distance and later on, it has no bearing on one's existence here and now—the moment in which one can only say (or not say): "Here I am." In his *Concluding Unscientific Postscript* Kierkegaard clarifies the difference between system and existence: "A system of existence cannot be given. Is there, then, not such a system? That is not at all the case. . . . Existence itself is a system—for God, but it cannot be a system for any existing spirit. System and conclusiveness correspond to each other, but existence is the very opposite. . . . In order to think existence, systematic thought must think it as annulled, and consequently as not existing. Existence is the spacing that holds apart; the systematic is the conclusiveness that brings together."[11]

"System," by sucking the temporality out of existence—replacing the temporal spacing that separates with the conceptual framing that binds—transforms the risk of unknowing into grids of knowledge. It thus dominates three parallel realms in Kierkegaard's thought universe: the universal, the ethical, the linguistic. "The ethical as such," he writes in *Fear and Trembling,* "is the universal, and as the universal it applies to everyone, which from another angle means that it applies at all times" (54). At all times: modeled on the Kantian imperative, the ethical does not vary.[12] More, it is enduringly sayable, graven in stone, an affair of understood, shareable laws. On this basis Kierkegaard distinguishes between the tragic hero—Agamemnon pressed to sacrifice his daughter Iphigenia—and the knight of faith: Abraham called to sacrifice his son Isaac. The motive of the former sacrifice is as ethically clear and open to language (only this extreme deed can end an otherwise endless war) as the motive of the latter sacrifice is unspeakable. To whom could Abraham speak of God's charge? To Isaac whom he is about to murder? To Sarah whose only child he is taking from her? To others who are somehow to understand that God would demand this deed? Abraham has no clue as to why God would demand it: how possibly explain it to others?

The deed to which Abraham is committed is, ethically speaking, a murder pure and simple, and Abraham is a man of ethics: he loves his child more than himself. "Humanly speaking," Kierkegaard writes, "he is mad and cannot make himself understandable to anyone" (76).

When, over a century later, the French philosopher Emmanuel Levinas takes up the Abraham drama, he sees in it the core difference between a Christian metaphysics of recovery (you shall find yourself in Christ, the return of the prodigal son, the blind shall see) and a Judaic metaphysics of errance (exile, darkness, the desert). For Abraham cannot enter this crisis and return as *himself*. What, for Kierkegaard, makes Abraham a scandalous betrayer of the ethical—Abraham's exit from the norms of his own acculturated ego structure—makes him for Levinas exemplary. "In Levinas's reading," as Jill Robbins argues, "Abraham's departure without return figures the very departure from self and from self-reference that is the movement of ethics and responsibility. Responsibility to the other is not something that is first filtered through the self; it is not an imperative that I deliver to myself. Rather, it is a being delivered over to the other" (78).

The implications of such departure from selfhood are considerable for Kafka, Proust, and Faulkner. Their fiction circulates around the dilemma of exposed or collapsed systems of meaning—systems that cannot be restored. The novels therefore center, like the Abraham narrative, on shattering encounters in the present moment, self-altering events for which no restorative interpretive key can be supplied. Marcel describes thus the moment when Swann learns that Odette has betrayed him "two or three times" with other women: "Swann had prepared himself for every possibility. Reality must therefore be something that bears no relation to possibilities, any more than the stab of a knife in one's body bears to the gradual movement of the clouds overhead, since those words, 'two or three times,' carved as it were a cross upon the living tissues of his heart."[13] In contrast to such implacable non-orientation, the more than two centuries of realist fiction that precedes modernism may be generally characterized as orientational, universal/ethical in its aims, focused on homecoming. (How often "treat others as ends in themselves, not as means" serves as the unexceptionable ethical spine of realist literature.) Such ethically charged fiction, moving steadily toward epiphanies of self-understanding, performs, as it were, a ransoming of time's passage. However lost during the process, one recovers in the end. The "I" proceeds continuously, in Levinas's language, by "recovering its identity throughout all that happens to it."[14] Try to make that fit for Joseph K. or Quentin Compson.

SWIMMING AND "SWIMMING"

> For my part, I presumably can describe the movements of faith, but I cannot make them. In learning to go through the motions of swimming, one can be suspended from the ceiling in a harness and then presumably describe the movements, but one is not swimming. (*Fear,* 37–38)

I asked above, how does Abraham's story deserve to be told? I now return to Kierkegaard's second answer: it cannot be told. It cannot be told because telling is a form of "swimming," and "swimming" never substitutes for swimming. Is it too much to say that modernism's first law of aesthetics is that language is a form of "swimming" that is honor-bound not to mistake itself for swimming? At any rate, Kierkegaard realized that, because the reality of his material was unsayable, he would betray it least by pretending least to say it adequately.[15] Because Abraham is a center that cannot be said, the text circles him instead, in speculative and unsanctioned ways. *Fear and Trembling* thus proposes four mutually incompatible "exordia" for saying Abraham: the father who would save his son's belief in God by telling him that this violence is the father's desire (rather than God's command); the father who returns from Mount Moriah faithful to the ordeal but ruined by it ("Abraham's eyes were darkened, and he saw joy no more" [12]); the father who returns to Mount Moriah after the crisis, consumed by the sinfulness of what he was prepared to commit; and finally the son who, in experiencing his ordeal, "had lost the faith" (14). Each of these (mutually incompatible) mini-narratives subjectifies—and in so doing falsifies—the story by supplying what Genesis omits: the traumatic charge of the crisis as it enters and alters Abraham. We are close to Friedrich Nietzsche's (proto-modernist) insistence that all seeing is perspectival rather than comprehensive, an insistence that Faulkner turns later into narrative form in the four perspectival chapters of Compson reality in *The Sound and the Fury*.

There is no ultimate coming to know in any of these tellings, for "swimming" is not swimming. Kierkegaard's text opposes from its opening page the easy translation of experience into profit, referring sarcastically to "bargain price[s]" and a society that believes it has gone deeper in doubt, further in faith, than all previous ones. But there is no going further than Abraham, there is not even a getting to him: "despite all its [Abraham's life's] passion," Kierkegaard writes, "my thought cannot penetrate it, cannot get ahead by a hairsbreadth. I stretch every muscle to get a perspective, and at the very same instant I become paralyzed" (33). Paralysis, trauma, scandal: Abraham haunts his writer in the measure that he is beyond knowing, mastery, articulation. No profit emerges from obsessing over him, no problem gets solved, nothing exemplary comes into focus. "During the time before the result" (66)—where the text keeps placing us, where life always places us—we are still in the beginning, the leap remains before us, it is all still to be done. Kierkegaard, like the modernist writers I shall be analyzing, remains "conscientious about time" (100) as a medium that cannot be honorably converted into profit or progress; his text takes us not into recovery but deeper into expenditure.[16] This time, though, an expenditure not recovered but illuminated *as* expenditure. I close this "leap" into Kierkegaard by citing once more Levinas: "To the myth of Odysseus returning to Ithaca, we wish to oppose the story of Abraham, leaving his fatherland forever for a land yet unknown and forbidding his servant to bring even his son to the point of departure" (cited in Robbins, 106). "Returning to Ithaca": what is that but the return to an enlarged self-knowledge—the progressive story of Western reason and imagination finding themselves fulfilled in time, from Descartes to Kant and the Romantics and beyond? Before clarifying modernist narratives of expenditure and exile—the extensive poetics of unknowing—we must first attend to the two-hundred-year project that precedes modernism, the Enlightenment project of knowing.

PART I

Knowing

"Sapere Aude!"—The West Dares to Know

Genealogy of Realism

An Enlightenment Narrative in Five Stages

It has long been recognized that Western realist fiction, rising into prominence in the eighteenth century and reaching its acme in the nineteenth, is
broadly indebted to earlier Enlightenment premises.[1] Current cultural work,
however, tends to stay closer to the practices of the place and time in question.
The significance of realism, like that of modernism that follows it, is typically
assumed to be inextricable from the contextual weave of contemporary social
and conceptual procedures. It is true that the nineteenth-century genre whose
protagonists journey relentlessly toward discovery (and self-discovery) has
numerous contemporary discursive siblings and cousins. But its parentage is
to be found two centuries earlier, in the rise of Enlightenment thought.

Can one speak responsibly of more than two hundred years as "a
period"? On the one hand, the most enormous changes—socially, politi-
cally, technologically, intellectually—took place during this time frame. Yet
(restricting the field of reference to Western Europe) the increasing empowerment of the bourgeoisie, the burgeoning of capitalism, the advent and
institutionalizing of science (a term appearing only in the early eighteenth
century, although its increasingly systematic practice begins a hundred years
earlier), the emergence and gradual hegemony of the realist novel as a fictional form: this constellation of interrelated phenomena spans the two centuries in question and gives them a certain minimal coherence. Stephen
Toulmin writes, "After 1660, there developed an overall framework of ideas
about humanity and nature, rational mind and causal matter, that gained
the standing of 'common sense' for the next 100, 150, or 200 years; the main

timbers of this framework of ideas and beliefs . . . we may refer to as the Modern world view."[2] Toulmin's *modern* designates the more or less stable contours of a Western "common sense" operative since the Enlightenment; it does not refer to the later *modernism* that calls such "common sense" into question. As to the advent of *that* challenge, Henri Lefebvre writes: "Around 1910 a certain space was shattered. It was the space of common sense, of knowledge . . . a space hitherto enshrined in everyday discourse. . . . Euclidian and perspectivist space have disappeared as systems of reference, along with other former 'common places' such as town, history, paternity."[3]

One can quarrel with the dates (Lefebvre may be remembering Virginia Woolf's famous proposal of December 1910 as the moment of cultural rupture), but it is harder to quarrel with the change itself. A traditional way of knowing comes into question, along with the familiar spatial-temporal frame—"town, history, paternity"—that it draws upon. In the realm of fictional practice, realism is crafted to tell that "common sense" story (even as modernism is crafted to call it into question)—the story of *a subject coming to know the territory.* The subject comes to know by learning (through trial and error) to recognize and exploit the arrangements of the external world (nature or culture, objects or others) in which he or she moves. For this project to succeed, a cultural consensus must obtain, as to who subjects are and what the world they seek to know better is likely to resemble. "The enlightened predictability of the world," writes Timothy Reiss, continues "in an uninterrupted line from Descartes to Laplace, passing through Newton and Kant."[4] The world must be objectively knowable but (to the questing subject) not yet known. There comes into being, in other words, a "common sense" narrative about subjects moving toward knowledge and self-knowledge through familiar space and time.[5] This chapter is about the story of the knowing subject that the Enlightenment launched and sustained for over two centuries.

There is no shortage of salient Enlightenment thinkers who might serve as architects of this broadly shared model. In the interest of manageability—for my book centers on modernism, not realism—I attend mainly to four of them: Descartes, Newton, Locke, and Kant. Others might stress Bacon or Leibniz or Voltaire or Diderot; others yet would oppose any top-down, "great man" approach to identifying core Enlightenment values.[6] But during the eighteenth and nineteenth centuries the four thinkers I have chosen remained significant references—symbolic markers—within Western Europe's shared high cultural assumptions about how human subjects engage space and time, objects and others. (Testifying to the resonance of Newton's *Principia* almost a century after its publication, Voltaire declared in 1776 that "we are all his disciples now."[7] No less telling, Diderot and d'Alembert dedicated their seventeen-volume *Encyclopédie* [1762–77] to Bacon, Descartes, Newton, and Locke—suggesting a certain consensus as to the "founding fathers" of Enlightenment thought.) My aim is not to offer a new interpretation of these four thinkers' concerns, but rather to draw on their thought in such a way as to delineate the emergent narrative (its constituent powers and limits) of the subject coming to know.

TRANSFORMING PREMODERN COSMOS INTO BACONIAN NATURE

In the Aristotelian/Scholastic worldview, subject, space, and time were joined in a different configuration.[8] Indeed, the idea of the questing individual, as such, did not exist (neither Greek nor medieval culture has a term designating "the subject").[9] The single figure was absorbed into a larger god-ordered cosmos whose form and purposes sanctioned his own. He was not separated out enough to be thought of as a subject.[10] The order of things—macrocosmic and microcosmic—was already posited rather than (to be) discovered. (One traversed that order not to come upon its secrets, inductively, but to confirm its patterning, deductively. Seen through Cervantes's early modern eyes, Don Quixote reveals the madness of this premodern procedure. Quixote is incapable, precisely, of learning from experience.) "One result of this Aristotelian picture," John Cottingham writes in his discussion of Descartes, "is that there is a kind of continuity between all living things. Plants, animals and man, all things which are alive or 'ensouled' . . . belong on a continuum, where matter is progressively organized in a hierarchy."[11] Such a cosmos operates on the principles of resemblance and relatedness. Its discourse employs "the 'images of things' not for the sake of a knowledge and use of things in themselves, not to gain power over them . . . [but rather to indicate] a certain relation within a totality of which man himself was but a part" (Reiss, 354).[12] The discursive procedures appropriate to this premodern cosmos are sustained by propositions and syllogistic argument. It has no central place for empirical observation as a generative process; it is not inductive, thing-oriented.

Bacon rails against this antiquated system of knowledge: "It commands assent therefore to the proposition, but does not take hold of the thing."[13] It is the thing that should compel attention, the thing considered not as a concept but as a *fact*. As Lorraine Daston writes, "Experience we have always had with us, but facts as a way of parsing experience in natural history and natural philosophy [i.e., science before it was called science] are of seventeenth-century coinage."[14] To attend to the fact responsibly—to learn something from it—requires unremitting self-discipline. "Man always believes more readily that which he prefers," Bacon complains; "he therefore rejects difficulties for want of patience in investigation."[15] By dint of patience, self-discipline, and severely methodical investigation, however, man can uncover nature's long-hoarded secrets. Man becomes the inductive knower, nature the inductively known.[16]

But—and this is as critical as it is often forgotten—what he discovers in a realm of nature no longer conceived on a micro-macrocosmic basis is less nature as she is (as sharing the fabric of his own being) than *nature as she can be known.* "Experimental discourse is not at first an attempt to describe the thing itself so much as a description of the human *sighting* of the thing" (Reiss, 34). That sighting is laden with possibilities, for Bacon—a little like Karl Marx later—wants less to describe the world than to change it. More precisely, he can do something with it only if he has accurately observed it, in its otherness. Such observation is objective in the sense, not that it captures the object as it is in itself, but that local subjective distortion is expunged from the human "sighting"—a stance of arduously achieved disinterest that will dissolve in modernism and disappear in Lyotardian postmodernism. In sum, to move from Aristotelian/Scholastic premises to Baconian/scientific ones involves a "passage from what one might call a discursive *exchange within* the world to the expression of knowledge as a reasoning *practice upon* the world" (Reiss, 30; emphasis in the original). "What in operation is most useful," Bacon writes in *The New Organon,* "that in knowledge is most true" (cited in Reiss, 211).[17] The rudimentary elements of a modern narrative of knowing are beginning to emerge; indeed, Michel Foucault's power-knowledge paradigm is on the horizon. An inductive investigative procedure is announcing itself. A physico-spiritual cosmos understood within the logic of resemblance and relation is being jettisoned; a natural world composed of inhuman matter and harboring facts at once unknown, knowable, and usable—answering to law but not yet mapped—is coming into view. Knowledge will result from, and be vindicated by, a set of practices upon the world. What is missing is a discourse of the subject as one who comes to know. Enter Descartes.

DESCARTES BIRTHS THE SUBJECT

Descartes announces the motor that drives modern science and realist fiction: systematic doubt. He begins by doubting all. "Anything which admits of the slightest doubt," he writes in his *Meditations,* "I will set aside just as if I had found it to be wholly false."[18] As Ernest Gellner has proposed, "Descartes wishes, cognitively speaking, to be a self-made man" (3). Gone are custom and history; departed are parents, siblings, and friends; in doubt is the reality of his body itself. A radical dualism operates: *res cogitans,* the thinking thing that is soul and that alone withstands corrosive doubt, on the one hand, and *res extensa,* the vast domain of extended material nature, on the other. Body, as part of that domain alienated from soul, becomes corpselike, calculable, will-less, gradually (but grudgingly) admitted as one's own: "since there is no other equally suitable way of explaining [my] imagination [of my body] that comes to mind, I can make a probable conjecture that the body exists. But this is only a probability. . . . First of all then, I perceived by my senses that I had a head, hands, feet and all other limbs making up the body which I regarded as part of myself, or perhaps even my whole self" (*Meditations,* 52). What tone does Descartes intend here—scientific methodicalness? pre-Beckettian absurdity? Either way, this remains a hypnotic moment of Western self-reflection. By way of doubt Descartes launches his (and fiction's) foundational narrative.

Before unpacking the alienation wrought into this stance of radical doubt, let us consider its fictional possibilities. Doubt gives birth to the premise of the fictional subject. One who will come to know must call into question what he thinks he already knows. Doubt reconfigures the canvas on which the subject moves by turning the subject's prereflective understanding of its props into misunderstanding, thus launching storytelling as a protean narrative of error-to-be-overcome. Forward motion—progress—is on the horizon. Space and time enter conditions of narrativity: objects in (lawful but not yet mapped) space will need to be (re)calculated; time is the (lawful but not yet unfolded) medium permitting the (re)calculation. Indeed, doubt gives birth to the subject in a more fundamental sense, not just as one who is suddenly noncoincident with himself and will have to recover his "properties," but more resonantly as one who invents himself by doubting himself. A move of "hubristic modesty" (Levine, *Dying,* 49), radical doubt siphons off—relegates to marginality—everyone and everything that previously peopled the subject's scene.[19] He is now larger than life, sublimely alone on the stage, alone undoubtable because he *knows* he doubts. God is eventually shown to underwrite his identity, so he is not entirely alone. But, leaving God aside, he is alone enough: "Lastly, as regards my parents, even if everything I have ever believed about them is true, it is certainly not they who preserve me; and in so far as I am a thinking thing, they did not even make me" (*Meditations,* 35). All those orphaned and wandering subjects that dot the realist canvas: are they not the unclaimed offspring of Cartesian doubting?

This emergent subject who would know is, suddenly, alienated. His doubt has othered everything that might earlier have participated in his identity. He shares now with God, and potentially with other human beings, only the capacity to think in a methodological manner: *cogito ergo sum.* Nothing material that he thinks about possesses this divinely bestowed resource—none of it is of his kind—and he is free to probe it fearlessly. "But first, so there may be less difficulty in understanding what I shall say," Descartes writes in *Discourse on the Method,* "I should like any- one unversed in anatomy to take the trouble, before reading this, to have the heart of some large animal with lungs dissected before him (for such a heart is in all respects sufficiently like that of a man)."[20] Dramatic ploy? tongue-in-cheek outrageousness? humorless scientific procedure? What- ever it is, the animal is detachedly othered in order to be entered, meas- ured, and mapped. As Francis Barker notes, "Before this inception of the new order and of modern subjectivity, the flesh was the immediate, the unmediated."[21] Now "the flesh is made to contribute, as a material, to the science which is to dominate it" (96–97). If Foucault is on the horizon of Baconian procedures, Claude Bernard's relentless materializing of human processes follows hard, two centuries later, upon Descartes's readiness to pierce the body in search of its secrets. "The passageway to knowledge goes through the kitchen of slaughter," George Levine writes of both scientists (*Dying,* 64). Put otherwise, the emergence of *the subject who would know* establishes, in pure alienation, the identity of the object as *what is to be known.* The relation between the two is instrumental, the object as means to the subject's ends.

Alienation and instrumentality are not just liabilities of Cartesian knowing, they are its necessary conditions. Together, they energize a proj- ect of enormous power. Finally, so great is the prestige of Cartesian (and later scientific) clear and distinct methodology that the object of human "sighting" tends to be read as the object *tout court.* "Word and thing are brought to coincide in the sense that the former is a completely adequate and transparent representation of the latter" (Reiss, 36). The object slides from its intrinsic object status of "what is to be known," toward its instru- mental status for the subject: *what it is known as.* As John Yolton and others have emphasized, early modern thinkers themselves labored hard to keep this distinction clear. Characterizing the epistemological tradition from Descartes to Kant, Yolton writes: "We cannot see or experience the physi- cal aspects of objects as physical, only as known."[22] Making matters more difficult, Descartes speaks of the "object in the mind" as "objective reality," as distinguished from the object's "formal reality" (its existence in itself, apart from the subject's knowing). Locke picks up this same cautionary stance about the subject's irreducibly mediated relation to the material world, and Kant honors Lockean-Humean skepticism by turning it into a transcendental regulative principle: All we know is what *we* know (although that "we" remains subjective, it is subjective only—if sufficient care be taken—in universal, law-governed ways). But the more common take is that, thanks to scientifically rigorous observation and experiment, the subject can indeed determine the object as it is. In so believing, the subject comes into his birthright as one capable of knowing, and the career of Enlightenment-spawned epistemology is launched.[23]

At the heart of this vexed epistemological issue is the question of adequation. Can the trained mind produce schemas adequate to the real world that it seeks to map and affect? Scientific progress during this entire period seemed resoundingly to answer the question positively. As Ernst Cassirer, Alexander Koyré, Yolton, Reiss, and others note, mathematical thinking— central to the analytico-inductive procedures of Descartes and later of Newton—does indeed achieve a purchase on the behavior of the real world itself. But the cost of such knowing can be stark. A value-laden Aristotelian cosmos—whose fabric one shared—is replaced by a value-empty realm of material extension: alien, knowable only in terms of quantity. Cassirer puts it thus: "Every mathematical operation, according to Descartes, aims . . . to determine the proportions between an unknown quantity and other known quantities. . . . Both elements . . . must be reducible to quantity."[24] Reduction to quantification enables adequation—an "adequation," as Levinas puts it, "between thought and what it thinks."[25] Beyond this, achieved adequation transforms knowledge of the object into something subtler, yet revolutionary. It permits a reflexive doubling back of the subject upon itself, *confirmed in its self-knowing by its capacity to know the object.* Here, finally, is the subject-caressing magic attaching to the Enlightenment knowledge project. For "the knowledge of nature does not simply lead us out into the world of objects," as Cassirer says; "it serves rather as a medium in which the mind develops its own self-knowledge" (44). I claimed above that the Cartesian relation of subject to object is purely instrumental, but its deeper and undeclared payoff may now emerge. In coming to know the object as an other reducible to the terms of one's own measure and scale, one comes, reflexively, to know oneself as oneself.

Let us compose the subject birthed by Cartesian premises and procedures. It is a subject at once alone, empty of values, capable of reasoning methodically and thereby measuring—mastering—the realm of *res extensa* that surrounds it. It is a subject without history, without interest in the benightedness of history, but latent with a future. It is a subject whose adequation-based knowledge of what lies outside furnishes, at the same time, satisfying self-knowledge. Protocolonial, the project of knowing launches the recovery of "territories" earlier put in question by doubt. Fantastically self-conceiving, this male subject generates its own essential identity, no female womb needed for parturition. Everything it encounters is grist for its mill, potentially transformable into the knowledge that yields self-knowledge. This intrepidly reasoning individual is the darling of the Enlightenment: "There is a profoundly radical individualism at the heart of Enlightenment thought. Its rationalism led Enlightenment philosophy to enthrone the individual as the center and creator of meaning, truth, and even reality" (Kramnick, xv). In sum, this subject's life history unfolds as a series of encounters with the other—encounters that, in the form of knowledge, risk transforming that other into a mere dimension of the same. Might such knowing actually reduce to no more than the various dimensions of an incessant ego-logy that never leaves the precincts of self-sameness? No one has more penetratingly asked that question of Cartesian clarity/adequation than Emmanuel Levinas: "In clarity the exterior being presents itself as the work of the thought that receives it. Intelligibility, characterized by clarity, is a total adequation of the thinker with what is thought, in the precise sense of a mastery exercised by the thinker upon what is thought in which the object's resistance as an exterior being vanishes. This mastery is total" (*Totality,* 123–24).

I do not claim that such a monster is the protagonist of classic realist fiction. I contend only that the monster of *ego-logy*—a knowing (logos) that is essentially ego-commanded—threatens permanently the assumptions and procedures of Descartes's subject-centered universe and the Enlightenment narrative that follows from it. Such a monster openly surfaces in Hobbesian cynicism, reemerges in Locke's cautionary stance toward what lies outside us, mandates the ethical project of Kant's *Critique of Practical Reason,* and issues into the constituent, creative paradox of realist fiction. A subject seeks to know the otherness of the world: is the otherness that comes to be known truly other, or merely a guise of the subject seeking to know? We shall return to this conundrum again and again. Meanwhile, we have now sketched in both the epistemological practices that arose in the seventeenth century and the birth of the subject who would achieve knowledge and self-knowledge by operating them. Still missing in our emergent narrative is the stabilization of nature as a uniform and lawful spatial/temporal scene suitably accommodating such subjects and their practices—the articulation of a "System of the World." Enter Newton.

NEWTON FIXES MATTER AND MOTION IN SPACE AND TIME

It would be hard to exaggerate Newton's importance for Enlightenment thought. Alexander Pope spoke not for himself but for eighteenth-century culture when he wrote: "Nature and Nature's law lay hid in Night: / God said, Let Newton be! and All Was Light" (*Essay on Man*). In a single scientific text—*Mathematical Principles of Natural Philosophy* (1687)—Newton was seen to have "unified disparate phenomena, laid bare age-old secrets, and with one almost incredible intellectual effort, compelled nature to order" (Gay, 129). He draws, of course, on the "new philosophy" (discoveries based on a "mechanics" model) of others—Nicolaus Copernicus, Galileo, Johannes Kepler, Descartes, Robert Boyle, Pierre Gassendi—and like them, he proposes a world system whose procedures are strictly immanent and quantifiable. That system moves, as Galileo showed, according to the principle of inertia: "that motion perseveres and [unlike the traditional conception of an external agent needed to propel objects] requires no agent."[26] Exterior hypotheses are neither needed nor tolerated: "For Hypotheses are not to be regarded in experimental Philosophy," Newton famously declared (*Optics,* query 31, in *Newton,* 55). No more of propositions and syllogisms smelling of rhetoric rather than tested by observation and arrived at by method. A material world without the need of God to make it run is being conceived, described, and demonstrated.

No God needed to make it run: this is a crucial dimension of Newton's commitment to experimentation and the knowable facts.[27] Yet Newton was, at the same time, fervently committed to Christianity.[28] He never ceased to claim that the truths about the natural world promul gated in the *Principia,* however independent of God's powers for their cogency, were God-compatible—indeed, God-supportive: "To make this systeme therefore with all its motions, required a Cause which understood and compared together the quantities of matter in the several bodies of the Sun and Planets and the gravitating powers resulting from thence ... And to ... adjust all these things together ... argues that cause to be not blind and fortuitous, but very well skilled in Mechanicks and Geometry" (letter to Richard Bentley, in *Newton,* 332). Newton's God may not interfere, but he knows all he needs to about contemporary "Mechanicks and Geometry." What looks like a contradiction is actually a constitutive tension of Newton's worldview: God is not needed to make this thing run, but the sublime coherence of its way of running implies a mathematically informed Creator.

Seen from within the Enlightenment imaginary, Newton seems less to have dethroned God than to have replaced him. "Let Newton be! and All Was Light": thanks to one man's intellectual power, a Godlike order descends upon the world. It achieves—by way of his formulae—a transparency that is not only testable by experiment but even (apparently) commonsensical. As Ernst Mach later said of gravity's inexplicable capacity to act on objects without touching them: "the uncommon incomprehensibility became a common incomprehensibility."[29] Everyone *thinks* they understand it, though Newton himself never figured out why it works as it does, carefully calling it a "component" of his system rather than a clarified "element" of it.[30] Even Kant finds it difficult to refer to Newton without blurring the distinction between discoverer and creator: "Newton was the first to see order and regularity combined with great simplicity," Kant writes, "where hitherto disorder and multiplicity had reigned, and since then comets move in geometric paths" (cited in Cassirer, 153). As though he told them to, and they obeyed. Put otherwise, this secular model of natural knowing—immanent, anti-authoritarian—is at the same time received as an authoritative (quasi-divine) testament to the truth of things.

In Newton's mechanistic version the Creator generated the natural world from a blueprint quite different from that assumed in the Aristotelian/Scholastic tradition. "It seems probable to me," Newton wrote, "that God in the Beginning form'd Matter in solid, massy, hard, impenetrable, moveable Particles, of such Sizes and Figures, and with such other Properties, and in such Proportion to Space, as most conduced to the End for which he form'd them" (*Optics,* query 31, in *Newton,* 52–53). Beneath the scrupulous constraint of this claim—for Newton denies all understanding of the purposes underlying what he has found—one glimpses a portentous, culture-changing predication. At the heart of things, as Epicurus and Democritus had proposed long ago and as Boyle and Gassendi were arguing in Newton's time, there are *atoms.* Named for their invariant nature (*atom* comes from the Greek word for "indivisibility"), Newton's atoms emerge as the core of objecthood. "Solid, massy, hard, impenetrable," they are possessed of indestructible self-sameness. Indeed, they figure as the bedrock of identity. Deep down, far beneath what can be seen, atomically composed matter is inalterably what it is. Made of atoms, objects possess weight and measurable mass, thus entering the schema of quantification, prediction, and control. Knowability and material identity are reciprocal. Because objects have specific mass and weight, they are seriously themselves. They take on *gravity*.

Gravity is the linchpin of Newton's "System of the World." "The universal application of the law of attraction," writes Alexander Koyré, "restores the physical unity of the Newton universe and, at the same time, gives it its intellectual unity. . . . it is the same set of laws which governs all the motions in the infinite universe: that of an apple which falls to the ground and that of the planets which move round the sun."[31] Sunday principles are revealed to be the same as everyday ones; the natural world is a unified, demystified mechanical system. Gravity not only completes the image of the inalterable individuality of atomistic entities. It also inserts each individual entity into an infinite constellation of related entities. Every one of them is centered in its own mass; every one of them attracts, and is attracted by, the gravitational mass of the surrounding others. Perfect unity in perfect multiplicity.

Descartes once said, "Give me matter and I will build you a world" (cited in Cassirer, 51). It is Newton who remaps Descartes's matter and arrives, by way of that remapping, at the blueprint of an exquisitely plausible world. To get there he requires, in addition to atom-constituted entities, Galileo's notion of inertial force, algorithms for plotting entities' motion in terms of their mass and velocity, and a stabilized frame for the space and time within which such movement lawfully occurs. Space and time must therefore become neutral and absolute. Newton declares: "Absolute space, in its own nature, without relation to anything external, remains always similar and immovable" (scholium, in *Newton,* 232). Likewise, he insists that "absolute, true, and mathematical time, of itself, and from its own nature, flows equally without relation to anything external, and by another name is called duration" (232). Both realms are uniform: "all things are placed in time as to order of succession; and in space as to order of situation" (233). As such, lawful themselves, they permit the "enlightened predictability" of the movement of all matter in the universe.

The players and the realm within which they play are thus brought to the board of knowledge. Newton's calculus is prepared to plot the moves on that board with unfailing accuracy. With the introduction of the all-clarifying final key—gravity—the game can begin, the motions open up to measurement. Here Newton arrives at his most elegant declaration of law:

Law 1—Every body continues in its state of rest, or of uniform motion in a right line, unless it is compelled to change that state by forces impressed upon it.

Law 2—The change of motion is proportional to the motive force impressed; and is made in the direction of the right line in which that force is impressed.

Law 3—To every action there is always opposed an equal reaction: or, the mutual actions of two bodies upon each other are always equal, and directed to contrary parts. (*Newton,* 234)

All bodies in a state of rest or inertial motion continue, if left alone, as they were. Only other forces impressing upon them can alter their state. That alteration, moreover, matches precisely the impressing force, the one body moving in recoil according to the other's advance. Finally, a body striking another body always recoils, itself, with exactly the amount of force that it has brought to bear on that other body. The beautiful simplicity of these laws has long been recognized, but we might note as well the ethics implicit in this drama of force and counterforce. As you strike, so are you stricken—and by exactly the force of your striking. Kant will later, in the categorical imperative, articulate and reconfigure the moral law lurking in the Newtonian paradigm. Yet "lurking" is the right term: Newton states only the sheer intelligibility of bodies in motion and commotion. This map deals with the interplay of amoral forces, one moreover in which the bigger objects attract imperiously the smaller ones. Their "will" is, so to speak, irresistible.[32]

If this was indeed, as Newton scholars claim, "the most famous generalization of the Scientific Revolution and a central feature of the science that dominated Western thought until the twentieth century,"[33] what are its larger implications for fictional practice? One might begin by noting that Newton's "System of the World" is as temporally continuous as Kierkegaard's vision of crisis on Mount Moriah is not. Johannes de Silentio muses that Abraham's "three and a half days could be infinitely longer than the few thousand years that separate me from Abraham" (53), but Newton's absolute time envisages no such subjective glitches. First point: the Newtonian world picture is comforting in its very cohesiveness. Not only does the conviction that Newton *knows* obtain (for over two centuries) throughout the educated West, but the behavior of the natural world proposed by his paradigm of knowing seems (in its broad outlines) eminently commonsensical.[34] The trajectory of everything physical can (in theory) be accounted for.

Next, let us return to those hard, glossy, and imperishable atoms that are the bedrock of matter and that house the force of gravity. This arrangement

(at once local and universal) suggests—at the level of the cultural imaginary—a centripetal schema in which entities cohere by always sustaining, so
to speak, their own center. It is therefore an understandable, if unjustifiable,
stretch when Alexander Innes prefaces Archibald Campbell's *Inquiry into
the Origin of Moral Virtue* (1728) as follows: self-love will "as clearly resolve
and explain all the *Moral Relations* and *Propositions* between the several
Agents in the Intellectual World; as the Incomparable *Sir Isaac Newton,* by
his Noble Principle of Attraction (which we may call the *Self-Love* of Inanimate Beings) has unravell'd the several *Phaenomena* of the Material
World."[35] Gravity is figured here as a sort of abiding attachment to one's
inner core, the natural (amoral) grounding of inextirpable self-love. To go
further, is it likewise an understandable (but even more unjustifiable)
stretch to see a Newtonian paradigm lurking in Adam Smith's (in)famous
conviction that "the individual intends only his own gain, and he is in this,
as in many other cases, led by an invisible hand to promote an end which
was no part of his intention"?[36] Does the Newtonian paradigm lurk in
Smith's casual legitimation of the individual's centripetal egotism, as well,
perhaps, as in the comforting notion of an objective structure (an "invisible
hand") turning that egotism to benign (though unintended) ends? God does
not underwrite the *Principia,* Newton is careful to say, but it is thought that
he would be comfortable with its arrangements.

Finally, and this may be the most impermissible stretch of all, does the
beauty of Newton's mechanically ordered universe lodge in the tensions it
figures between stasis and motion, isolation and community, balance and
longing? Objects would tend toward their own gravitational centers—a
suicidal excess of self-love?—were it not for the continuous counterattraction exerted by other objects, a counterattraction not sought but irresistible.
The imbalance of each establishes the balance of all. Each body, seeking
and sought, is caught in a mesh of attractions beyond its own comprehension, though knowable, indeed known to the great mapmaker. The gravity
lodged in each serves at once as its organizing core and its myopic limit, the
inward-focused longing that can conceive only in distorted fashion the
greater (but distant and seemingly irrelevant) force field of the whole.
Finally, the arrangement of parts and whole on the Newton canvas is as
pitiless as it is poetic, the price of cosmic coherence being the objective erasure of freedom within the puny individuals who subjectively fantasize it
nevertheless. I am aware of what is impermissible about this stretch: its figurative application of a Newtonian calculus of moving bodies to the
human scene of self and others. But isn't a carryover to unintended
domains exactly the work that supreme paradigms illegitimately effect

upon the cultural imaginary that absorbs them? Isn't this transfer of New-ton's thought abusive on a minor scale, given the distortions social Darwin-ism was to impose on Darwin's thought two centuries later?

In any event, it is safe to say that Newton's gravitational paradigm dom-inates the image of knowing for over two centuries, contributing centrally to the realist narrative I argue to be in the making.[37] Taking stock, we note the following elements of that narrative that are now available. A power-ful, observation-fueled testing procedure has emerged. A subject who would know the material properties of the external world has been con-ceived and birthed. A spatial-temporal canvas on which he will move has been rationalized, answering to the calculation of motion as trivial as an apple's fall, as sublime as Jupiter's orbit. The narrative is taking shape; the empirical method, the knowing subject, and the rationalized scene are in place. What is missing are the fuller contours of the plot to be enacted. Enter Locke.

LOCKE ESTABLISHES EXPERIENTIAL PLOT

Locke not only knew Newton and his work—both were members of the Royal Society—but published his *Essay concerning Human Understanding* (1690) within three years of Newton's *Principia*. The two thinkers are regu-larly paired in eighteenth-century commentary. D'Alembert proclaimed in mid-century that Locke "created metaphysics almost as Newton had cre-ated physics"—such "creation" being understood as no less an abolition of Aristotelian "metaphysics" than Newton's physics was an abolition of Aris-totelian cosmology. For Locke's empirical approach "reduced metaphysics to . . . the experimental science of the mind."[38] Experimental: one under-stands the mind not by deducing its procedures from untestable first prin-ciples, nor by calling everything into doubt. (Locke's conceptual frame is as peopled as Descartes's is solitary.) Rather, one observes with care, and one continues to observe, assuming as little as possible in advance of the observ-ing. "Instead of presuming what we know not," Voltaire wrote of Locke's procedures, "he examines gradually what we want to know. He takes an infant at the instant of his birth; he traces step by step the progress of his understanding" (cited in Kramnick, 192). An infant at birth, the step-by-step progress of his understanding: it trembles on the verge of fictional plot. The temporal gap from Locke to the opening chapter of *David Cop-perfield*—"I am born"—is considerable (160 years), but the gap in develop-mental models is slight.

"This, therefore, being my *Purpose* to enquire into the Original, Certainty, and Extent of humane knowledge; together, with the Grounds and Degrees of Belief, Opinion, and Assent."[39] So Locke opens the *Essay,* intent upon distinguishing knowledge from belief or opinion, inquiring into the rational conditions justifying (or prohibiting) assent. What can one know, and how should that bear on living one's life?—these are already visible as the questions driving Locke's treatise. Although Richard Rorty has accused Locke of epistemological naïveté—asserting an indemonstrable capacity of the knower to grasp the contours of the known—Locke is quite cautious. We begin life ignorant, as blank slates, for all ideas come from sensation or reflection: "Let us then suppose the Mind to be, as we say, white Paper, void of all Characters, without any *Ideas:*—How comes it to be furnished? . . . To this I answer, in one word, from *Experience*" (2.1.2). Experience is how we gradually come to know—no authorized program pre-exists or supersedes it—and we are overwhelmingly likely to mislearn through experience. The light of the outer world reaches us only modestly. In a well-known passage employing the analogy of a camera obscura, Locke speaks of "external and internal Sensation . . . [as] the Windows by which light is let into this *dark room*. For, methinks, the *Understanding* is not much unlike a *Closet* wholly shut from light, with only some little openings left, to let in . . . *Ideas* of things without" (2.11.17). Note that what is let in (and only parsimoniously) are *ideas* of things, not the things themselves. We understand objects only in the form of the immaterial ideas our minds propose for them. We grasp what Kant will call the object's *phenomenal* qualities, qualities belonging to our way of knowing it, not to the object itself. We may refer to this, as Descartes did, as "the very being of the objects known," yet that kind of being is never more, tautologically, than "the being of objects as known" (Yolton, 169).

Lockean experience, then, is not an affair of unmediated reception of the outside world (his is in no simple sense a "mind-as-mirror-of-nature" philosophy).[40] Rather, experience is mediated through and through by ideas (our internal grasp on things) abidingly subject to error. What we possess as an idea—insofar as it concerns material nature and not mathematical propositions—is only the "nominal essence" of the thing. This tells us what we mean by the thing but not why it is as it is. By contrast, as Roger Woolhouse puts Locke's position, "[t]he real essence of something is its 'very being . . . whereby it is, what it is.'"[41] Locke goes on to distinguish real essence from nominal essence by comparing how a clockmaker would view the Strasbourg Cathedral clock with how a "gazing Country-man" would view it (3.6.3, cited in Chappell, 158). Both men would know what the clock does, but only the clockmaker would know why it does it. With respect to the great bulk of our experience, Locke concludes, we are as gazing countrymen, not as clockmakers.

Locke finds nothing depressing in these epistemological constraints. In Woolhouse's words, "Not only [in the Lockean frame] have we no need to know much of what we do not know, we also are not suited for it" (in Chappell, 147). God gives us "not the knowledge that is necessary and useful, but rather the means to acquire it" (148). The grandeur of Locke's conception of experience inhabits, so to speak, the far side of certain knowledge. Because we are not equipped to know with certainty, we must learn to know by trial. Our lack is our stimulus. Locke stresses not the knowledge we cannot have, but the resources we have in abundance—as though the human figure were supremely fitted for making a great deal out of the "dark room" of his meager knowing. This is not Descartes's insistence on radical doubt, in which the search is interior and isolated, but rather a potentially comic vision of the common human enterprise as a darkened but enlightenable project we are enjoined to undertake. In giving us the means to acquire knowledge, God launches, so to speak, our adventure through space and time as a process open to learning and to acquisition. On this adventure we must proceed inductively, without proofs or theorems, shedding false ideas and finding our way into true(r) ones. "*Experience here must teach me,* what Reason cannot: and 'tis by trying alone, that I can certainly know" (4.12.9).

This drama of trial is social to the hilt. We are not enjoined into "that Abyss of Darkness, (where we have not Eyes to see, nor Faculties to perceive anything) out of a Presumption, that nothing is beyond our Comprehension" (4.3.22). We learn, instead, through our secular encounters with palpable others, not our metaphysical wrestling with the untouchable godhead. "The Faculty, which God has given Man to supply the want of clear and certain Knowledge in Cases where that cannot be had, is *Judgment*" (4.14.3). Judgment is social, approximate, revisable: civil. Though Locke does not speak of the religious violence that ravaged England throughout the seventeenth century, it is pertinent that he composes the *Essay* at the very time (late 1680s) that William of Orange comes to the British throne, putting an end to over a century of sectarian barbarities sanctioned by the name of God. What we cannot know, Locke believes in good Enlightenment fashion, we do not need to know: "the proper study of Mankind is Man" (Pope, *Essay on Man*).

This sense of public trial and shareable judgment as civic undertakings enters into Locke's understanding of selfhood. "*Person,* as I take it, is the name for . . . *self*. Where-ever a Man finds, what he calls *himself*, there, I think, another may say is the same *Person*. It is a Forensick Term appropriating Actions and their Merit; and so belongs only to intelligent Agents capable of a Law, and Happiness and Misery. This personality extends it *self* beyond present Existence to what is past, only by consciousness, whereby it becomes concerned and accountable" (2.27.26). Unlike Descartes, Locke envisages the establishing of one's claimed selfhood in terms of the corroboration of others. My being selved opens onto the stage of another's appropriate judgment. Though denoting me alone, my selfhood proceeds in a forensic manner, clothing me, so to speak, with my actions and their cumulative merits, over time past, present, and to come. Lockean selfhood is thus an overarching, socialized, responsible concept; it turns individuals into agents. The scene he characterizes is plural. Not only do I accede to my selfhood by way of trial (trial as error, but also as trying again and again), but my selfhood is also open to trial by others, accountable to them even as their selfhood is by implication accountable to me.

Here, perhaps, lies the considerable appeal of the Lockean conception of human understanding. Not only does he recognize that during most of the trials and accomplishments of our lives we are as gazing countrymen rather than experts. He also writes for those countrymen, distilling (wherever possible) his own insights into common terms, proffering familiar analogies when the concepts in question are recondite. In this procedure his coming role as "America's philosopher" can be glimpsed, for Locke conceptualizes the emancipation of the common (white, male) individual. Life, liberty, and the pursuit of property become, in his thinking, the birthright of all men—a proclamation only slightly reworded in the American Declaration of Independence. As Hans Aarsleff puts it, "His great message was to set us free from the burden of tradition and authority, both in theology and knowledge, by showing that the entire grounds of our right conduct in the world can be secured by the experience we may gain by the innate faculties and powers we are born with" (cited in Chappell, 252). Faculties we are born with, experience all of us may gain: "Natural philosophy can only admit knowledge that is open to all, that is, drawn from the shareable experience of reflection and sensation, of reason and the senses" (256). The realm of common democratic values is summoned here, though we must recognize that, for all its reach, the Lockean adventure takes root in that "dark room" of individual consciousness. For all its sociable sunniness to come, this remains a philosophy of the questing subject, others stationed all around him as he comes into his own.

The narrative is all but complete. Drawing on representative Enlightenment propositions, we have identified the emergence of a powerful observational procedure for doing things to nature, the birth of an unhampered
subject who seeks to know, the authoritative ordering of the material universe (from apples to stars) in uniform space and time, its force and
motions open to exact measurement. Procedure, subject, and setting are in
place. Locke takes these and sets them in motion by way of a plot that has
proved to have abiding appeal—launching novels and compelling audi-
ences from his time to our own. The plot goes like this, moving progressively from dawn to day (but rarely far into the evening): I am born; I learn
swiftly that I do not yet know but am capable of knowing; I am not predicated (no inherited schema contains me), but the world I inhabit *is* predicated, that is, knowable by way of trial and error, God-given perhaps but
secular in its operations; I can learn to negotiate objects and others in the
familiar space and time of this schema, obtaining property as I go; my
doing this confirms reflexively my identity as an agent in my own life
(property referring simultaneously to what I own and to what is "proper to
me," mine alone); I cannot obtain everything, but if observant, prudent,
and self-aware, I can get what I deserve. I am, it seems, everyman. I am
also white-male-bourgeois-developmental acquisitiveness. Therefore one
last element is required of this narrative, something that will allow it to
continue speaking to my dreams while at the same time honoring my
Judeo-Christian conviction that the systematic career of selfhood is an
exercise not of virtue but of vice. The narrative must be effectively moralized, yet without repudiating the earlier givens. This is not only not easy, it
is probably impossible. Enter Kant.

KANT MORALIZES THE ENLIGHTENMENT NARRATIVE

I shall begin by stressing epistemological Kant, the thinker who liked to
see himself as the Newton of the mind. Kant's transfer of Newton's external scene of lawful heavenly bodies to an internal scene of lawful subjective necessities is a stunning leap. Lawful necessity is, for them both, the
keynote: "Everything that happens is hypothetically necessary; that is a
principle that subjects alteration in the world to a law . . . without which
not even nature itself would obtain."[42] Newton's outer world is here
reprised, mentally, according to its uniform necessities, inasmuch as these
appear to human consciousness—the world's *phenomenal* nature (which is
all we shall ever know of it). Nature assumes conditions of necessity and

rule-governedness because consciousness could not conceive it otherwise. The interplay of inner and outer can be confusing, but Kant's logic does not falter: "Thus there may very well be something outside us," he writes later in the *Critique,* "which we call matter, corresponding to this appearance; but in the same quality as appearance it is not outside us, but is merely a thought in us, even though this thought . . . represents it as being found outside us" (A385). In Paul Guyer's words, "Kant ultimately came to see that the validity of both the laws of the starry skies above as well as the moral law within had to be sought in the legislative power of human intellect itself" (2). Legislative: Kant's starry skies are as rule-driven as Newton's obedient comets. For, as Guyer claims, "the possibility and indeed the certainty of the spatiotemporal framework of Newtonian physics could be secured only by recognizing it to be the form of our own experience" (10).[43]

Space and time, thus fixed as regulative coordinates imposed by human consciousness, are more than merely "the subjective condition under which alone all intuition can take place in us" (B49, cited by Charles Parsons, "Transcendental Aesthetic," in Guyer, 82). *Their lawfulness buttresses the unity of consciousness itself.* This reciprocity is crucial. As in Descartes, the apprehension of an object's identity—its calculability in specified space and time—coheres reflexively the identity of the subject coming to know. Suturing the self is an inestimable "byproduct" of cogently apprehending the other. Kant's claim is perhaps more basic—at the level of mental acts of representation itself—but its insistence on the unity and continuity of consciousness as the ground of cognition of anything external implies a similar reciprocity. Kant writes: "We are conscious *a priori* of the thoroughgoing identity of ourselves with regard to all representations that can ever belong to our cognition" (A116). Or, as he puts it elsewhere, "the *I think* must *be able* to accompany all my representations" (B131–32, emphasis in the original). The logic is compelling inasmuch as representations do not just "occur" to me as random marks upon a substitutable blackboard; rather, "I think" these representations actively, they are mine, testifying to my "thoroughgoing identity." Thus, insofar as Kant ends by assuring my inner coherence as a necessary precondition for the logic of my outer representations, one may wonder: is the baby (centered selfhood) being brought in by way of the bath powder (ordered spatial/temporal representations)?[44] At any rate, within the transcendental framework of subjective consciousness rather than the mechanical one of objective mass and motion, Kant establishes a law-governed traffic in space and time as absolute as Newton's "System of the World"—in both cases a scene of necessities.

Within such unremitting constraints, how does Kant propose to establish a realm of unpredicatedness that we could call freedom? What conceptual room exists that might permit *human* entities to claim autonomy?
They cannot otherwise be ethical agents. How can Kant find the Christian
God in a Newtonian universe? If I follow him here, Kant's response does
not involve finding God. It centers, first, on Kant's ethical notion of human
requirements, and then on his epistemological conviction of the (radical)
limits of human knowing. First, as beings who must be moral agents if we
are to remain human, we require the notion of freedom. Then, as beings
who can know nothing of the *noumenal* world (things as they actually are,
independent of our knowing), we know the world only as it appears, phe-
nomenally, to human consciousness. It follows that we ourselves are thus
determined—rather than free—only *apparently* (according to how we
must appear). Because we cannot reach knowledge of our own essence, we
cannot know that we are not free: which means we can and must act as
though we are free. As Locke sees the limits of our knowing calling into
play our faculty of judgment, so Kant sees the limits of knowledge making
possible moral and religious life: "I had to deny *knowledge*," Kant famously
declared in the *Critique of Pure Reason,* "in order to make room for *faith*"
(Bxxx, emphasis in the original).

This claim appears, but is not, defensive. Rather, the human mind, for
Kant, just *is* legislative. As it cannot function in a material world without
nature-regulative categories, so it cannot function in a moral world without behavior-regulative categories. "No authority external to ourselves is
needed to constitute or inform us of the demands of morality," J. B.
Scheewind writes of Kant's moral philosophy: "We can each know without
being told what we ought to do because moral requirements are requirements we impose upon ourselves."[45] Thus Kant arrives at the categorical
imperative: "Act in such a way that you always treat humanity . . . never
simply as a means, but always . . . as an end" (Scheewind citing *Ground-
work,* in Guyer, 322). Others conceive and pursue their ends, even as I conceive and pursue mine. Newton's famous Second Law of Motion becomes
moralized. It is no longer that what I do to you rebounds on me, but rather
that I am to leave you untouched, even as I would want you to leave me
untouched, for we each have our own motions in mind.[46] On this schema,
all human lives proceed, precisely, as not-just-matter. "The inertia of matter is and signifies nothing else but its *lifelessness* as matter in itself. Life
means the capacity of a substance to act on itself from an inner principle."[47]
Acting from one's own inner principle, determining one's ends, as opposed
to being determined by external forces (being a means to other and more

powerful ends): this is the Kantian moral drama. It is likewise a central moral drama of realist fiction.

The keynote of Kantian politics, as of Kantian ethics, emerges as *autonomy:* in Onora O'Neill's words, "the principle of not submitting to groundless authorities . . . [thus] the core of reason, hence of enlightenment."[48] Autonomy is the birthright of free individuals entitled to generate their own ends, capable of assuming full responsibility for their own lives. If reason is enlightenment, O'Neill goes on to posit, then "enlightenment is no more than autonomy in thinking and in acting—that is, of thought and action that are lawful yet assume no lawgiver" (in Guyer, 299). Here, I believe, we reach the creative paradox at the heart of the Enlightenment imaginary. On the one hand, philosophy and science have established a fundamental force field determining the behavior of matter. On the other, that same philosophy and science, as well as liberal ethics, require a no less fundamental commitment to the value of the subject's free-moving power and autonomy. All matter is wholly bound, embodied individuals must be essentially free. "Enlightenment is man's release from his self-incurred tutelage. . . . *Sapere aude!* 'Have courage to use your own reason!'" Kant proclaimed ("What Is Enlightenment?" cited in Kramnick, 1). Dare to know, free yourself, rise into your estate.

Autonomy, individuality, freedom: tellingly absent from this trio of values is any sense of *community.* And for good reason: from Bacon and Descartes through Locke and Kant the central player in the emerging narrative is an independent subject who wants to know, a subject who accesses others or objects outside himself only by way of mediating schemas, a subject whose coherence is reflexively underwritten by coming to know others in their subsidiary otherness. In Alasdair MacIntyre's trenchant terms, "Each moral agent now spoke unconstrained by the externalities of divine law, natural teleology or hierarchical authority; but why should anyone else now listen to him?" (66). Such absence of communal values sounds more like Hobbes than Kant, yet this seems the unspoken base note driving Kant's insistence on the autonomy of *all* subjects. Only in a world conceived at the most basic level as an interplay of conflicting individual projects does Kant's plea to respect the autonomy of others reveal its urgency. I myself am free, empowered, unpredicated; you, however, are other, determinable, a possible means for my ends, just as other things serve as possible means for my ends. My being comes before yours. You may well be something real outside me, but I apprehend you only as a thought existing within me—spectral, secondary.

The Enlightenment individual whose birth and pathways I have here sketched pre-exists, so to speak, the realm of others and objects in which he moves. Indeed, Cartesian liberation of the subject involves a virtually *ontological* move. The individual occupies a prior space of inner being; what is outside this space is speculative. The need to correct this lopsided figure/ground ratio—the I so large, the other(s) so small—obviously supplies the ethical project of realist fiction. Less obviously, such lopsidedness itself is in a measure constituent of Enlightenment narrative. As such, it is incorrigible, fueling thus a genre whose deepest commitments seem to run at cross-purposes, as though the realist novel—at its most revealing moments—were to resemble a creature whose feet moved resolutely in the opposite direction of its arms.

SUBJECT, SPACE, AND TIME IN THE ENLIGHTENMENT NARRATIVE

If I have properly sketched in this "commonsense" narrative about subjects moving toward knowledge through familiar space and time, it will appear richly ambivalent: a narrative we cannot do without, yet one whose disturbing priorities we cannot ignore. We cannot do without it because the drama of individuals coming to know is irreplaceable. Once the Enlightenment in its thought and practice had delegitimized the authority of crown and church, it could put in its place only a story of adventuring subjects, each with an unforeclosed future. The telos of this story, for the Enlightenment, is *education:* escape from self-incurred tutelage, daring to know. The central text of the Enlightenment is surely the seventeen-volume *Encyclopédie* edited by Diderot and d'Alembert. What greater testimony to the value of education could there be than an encyclopedia? Coming to know takes on its resonance only when a sanctioned natural/spiritual cosmos is replaced by an unsanctioned physical realm other than us, open to both our knowledge and our mastery. Unsanctioned: human life begins in doubt, ignorance, and orphanhood. It takes on value by way of the orientations and recognitions that one manages to acquire over extensive time and space. This forward-moving drama proceeds by a gradual familiarization of, and negotiation with, the conditions we encounter. It binds the subject's passage through space and time into what the Greeks called *paideia* (education, leading out of the spirit)—the etymological root and humane dream behind Diderot and d'Alembert's *Encyclopédie.*

Yet the "analytico-referential" discourse that arose in the seventeenth century and dominated Western scientific thought for the next two hundred years is, as we have seen, fraught with trouble. It must "disenchant" the world (Max Weber's great verb) before it can subjugate it to knowledge;

the natural sphere, emptied of value, enters the conditions of pure quantification. The emergent subject alienates himself from family and custom in order to practice effectively upon this world; the world practiced upon is likewise alienated. More, the referentiality of such discourse, when approached more closely, is fraught with trouble as well. This language can say the world not as it is but only as it is known. (Things as they are have departed from the wordscape of Western science, not to reappear.) But apprehending things only as they are known risks reducing the things to mere items within the subject's lexicon for knowing them. Does all our knowing reduce to an ongoing ego-logy?

The spatial and temporal coordinates of such a worldview are insistently tailored to the interests of the knowing subject. Space is traversed in ways that promote recognition, empowerment, education. Time is even more powerfully domesticated for progressive purposes. Experimental science, committed to the project of repeatable procedures that will reproduce the same results, provides a resonant model for countering time's dispersive power; it invokes time always in the interest of human mastery. Put more broadly, the Enlightenment narrative of coming to know—of moving past error into accuracy—fixes space and time as conditions permitting human empowerment. But undomesticated space, in reality, dwarfs the puny human traces made upon it. And unplotted time, in reality, is the frame in which human identity alters and individual lives move toward their end. Arguably, all fictional narrative exists to avert a recognition of human unraveling: by *plotting* time rather than conceding its unplotted power. (Peter Brooks has made such an argument.)[49] In any event, realist narrative follows hard upon the progressive strand in Enlightenment thought that has been so stressed in the foregoing pages: that the subject's movement through space and time is an adventure, and a profitable one at that.

Modernist and postmodern narratives, as I explore in later chapters, repudiate in various ways the "common sense" of this Enlightenment/realist narrative. They refuse to endorse the economy of the same that covertly subtends the realist subject's encounter with the other. They do this by attacking realist narrative's constitutive compact joining subject, space, and time. First, they sabotage realism's spatial premise that representational language somehow makes reliable contact with the real world (signaled by that language) of objects, others, and the reader (the protagonist achieving enlightening encounter with others and objects outside himself, the reader being enlightened by participating in these encounters). The meaning of such sabotage? *In knowing others I colonize rather than encounter them / the language*

I use cannot cross into the space of the other. Second, they refuse realism's temporal premise that the subject (in the narrative) and the reader (by engaging the narrative) retain continuous identity over time. The meaning of such refusal? *"I" is an illusion of sustained identity that representational language is crafted to create / the identity of subjects living in real time is unfixed, if not fictional.*

Foucault and Levinas both explore critically how suasions of conventional representation are linked with the premises of sustained identity. Foucault writes that even though time imposes a linear sequence on representation, representation nevertheless is able "to reconstitute itself for itself in imagination and thus . . . to subjugate time . . . [and] to recover what had been conceded to succession" (*Order,* 335). Foucault sought repeatedly to compose analytic histories that would dislodge this fantasy of the subject's self-restitution over time: "My aim was to analyse this history . . . to map it in a dispersion that no pre-established horizon would embrace; to allow it to be deployed in an anonymity on which no transcendental constitution would impose the form of the subject."[50] For his part, Levinas has argued that "[t]he positing of a pure present without even tangential ties with time is the marvel of representation. It is a void of time. . . . To be sure the I who conducts his thoughts *becomes* . . . in time. . . . But this becoming in time does not appear on the plane of representation" (*Totality,* 125, emphasis in the original).

More, Levinas grasps the progressive logic at the core of the Enlightenment subject's passage through space and time. A rhythm of apparent self-loss (wandering through space and time) is actually one of self-recovery: "It is as though subjective life in the form of consciousness consisted in being itself losing itself and finding itself again so as to *possess itself.* . . . The detour . . . leads to coinciding with oneself, that is, to certainty, which remains the guide and guarantee of the whole spiritual adventure of being. But this is why this adventure is no adventure. It is never dangerous; it is self-possession, sovereignty."[51] Sovereignty because consciousness converts—by way of knowing—the otherness of everything it encounters into aspects of its own (reconfirmed) self-sameness.

I conclude this genealogy by speculatively aligning the "ego-logy of realism" with the procedures of an exemplary novel of the eighteenth century, Defoe's *Robinson Crusoe.* Defoe is no philosopher, nor is Crusoe, yet the novel's moves reprise in a number of ways the generic Enlightenment model of subject/space/time set forth above. First, it is narrated in a transparent prose that seems to take us effortlessly into the world represented within the fiction. As Defoe's commentators long ago pointed out, he has the capacity apparently to remove himself and to insert his readers into his scenes as though they were there.[52] The wildest fantasy—that a ship-wrecked man would end up wealthy and successful rather than dead through starvation or depression—comes across as plausible while we are reading it. Defoe's language of representation conceals its status as representation; the reader seems to journey unhindered in real space and time. Reprising Foucault's and Levinas's concerns about the reconfirmed subject and its shored up sovereignty, but in a lexicon pertinent to Defoe and to fiction more generally, we might ask the following: does the representational logic of such a narrative provide anything more than a delicious ego-logy—a stroking of the subject's fantasy of invincible self-possession, not to mention imperial possession of others—disguised as a voyage of genuine encounter?

Further, although Crusoe's adventures are empirical and unplanned, every crisis somehow turns to profit. As Reiss has argued, Crusoe's recurrent spiritual concerns are neither a hypocritical dodge nor a central motivation. He does care (intermittently) for the welfare of his soul, he also cares (intermittently) about the success of his projects, and he is not eager to work out the implications of this tension. Though Providence hardly underwrites his contingent adventures, they end by seeming . . . providential. "'Sin' there is not," writes Reiss; "rather there is a process of learning, of acquisition, of making, of coming to power and authority" (304). Crusoe's purposiveness lies shrouded in contingency. His concern for his soul cohabits, in inexplicably untroubled ways, with his focus on material gain. Like Crusoe's continuous but "unintentional" profiting, the prose in which his story unfolds—apparently unauthored—also "goes of itself," testifying to a seemingly objective and free-standing world. In Reiss's words, "The 'individual' now makes a place for 'himself' within an order 'he' shows and uses as if it had existed from all time. . . . Crusoe acquires his power and authority—and all his property—'*passively*' because he follows that order (even thought he needs must 'activate' it)" (327; emphasis in the original).

What masterplot—an "order" so familiar as to lodge beneath recognition—shapes this model of the subject's fortuitous prospering over docile time and supportive space? Does Weber's Protestant ethic meet the spirit of capitalism in the form of Crusoe? Is doing well related to doing good in ways that are here inextricably blurred—the ongoing life of secular success testifying to the atemporal (but unknowable) assignment of grace, yet success and grace remaining necessarily different from each other? What would it mean to say—with respect to such a representational schema—that the atemporal significance of a life is known to its maker, though not to the one living it as he moves through time, thus assuring that he continues to move through the time unknowing, yet silently oriented by the conviction that his significance is, though undisclosed, known? What such a subject experiences in the present as obscure—caught up in trial and error—has actually already reached conclusion and clarification. To be sure, a clarification not known to the protagonist (though Crusoe as narrator must know without telling), nor—as is mandatory in realism—fully known to the reader either. But the reader knows that what is to come is already written, and that this deferral/duplicity—this playing with time as both ongoing and mastered—constitutes a delightful adventure.

Put in other words: what shall we say of realism's seeming to move forward contingently, as though it were respecting time's concealed futurity, even as its deployment of verbs in the past tense keeps subliminally reassuring the reader that this not-yet-future is a retrospective past, has already happened and been written? Does this double-edged movement through time constitute the illegitimate magic, not just of realism, but in a certain measure of narrative—of representation—itself? Is Defoe's seemingly transparent prose that draws us into the scene as though we were transplanted there and then more broadly emblematic of narrative's power not so much to recover time as, in Brooks's words, to "pervert" it? However we read such playing with time, we are far from Kierkegaard's insistence on being "conscientious about time," his refusal to represent our immersion in time as an adventure still unfolding yet safely seen through and end-clarified. (As Levinas saw, such an "adventure is no adventure. It is never dangerous; it is self-possession, sovereignty.") Juxtaposing Defoe's realist practice, Kierkegaard's protomodernist practice, and Levinas's modernist strictures allows us to ask one final question. When modernist and postmodern narrative refuse to rehearse these centering (indeed, imperial) moves of the subject journeying productively through space and time, is this a correction we require, or is it a reneging on narrative's most precious gift? I cannot answer all these questions, but I can guarantee that, in the considerations of fictional practice—realist, modernist, and postmodern—that lie ahead (but that, dear reader, are already written), they will get their hearing.

CHAPTER THREE

Anatomy of Realism

Coming to Know, from Defoe to Dostoevsky

REVISITING REALISM AND ITS DISCONTENTS

Many of the claims I have begun to make about realist fiction involve the reader's participatory stance toward the scene of representation. It is therefore pertinent briefly to survey the attack on realist representation mounted by university critics during the later decades of the twentieth century. Deconstruction's narrow target was realism, the broader one was representation itself. Based on the Saussurean view of language as a system of empty differences (nonreferential, functioning by way of words' differential relation to other words), deconstruction indicted the epistemological naïveté of realism—its pretense that it could reliably represent reality through words. Worse than naïveté, realism was—so Roland Barthes argued—sheer ideology masking as objective representation. What is called the real is what hegemonic power calls the real; such a claim is to be contested wherever encountered, so that the ideology driving the claim may be exposed. Barthes attacked literary realism at its citadel—Balzac—and produced in *S/Z* a discourse on Balzac's "Sarrasine" in which neither Balzac nor Sarrasine emerged with a shred of subjective agency, innocence, or familiarity still intact. Reconfiguring author, character, plot, and language to the point where the contract binding them together as a singular intentional act burst asunder, Barthes divided the text into five impersonal, meaning-productive codes. Realism emerged as a composite creature of these codes, the codes themselves repositories of

cultural stereotype, not cultural wisdom.[1] Barthes's stance toward literature mandated, on the part of the critic, a judgmental binary. On the one
hand, the "readerly" text—reader-friendly, realist—was reactionary, a
product of the dead hand of authority. On the other hand, the "writerly"
text—antirealist, slipping past or subverting conventional codes—was
uncoopted, a blow for freedom. For more than a decade one of the great
games of literary criticism consisted of taking texts previously assumed
"readerly" and showing them to be "writerly." (A text that nevertheless
remained "readerly" was seen to be a mere repository of stultifying norms;
most realist texts were placed in this category.)

Barthes's attack was enjoined by a larger battery of French intellectual
heavyweights of the later twentieth century—Foucault, Gilles Deleuze,
and Jean-François Lyotard—all four concurring that the premise of representation itself was untenable. As Christopher Prendergast reprises the
argument, any pretense, on the part of language, to *represent* reliably something nonlinguistic amounts to a laying down of the law: "It is the Law
which regulates the economy of mimesis. . . . As such, it is closely aligned
with forces of repression and censorship."[2] Jacques Derrida went the next
step and claimed that "all organised narration is a 'matter for the police'"
(from "Living On," cited in Prendergast, 39). Foucault's panopticon,
Deleuze's critique of "territorialization," Lyotard's crusade against "master
narratives": these related attacks on social and representational structures
as strategies of surveillance—concealed policing—were enormously influential in literary-critical quarters. Jonathan Culler's ingenious reading of
Gustave Flaubert (*The Uses of Uncertainty*) rescued the novelist from complicity with the police—showing his seemingly denotative/realist style to be
scrupulously opaque, and inspiring a virtual industry of commentary that
either attacked realism for its complicity with the Law or applauded it for
its escape from the prison-house of referentiality.[3]

I shall not pursue this past academic history in detail, although, as a professor of literature, I believe that the nihilist dimension of deconstruction's
attack on representation-as-fraudulence has had (within the humanities
domain of higher learning) sustained consequences.[4] Saussurean "arbitrariness" was repeatedly cited as proof that texts can mean whatever anyone wants them to mean—as though the rules are anyone's to change at
will, as though pre-Saussurean linguistic thought were trapped in
deplorable naïveté about the word's purchase on the thing. We have
already noted how Locke distinguishes between things, on the one hand,
and our ideas of things, on the other. This distinction cannot be overrid-
den. As John Yolton puts it: "But we can no more talk or write with objects

than we can know or be aware of objects directly. The word 'directly' here would mean 'without being aware,' just as writing or speaking with objects would be not to write or to speak. The difficulty with the Swiftian notion of carrying a bag of objects as a medium of discourse is not the weight but the inability of objects to form a language. To replace ideas as cognitive contents with objects would similarly result in the loss of perceptual aware-ness" (75). Objects and discourse ride on parallel tracks continuously in relation but never meeting.

The arbitrary connection of word to thing is hardly news. Language's conventionality, Foucault claims, was a familiar feature of the "classical episteme" arising in the seventeenth century. Reiss argues that "the very arbitrariness of the word [in early modern thinking] permits the assimila-tion of the phenomenon it denotes to a mental order, to a discursive system . . . within whose . . . relationships it may be *known*" (32). Again, the object not as it is, but as it may be *known*. Such arbitrariness renders suspect the stubborn gravity this culturally supplied significance takes on—yet not wholly suspect. Who could live for more than a few days in a world where words were not in some measure tethered to their (broadly agreed upon but socially imposed) reference? A modicum of respect for the reliability of predications proposed by specific usages of language is often missing in deconstruction (and, to some extent, in its cultural studies successors as well). Instead, pervasive language norms, culturally assigned, are seen to operate tendentially as a binding "contract which, from the point of view of the individual," as Prendergast writes, "is drawn up, signed and sealed long before he himself is engaged in its clauses" (38).[5] Suspicion reigns. So long as mimetic enterprises (pretending to represent something credibly, so that it will be broadly familiar) lodge near the prison-house, realism—and representation more broadly—is unlikely to get a sympathetic hearing.

I want to give it that hearing, even though I argue later that modernist practice refuses many of realism's procedures for securing recognizability. Yet realism is hardly as epistemologically naïve as its critics have charged. Let us return to Prendergast's warning that the contract of language is "drawn up, signed and sealed" long before anyone makes use of it. Cultural codes do lodge "naturalized" in the norms of language, and this situation is anything but innocent. But Prendergast's own reading of Flaubert makes it clear that apparently "contractual" language is plausibly full of interpretive loopholes, evading any assignment of monologic meaning. Syntax and grammar are flexibly regulatory conditions that enable surprise (on the part of receiver as well as of sender) surely as much as they disable it. Without a net, no tennis; without norms of usage, no meaningful transgression of them. Yet the deconstructive stance remains suspicious. There is "no end to the process of interpretation," Prendergast insists; "all possibility of a final or settled relationship between language and the world is, as Derrida will put it, permanently 'deferred'" (67). Note the extreme positions: either endless process or final relationship. What happened to the space in between (the space where language's relation to the world typically operates)—representation as both determined and free, world-predicative yet open to contestation? Note further the way in which Derrida's "permanent deferral" reprises the feared "final settlement": who is the policeman in this scenario?

What does it mean to call a particular deployment of language representational? Two extreme answers to this question breed only further confusion. First is the naive claim that language faithfully re-presents nonlinguistic experience, enacting a *recovery* of that experience. This stance of *language-as-recovery* serves as the whipping boy of the other extreme, *language-as-loss*. It would be hard to exaggerate the currency today, among literary critics, of the premise of language-as-loss. According to this premise—against which much of my book is written—when we speak or write, we unknowingly concede the loss of what we think we have summoned/recovered. I contend, however, that when we speak or write, the language we use and the events to which it refers are neither fused as recovery nor severed as loss. How might we transpose this way of thinking to realism's representational practice?

Realist writers rarely conceive their enterprise as simply re-presenting some nonverbal reality. To "write" experience is to do many wonderful things to it; among them, however, is not re-presentation. Because writing is continuously other than the experience it "puts into" words, *imitate* is an inadequate verb for this relation. Indeed, no single verb can cover the range of what writing does with (and to) experience. Here are two alternatives: writing *entertains* or *processes* nonverbal experience. Writing "entertains" in that it posits experience in a speculative "let's see" manner, an "as if" not to be taken as "almost coincident" but rather as richly *non*coincident. Noncoincidence permits tone, stance, attitude toward what is being represented. Writing may also entertain by *entertaining;* its playfulness and guile, its variable tone contribute to a pleasure neither separable from the seriousness of representation, nor collapsible into it.[6] The verb *processes* likewise conveys the sense in which an articulation of nonverbal experience adds as much to the original experience (*processing* it) as it subtracts. But it is not a question of adding or subtracting; writing is other than the nonverbal material it represents. It is crude to think of language's inexhaustible interplay with the world as reducing to either recovery or loss. Like *imitate,* my two alternatives are transitive, but the kind of relation they propose— unlike that proposed by *imitate*—may elude the naïveté of a claim for objective grasp of the nonverbal real, on the one hand, as well as the countercharge of surreptitious imposition of ideology, the Law, on the other.[7]

Rather than straitjacket realism into the binary of either re-presenting the objectively real or remaining within an ideological web of words alone, we can more flexibly characterize realism as a genre that proceeds by way of *verisimilitude.* Verisimilitude invokes the reader's growing sense of familiarity with the nonverbal scene being put into words, but not by pretending belief in some "imitation of the real." Lilian Furst's *All Is True* argues (as many studies do) that realism's strength is its true-seeming imitation, while its embarrassment is its status as artful, counterfeit. She entitles her opening chapter "Let's Pretend," claiming later that realist writers "conceal *poiesis,* and they do so by pretense, more specifically by pretense of mimesis" (189–90). But artworks—including realist ones—do not pretend to deliver the real. As Adorno puts it unanswerably, they "do not feign the literalness of what speaks out of them."[8] They "know" they are art; they "know" we know it too. Belief in the pretense involves a confusion of realms, a taking of the imitation for what is imitated. We do something more interesting when we read *Tom Jones* or *Pride and Prejudice* or *Madame Bovary* or *Crime and Punishment.* Such novels entertain/process nonverbal experiences in complex ways that move us because the experiences are richly recognizable. They participate in verisimilitude so that we can relate to—not believe or believe in—them. As Charles Altieri has argued, realistic representation involves "not the desire to copy particulars, but the commitment to using art's likeness to the world of appearances in order to achieve a wide range of interpretive . . . effects that might have ethical consequences."[9] Likeness functions as a strategy, not an alibi.

Prendergast writes: "Literally, as Julia Kristeva reminds us, it [verisimilitude] means 'resembling the true' (and not, as is sometimes thought, 'resembling the real')" (68). Figuratively, however, an art of verisimilitude delights less in the apparently true or real than in *seemingness* itself. Inhabiting a realm of seeming allows realist art to exploit the speculative space of detachment that writing requires (and to which it is in any event condemned) in its intricate relation to the real. Unlike imitation, verisimilitude invokes not (the pretense of) truth but familiarity—what Northrop Frye calls "the continuous recognition of credibility" (cited in Furst, 16). Not that we *believe* it, but that it be shaped so as to be the sort of thing we recognize as *credible.* Credibility, finally, is valuable to the writer, as belief is not, because it invokes the reader's *trust*—not preemptively, but in the form of a willingness to grant that something of interest may come from this engagement, a willingness to "entertain" the realist text. Thus to return to the opening claim of this section, securing the reader's participatory stance is an elemental goal of realism, the bridge enabling subsequent acts of identification.

I have here meditated on late-twentieth-century debates (occurring within the professional academy, to be sure, not in the marketplace) about realism and representation for a number of reasons. First, such meditation focuses the anatomy that follows on realism's procedures for enabling recognizability and recognition. (Against these strategies modernism crafts its counterstrategies.) Next, I want to make clear my unwillingness to condemn realism as a set of mistaken premises eventually seen through and replaced by modernist ones. If realist fiction goes by the boards, so ultimately do modernist and postmodern fiction. No fiction can succeed without a minimal assumption (however modified and self-conscious) of the value of linguistic representation as an engagement with something more than words. (The deeper issue is not realism but fiction as such.) Analysis of realism benefits less by a putdown of its pretensions to achieved objectivity and confirmed subjectivity than by a putting into question of these moves and their motives. The aims of this inquiry are interrogative.

INTRODUCING THE SUBJECT

Christian in John Bunyan's *Pilgrim's Progress* would never be mistaken for the protagonist of a realist novel. "As I walked through the wilderness of this world, I lighted on a certain place where was a den, and I laid me down in that place to sleep, and as I slept I dreamed a dream."[10] So the text opens, placing the reader in biblical dreamscape, not natural landscape. Within the next three pages one comes upon, not Christian in his setting, but brief citations from Matthew, Psalms, Peter, Genesis, Isaiah, Luke, Proverbs, and Revelation, as well as characters named Obstinate and Pliable—all this before arriving at the first natural landscape of the text: "they [Obstinate and Pliable] drew near to a very miry slough that was in the midst of the plain, and they, being heedless, did both fall suddenly into the bog. The name of the slough was Despond . . ." (22).

We know to read this fictional procedure as allegorical rather than realistic for several reasons. The protagonist's name tells us he is only apparently an individual, he is really Everyman (every Christian, that is). The "miry bog" he must traverse is only apparently natural, it is really the Slough of Despond separating Everyman from his final Home. (Bacon could tell us nothing about the kind of space here represented.) The others he has already begun to meet are only apparently adventitiously encountered, they are really a Christian-deducible roster of human failings one encounters in life. (His meeting them unfolds not as empirical adventure but as allegorical necessity.) The travails he undergoes are only apparently a local plot, they are really the travail humanity must undergo if it would enter Heaven. (His duress is not tailored to his specific individuality.) All these "reallys" lift Bunyan's seventeenth-century book out of the mode of experiential observation, depriving it of a sense of singular, secular unfolding. By contrast, as Ian Watt writes, "[m]odern realism . . . begins from the position that truth can be discovered by the individual through his senses: it has its origins in Descartes and Locke" (12). Watt goes on to pinpoint the crucial premise of an individual located in a specified here and now: "The 'principle of individuation' accepted by Locke was that of existence at a particular locus in space and time" (21).

This premise is fundamental, more so than Watt grasped. Realist fiction did not invent the individual (epic and poetry deal memorably in individuals), but realism introduced him as he had never been introduced before. It did this first by inserting him into a particularized space that is familiar (or more precisely, seeming-familiar) and into a specified time that seems to proceed as now, even if (as in Scott) a time of "sixty years ago." As yet unknown, he is located in a space and time whose contours we seem to recognize immediately. Though he be unpredicated, his conditions are not. We are already halfway toward knowing him because we have assimilated the cogency of the canvas on which he moves. We do not know what he will do, but we are confident—without thinking about it—that his actions will unfold along familiar (Kantian) axes of space, time, and causality. To reprise Reiss's term, the realist framing of the subject in space and time already possesses an "enlightened predictability."

Realism introduces this subject by bringing him close-up; the figure/ground schema is shaped to make him swiftly take on salience. Close-up, but not too close-up—as Benjy Compson of *The Sound and the Fury* and Stephen Dedalus of *Ulysses* are too close-up: in our face before being introduced, causing readerly anxiety, as though we were nearsighted, too many elements rushing into our field of vision before we are prepared to place them. Close-up, but "dressed," composed, already his introducible self and, so to speak, emitting signals to the reader that he is approachable. Further, realism introduces the individual reliably close-up, not like

Kafka's K., whom "someone must have traduced, for without having done anything wrong he was arrested one fine morning":[11] a narrative situation putting us in a familiar bedroom with the protagonist all right, but there is something wrong with that room, something that was never before wrong with it, something (we do not yet know) we are never going to find out. In realism, we will find out fully what is "on his mind" or "in his path"; we already know we will and are looking forward to it. Put otherwise, realism situates its protagonist in a compelling here and now. Composed so as to be knowable though not yet known, the subject is cleanly figured against a ground of familiar space and time, pregnant with a future.[12] He is thus birthed as one who will in time rebirth himself, by way of an achieved self-knowing—one who, creator-like, will negotiate (in the form of recognition) all that he has passed through.[13]

My protagonist pronoun has been masculine, despite the figure of pregnancy, but consider Diderot's testimony to the impact made on him by Samuel Richardson's *Clarissa:* "My soul was held in a constant state of agitation. . . . I had encountered in the space of a few hours a great number of situations such as the longest life scarcely offers in its fullest span. I had heard the true accents of passion; I had seen the motive forces of self-interest and self-love working in a hundred different ways; I had been the spectator of countless incidents, I felt I had acquired experience" (*Eloge de Richardson* [1762], cited in Watt, 26–27). This breathless rhapsody has nothing to do with "let's pretend." Diderot knows that Richardson's pages are not an imitation of the real; he knows it is "not happening." Indeed, life cannot "do" to the reader what Richardson's novel does. The longest life is too short to make available the range of experiences Richardson distills into words on pages. What has caught Diderot is the unprecedented immediacy that Richardson achieves in both Pamela and Clarissa; as reader, you are there with them. You are there in part because, though the spatial specification is occasionally meager, Richardson's temporal specification is hallucinatorily precise and enfolding. This is verisimilitude indeed, by which I mean truth-seeming. In fact, these distressed women could hardly write to the moment as they do, with their predators breathing down their necks. Yet the pulsating moment of crisis is utterly credible (in a way that only worded experience can be credible). In reading Richardson one engages subjective dramas unfolding from moment to moment, hour to hour, day to day, week to week. In a manner that is novel, these are fictions of unfolding time. The present crisis explodes with—there is nothing else to call it—presence, a presence alarmingly intense because linked to a past crisis just moments ago, a future crisis just moments away. The drama inside the mind could hardly be more private, but its privacy depends on specified, familiar, public space and time. We are located in a bedroom, a kitchen, a garden, or an inn on a country road; these indices send a normative signal of impersonal "thereness."

Robinson Crusoe opens as follows: "I was born in the Year 1632, in the City of *York*, of a good Family, tho' not of that Country, my Father being a Foreigner of *Bremen*, who first settled at *Hull:* He got a good Estate by Merchandise, and leaving off his Trade, lived afterward at *York*, from whence he had married my Mother, whose Relations were named *Robinson*, a very good Family in that Country" (5, emphasis in the original). No one needs to believe this, but what Western reader finds it unbelievable? The verisimilar is at work, both spatially and temporally, giving us what we have learned to expect of chronology, geography, travel, labor, and family to get our bearings, achieve an orientation. All is as secular/material here as it is spiritual in Bunyan. The frame of values is weekday rather than Sunday, horizontal rather than vertical. Such an opening sentence has, as Robert Frost said of conversation one overhears without catching the words, the already familiar sound of sense. We recognize the narrative of family genealogy, even as we expect the genealogy to precede the protagonist's plot. None of this, of course, is free of cultural patterning. "The language of mimesis," Prendergast reminds us, "re-presents not the world but the world as already organised in discourse" (68). To be, in *Robinson Crusoe,* is to be born at a specified time in a specified place, of a specified father and mother also occupying one or more specified sites and practicing one or more familiar occupations. More deeply, to be is to be launched on the path of self-fashioning, toward becoming something more. The discourse operating here is transparently patriarchal (father before mother), family-punctuated (how the parents met, the legitimacy of their union), income-sensitive (a good estate allowing retirement), forward-slanted toward a knowable but unknown future (Robinson will leave, he has—as narrator—already left): in sum, a familiar bourgeois narrative of subject development, the sort the Enlightenment specializes in.

Austen's *Emma* opens with chiseled concision, the first sentence telling us not everything we need to know, but the stakes of what is to come. The governing narrative contract is secured in under forty words: "Emma Woodhouse, handsome, clever, and rich, with a comfortable home and happy disposition, seemed to unite some of the best blessings of existence; and had lived nearly twenty-one years in the world with very little to vex her."[14] A close-up portrait: not only psychological (Emma's vanity: unknown to her, exposed to us), but structural—the text authoritatively summarizes her traits and possessions, giving us Emma as center with concentric circles to be established later. Austen's novel assumes on every page—as Defoe's did not—the interestingness of the interior life of an individual subject, her gradual, resistant coming to know better who she is, thanks to the most carefully orchestrated set of surrounding and supportive props. Emma travels widely without going far. In the next part of this anatomy of realism, I inquire further into the logic of these props, but for now it is enough to say: no Emma-development without them, and more important, no sense to the props without a larger-than-life Emma at their center and motivating them. As that first sentence implies (and as Kant feared), the centrality of the subject who would know is structural before it becomes ethical. The only unfolding the Enlightenment narrative is prepared to moralize is the foregrounded adventure of a liberal, free-moving subject commanded (by everyone, by no one) to come to know herself and her world better.

There are countless ways for realist novels to begin, yet such unpredictable beginnings tend to be easily recognizable as beginnings. A human subject is being introduced, approached close-up. Unpredicated, his or her future is opaque for now, but not wholly unpredictable. Located in specified, familiar-seeming space and time, the figure comes alive for us, as a salient presence and a latent promise. A waiting but undetermined destiny will grow out of the figure's characteristic interactions with others; when it arrives, it will seem fitting. Such a destiny already possesses "enlightened predictability." Whether it be Frédéric Moreau on a passenger boat moving down the Seine, or Michael Henchard walking (with wife silently behind him) on a lonely Dorset road, or Raskolnikov nervously exiting from his coffin-like flat and moving "somewhat irresolutely in the direction of Kamenny Bridge," the drama to come is saturated in the continuous intelligibility of time and space as shaped to the developmental drama of the subject in question.[15] Formally innovative as James's last three novels are, nothing could be more classically realist than this opening: "She waited, Kate Croy, for her father to come in, but he kept her unconscionably, and there were moments at which she showed herself, in the glass over the mantel, a face positively pale with the irritation that had brought her to the point of going away without sight of him. It was at this point, however, that she remained."[16] Though *The Wings of the Dove* will proceed in the most circuitous and backtracking ways (moving into Kate's past relations with Aunt Maud and Densher, into Densher's own rich interiority and history, then into Millie's completely other interiority and history), and though James rarely specifies subsequent settings as minutely and objectively as he does Lionel Croy's "shabby sofa upholstered in a glazed cloth" at once "slippery" and "sticky," yet Kate Croy's voyage of becoming is unmistakably launched in this first sentence. Robinson, Emma, Frédéric, Henchard, Raskolnikov, Kate: they are recognizably there before us within a page or two, figures silhouetted against— grounded by—familiar space and time, ripe to be plotted, dreaming or conceiving or fearing or resisting a future that is, even within that page or two, starting to burgeon within them. Already clothed in identifying characteristics—already themselves as (in both senses) potentially moving subjects—they inhabit a canvas shaped to make the crises that will come compelling and familiar.

FAMILIARIZING THE SUBJECT

I intend the process of "familiarizing the subject" to be understood in three interrelated ways. There is first realism's energetic production of the larger world of people, places, and objects with which the protagonist is to become familiar. Second, there is the reflexive counterpart of such famil- iarizing—that in which the reader grasps the particularity of the protago- nist by coming to know the particulars of his world: the protagonist becomes familiar to the reader. Is it possible that the reflexivity does not stop there—that the reader subject thus in possession of the textual subject is thereby, in a certain measure, confirmed in his own self-possession? Is it a hall of mirrors, in which the familiarity enabling self-confirmation at one level nourishes self-confirmation at other levels? Is one reason that West- ern novels have proved so popular for three centuries that the act of *reading them* sustains, by way of rehearsing fantasy reciprocities and possessions, the sense of continuous identity itself?

Such a process of familiarizing posits individual identity as not only compatible with others in social space and time, but dependent on their encounter for its flourishing. The canvas is immediately peopled with oth- ers (and the social norms they carry). The protagonist's familiarity with their territory is doubled by the reader's familiarity with the protagonist's territory; the capacity to recognize others (both literally and figuratively) proceeds swiftly. Perhaps too swiftly: suppose that traffic in fluid identifi- cations were not so docile, suppose movement into the field of the (fic- tional) other were either intricately delayed, on the one hand, or revealed to be egotistic fantasy, on the other—stances that modernist and postmodern fiction will respectively explore. Realism explores such misrecognitions too, of course, but mainly in the form of mistakes set right eventually for the protagonists (and typically much earlier for the privileged reader): a host of Wickhams in time replaced by Darcys. Misrecognition in modernism tends to be more stubborn, even irreversible; in postmodernism it becomes normal.

Finally there is a third sense of "familiarizing": providing the subject with a family. As Michael Holquist writes, "Family culture is every child's first culture."[17] In a number of realist texts this third sense of "familiar" seems to command the other two by supplying the key in which the realist novel will most often *familiarize* the Enlightenment narrative—by humanizing its Kantian commitment to the universal as a *drama of family*. Orphaned though they often are or become, what realist subject does not emerge from the web of a birth or foster family? How would we know they had achieved the freedom and gravity of selfhood, did we not know what they had freed themselves from—and often at what cost? But do they do so only to return, at the end, into a kindred web, this time on chosen rather than imposed terms—an exiting shaped so as to permit a reentry? Does the adventure of exiting from family, no less than the adventure of subjectivity, end by being (in Levinas's terms) no adventure at all? Does it operate as a concealed economy of the same? Is family culture, in realism, also every adult's last culture—in such a way that the drama of individual flowering is recontained (peacefully if possible, violently if necessary) within the stability of family values? Surely not always, but often enough to justify the following further reflection.

Consider how two supreme realist novels stage subjectivity as an inner space at once unbearably singular and familiar. Both of them envisage subjective agency as the woman's taking of responsibility (by way of memory and conscience) for the entire temporal arc and spatial reach of her experience. Wherever it travels, subjectivity must end, as it began, family-inflected. Eliot's *The Mill on the Floss* spends some four hundred pages attending to Maggie Tulliver's childhood, while Tolstoy's *Anna Karenina* spends no time on Anna's, but they each immerse their heroines in inescapable family complications. Maggie's impetuous father, commodity-fixated mother, censorious aunts, haughty and adored older brother: these figures form a constellation of rooted emotional linkages and memories, against which her own later developments in social space and time, however urgent, must come to naught. Her immovable family so implacably frames the mirror in which she is able to recognize herself that life outside this familiar mirror is, finally, intolerable. Anna Karenina, by contrast, is never seen as a child herself, but she is fatally accompanied by one, her son

Serezha. Her husband Karenin, her son Serezha, and the judgment-bearing society she lives within: these end by poisoning her love for Vronsky, for her new child, and ultimately for her own life.

Both novels produce their heroine's flourishing outside the mirror of familiarity as developments mandating suicide. Maggie enters that final water thinking she is still Maggie (rather than someone other than the fantasy/childhood Maggie who has actually long since ceased to exist, but whom the older Maggie cannot relinquish for fear of an unendurable vertigo of conflicted identity). Anna, by contrast, heads toward her fatal encounter with the oncoming train knowing she has betrayed familiar Anna—a betrayal both terrifying and revelatory. Here is Anna telling Vronsky what would happen if she were to let her husband know of her affair and beg him to let her go:

> "Do you know what the result will be? I will tell it you all in advance," and an evil light came into her eyes which a minute before had been so tender. "'Ah, you love another and have entered into a guilty union with him?'" (mimicking her husband, she laid just such a stress on the word *guilty* as Karenin himself would have done). "'I warned you of the consequences from the religious, civil, and family points of view. You have not listened to me. Now I cannot allow my name to be dishonoured . . .'" my name and my son she was going to say but could not jest about her son . . . "'my name to be dishonoured' and something else of that kind," she added. "In short, he will tell me clearly and precisely in his official manner that he cannot let me go, but will take what measures he can to prevent a scandal. And he will do what he says, quietly and accurately. That is what will happen. He is not a man, but a machine, and a cruel machine when angry," she added, picturing Karenin to herself with every detail of his figure and way of speaking, setting against him everything bad she could find in him and forgiving him nothing, on account of the terrible fault toward him of which she was guilty.[18]

One sees how deeply the model of identity-as-familiarized-by-others can penetrate. Anna has absorbed, as a central dimension of herself, the voice of the family/culture judging her. (Elsewhere she finds herself unintentionally trying to pull her hair out: she is simultaneously her embodied self and her familiar angry attacker.) Here she does more than quote Karenin, she speaks Karenin, becomes Karenin. She relinquishes her agency as speaking subject, becomes instead the guilty object addressed by her husband, the enraged subject. More, she does it all by herself, speaking her spokenness, sharing Karenin's familiar indictment of her passional being. He could not loathe her more than she loathes herself; he is all the more loathsome for doing so. As beleaguered subject, Anna lacks even a shred of any nonfamiliar discourse that might let her explore (let along affirm) her love of Vronsky. The dimensions of that love can find in *Anna Karenina* no language sympathetic to their intricate subjective reality, thus can be engaged only as socially assigned guiltiness, as violation of *familiar others* (even as Tolstoy's genius is to show, throughout this passage, how she is violating herself). Karenin (and the larger Russian society) deploys a language of morality that is indifferent to individual desire. Anna is wholly convinced of this language's truth. "That is what will happen," she thinks, foreseeing her fate shaped by the self-lacerating optic of others whose alienating judgment she shares. What finally does happen, some six hundred pages later, bears her out by severing her head from her body.

Both novels reveal the potential violence wrought into a model of individual identity held to the terms of family identity. Do we not glimpse, once again, the irresoluble conflict at the heart of the Enlightenment narrative? Subjecthood emerged there as primary, all-engrossing, freed from the dictates of church, state, and family (recall Descartes's birthing of the subject who would know). It has but one destiny—to unfold itself, reach its potential. Who has understood this burgeoning of individual energies better than Tolstoy in his portraits of Natasha or Nicholas Rostov? Yet selfhood released on such a scale is tantamount to displaced godhood: we become creators within our own fiefdom. Why else would Kant so belabor the categorical imperative, insisting that self is meaningful only as it learns to respect the ends of others as equal to one's own? Thus the clash of irreconcilable absolutes: Anna's radiant individual entitlement, Anna's mandated social annihilation. Anna and Maggie both read their own life force in the light of a social narrative that sentences them to death. "Sapere aude!" Kant urged. But what one comes to know must, on pain of self-extinction, accommodate a model of familial, social values—accommodate them once and for all. No deviations permitted, no lapses allowed. The drama of self-creation just is one's learning to take on, find terms for, whatever challenges have occurred in space and time: to do this and remain oneself. Anna and Maggie prefer annihilation to the acceptance of altered identity. Tolstoy's Kantian morality subtends Anna's crisis, concluding the passage cited with the same judgment—*guilty*—that appeared ten lines earlier as the abusive term Anna envisages Karenin using to wound her. In the name of the same encompassing morality Eliot, likewise, has Maggie immolate herself.

Coming to know occurs, in these two novels, with a cumulative vengeance; they are charged with pedagogic warning. As Levine (recalling Novalis) puts it, "character becomes fate": realist denouements imply "a meaningful universe . . . [in which] characters must be seen . . . to create or place themselves in the conditions that correspond to their natures" (*Realistic,* 147). This long view can be a fatal one, revealing the rigor of the constraints reining in the Enlightenment narrative of released selfhood. The God whose perfection is mirrored in Newton's secular "system of the world" is a *deus absconditus:* wrought into the perfect ordering of the setting but banned from the cast of characters. He cannot intervene upon his own canvas. Within that canvas, "enlightened predictability" presides—a world of uniform lawfulness, of forces endlessly calculable, of subjects incessantly in motion. Neither mercy nor contingency obtains. Subjectivity is primary (nothing preempts it), yet equally primary is the gravity-supplying weight of the lawful social scene these subjects cohabit. They are wholly free and wholly bound. What does "character is fate" mean but that who you are translates into—exactly what surrounds you and happens to you? Every move you make is your own, yet it is simultaneously responsible to, and for, the equal and opposite reactions of an inexhaustibly meaningful universe.

By the time of the late twentieth century, postmodern Salman Rushdie can have one of his characters say: "in these days, character isn't destiny any more. Economics is destiny. Ideology is destiny. Bombs are destiny. What does a famine, a gas chamber, a grenade care how you lived your life?"[19] But in the subject-centered, subject-moralized world of nineteenth-century realism—in that unforgiving space of total emplottedness—no seeing past the drama of character is possible. *Anna Karenina* puts into play all the props enabling Kantian maturation, yet insists that character is still fate, paying the price this premise exacts. Levin, at any rate, is left alive, saved by the family orientation that destroys Anna, saved as well by a set of activities usually sufficient to let realist protagonists make sense of their trial and achieve maturation: travel through space and time.

SPACE TRAVEL, TIME TRAVEL

The realist journey of individual emancipation is iterative and meandering. It seems familiar early on, but appearances can deceive; actually to learn from experience takes a lot of space and time. In realism, as Elizabeth Ermarth writes, "[t]he identity of anything . . . can only be discovered in relationship, and so . . . discrete forms are replaced by continuities, stasis is replaced by implied motion, and hierarchy is replaced by horizon."[20] More, the protagonist inserted within a social web of familiar objects and others is—however salient and gathered unto himself—insensibly altered by that insertion. "Are not our sentiments," Balzac wrote, "written on the things that surround us?" (cited in Hemmings, 46)—a question that hauntingly suggests two-way traffic. We become in relation to the familiar realities we move within, marking them as they mark us. Sometimes, as in *Persuasion,* none of those surrounding realities is essentially altered—Wentworth is Wentworth, Lyme is Lyme, Anne's father is forever the vain and impossible Mr. Elliott—yet the passage of time itself allows Anne to reconceive this sameness, and in a life-altering way to change her mind. At other times—a memorable instance is Lydgate in *Middlemarch*—the aspiring individual, however admirable his intentions, is gradually worn down and destroyed, by his own "spots of commonness," to be sure, but these "spots" as writ large and lethally activated, thanks to the individual's enwebbing responses, commitments, and encounters.[21]

The realist world of space and time, because lawful, accommodates a series of Lockean trials—horizontal and civic rather than vertical and divine, incremental rather than occurring once and for all. As "gazing countrymen" we must see others over and over again if we would learn to read appearances. Repetition (seeing the object more than once, becoming familiar with it) punctuates realist practice. Prendergast speaks of such repetition as "a re-presenting of the object in ways that keep its criteria of *identity* intact" (76). That last verb should be stronger: re-presenting the object *establishes* its identity. The first sighting prepares the second one. As Descartes established doubt to be initiative, and as Locke stressed ignorance to be the first step toward knowledge, so certain entities on the realist canvas will be misread when first presented, so that they may be reread when re-presented. What one comes to know is painstakingly winnowed of distortion, disinterestedly re-cognizable, finally, in its invariant identity. Anyone observing from a neutral position would concur in such eventual knowledge. The realist enterprise gradually coheres in the form of a larger system of mutual investments and engagements operating over time. The widely cast net joins the large roster of characters—seen and reseen, refracted from different angles—so as to intimate finally: this is how things are, you need not take any single person's word for it.

Watt noted long ago that a common epistemological stance operates in the realist novel and "the jury in a court of law . . . both want to know 'all the particulars' of a given case—the time and place of the occurrence; both must be satisfied as to the identities of the parties concerned" (31). All the particulars: the singular detail (in the frame of its singular moment) may count, of course, but it is the accumulation of details that *tells* in a court-room—an accumulation built upon the testimony of several different observers. The striking moment, as such, has no priority. It matters only as it enters a composite narrative broader in scope (verifiable by others) and extensive in time (a moment prepared by earlier moments, secured to later ones in the form of a developing motive). Trials, like realist novels, special-ize in producing narratives of individuals traveling in highly specified ways through uniform spaces and times. The uniformity is key, for it guar-antees space and time as reliable conditions, thus rendering subject-behav-ior within them *consequential*—in both sense of that term. Like realist novels but more drastically, trials edit the messiness of life histories into the selective clarity of a developmental line. Both the protagonist of such nov-els and their readers engage in a jurylike trying out of materials encoun-tered, sifting through appearance, zeroing in on the shape of the real.

All of these premises will be stood on their head in Kafka's trial of a trial called *The Trial*. But in the pre-Kafkan realism with which we are here concerned, matters are arranged so as to permit successful trying—and retrying—to take place. I have therefore used the phrases "space travel" and "time travel" to emphasize the almost science-fiction con-structedness of arrangements we have been trained to read as natural. Realism narrates space not only so as to make it familiar, but also to make specific places within that space leap into significance, either by their revealing difference from other places, or by their gradual revelation of interior meanings at first concealed. The point is so obvious as to go unnoticed. How can Balzac get his reader better to grasp the difference of Paris than by juxtaposing it with Rubempré's and Rastignac's provincial places of origin? How can Dickens convey the ramifications of either Tom-all-Alones or (its apparent opposite) Chesney Wold, except by even-tually showing them to be scandalously interrelated? How can Isabel know what Gardencourt means until, years later and now juxtaposed with Osmond's Roman palazzo, she returns to it in order to see the dying Ralph, and (finally) she hears the ghost? How could Forster hammer home the stultification of anemic England, without the inexhaustible contrast of robust, enfleshed Tuscany or Venice? Usually the protagonist is provided the necessary time and space travel to recognize these mas-sively coded differences; always, by imaginative entry into the narrative, the reader is. Space and time are uniform, and pedagogic, in realism. It takes travel through them for Elizabeth Bennet to make the connection between Darcy and Pemberley, but when she makes it she has found their invariant mutual identity.[22] Of course *Pride and Prejudice* is a narrative shaped by class investments; my aim here is merely to suggest its spatial logic. Its temporal logic is even more imperious. The final, all-cohering element in this speculative anatomy of realism is recognition.

RECOGNITION

Recognition is the indispensable term in a realist lexicon, for it enacts realism's cardinal premise—without which it would have few readers—that human life takes on precious focus in time. Repetition of pertinent entities or actions permits a later recognition made possible by their prior familiarity. Here lies the mission of verisimilitude: to provide realist fiction with familiar objects and others poised to play their role in that sudden move of the mind (over space and time) which is recognition. Repeated sightings enable insight.

Realism, of course, did not invent recognition. Aristotle identifies it in the *Poetics* as the pivotal moment of plot—the moment, for example, when Oedipus goes beyond *seeing* the man he killed, the woman he sleeps with, and himself: he finally *recognizes* all three. Recognitions are reciprocal: if that is really who they are, then this is really who I am. I deliberately flaunt a word that is unavoidable in a discussion of recognition: *really.* The question subtending my exploration of recognition is this: can either life itself, or fiction that seeks to be profoundly "about" life, do without a discourse of "really"? Is it possible—let alone desirable—for humans to proceed through the space and time of their not-to-be-repeated lives, without seeking a sense (revisable though it be) of what experience has been yielding, what seems "really" the case with respect to the identity of oneself in relation to others? Is fictional narrative itself one of the privileged cultural forms for rehearsing identity as a something confirmed and deepened by recognitions over space and time? I argue, in part 2 of this book, that modernism is shaped to articulate a new pathos and urgency to this issue of "really"—by producing a fiction that raises "really" as a question newly disturbing because unanswerable. Later, postmodern practice, taking that modernist move to the logical next step, often seeks to repudiate the entire program of "really" as representation's attempt to grasp the real—an attempt at once futile, tiresome, and wrongheaded.[23] But can the activity of reading compel a reader's attention when "really" is no longer imaginatively at stake, when recognitions cease to be sorted out from misrecognitions? Claims of knowing better now, of having come to know, always lodge in discourses featuring "really." Can we live without such claims?[24] Can we make these claims in nonlegislative ways so as to be able to live with them?

The Enlightenment narrative of coming to know the other posits, as we have seen, a reciprocal self-knowledge. In realist fiction, the two are joined objectively. (It goes otherwise in modernism: in the act of knowing, the knower tends, all unawares, to "bleed into" what comes to be known.) Realism's sublime moments center on recognition. Consider Pip's withheld re-encounter with Magwitch, that stormy night in Pip's chambers. Virtually everyone who matters—Miss Havisham, Estella, Magwitch, Joe, and most of all Pip himself—comes suddenly into a new and disturbing focus: "But, sharpest and deepest pain of all—it was for the convict, guilty of I knew not what crimes, and liable to be taken out of those rooms where I sat thinking, and hanged at the Old Bailey door, that I had deserted Joe."[25] This is not a final recognition. Pip will later grasp not only Magwitch's deception but his bumbled kindness, his desire to promote a child as he has never been promoted, as he has been unable to promote his own child. But Pip's new take on both Joe and himself, dating from this moment, is proffered as permanent, and permanently reshaping. Consider as well Pierre's accumulated recognitions during the battle of Borodino, the firing of Moscow and his near execution there, the misery of his forced march through the frozen countryside—a prisoner held by fleeing French troops and threatened by starvation, illness, and the violence of a desperate army. Possessing nothing except his punished body and his free-moving mind, yet still alive, Pierre comes to a stoic self-acceptance that places him, finally, on the other side of the temptations and mirages that have beset him throughout *War and Peace*. My point is not that these recognition scenes are invulnerable to criticism, but that they appear as crescendo moments of realism—credible clarifications of an entire life, made possible by coming to know one's world better, and thus oneself better.

How does the realist protagonist manage to rise above the flow of his own life in time and startlingly see who he really is? First, he is positioned to benefit by extensive travel through space and time, enabling comparison and return. Yet such travel would be pedagogically fruitless were the protagonist's identity not assumed to be a coherence not only unharmed by passage through time, but clarified by it. Space and time in the Enlightenment model, as we have noted often, are uniform and objective frames that permit free-standing subjectivity: *they are not constituent conditions of subjectivity*. Time is a disinterested friend of Enlightenment subjectivity. The

Lockean adventure that begins with a blank slate looks forward, progressively, to the wayfaring subject's managing of experience so as to mark that slate richly, wisely, self-consciously.

Next, if we ask how this is possible, we come to an indispensable assumption: the conscious I of the Enlightenment possesses *reliable memory*. Locke insisted on "personality" as an entity extending "beyond present Existence to what is past, only by consciousness, whereby it becomes concerned and accountable." Continuous consciousness is the assumed ground whereby memory attains to accountability and permits recognition. Realist protagonists gradually cohere, come into focus and self-focus, thanks to their accurately *remembered* travel through space and time. This model of identity, as Ronald Schleifer has pointed out, is rooted in "the methodological epistemology [of] Descartes's quest for certainty"; its founding premise is "an atemporal subject, one who stands outside the experience he comprehends."[26] If not atemporal, then at least a subject whose identity comes to be more fully centered in time; his very changes are compatible with a more extensive self-sameness. No modernist unconscious here; as in Kant, the "I think" that subtends knowing is present to itself—not only now but reliably over time, a coherence that perdures. Pip has to (and *can*) remember his past accurately, as Pierre remembers his, as Maggie and Anna suicidally remember theirs (Anna psychotically confusing her new child with her lost Serezha shortly before killing herself). Memory, severely pedagogic, cannot be evaded; realism launches all its recognitions by way of that resource. Was blind, but now I see.

The preconditions that enable such seeing are menaced, however, by a pair of objections so recurrent as to be, perhaps, unanswerable. The first objection we have already considered (and, with modernism, will consider further): that recognition of the other—what realism takes to be *knowing*—might actually erase the other-as-other and substitute for it the other-as-known. This objection—inherited from the Enlightenment narrative of a world knowable only in its appearances—may be seen as *spatial;* one does not so easily travel from here to there, from self to others, and come to know their nature. The second objection is *temporal:* the mind does not so securely travel backward from *now* to *then* and come to grasp—as recognition—the past as it really was. In realism, the mind is conceived as a unitary, continuous consciousness capable of remembering life experiences over time.[27] The word to stress is "over"—"over" as temporally extensive but also, so to speak, spatially above. Perhaps narrative's primordial purpose, as we broached earlier and consider more directly now, is to order time—to bring order to our immersion in the medium in which we undergo disorder, a continual going-away. The challenge that time poses to human identity predates realism and will be with us after postmodernism. It is a constitutive challenge, wrought into the differences between living life and imagining it coherently. Narrative is precious, and deceptive, in the ways in which it meets this challenge—was invented to meet it.

No one has better understood the motive for narrative as a response to time's menace than Augustine, some sixteen hundred years ago. Augustine conceptualized memory as a distension of the soul—an interior stretching that permitted the mind to link what is past with what is present and what is yet to come. As a written configuration of the resources of memory, narrative binds the past (looked back upon and seen as formative), the present (taking place now, but motivated and motivating, no longer blind), and the future (anticipated as a project of the present). Augustinian narrative permits a written subjective coherence over time, at the human level, that is, in Genevieve Lloyd's words, "modeled on God's eternal self-presence" (16). Memory secures the entire project. As narrator of his *Confessions* Augustine succeeds in "seeing each event in a fixed relation to a past which has achieved its final form" (16). The rub is this: the final form of what has been lived through can be recognized—the verb is unavoidable—only from the vantage point of an all-clarifying later event (Augustine's conversion to God). This later event sheds the light that reveals the past in its recognized shape. To bind time into meaning, you have to know how it comes out later. Narrative's crucial activity—*representation*—enacts the perversion of time (Brooks's term) that makes realist fiction possible.

Realism most effectively secures its trick of time through a single procedural device to which I have already alluded in my discussion of Defoe, as unnoticed as it tends to be far-reaching: the use of verbs predominantly in the past tense. That past tense reads doubly. On the one hand, events seem to be freely unfolding in a forward motion, toward an undeclared future. On the other, events have already unfolded (the past tense tells us this), though not yet been narrated. *The unannounced end underwrites the developing coherence of everything prior to it.* This is the crucial coordinating work of the realist narrator. As Ermarth puts it, "Such 'Nobody' narrators literally constitute historical time by threading together into one system and one act of attention a whole series of moments and perspectives."[28] Superior to the vicissitudes of time because positioned both before and after, such a narrator has, precisely, *come to know.* No one is more alert than Foucault to the ways in which such subjective coherence—and the myths of knowing that follow from it—rely upon this trick of mastered time: "Continuous history is the indispensable correlative of the founding subject: the guarantee that everything that has eluded him may be restored to him . . . the promise that one day the subject . . . will once again be able to appropriate . . . all those things that are kept at a distance by difference, and find in them what might be called his abode."[29] Foundation, restoration, unity, abode: what is this but the grandeur of recognition, of domesticating time's dispersive power by (re)possessing one's lost estate and coming, finally, to know?

CRIME AND PUNISHMENT: MISRECOGNITION AS RECOGNITION

As the satyr play follows the great tragedies, so the possibility of misrecognition dogs the sublimities of recognition. Suppose one got it wrong? Suppose that one's progressive journey through space and time were not satisfyingly rewarded by coming to know? *The Mill on the Floss* and *Anna Karenina* reveal the austere price this Enlightenment narrative can impose, the death sentence (freely chosen by the protagonist, in good Kantian fashion) at its disposal. I conclude this discussion of realism by examining a canonical Western novel that puts the genre's epistemological premises under even greater pressure. Greater pressure because no novel has worked harder at producing self-knowledge than this one—or produced stranger results. Dostoevsky's *Crime and Punishment* inhabits an underground territory between knowing and unknowing—between Kant and Freud—in which recognition and misrecognition, rather than getting sorted out, turn into each other.

Crime and Punishment is amply endowed with realist procedures. To begin with, entities on its canvas are spatially arrayed in unambiguously pedagogic fashion. All Raskolnikov has to do is walk out of his apartment, to encounter others who supply insight into his dilemma (sometimes to him, always to the reader). Some examples will suffice: (1) On the street he passes by an intoxicated young woman about to be abused by a scoundrel (the coding leaps off the page); his finer instincts are aroused, he unthinkingly gives her twenty kopecks, then wonders why he did so: we learn that he has a good heart. (2) He enters a bar and encounters (as though waiting for him) the drunken Marmeladov; he hears Marmeladov's story of humiliation and perversity, learns of Marmeladov's daughter Sonya and her saintlike submission to prostitution to help the family, accompanies the intoxicated man to his flat and meets his wife and three needy children: again his spontaneous generosity is revealed, along with the introduction of "familiars" who will help us make sense of him (and in the case of Sonya, help him make sense of himself). (3) His mother in the country lets him know his beloved sister Dunya is "prostituting" herself—by marrying a petty and egotistical businessman (Luzhin)—so that Raskolnikov can continue his education; this sister and mother come to St. Petersburg where he sees them and must work to free Dunya from Luzhin's clutches. (4) He wanders dazedly toward the lodging of his one friend in St. Petersburg (Razumikhin), finds him there and is from that point forward shepherded by Razumikhin—the latter a sort of cleaned-up version of Raskolnikov who admires his intellect and will eventually replace Luzhin as Dunya's appropriate suitor. (5) He hears from his mother about Svidrigaylov, a multimotivated older man who both lusts after Dunya and unaccountably gives away large sums of money to the Marmeladovs and others, a man at the same time sufficiently amoral—interested in toying with others, perhaps killing them too—to be a telling foil for the younger man's project of going beyond good and evil.

The deployment of time in this novel likewise seems familiar. The narrative moves steadily forward (apart from one brief flashback), taking that "somewhat irresolute" young man of page 1 inexorably toward the pawnbroker's apartment, where he will—to his own amazement, despite its being his plan—brandish his axe and murder her. Thereafter the days follow in linear fashion, as he seeks out Sonya to ease his troubled mind, tries to remain unsuspected while being surrounded by others. Seeing Sonya leads to confessing to Sonya (a clarification that progresses in three charged scenes), just as meeting the detective Porfiry leads to being tracked and identified by Porfiry (a clarification that likewise progresses in three charged interviews). His hearing about Svidrigaylov in part 1 leads to meeting him at the end of part 3 and then to sustained interaction with him throughout part 6. This struggle with his double resolves, almost simultaneously, in Svidrigaylov's suicide and Raskolnikov's confession. He goes to prison, sentenced to eight years. While there he becomes recurrently ill and is cared for by Sonya. One day he actually grasps the meaning of her enduring faith, and, suddenly thereafter, he is reborn: "there glowed the dawn of a new future, a perfect resurrection into a new life" (463). This is the realist temporality of error, consequences, recognition, and resolution.

Raskolnikov's subjectivity, as his Russian name tells us (*raskol,* "schism, split"), is riven by conflicting stances. The Cartesian methodologist in him plots a murder along rational, instrumental lines. He hardly knows the pawnbroker—she is an abstract target—but her battening off urban misery means that she does not deserve to live. More, he aspires to a Western model of achieved selfhood at any cost. Napoleon is his ideal, the

Napoleon who, ignoring conventional morality, stopped at nothing to impose his will. This intellectual stance divides the world into two camps: a few unhampered individuals with something new to say or do, and all the sheeplike others lost in their mediocrity. His deed of murder will prove that he is one of the free individuals. "Sapere aude!": Raskolnikov dares to know—the world as it really is, himself as he might be, could he release his inner promise. Against this stance, there is the spontaneous, good-hearted, Russian Orthodox youth. Recurrently we see how his generous feelings overturn his calculated ideas and are then overturned by them. (He cannot *think* ethically, but he can act ethically without thinking.) His mother and sister are precious "familiars"; he cannot bear their suffering for his sake. His spontaneously giving Marmeladov's family all the money his mother has sent him contrasts decisively with Luzhin's systematic money-grubbing. Covered with Marmeladov's blood (after trying to save him from the consequences of a violent accident), Raskolnikov feels a "boundlessly full and powerful life welling up in him, a feeling which might be compared with that of a man condemned to death and unexpectedly reprieved" (159–60).

The premise of a protagonist who will come to know, through trial and error, is patently before us. Not only does his eight-year prison sentence echo Dostoevsky's own, so do the condemnation to death and the unexpected reprieve. All attentive readers would assent to the "enlightened predictability" of the following scenario: after committing his murder, Raskolnikov will come to recognize his crime, accept his punishment, and begin a new life, this time as a believing Christian rather than an iconoclastic intellectual. Such a reading is not wrong. Indeed, it summarizes the recognition drama so clearly wrought into these pedagogic materials. What it misses is the misrecognition haunting the entire narrative and accounting for its mesmerizing quality.

Our first glimpse of Raskolnikov's dilemma as irresoluble occurs by way of a vivid dream sequence. Raskolnikov dreams he is a child again, walking with his father in their rural village, and they come upon a brutal peasant beating to death the mare that pulls his cart—first overloading the cart beyond the mare's capacity, then smashing her with wood and then iron, finally bludgeoning her to death with an axe. The killing scene is surrounded by laughing, brutal peasants; it radiates a carnival insouciance. The distraught child begs his resistant father to intervene, then approaches the murdered mare and kisses it distractedly on its eyes and mouth. When Raskolnikov awakens, "his whole body felt bruised" (51); he cannot believe he will carry out his design. As such, the dream is clarifyingly pedagogic. At another level, however, it is provocatively confusing. For Raskolnikov identifies with all three of the dream's key figures: Mikolka the enraged axe wielder, himself the anguished child who looks on, and—most intensely— the mare struggling against a force too great for it, collapsing under the onslaught. To identify with all three figures is noncompossible; the dream thus hints at a deeper incoherence energizing Dostoevsky's protagonist. Raskolnikov is inextricably gazed at and gazing, victim and victimizer, wronged and wronging. His deed at once murders and makes him.

If we revisit space, time, and subjectivity in the novel, their unlawfulness comes into greater focus. The city's arrangements remain pedagogic in the ways described above; yet Raskolnikov wanders through St. Petersburg as in a dream. He is liable suddenly to collapse into unconsciousness while in midstride—as Joe Christmas will do in Faulkner's *Light in August*— even as he wakens with a start, not knowing when he lost consciousness, not sure he has regained it. (When he suddenly finds Svidrigaylov at his bedside, he thinks he may be still asleep.) The Porfiry interviews sound like a pedagogic deployment of characters in space—unfolding as an interplay of speech and counterspeech, headed toward dialogic knowledge but they read on the page otherwise. Dostoevsky keeps the reader locked inside Raskolnikov's frantic mind, as he seeks to preempt or decode Porfiry's gestures and utterances, terrified he is giving himself away, doing so despite himself. These three interviews are not dialogic but paranoid— registering as moment-by-moment assault (what will he say next? how will I parry it?)—phrases blurted out that suddenly turn and incriminate. Unframed, unmastered, the interviews read as torture, not pedagogy.

Time operates more broadly in *Crime and Punishment* as a medium of shardlike eruptions rather than the setting for progressive unfolding. Indeed, the book enacts unforgettably Raskolnikov's unpreparedness in time. He hears voices in his head, dreams and redreams the murder (it will not finish as a discrete event in linear time but unpredictably commands oneiric time). Feverish before the murder and after it, he lurches through his moments, barely able to grasp, let alone attend to, the contours of his flickering setting. This is hardly Baconian man setting up a practice upon the obedient natural world. Most tellingly, Dostoevsky cannot bring his protagonist to resolution within St. Petersburg time or space. Time in that space moves unprogressively, a sequence of interchangeable days and nights. He awakens in a sweat, it begins again. Likewise, space during that time lacks focus, subjective orientation; it is a territory he moves through myopically, his lenses lost. Raskolnikov's anxiety that Porfiry is suddenly going to spring someone from outside the walls into the interview room—any moment now!—in order to shock him into confession: this is a microcosmic figuring of Raskolnikov's insertion in unmasterable St. Petersburg time and space. To be brought to resolution, he has to be removed to another time, place, and mode of subjectivity.

The prison scenes in the epilogue occur eighteen months after his confession—enough time to lift the narrative clear of the hounded, claustrophobic subject in the city. More, the prison serves as a radically different space. Surrounded there by criminals and at last outed, himself, as a criminal, Raskolnikov appears as a different being. Not that he is now ready to know, but that the narrative has had to abandon the staccato rhythms of his urban consciousness—the suffocating locus of its point of view for the previous 450 pages—if it would produce recognition. The narrative can now access the long view—weeks or months pass by within paragraphs, retrospect is possible—and this telescoping of events enacts a different subject/space/time dynamic. Only this altered dynamic allows Dostoevsky to bring his protagonist to epiphany (a resolution, moreover, that many of the novel's readers greet with suspicion). Why has it been impossible to produce epiphany in any other manner?

First—and this is capital—Raskolnikov never feels remorse. Shame and humiliation for having botched it, but no remorse for having done it. This stubborn refusal to regret having killed the pawnbroker puts a considerable strain upon the Christian epiphany he finally experiences. No remorse, likewise no memory: "Everything, even his crime, even his sentence and his exile, seemed to him now, in the first rush of emotion, to be something external and strange, as if it had not happened to him at all" (464). No subsequent sentence revises this one in the direction of recall. As opposed to Augustinian recognition—the soul's attentive reach backward toward its earlier deeds, now clarified by the later conversion to God—Raskolnikov never reconceives his deed in his mind. This is not Maggie Tulliver or Anna Karenina, on the rack of suicidal guilt as they register inwardly the pain of those "familiars" they have betrayed. It is as though, despite the recurrent moments of spontaneous community that dot the novel, there occurred, simultaneously within Raskolnikov's consciousness, a repudiation of the structure of "familiarity" in which the larger society—including despicable pawnbrokers—might be recognized as ineluctably one's own. "Thou shalt not kill" is thus oddly abstracted in *Crime and Punishment*. He becomes a liberated man, but he seems unable to remember what he is liberated from.

It gets murkier. In perhaps the strangest utterance in the novel, Porfiry—the man of the law—says to Raskolnikov, in an intimately understanding manner: "It's a good thing that you only killed an old woman" (388). Thou shalt not kill, but yours was only a little-league murder. Behind such stunning casualness I glimpse two dark and unrepentant convictions coiling unspeakably in this text. One, the pawnbroker deserved to die. She was despicable, a leech upon the body politic: killing her is not wrong. If we further align the pawnbroker with Raskolnikov's own mother—the two elderly women in control of the purse strings, both of them cramping others' possible moves—then the darkness we are exploring only increases. Is the mother's death, late in the book, the suspended echo of the pawnbroker's murder, so many pages earlier? Does killing the one also and inevitably mean killing the other? (Is the pawnbroker not only doubled but tripled— not only *her* sister but *his* mother?). The logic joining them—the other dark and unrepentant conviction implicit in Porfiry's remark—is that Raskolnikov must be free at all costs, free to become himself. His own dependent creatureliness is what he cannot bear, his blood indebtedness to his mother and sister, his money indebtedness to the pawnbroker, his generic indebtedness to all the others who surround and impede him.

He fantasizes himself as a Nietzschean *Übermensch,* but he may more deeply reveal Nietzschean *ressentiment.* Sartre's *"l'enfer, c'est les autres"* is his stance as well. Everything cramps him, he flaunts his coffinlike flat as a metaphor of his soul's condition, the tiny and debased space he feels unjustly required to inhabit. He would mow others down, he does mow one of them down. Though surrounded by others, awake or asleep, he is rarely in sync with them, never in sync with them once his mind catches up with and disciplines his recurrent outbursts of spontaneous feeling. Indeed, his mind is an alienation machine. With Porfiry he spars; with Sonya he is alternately abusive and self-abasing. His speech pattern repeatedly conveys—by its three-dot ellipses—his nondialogic nonaddress of the other. A mumbler rather than a speaker, he talks mainly to himself throughout the novel (except in the epilogue where, significantly, Dostoevsky *silences* him, as he earlier had to silence the Underground Man to complete that narrative). Is this a gigantic ego-logy?

An ego-logy in the name of God: how could this be? If he *has* come to know himself, who is he? He told Sonya that he killed the pawnbroker because he had to find out if he had the courage to do so ("Sapere aude!" indeed). In a certain sense it has worked out accordingly: he did dare, and he now knows. We read (on the penultimate page) of Raskolnikov's new life as a something that "must be dearly bought, and paid for with great and heroic struggles yet to come . . ." (464). Great and heroic struggles: could this be, in the guise of Christian self-transcending, a reprisal of the Napoleonic dream?

If it is an ego-logy, rather than a Christian *imitatio,* then it reveals—with an exponential brutality that only misrecognition could allow—the implicit stakes of realism's Enlightenment narrative of coming to know. Luridly exaggerated, what are these stakes but the right to instrumentalize others (indeed, in this case, to off one of them), as the means toward self-knowledge? Such others can never be known in their genuine otherness. As Mikhail Bakhtin puts it in another context, "Everything that is . . . recognizable is fully dissolved and assimilated solely by the consciousness of the person who understands: in the other's consciousness he can see and understand only his own consciousness" (*Speech,* 143). Erasure in the name of recognition: the other as truly other is, finally, intolerable. *L'enfer, c'est les autres.* Does this unspeakable conviction fuel the Western drama of released individuality? If I comes first—ontologically and structurally— then you are in my way. I must *learn* to respect you: respect hardly follows immediately from a conceptual schema in which you are object to my subject, rather than co-equal within a community of beings. The Enlightenment narrative, as has been often pointed out, is stronger on universals than on community. If, in *Anna Karenina,* realism sentences to death the individual in the name of the other, in *Crime and Punishment* it sentences to death the other, in the name of the individual.

Is Raskolnikov going to be the great man after all? Can this question be answered? If we follow realist protocols, it cannot be answered, for it is alien to the very model of coming to know that those protocols are set up to enable. Raskolnikov's troubling resolution involves not a failure to achieve knowledge but a misrecognition at the heart of the novel's final recognition. For us to reconfigure the relation of recognition to misrecognition, to grasp the unknowing that coils within apparently achieved knowing, would involve considering Raskolnikov as a different kind of subject moving within the space and time of a different kind of narrative. A subject who is other than himself, a space he uncannily distorts by occupying it, a time no longer bound into linear progress. Dostoevsky's novel may allow this kind of reading, but *Crime and Punishment* is not shaped to invite it. By contrast, the modernist fiction of Kafka, Proust, and Faulkner is crafted to register knowing as unknowing—knowing as unknowing's most cunning guise. To make sense of a modernist deployment of an opaque subject's moves in uncanny space and unbound time, we must meet guile with double guile. As guide for this analysis we need not the Enlightenment thinkers but Freud.

PART 2

Unknowing

The Work of Modernist Fiction

CHAPTER FOUR

Plotting Modernism

Freud

"THIS IS NOT THE SYSTEM" II

What a system it often appears to be! Jean Laplanche and J. B. Pontalis's deliberately restrained "encyclopedia" of Freudian concepts (compiled in 1967) includes some 289 entries. As Freud (and his collaborators) continued to develop the theory and practice of psychoanalysis, the need to systematize—to bring it all into univocal order—only increased. In 1910, again in 1914 and in 1916–17, once more in 1933, and a final time in 1938, Freud produced comprehensive overviews that sought to bring under conceptual control the unruly monster he had begun to unleash in the 1890s. Now, over a century since it emerged, not only is the system under continuing attack from the widest range of discursive practices, but the psychoanalytic practice of therapy itself has been largely replaced by alternative practices unburdened by Freudian protocols.[1] The datedness of classical psychoanalysis looms so large today that a literary critic making use of Freud (Freud: not even Jacques Lacan!) needs to explain his enterprise with some care.

I begin with a couple of clarifications. The Freud who appears in this study is a modernist, not a scientist. As a scientist, he has long been under suspicion; ever since the 1960s—to take a vociferous example—Frederick Crews has been pillorying his work for failing to meet scientific criteria. One of his latest assessments—"Freud has been the most overrated figure in the entire history of science and medicine"[2]—states in an extreme manner a critique of psychoanalysis to which a wide range of respectable scholars (Henri Ellenberger, Phyllis Grosskurth, Adolf Grünbaum, along with Frank Sulloway and others) have more cautiously contributed. Yet the dimension of psychoanalysis that Crews centrally reproaches—Freud's placing his argument "beyond the reach of empirically based objections" (61)—is, however troubling, open to a different reading. For Bruno Bettelheim, the failure to meet empirical criteria is less the Achilles heel of psychoanalysis than its unavoidable condition. Unlike the natural sciences that "require verification through replication by experiment . . . [and that] ought to permit mathematical and statistical analysis,"[3] Freudian analysis is "idiographic" in its procedures. "Idiographic sciences deal with events that never recur in the same form—that can be neither replicated nor predicted" (42).[4] As Michel de Certeau has noted, the "golden rule" of psychoanalysis—that the analyst must care for his patient—means that "every psychoanalytic treatment directly contradicts a first norm, a constituent part of scientific discourse, which argues that the truth of the utterance be independent of the speaking subject."[5]

Second, I do not propose the Freud appearing in these pages as a determining *influence* on the modernist writers at the center of my inquiry. To a lesser or greater extent all of my writers were conscious of Freud's work (how, in the early-twentieth-century West, could an informed novelist not be aware of Freud?), but their work hardly derives from his. Though they creatively share his vision of "unknowing," they do not insist—as he does—on sexuality as the funding energy of neurosis. To put the matter otherwise, I am not interested in producing Freudian readings of literature. I do not invest Freudian categories with a normativity that would justify deducing fictional interpretations of novels from them: this is not the system. (The beast I have in view is not a sexually laden human prehistory that repeatedly subverts Western civilization's blueprints for maturation.) Finally, I am neither for Freud nor against him; my use of his work assumes neither complicity nor critique.[6]

Notwithstanding, this may be the place to suggest that, at a level I cannot prove but for which numberless testimonies would be available, we (Westerners) still tend to read our lives within a generic Freudian optic. We unthinkingly draw on his psychopathology of everyday life as a normative guide for our miscued words and deeds. A humble example may suffice. Several years ago, at a professional panel focused on Faulkner's centennial, I had occasion to deliver a paper. I had only fifteen minutes to speak, and I realized I had to overstate my points in order to get them across in so little time. More deeply, I was worried that the condensed theoretical frame of my argument would make me appear pretentious and thus increase the likelihood of failure. Addressing the first concern, I wrote down and planned to say: "Given the constraints of time, I intend deliberately to over-shoot my target, counting on you [the audience] to revise it as necessary." What I actually said, however—and heard with horror coming out of my mouth—was: "I intend deliberately to overshoot my audience, counting . . ." I never finished the sentence, turning beet-red as I saw my audience take in my words and respond with smiles, annoyance, and renewed atten-tion. My point is that, whether this was or was not what Freud deliciously calls a "failed performance" [*Fehlleistung*, ineptly translated by James Stra-chey as "parapraxis"], everyone in that room (myself included) took it as a Freudian slip of the tongue. He is with us still.

Let me clarify my stance further. Any literary analysis deploying Freud's body of thought must proceed with a sustained alertness to differ-ences between literary and psychoanalytic discourse, lest the commentary fall into predictable inanity. His core notions often annul the most valuable dimensions of literature. Here are a few examples. For Freud, the "scram-bling" achieved in the dream work proceeds involuntarily, by way of pri-mary processes, the most salient being condensation and displacement (both of these in the service of disguising the dreamer's unacceptable impulses). By contrast, the literary text artfully *deploys* condensation; such metaphoric activity (intimation of likeness among differences) is at the heart of its procedural insights (insights that go beyond authorial intention, but that are nevertheless launched by such intention).

More, *pace* Lacan and most of his deconstructive followers, one centers the work of art on the dynamic of unconscious displacement at one's own peril. The work's deepest investments are less those it furtively conceals from itself (and its reader), in order to avoid detection, than those its formal arrangements cunningly make available (though hardly self-evident)—this even though no writer brings under full control the shaping influence of cultural factors. Systematic distrust of the work's intentions is no less limit-ing than thoroughgoing trust in them. Put otherwise, a self-aware critical enterprise should remain alert to the ratio it maintains between insight and blindness. There is something comic (not to mention disturbing) in assum-ing the author's total blindness, as opposed to one's own total insight . . . Deconstructive readings of Freud's "The Uncanny" (like those by Sarah Kofman and David Ellison) typically proceed as though the essay's shaping motives fundamentally escape the author himself, without, of course, elud-ing the critic. Finally, Freud conceives artworks as essentially "about" the complex play of repression and sublimation operating in the psyche of their makers. The solipsism central to this stance effaces the cognitive dimension of art—the ways in which, as Adorno has persuasively argued, art sustains a tensile relationship with the social world it simultaneously encodes, interprets, and resists.[7]

Then why use Freud at all, why see him as "plotting modernism"? The reason is that, with exemplary seriousness, Freudian thought articulates, *conceptually,* stances toward the subject in space/time that modernist writers configure and deploy, *narratively.* He provides conceptual structures that bring into fresh focus the logic of modernist imaginary—structures that often shape modernist practice (the "plot" of modernism), however different the motives in play. (The motives differ significantly with each of my major writers, but the shaping structures remain.) I draw on Freudian concepts, then, not as a psychoanalytic cause that explains literary effects but rather, in Benjaminian terms, as co-elements within a larger, historical constellation of ideas and feelings that we may identify as modernist. This is why Lacan is irrelevant here (however useful he might be for postmodern investigations); it is also why current belief or disbelief in Freud is irrelevant. The constellation in question mattered then—for thinkers and novelists, for ideas and narrative procedures—and mattered regardless of whether it was perceived as a constellation. Attention to it lets us see how modernist fiction most tellingly revised realist assumptions.[8]

I have argued, throughout part 1, that a fundamental assumption enabling Western realist fiction is the value of *knowing.* Coming to know renders coherent—makes available for recognition—the trajectory (over space and time) that protagonists trace in their fictional passage. Such emergent orientation is fundamentally similar to the ego's task of aligning itself with the reality principle. Freud writes: "The ego's 'constructive function consists in interpolating, between the demand made by an instinct and the action that satisfies it, the activity of thought which, after taking its bearings in the present and assessing earlier experiences, endeavours . . . to calculate the consequences of the course of action proposed. . . . (Here we have the *reality principle.*)'"[9] All the terms necessary for a subject's profitable journey through space/time (the bread and butter of realist plot) are gathered together: ego as constructive agency, instinctual demand as desire/menace in need of mediation, assessment of earlier experiences and tentative new forays into the outside world as moves that together advise the ego whether to proceed, revise, or abandon project. The plot here sketched—didactic to the hilt—cannot function without secure *ego,* negotiable *space,* and linear, memory-traversable *time.* But suppose these three enabling terms were both unstable and latently interdependent? Suppose that prior to ego there was a something-else, and that something-else encountered and deformed space/time in ways foreign to the progressive moves of ego?[10] Enter the Freudian *unconscious* and the *primary process* that characterizes its activities.

As is well known, Freud arrived at his model of the unconscious only after sustained experience with hysterical patients and increasingly futile attempts to map their aberrant behavior onto a medical grid of somatically determined injuries. These were subjects who seemed to be experiencing a space/time different from that of healthy subjects: "then" was somehow still afflicting "now," "here" was eerily contaminated by "there." Not only had space/time, for Freud's patients, lost its lawfulness, but those patients' title to individuality (to undividedness, to ego identity) had lost its purchase: they seemed penetrated by absent others. To understand the logic of their behavior, Freud eventually decided to concentrate on their dreams, and even more on the ways in which their free associations revealed the invisible company they kept. Gradually he arrived at his poetics of the conflicted soul (his psycho-analysis), in which space, time, and subjectivity shed their Newtonian valences and take on a new configuration. *Space* here appears as no longer orientational but rather *uncanny* (reconfigured by the drives of the subject immersed in it). *Time* shows itself as no longer progressive but rather *traumatic* ("now" deformed by "then," for the same reasons space is deformed). The *subject* emerges as no longer individual but plural, inhabited invisibly by *other(s)* encountered—and unknowingly introjected—in the past.

FREUDIAN SPACE: THE UNCANNY

In a poststructuralist climate intent on undermining the legitimacy of boundaries, it is not surprising that the "uncanny" became one of Freud's most widely deployed concepts. Paul de Man's well-known essays on the subversion of conceptual borders in literature by romantic and modern writers—boundaries between literature and life, text and critic, fantasy and reality, figurative and literal—have encouraged recent interpreters of the "uncanny" to see it as the inclusive category within which literature itself resides.[11] Read from within a deconstructive optic, all literature exhibits a constituent *slippage,* a destabilizing of boundaries easily generalized as "uncanny." Thus, in a move whose logic is familiar, David Ellison reads Freud's attempt to define the uncanny as the necessary failure that obtains when one pretends to master the bounds of literariness itself. Instead of achieving mastery, Ellison claims, Freud comes under the spell of "that *energeia,* which, in pushing beyond clearly established boundaries of all kinds, ends up possessing the naïvely unsuspecting would-be possessor (interpreter)."[12] Ellison goes on to generalize: "the uncanny is that which cannot merely be an example . . . but which is a fall . . . into literariness" (58).[13]

Within this current reading, the specificity of "uncanny" disappears. Buttressed by a larger Derridean suspicion of the privilege lurking in all hierarchical oppositions, the term is now applied to the suspect construct-edness of any binary whatsoever. Along with this extension of the term beyond Freud's own usage, there is widespread deconstruction of his inter-pretation (in his essay "The Uncanny") of E. T. A. Hoffmann's "The Sand-man." Such deconstructive analysis first shows Freud's reading of Hoffmann to be perforated by his own unaccounted-for biases, then rejects Freud's claim that, within the literary domain itself, only fiction that pro-poses to "move in the world of common reality" ("The Uncanny," in *SE,* 17:250) is capable of producing uncanny effects.[14] Freud knew what he was doing in this essay, however, well enough to justify more attention to his claims. To wit, the Freudian uncanny is perhaps best understood as bear-ing not on all boundary instabilities, but, more productively, on boundary slippages that are *spatial:* scenes supposedly occurring "out there" but actu-ally being shaped from "in here." Shaped from "in here" because, when-ever the constructive ego ceases to operate according to the reality principle, the subject's relation to the outside world goes awry. For Freud, the fundamental task of an I-principle (be it his later term "ego" or his ear-lier "perception/consciousness system") is to manage the behavior of the (multiply solicited) subject in (external) space. He therefore has no trouble locating "the system *Pcpt.-Cs.* . . . on the borderline between outside and inside; it must be turned towards the external world" (*Beyond the Pleasure Principle,* in *SE,* 18:24.)

So crucial is this spatial claim that one might see Freud's earliest clinical experience as presenting him with a dilemma he was to probe throughout his career: how to distinguish with certainty between inner events (hallu-cinatory, psychotic) and those wherein the mind responsibly engages the outer world? Psychotherapy as a practice prioritizes this question; and ego, positioned on the "borderline," undertakes its challenge. The process it employs for doing so is what Freud calls "reality-testing," and the body of Western fiction centrally invested in representing this process is, of course, realism.[15] Thus Freud's remarks in "The Uncanny" about litera-ture focused on "common reality" are pertinent, for the eruption of the uncanny announces less the boundary slippage intrinsic to literature *tout court,* than a breaching of the conditions of world-engagement—of familiarity, of orientation—common to ego activity and to literary realism. When a writer pretends to move in the world of common reality, Freud writes, "he accepts as well all the conditions operating to produce uncanny feelings in real life; and everything that would have an uncanny effect in real life has it in his story" (*SE,* 17:250).

Freud invokes realism because realism privileges the moves of constructive ego. An uncanny effect occurs, therefore, when ego's spatial contract for engaging with "common reality" is suddenly invalidated. Fairy tales do not meet this criterion, because the subject is, so to speak, informed from the beginning that other rules for world-engagement are in force. By contrast, shock occurs when, and only when, the props that underwrite our commerce with "common reality" are removed, and ego's lurid prehistory is suddenly reactivated. Instead of "reality-testing," one registers (generated from within but seeming to come from without) assault and invasion, and one suffers anxiety.[16] For Freud, this anxious encounter is inevitably with something buried deeply in the past, something once friendly but now terrifying: "for this uncanny is in reality nothing new or alien, but something which is familiar and old-established in the mind and which has become alienated from it only through the process of repression" (*SE,* 17:241).

The underlying premise is painfully simple and basic to Freudian thought. Before we develop ego, we are in involuntary and unmappable relation to that which (in us and outside us) neither resolves into inner identity nor submits (by repression or conceptual boundaries) to outer negotiability. When this primitive subject state recurs, we experience "a regression to a time when the ego had not yet marked itself off sharply from the external world and from other people" (*SE,* 17:236). Put otherwise, whether it be a matter of the "omnipotence of primitive thoughts" or of "the return of the repressed," we register, as in the outside world, what is inside us, leaking out. Thus, *space* as the constructive ego knows it, as Newton mapped it, and as realism represents it is (in Freudian thought) a corollary of the "secondary system." All sutured (mature) egos live there, oriented and agential, but assaulted egos suddenly find themselves regressed somewhere else: in the uncanny.

One last terminological distinction needs to be made, in preparation for the following chapter on uncanny space in Proust, Kafka, and Faulkner. In seeking to understand the origin of sexual instincts, Freud distinguishes between *anaclitic* and *auto-erotic* activities.[17] Freud's narrow distinction is between the earliest infantile instincts that "lean upon" the mother's milk itself, and a later separation/sexualizing of these instincts as they move away from any necessary object. (First the infant instinctively seeks the life-sustaining milk, then, more playfully, the breast that contains the milk but is gradually becoming a sexualized object in itself, and thereafter any number of potentially sexualized objects unconnected with "milk"—a trajectory that launches the unplotted history of human sexuality.) The term "anaclitic" has, however, taken on a larger reference. It describes not the instinct's "leaning," but rather the *infant's* "leaning"—in Laplanche's terms—"on the *object,* and ultimately *a leaning on the mother*" (16; emphasis in the original). "Leaning on the mother": anaclisis figures a sort of primordial socializing or bonding between infant and mother. More broadly, I read as a form of anaclisis the relation of the subject to *already familiar* space, space previously "leaned on" and made safe by association, so to speak, with the mother's breast, space located on the path of ego maturation.[18] Uncanny space, by contrast, is space removed from familiarity, no longer breast-sanctioned, space you can do nothing with—like the space you find yourself in, for example, when you have become a noxious insect and your own bedroom is suddenly a prison.

FREUDIAN TIME: TRAUMA AND DEFERRAL

"Psychoanalysis, like archeology, is the quest for . . . anterior states," Malcolm Bowie writes; "for Freud *that which came before,* whether in the life of a civilisation or in the life of the mind, has a peculiar and unparalleled capacity to organize our perception of *that which is.* 'Le thème de l'antérieur,' Paul Ricoeur has said of the Freudian theoretical corpus, 'est sa propre hantise'" (18; emphasis in the original; Bowie cites from Ricoeur's *De l'interprétation: essai sur Freud*). As Freud put it in *Beyond the Pleasure Principle,* "In the last resort, what has left its mark on the development of organisms must be the history of the earth we live in and of its relation to the sun" (*SE,* 18:38, cited in Sulloway, 402). Thus emerges the first dimension of Freudian time: it is *backward-oriented.* Past contains the secret of present; psychoanalysis has only a thin sense of the future. Analysis gets under way in the conflicted now, working tirelessly backward. One could even say that psychoanalysis does not begin until the premises fueling the realist plot have bogged down in failure. Patients enter therapy less because they want help on future projects than because their present has become unbearably dysfunctional. The resonance of a backward temporality in my modernist writers is inexhaustible. Proust, Kafka, and

Faulkner—each in ways to be explored later—represent time in its anteriority, time as what has already passed objectively, yet not passed subjectively (in thought, feeling, and understanding). The great work of Proust
and Faulkner hardly moves past the time of the opening page, while that
of Kafka registers subsequent time as only the extension of present
impasse, never its resolution. Arrest—the keynote of Kafka's *Trial*—reappears as a foundational category (fixation, regression) in Freud's narrative
of the subject-in-time.

Freudian time is haunted by anteriority not only as a recovery project
(an archaeology), but also as a sort of perforation within presence; events
that occurred earlier remain unabsorbed, still registering their effects.
There are a number of reasons for the power of the past in Freudian
thought, of which perhaps the most lethal is this: the Freudian unconscious
does not know time. "We have learned," Freud writes, "that unconscious
mental processes are in themselves 'timeless.' This means . . . that they are
not ordered temporally, that time does not change them in any way and
that the idea of time cannot be applied to them" (*Beyond,* in *SE* 18:28).[19]
Freud thus proposes a model of mind that operates both outside time
(according to primary processes, the realm of the unconscious) and inside
time (according to secondary processes, the realm of consciousness, where
projects are conceived and pursued). In such a model the subject moves
forward in time, yet remains obscurely vulnerable to stoppages, visitations,
returns. Indeed, it becomes difficult after Freud to describe how human
beings do move in time. As Rachel Bowlby puts it: "For after the uncomfortable birth of psychoanalysis, time was no longer what it had been,
'before' and 'after' entering into new and hitherto unimagined relations of
complicity and interference. The unconscious is indifferent to the measure
of the ordinary time in which it never ceases to meddle, impinging with
some forgotten or unthinkable past events upon a now for which it is
always offbeat, untimely, untoward."[20]

The second dimension of Freudian time, then, invokes a kind of
moment rarely seen before, one in which before and after have forfeited
the healthiness of their linear sequence in realism. Past and present become
inextricable, glued together—most damagingly so when least anticipated.
The realist moment, securely bound and wrought into a progressive weave
of events that will eventually produce knowledge and self-knowledge, here
cedes to the moment as unmanageable stage for visitations from elsewhere.
To grasp the fictional possibilities of this newly conceived moment, one
might compare James's Isabel Archer with Kafka's Joseph K. At a critical
moment Isabel glimpses Gilbert Osmond sitting while Madame Merle is

standing next to him, and the intimacy revealed is pregnant with a plot eventually to be disclosed. Likewise at a critical moment Joseph K. wakes up to find two warders in his bedroom, and the moment is . . . never unraveled to him, however fatal its implications. In the one case, the text delivers an insight that is launched in present time and will be developed in future time. In the other, what Freud calls "a protective shield" (*Beyond,* in *SE,* 18:29) has been breached, and one's experience is no longer taking place, so to speak, in time at all.

The third dimension of Freudian time, closely connected with the unruliness of the modernist moment, is the unleashing of psychic trauma. The behavior of Freud's patients traumatized by World War I led him to revise fundamentally his model of mind. In *Beyond the Pleasure Principle,* he concludes that his shell-shocked patients' "compulsion to repeat"— manifested in painful dreams embodying the organism's desire to restage a terrible event and this time be ready for it—evinced a mental principle deeper and older than that of pleasure. Here is perhaps Freud's keenest insight into the psyche's troubled drama in time: that trauma unfolds as "an event in the subject's life defined by its intensity, by the subject's incapacity to respond adequately to it, and by the upheaval and long-lasting effects that it brings about in the psychical organisation" (Laplanche and Pontalis, 465).

Freud himself seems indifferent to the larger social framing of trauma—the failure of ideology revealed when a subject's cultural furnishing for managing stimuli comes undone—but Faulkner explicitly (and Kafka implicitly) conduct their most far-reaching social diagnosis through the subject-arrest attendant upon trauma. "Wait! I'll get used to it, I'll—": Quentin Compson's interior cry in *The Sound and the Fury* echoes a more broadly shared incapacitation of modernist protagonists. Not only do they lack the social resources to "get used to it" (to transform the traumatizing assault into digestible experience), but their authors' signature narrative moves consist in *writing* arrest (as in Faulkner's 'arrested' sentence above), in articulating not the renewal of movement but the compulsion to repeat. As we generalized modernist space, so may we generalize modernist time: *time,* as the constructive ego knows it, as Newton mapped it, and as realism represents it, is a corollary of the "secondary system." All sutured (mature) egos live in lawful linear time, but assaulted egos suddenly find themselves regressed somewhere else: in the realm of psychic trauma.

Psychic trauma displays an elusive temporal structure not seen in physical trauma. The latter operates unambiguously: an accident now produces traumatic consequences later. The former operates in undecidable time—in both past and present, and yet in neither. For an event that occurred in the past may not have been traumatic then, yet may become traumatically charged later. Freud's oft-quoted early claim—"Our hysterical patients suffer from reminiscences"—needs to be understood narrowly: it is in *remembering* that they suffer.[21] This takes us to the dimension of Freudian time that is in many ways the most fraught of all: deferral (German: *Nachträglichkeit*), the recognition only later of what was forgotten or repressed earlier.

Freud's understanding of deferral is based on the tension-filled model of memory described above. On the one hand, one forgets things, all during one's life. On the other, "we have been inclined to take the . . . view . . . that in mental life nothing which has once been formed can perish" (*Civilization and Its Discontents,* in *SE,* 21:16). Thus, one's forgetting (even when healthy) is strategic, motivated by repression and one's system of defenses. In *Beyond the Pleasure Principle* Freud seeks to conceptualize more fully the operations of memory that make this simultaneous forgetting/remembering possible. He proposes a pair of organic systems, one (nearer the body's surface) for the reception of excitations (a becoming-conscious system), the other (deeper within) for their storage (a memory-trace system). He goes on to suggest "that becoming conscious and leaving behind a memory-trace are processes incompatible with each other within one and the same system. . . . If this is so, then, the system *Cs.* is characterized by the peculiarity that in it . . . excitatory processes do not leave behind any permanent change in its elements but expire, as it were, in the phenomenon of becoming conscious" (*SE,* 18:25). The mental structure that receives stimuli from the outside world—consciousness—must manage to empty itself regularly (to relay elsewhere, for storage, what has been received). Otherwise it would swiftly become overwhelmed by the incessant arrival of new stimuli (to which it must respond). Consciousness and memory-traces thus operate, for Freud, fully independently of each other. It follows that narratives reliant on conscious memory would be, in effect, a tissue of pragmatic inventions, rather than an accurate recovery of stored (unconscious) memory-traces.

The implications of this model are considerable and disturbing, both for a general problematic of memory and for Freud's own understanding of subject development over time. As we know, Freud first believed that the infant's parental interactions were not, at the time, registered as sexualized, but were remembered later as sexually charged: "Here we have an instance of a memory exciting an affect which it had not excited as an experience, because in the meantime the changes produced by puberty had made possible a new understanding of what was remembered. . . . We invariably find

that a memory is repressed which has become a trauma *after the event.*"[22]
Long after the event—deferral, *nachträglich*—is when the event picked up
its traumatic charge. Glimpsed here is the nightmarish underweave of
Freud's dream of archaeological bedrock: that the origin is not the origin
until it is *later* posited as such. Indeed, the scenario deepens in deceptive-
ness, for Freud soon came to believe that the "origin" of what was later
taken as the infant's sexual assault was neither remembered nor misre-
membered, but *invented* by infantile desire. This emergent oedipal model
joined his ongoing work with patients' dreams as preparation for understanding the elusiveness of past experience, for in analyzing their dreams
he focused not on the (past) dream's recovered accuracy, but rather on the
patient's (present) associations. Thus he would, I think, have been deeply
skeptical of the massive social movement of the 1980s and 1990s that insistently reprised (for its own purposes) his model of unconscious memory:
the phenomenon of recovered memory therapy.[23]

If the dark side of deferral is the possibly fictitious "recovery" of forgotten memories (the irreducible liability that "recovery" is present-suggested
rather than past-authentic), the bright side is no less resonant. Later is
when we make sense of earlier. The project of realism thus depends crucially on what *seems* to be the same model of temporality. It would be hard
to overestimate the number of realist novels honoring the premise of "was
blind but now I see." (And not just realism: it would be difficult for anyone—present author included—to endure the passage through time without believing that, somehow, greater self-knowledge comes with later
retrospection. For further analysis of this issue, see my earlier comments on
"recognition" as the culminating moment in the realist narrative.)[24]

Yet this premise, however indispensable, requires belief in lawful, linear, ego-remountable time. I emphasize *"seems* to be the same," therefore,
because such belief is precisely what is missing in the Freudian model of
memory. Its absence makes recognition—always fraught—suddenly, expo-
nentially, more so. The notion of *unconscious* opens up a Pandora's box of
troubles insofar as it makes abidingly unreliable the notion of *conscious.* To
credit the one is always, potentially, to discredit the other. Freud's theory of
mind, I believe we can now see, simultaneously—and somewhat incoherently—*sabotages* and *sacralizes* the premise of temporal recovery. On the
one hand, we are self-deceived in time, our memories fallacious, our psyches distorted by the very defenses and repressions required for us to make
our way projectively through ongoing time. On the other hand, nothing is
lost, thanks to an unconscious that has never ceased to store (all unawares)
our memory-traces. I write about Freud, but who can read this without

thinking of Proust? Indeed, as I shall argue in the following chapters, only modernist fiction—not realism—truly takes the illumination that comes *afterward* into formal account. For only modernist fiction regularly represents the present *before* the past, such that the confusions of presence (its opacity without reference to the past from which its legibility follows but which this fiction has withheld) *remain confusing,* until the present is illuminated by belated flashbacks into the past.[25] Although Freud would have been dismayed by the reckless vehemence of the recovered memory therapy movement, he could hardly have repudiated the logic of modernist deferral: that logic was his as well.

FREUDIAN SUBJECTIVITY: SELF AND/AS OTHER

The Freudian subject is intrinsically divided (not an in-dividual), and this dividedness needs to be understood in a number of ways. Freud conceives the psyche, from the beginning to the end of his writings, as internally conflicted. The original consciousness/unconsciousness dichotomy cedes, eventually, to the trio of ego, id, and superego. As Freud continued to reflect on these agencies (especially in *The Ego and the Id* [1923]), he proposed among them not only irreducible differences, but also treacherous channels of communication: internal hostility made more ominous by internal betrayal. He envisages the ego as not only largely unconscious and libidinal, but camped out on the precincts of the id. It is the part of the id engaged in negotiation with the outside world and therefore conscious. More, the superego—that moralizing agency inaugurated by the abolition of the Oedipus complex— is likewise camped on the precincts of the id, thus punitively in touch with the renounced desires of the ego: "It is simply a continuation of the severity of the external authority . . . which it has in part replaced. . . . Here, instinctual renunciation is not enough, for the [child's] wish persists and cannot be concealed from the super-ego" (*Civilization,* in *SE,* 21:127). Thus the Freudian subject emerges as an internally beleaguered entity, rebuked no less for impulses unacted than for those released.

Interior conflicts go further. The Freudian subject moves in the most unknowingly guileful of ways. Repression and defenses—psychic energy deployed to prevent unpleasurable impulses from reaching consciousness— keep this subject in a sort of constant fog of self-unknowing. (This is not a heavy fog that brings subject movement to a halt, but a light one that, so to speak, allows the subject strategically to misread the shape of things.) Meanwhile, condensation, displacement, and symptoms shape the arabesque of

censored/disguised impulses. Finally, within the subject's array of resources
for negotiating ambivalence, speech itself emerges as uniquely duplicitous,
creatively overdetermined. Speech is not, on the Freudian model, hypocritical; that category of deliberate deviousness belongs to a nineteenth-century
model of ego-conducted behavior transparent to consciousness. Rather, the
Freudian subject's language, riven by the need to negotiate the disowned
even as it expresses the owned, achieves a certain poetic opacity, revealing—
as realist speech rarely does—intricately incompatible motives.[26] In Kafka
we will find a fictional version of such linguistic undecidability: sentences
that both do and do not mean what they say, sentences that torpedo the realist contract of responsible (ego-driven) utterance.

The traffic patterns so far described are intrapsychic. No less pertinent
for modernist fiction are the interpsychic ones. Despite the critical commonplace of narcissistic self-involvement, the Freudian subject is ceaselessly implicated in the world around him, in ways inconceivable on the
realist model. The assumption explaining such incessant two-way interaction is common to Freud and other modernist writers. Unlike all other
animals, human beings come into the world radically unprepared: "The
instinctual setups are insufficient," writes Laplanche, "and in any event
they appear too late, with a gap: they are not there when one would
expect: i.e., at birth. From birth onward . . . there occurs a kind of *disqual-
ification of the instinct* [and thus] satisfaction must pass from the beginning
through intersubjectivity; i.e., by way of another human, the mother"
(*Life and Death*, 60).

Intersubjectivity, satisfaction by way (first) of the mother: the human
subject envisaged by Freud is—by virtue of instinctual insufficiency—
divided, mimetic, absorptive. Engaged variously in identification with
others and projection upon them, the subject activates previous social
frames in every individuating move.[27] From birth forward, this needy
being engages the world; there is no alternative. One could say that
Freudian theory is a study in slow motion of the interactions complicating
that journey, even as much modernist fiction centers on the journey's
derailment, not its accomplishment. As I show in the following chapters,
few differences between realist and modernist narratives are more salient
than this one. If we return to the title of *David Copperfield*'s first chapter—
"I am born"—the distinction between a realist and a modernist launching
of the subject may be more clearly glimpsed. The realist subject is represented as patently destined for—already entitled to—"majority" status (an
individualized "I" assumed as birthright). His/her moves on the fictional
canvas register as satisfyingly discrete, coherent, supporting the notion of

a selfhood inaugurated at birth though still in the making.[28] Modernist narratives, by contrast, launch subject-making as a more troubling enterprise, prone to arrest rather than to development. Their subjects' symbiotic relations to the external world tend to remain conflicted and confused, in the realms of space, time, and the other.

The Freudian subject-drama we have been considering—like the modernist fictional dramas that follow—is radically intersubjective. However approached, it involves the co-presence within the "individual" of elements that de-individualize him. Constructive ego only goes so far; it may not even be first among equals. The insult to Western Enlightenment assumptions (and to the realist project funded by them) could hardly be clearer when juxtaposed with Kant's stirring call: "Enlightenment is man's release from his self-incurred tutelage. . . . *Sapere aude!* 'Have courage to use your own reason!'" ("What Is Enlightenment?" cited in Kramnick, 1). Insofar as the Enlightenment was a program for promoting individual, unsponsored maturation—for launching subjects toward their "majority" and their entitlement—Freud's symbiotic countermodel emerges as profoundly disruptive. De Certeau hammers the point home:

> Freudianism dismantles individualism. It destroys its truth-seemingness. . . . In 1784 Kant enumerated the rights and obligations of an enlightened consciousness: "a full liberty" and responsibility, an autonomy of knowledge, a "move" which enables man to "transcend his minority." The ethic of progress depends upon the postulate of individualism. A century later Freud reverses one by one all the Kantian affirmations. In his analysis, the "adult" appears to be defined by his "minority"; knowledge, by desire mechanisms; liberty, by the law of the unconscious; progress, by originary events. (*Heterologies,* 24; Kant's phrases taken from "What Is Enlightenment?")

Up to this point I have juxtaposed the Freudian model of the mind in space/time only with an Enlightenment/realist one that precedes it. Let me conclude by glancing ahead, to its salient difference from a Lacanian/postmodern model that will replace it. Drawing on surrealism as well as the least humanistic dimensions of Freud's own thought, Lacan simply does away with ego as the subject's always-fragile orientational agency for managing space/time. (This move has made Lacan the darling of many postmodern thinkers.) Ego is imposture; the aim of Lacanian analysis is not to shore it up but to go beyond (but where would that be?). It is thus instructive that Jean Laplanche, Lacan's sympathetic fellow critic of American "normalizing" of Freudian thought, nevertheless worries over the cost of

Lacan's enterprise: "But making the ego a 'simple' metaphor—i.e., an image whose role in the psychical apparatus would be restricted to delusion and 'lure' [*leurre,* Lacan's term]—would entail underestimating the effectiveness . . . taken on by that image . . . [and would lead us to] neglect one of the principal discoveries of psychoanalysis: *the constitution within the subject of veritable internal objects*" (*Life and Death,* 136; emphasis in the original).

Internal objects: real others, phantasmatically inside us. Deluded, invaded, caught up in ceaseless inner and outer commerce, the ego nevertheless remains an irreplaceable component of any model of the subject intent upon grasping its place in a real world populated by others as well. That such others are in us (including primitive unconscious residues incompatible with civilized identity) is, for Freud, less the sign of illusory identity than the index of anxiety besetting identity. We would be cohesively one, we are ambivalently plural. The subject trembles in Freudian discourse not (as in Kierkegaard) because of an inscrutable God's call upon it, but because its need of coherence, in the face of such introjections, is as menaced as it is clamorous. The path toward coherence requires painful acknowledgment of the others lodged inside. That it takes another to help us locate these others—that psychoanalysis is in several senses a discourse of the other—points not to the master/slave scenario invoked by Freud's critics. Such interdependence intimates psychoanalysis's most enabling insight: only our capacity to identify with others, however damaging, may yet set us free. What registers as assault may be reconfigured as annunciation.

CHAPTER FIVE

Uncanny Space

Flaubert to Beckett

"I have experience and I am not joking
when I say that it is a seasickness on dry land."
KAFKA

"BY ANOTHER *DÉTOUR*"

As I was walking, one hot summer afternoon, through the deserted
streets of a provincial town in Italy which was unknown to me I found
myself in a quarter of whose character I could not long remain in doubt.
Nothing but painted women were to be seen at the windows of the small
houses, and I hastened to leave the narrow street at the next turning. But
after having wandered about for a while without enquiring my way, I
suddenly found myself back in the same street, where my presence was
now beginning to attract attention. I hurried away once more, only to
arrive by another *détour* at the same place, yet a third time. Now, however, a feeling overcame me which I can only describe as uncanny . . .
("The Uncanny," in *SE,* 17:237)

We begin analysis of the uncanny space of modernism by way of Freud's
well-known vignette. What is happening in the passage? What in its spatial arrangement identifies it as modernist?

The vignette is narrated in such a way that the reader is not sure what is
(really) happening. A subject is moving through previously orientational
space and time, but his relation to those two Kantian axes of human experience has become troubled. Is he lost, and more so each time he erroneously
returns? Or is he found (out), and increasingly so, in ways he cannot admit

to himself? Is his spatial situation unmappable, or coyly in sync with unconscious intentions? Unless we can answer these questions we do not know how to read the vignette, from which rule number one emerges. In narrative the coherence of subjectivity is grounded in purposeful movement through space and time. Textual alignment of subjects within these orientational axes works to establish their identity and reveal it to the reader. No realist narrative refuses to honor this precondition of plot.

At crucial moments in modernist narrative, however, a subject's movement through space becomes uncanny—for the protagonist, sometimes for the reader as well. The intentional ego's spatial contract is rescinded; the subject is suddenly "on another scene." In postmodern fiction, as I suggest at the end of this chapter and explore more fully in part 3, anxiety about negotiating space tends to disappear. Such anxiety marks only, and profoundly, the subject of modernist fiction. The project-driven subject of realism hardly encounters obstacles at this elemental level (how *literally* to domesticate space). The subjunctive or linguistic subject of postmodern fiction is typically beyond orientational problems altogether. There is no body substantially there, to be lost in space, no "here I am" suddenly turned into "where am I?"

In the work of Kafka, Proust, and Faulkner, the relation of the subject to space becomes—at crisis moments—dysfunctional. Insofar as the elemental furnishing that cultures bestow upon subjects is orientation in space and time—what Pierre Bourdieu calls "habitus"—the unfurnishing of modernist subjects portends a something deeper than a bankruptcy in the plot: portends the bankruptcy *of* plot (as realism knows plot).[1] To open this claim further, let us reprise our earlier discussion of Freud and liken the subject's entry upon suddenly alienated space to the disorientation occasioned by removal of the mother's breast, the collapse of anaclisis.[2] Anaclisis, we recall, defines the infant's earliest experience of the world-become-familiar—a trust-suffused leaning upon the orientational breast that we explored both in Freudian theory and in realist procedures ("familiarizing the subject"). In the modernist instances here examined, the viability of space—supposedly furnished by the mother/culture—is being withdrawn. Yet no project, no capacity to *project* selfhood into the future, is possible unless a subject can count on space. The analogy with the mother's breast intimates as well the *temporality* of trust. The infant's familiar path toward the breast inaugurates the later familiar path toward conventional object choice and subject-maturation. Introduce a different space/time, and a different subject trajectory follows.[3]

THE CANNY SPACE OF REALISM

I here reprise, in brief, the implications of the realist protagonist's canny awareness of how thing go in space/time. Despite Victor Shklovsky's insistence that *Tristram Shandy* is the most typical of European novels, and despite the predilection of romance and the gothic for the fabulous, the representational norm for over two centuries of Western fiction is *verisimilitude*, a textual weave of the familiar, the lawful.[4] Within such a weave, as I argued above, the subject moves securely and acquisitively through space and time; epistemological confidence is a birthright of the Enlightenment.[5] In the domain of Cartesian thought, as Charles Taylor puts it, "we demystify the cosmos as a setter of ends by grasping it mechanistically and functionally as a domain of possible means" (149). The object enters classification within an instrumental schema: "This defines a new understanding of subject and object, where the subject is, as it were, over against the object" (188). In this new understanding there is nothing uncanny; the world is there to be known, mapped, and exploited by venturing subjects. The mastery that obtains is the glory of Western science, but it is simultaneously the source of abiding alienation: objects withdrawn from subjects, knowable only through internal schemas of representation and insofar as manipulated and classified—an outer world answering to the calculus of instrumental procedures.[6] Though the path of individual maturation may be (metaphorically) breast-launched, it is no less constitutively plotted (within Western culture since the Enlightenment) by a logic of acquisition and commodification. Knowledge-power (reading objects in space accurately, profiting by one's reading) typically motivates behavior in Enlightenment-derived realism. As the arch anti-Kantian Madame Merle says to Isabel Archer (in James's *Portrait of a Lady*), "I don't pretend to know what people are meant for; I only know what I can do with them."

For the next two centuries of Western fiction the project of self-realization is hegemonic. Insofar as this project tends toward a Hobbesian scene of unchecked aspiration—of ambitious individuals sprung free from the compelling fiat of church and state—insuperable moral dilemmas arise.[7] What values beyond self-empowerment do such liberal subjects recognize? The "democratised subject which has no necessary social content and no necessary social identity," Alasdair MacIntyre writes, "can then be anything . . . because it *is* in and for itself nothing" (30). Such a subject is only what it can contrive to become or acquire. For this subject, "reason is calculative; it can assess truths of fact and mathematical relations but nothing more. In the realm of practice therefore it can speak only of means. About ends it must be silent" (52). The most compelling goal is freedom to become, in time and space, all one can, the best way one can.

As I argued in part 1, this is a world of developing subjects—Moll Flanders, Joseph Andrews, Julien Sorel, Maggie Tulliver—each pregnant with a future. The drama in which these subject pregnancies are either aborted or fulfilled occupies the canvas of realist fiction. "Individuals were now assumed to be active participants in their own biographies and in history itself," Roger Friedland and Deirdre Boden write: "The ability to shape the future thus made . . . 'lifescripts' a necessary component of modernity" (in Giddens, 9). Because such developmental lifescripts privilege the release of energy more than the constraints of ethics, the need to moralize this scene of competing desires becomes acute. Kant's categorical imperative supremely articulates the ethical discipline required to rein in this game of self-flourishing. For Kant recognized that, though freedom and empowerment are the definitive and legitimate goals of all subjects, though subjects move through a field of others they can never know "in themselves," they must treat those others as they would themselves be treated: as ends, never as means.

As we noted above, this balancing act is easier said than done; realist narrative is constitutively invested in opposing core values. On the one hand, the Enlightenment dedication to subject empowerment in a lawful world underwrites realist plot. On the other hand, the categorical imperative hovers over that plot, rebuking subjective excess. The great realist novels negotiate intricately the tension between materialist career and spiritual demand, between acquisition and relinquishment. The canvas produced by realism thus reveals—one might generalize—a tripartite grid of assumptions: a Newtonian physics in which what the subject encounters likewise encounters the subject (with an equal and opposite force), a Cartesian/Lockean epistemology in which (with sufficient reason, method, and attentiveness) the subject can learn to map and master the world, and a Kantian morality in which the subject's humanity is measured by a capacity to acknowledge the kindred humanity of others. However unpredictable the range of moves made by realist subjects in space/time, the consequences emerge as familiar and lawful.[8]

By the mid-nineteenth century, for writers like Flaubert and the naturalists who follow him, realism's constitutive tension has become unnegotiable. Material acquisition (in a capitalistic world apparently responsive to instrumental reason alone) routinely overpowers spiritual aspiration (doomed within such deadeningly familiar arrangements). The spatial canvas of such

narratives, obedient to the protocols of the Enlightenment narrative of coming to know, remains technically lawful. Canny subjects continue to exploit
that lawfulness, coming to know with a vengeance. But the underlying
Enlightenment premises reveal more openly their moral vacuity; the masterplot of realism (ambitious subject-dramas occurring within a Newtonian
universe), tends to suffer from spiritual bankruptcy. In these paragraphs I
have sought to describe the exhaustion of realist norms of representation in
such a way that we might grasp more fully the need of a *new representational
schema*. Rather than tweak that familiar plot of knowing and mastery, modernist practice liberates narrative from the blandishments *of* plot. Attending
to the dilemma of subjective energies in a realm of unmastered space, discontinuous time, and unfamiliar objects, modernist procedures probe
beneath the otherwise ironclad lockstep of the knowing subject's orientational moves in familiar space/time. Before examining in detail how they do
this, we might take a last look at how suffocating that lockstep can be. Here
is Emma Bovary at table with her husband Charles:

> But it was above all the meal-times that were unbearable to her, in this small
> room on the ground-floor, with its smoking stove, its creaking door, the
> walls that sweated, the damp pavement; all the bitterness of life seemed
> served up on her plate; and with the smoke of the boiled meat there rose
> from her secret soul waves of nauseous disgust. Charles was a slow eater; she
> played with a few nuts, or, leaning on her elbow, amused herself drawing
> lines along the oil-cloth table-cover with the point of her knife.[9]

Erich Auerbach and Georges Poulet have identified this as a specimen passage of Flaubertian narrative. Subject and object enact a marriage made in
hell perhaps, but a marriage nevertheless, from which there can be no
divorce. Novalis had claimed character to be fate; we see in Flaubert just
how claustral the equation can be. In George Levine's terms cited earlier,
"a meaningful universe . . . [operates in which] characters must be seen . . .
to create or place themselves in the conditions that correspond to their
natures" (*Realistic,* 147). Contractual to the hilt, Emma's earlier acceptance
of Charles's proposal leads to this scene of provincial suffocation. Anaclisis
can go no further, we know exactly where we are. Just as Bournisien's
sweating face and food-stained cheeks reveal, objectively and inalterably,
who he is, so the details of this room reveal, objectively and inalterably,
why one with Emma's escapist dreams must suffer within it. Who she is
explains why she suffers. Point for point—stove, door, walls, tiles, steam,
meat, Charles—the familiar objects composing the setting of Emma's daily

meal (its dailiness makes it deadly) announce the fate of Emma-as-subject, telling us that she is lying on a bed she has made. This scene of constriction is lawful; Emma's actions have produced their appropriate equal and opposite reactions.

Matter follows its tendential course, as Flaubert narrates Emma's collapse through two events that convey the extinction of spirit in a world of Newtonian necessity: first, the bailiff's confiscation of her precious things (objects she has tried to impregnate with spirit, make her own), and then the self-poisoning that progressively reduces her to inanimate body. Objective space remains familiar in *Madame Bovary,* but only the novel's self-aggrandizing males—canny Cartesian manipulators like Homais and Lheureux—negotiate it profitably. As Charles Du Bos says of Flaubert's sentences, we may say of the realism Flaubert writes and the naturalism he foreshadows: the spirit has gone out of things, instrumental reason and materialist projects alone thrive. The subject's moves in alignment with commonsensical Newtonian laws have become lethal; falling bodies fall.[10]

Flaubert is an indispensable reference for the modernists who follow. In him they read the bitter comedy of the spirit enacted within a commodity-charged spatial/temporal continuum faithful to the logic of Cartesian empowerment and Weberian disenchantment. (Consider, in this regard, how Flaubert keeps his eye on the commodification operative in converting lyrical Lucia di Lammermoor into materialist Emma Bovary, or in converting Charles's purchased set of medical books, embodying scientific knowledge, into the displayed furnishings of his office: the pages of the books still uncut, their sole purpose—as commodities—to advertise his learning rather than enable it.) The entire materialist scenario is tight as a drum, inescapable as a theorem: endgame. His followers see in his work the spiritual insolvency of a realist program of representation in an age of acquisition. The very authority of such bankruptcy announces the need of an *otherwise:* not an other place (that is sentimental *Bovarysme*), but an other set of procedures. *Bouvard et Pécuchet,* that ironic encyclopedia replacing the Enlightenment's aspirational one, reprises every entity a realist subject might seek to know (and possess), reconfiguring it as either chimerical or slipshod. This last text of Flaubert serves as virtually a tombstone on which is written for those who come after: *proceed otherwise.* These other procedures, operating not thematically but within the scene of representation itself, permit the modernist drama of the uncanny.

"HOW COULD HE HAVE FAILED TO NOTICE THAT?": KAFKAN UNCANNY

Kafka's text is limpid, his vocabulary simple, yet he time and again eludes conditions of familiarity. At critical moments he revokes the anaclitic assumption; canniness and cultural training no longer get anyone anywhere. "What we need," he once wrote, "are books that hit us like a most painful misfortune, like the death of someone we loved more than we love ourselves. . . . A book must be the ax for the frozen sea within us."[11] Only a wound will do, for we are unaware of our ongoing stupefaction. The wound, insofar as it is Kafka's theme, may be lethal (as in *The Trial*); but at the level of formal procedure—on the plane of representation—the lesion can be miniscule, yet quietly devastating. Consider the following passage from the first chapter of *The Trial,* after K.'s arrest:

> "You are only under arrest, nothing more. I was requested to inform you of this. . . . That's enough for today, and we can say good-by, though only for the time being, naturally. You'll be going to the Bank now, I suppose?" "To the Bank?" asked K. "I thought I was under arrest?" K. asked the question with a certain defiance, for though his offer to shake hands had been ignored, he felt more and more independent of all these people, especially now that the Inspector had risen to his feet. . . ."How can I go to the Bank, if I am under arrest?" "Ah, I see," said the Inspector, who had already reached the door. "You have misunderstood me. You are under arrest, certainly, but that need not hinder you from going about your business. Nor will you be prevented from leading your ordinary life." "Then being arrested isn't so very bad," said K., going up to the Inspector. "I never suggested that it was," said the Inspector. "But in that case it would seem there was no particular necessity to tell me about it," said K., moving still closer. The others had drawn near too. They were all gathered now in a little space beside the door. "It was my duty," said the Inspector. . . ."I was assuming that you would want to go to the Bank. . . . And to facilitate that . . . I have detained these three gentlemen here, who are colleagues of yours, to be at your disposal." "What?" cried K., gaping at the three of them. These insignificant anaemic young men, whom he had observed only as a group standing beside the photographs, were actually clerks in his Bank, not colleagues of his—that was putting it too strongly and indicated a gap in the omniscience of the Inspector—but they were subordinate employees of the Bank all the same. How could he have failed to notice that? (14–15)

Above, I characterized rule number one in realism as dictating that we come to understand subjects by understanding their movement through space and time. Rule number two is that narrative space in realism is reliably inventoried: not that everything is identified, but that everything *pertinent* to the subject's orientation is identified. The realist narrator silently performs this task of domesticating space in the moment of describing it, making it legible so that progress may occur. Kafka breaks this rule; his text is unpredictably "mined," and the result (as in the Freud passage) is uncanny. The three "anaemic young men" surge into recognizability well after K. has already entered the room, and we ask: How did they get there? Do they belong to the Bank or to K.? How can he have "failed to notice" them? (It is more than a question of bad lighting.) If we resurvey the passage, we note that it is suffused with orientational spatial gestures. The Inspector who rises to his feet and reaches the door, K. who goes up to him and moves still closer, the others who gather together beside the door: all these details that would facilitate a scene of clarification in realism carry here a tinge of epistemological menace. The orientational assumptions of social life dependent on shared spatial convention—the handshake, the privacy of the bedroom, the meaning of arrest if it does not signify disruption in K.'s ordinary management of space and time—are being sabotaged.

Without orderly space, no orderly time; without these, no subject development. K. can learn nothing.[12] Later, while discussing his case with the lawyer Huld, the spatial trap is sprung again: "'For example,' Huld says, 'there's a dear friend of mine visiting me at this very moment,' and he waved a hand toward a dark corner of the room. 'Where?' asked K., almost rudely, in his first shock of astonishment. He looked round uncertainly . . . [a]nd then some form or other in the dark corner actually began to stir" (104). Not so unmotivated this time: K.'s lapse is partially explainable. But the point is that Kafka represents him as *no longer in perceptual control of his space;* he has lost his road map. Other spatial surprises abound—the building (it could be any building) where he enters on the fifth floor and the hearing is being held, the discovery of court doors in Titorelli's apartment, the performance of the Whipper scene within the precincts of the Bank itself.

Although I concentrate in the next chapter on the deformations of modernist time, I cannot leave the Whipper scene without noting the scandal of its temporality. When K. returns to the lumber room the next day and opens the door again, "what confronted him, instead of the darkness he had expected, bewildered him completely. Everything was still the same . . . the Whipper with his rod and the warders with all their clothes on were still standing there, the candle was burning on the shelf" (89). Newton is stood on his head, not to mention the law of thermodynamics mandating that a normal candle lighted yesterday will necessarily burn down by today. If neither the candle nor the figures in the scene have changed at all, and yet a day has elapsed, then space and time are operating here in ways that no Enlightenment thinker is prepared to explain.[13] Perhaps Einstein comes to mind—he who argued that space-time is subject- and velocity-relative rather than Kantian-absolute—and indeed Walter Benjamin draws on Einstein (by way of Arthur Eddington) to characterize Kafkan space:

> I am standing on the threshold about to enter a room. It is a complicated business. In the first place I must shove against an atmosphere pressing with a force of fourteen pounds on every square inch of my body. I must make sure of landing on a plank travelling at twenty miles a second round the sun—a fraction of a second too early or too late, the plank would be miles away. I must do this whilst hanging from a round planet head outward into space, and with a wind of aether blowing at no one knows how many miles a second through every interstice of my body. The plank has no solidity of substance. To step on it is like stepping on a swarm of flies. Shall I not slip through? No, if I make the venture one of the flies hits me and gives me a boost up again; I fall again and am knocked upwards by another fly; and so on. I may hope that the net result will be that I remain about steady; but if unfortunately I should slip through the floor or be boosted too violently up to the ceiling, the occurrence would be, not a violation of the laws of Nature, but a rare coincidence. . . .
>
> Verily, it is easier for a camel to pass through the eye of a needle than for a scientific man to pass through a door. And whether the door be barn door or church door it might be wiser that he should consent to be an ordinary man and walk in rather than wait till all the difficulties involved in a really scientific ingress are resolved.[14]

Dizzying as Eddington's spatial scenario is, it is easier to assimilate than Kafka's, for at least it is boundary-consistent (i.e., not uncanny). The trouble remains "out there"—a storm of atomic activity that, mercifully, an ordinary man need not consider in order to enter a room. Ordinary man need not rethink his identity, is permitted to remain coherent, project-sustaining, even pious. Kafka's subject/space/time scenario plays out otherwise, remains undecidably treacherous and normal, inside and outside, disabling for K. yet conventional enough for the fiction's others. Writ large, writ small, the Kafka text is beset by spatial instability. Georg Bendemann is suddenly "surprised" at "how dark his father's room was even on this sunny morn-ing"; soon he discovers his father's newspaper to have "a name entirely unknown" (Kafka, *Metamorphosis,* 54, 62).

Klamm in *The Castle* is fiendishly repositionable in space: first seen through a peephole (seemingly reliable knowledge, this, and consistent with realist practices), but shortly thereafter we are told (I do not say: we learn) that he sleeps with his eyes open: so *he* was not seen, only (so to speak) his eyes were. Thereafter we get an endless series of screens and substitutions. There is Klamm's awaited departure (a prolonged scene delivering not Klamm but only an increasingly frustrated K. who slips into Klamm's attending carriage, swigs some brandy he finds there, half passes out, never comes upon his quarry); there is Klamm as "dispersed" in others (Frieda, the assistants: they emanate his aura); and there is Klamm as ver-bally represented by Erlanger and others. Nor does it help to hear from Olga the following: "an image of Klamm has been constructed which is certainly true in fundamentals. But only in fundamentals. In detail it fluc-tuates, and yet perhaps not so much as Klamm's real appearance. For he's reported as having one appearance when he comes into the village and another on leaving it, after having his beer he looks different from what he does before it, when he's awake he's different from when he's asleep" (230–31). In the face of visual indeterminacy at this level, canniness becomes irrelevant; one is no longer capable of measuring. The local irony of *The Castle*'s K. being trained as a "land-surveyor" has been noted by many critics; less noted is the irony's larger resonance. For "surveying the land" is the figurative project of every realist subject, and it comes a crop-per in Kafka. We remember his parables: "There is a goal but no way. The rest is hesitation," says one of these, while another concludes pithily: "Give it up." "Give it up": you can't get from here to there. To leave this village and find your way to the next one requires more than a lifetime.

Give it up: what might Kafka's fiction be asking us to give up? It is tempting to allegorize this question, or to blunt it by reading the spatial vertigo in Kafka as a conceit—which is how Jorge Luis Borges will rewrite Kafka—but what would it mean to read this anxiety literally?[15] To believe, contradictorily, that space is both lawfully given (outside us) and insidi-ously shaped (from within), operating differentially according to subjects, according to the same subject? Perhaps Kafka's purest narrative of spatial lawlessness appears in a 1914 diary entry:

> It was around midnight. Five men held me, behind them a sixth had his hand raised to grab me. "Let go," I cried, and whirled in a circle, making

them all fall back. I felt some sort of law at work, had known that this last effort of mine would be successful, saw all the men reeling back with raised arms, realized that in a moment they would all throw themselves on me together, turned toward the house entrance—I was standing only a short distance from it—lifted the latch (it sprang open of itself, as it were, with extraordinary rapidity), and escaped up the dark stairs.

On the top floor stood my old mother in the open door-way of our apartment, a candle in her hand. "Look out! Look out!" I cried while still on the floor below, "they are coming after me!"

"Who? Who?" my mother asked. "Who could be coming after you, son?" my mother asked.

"Six men," I said breathlessly.

"Do you know them?" my mother asked.

"No, strangers," I said.

"What do they look like?"

"I barely caught a glimpse of them. One has a black full beard, one a large ring on his finger, one has a red belt, one has his trousers torn at the knee, one has only one eye open, and the last bares his teeth."

"Don't think about it any more," my mother said. "Go to your room, go to sleep, I've made the bed."

My mother! This old woman already proof against the assaults of life, with a crafty wrinkle round her mouth, mouth that unwittingly repeated eighty-year-old follies.

"Sleep now!" I cried—[16]

What can be said of the investments in such a piece of narrative? As with Freudian uncanny, the loss of spatial reliability sabotages the very project of knowing. Subject and object bleed inextricably into each other. These six men emerge from nowhere and appear both accidental and necessary, the door latch springs open half magically (as though it were obscurely in on the event—but what is the event?), the protagonist's mother is both terrified and disbelieving (a real threat? a child's delusion?), the vignette closes on his furious, incommunicable estrangement, it all happens in an unbound moment. The subject in this vignette is nakedly unfurnished. All we know for sure is that the way of the world instituted by realism—the cultural furnishings it continuously supplies—does not operate here. This subject, like the Proustian and Faulknerian ones I shall discuss next, will get no sleep this night.

Give it up, the parable admonishes. Give up what? Our certainty that space and time submit objectively to familiar mapping? That the spatial-temporal pact underwriting the twin insistences of Western science and

Western colonialism—those two supreme impositions upon global space—
is founded on objective nature? That narratives of maturation, coherence,
and gathered wisdom (the precious stories we tell ourselves) depend upon a
model of subject/space/time indebted to nature rather than to Newton?
That sanity is given, not produced, not some fragile mental arrangement
dependent on Freud's secondary process? Freud was certain that, at issue
in any outbreak of the uncanny, one would come upon traces of the primary process, of the not-yet-individuated infantile psyche clamoring
within the adult psyche.

Kafka, for his part, scrupulously refuses to say—a silence that has pro-
voked in its train an inexhaustible supply of speech from the commentators. Rather than simply add to the supply, I prefer to remain attentive to
Kafka's *form,* his telling refusal to tell a certain form of story. That form
he refuses, in its insistence on the subject's canniness—his coming to know
spatially, and to claim his viable place in the external world—is realism.
Its telos is progress. Next to such confidence, one remembers Kafka's
aphorism, "to believe in progress is not to believe that progress has already
taken place." Or, more tendentiously in Adorno's words, "the further real
domination of nature progresses, the more painful it becomes for art to
admit the necessity of that progress within itself. In the ideal of harmony,
art senses acquiescence to the administered world" (*Aesthetic,* 158).[17] If art
"gives up" harmony—as a mimesis not of nature but of the meretricious
effects of "the administered [bourgeois] world"—what does art supply in
its place? Provisionally, let us call it a radiantly diagnostic refusal to con-
sole. Adorno again, on the dark masterpieces of modernism: "Even artworks that incorruptibly refuse celebration and consolation do not wipe
out radiance, and the greater their success, the more they gain it. Today
this luster devolves precisely upon works that are inconsolable" (*Aesthetic,*
82). We turn to Proust.

"IT IS OUR NOTICING THEM THAT PUTS THINGS IN A ROOM": PROUSTIAN UNCANNY

I was half dead with exhaustion, I was burning with fever . . . I should
have liked at least to lie down for a little while on the bed, but to what
purpose, since I should not have been able to procure any rest for that
mass of sensations which is for each of us his conscious if not his physical
body, and since the unfamiliar objects which encircled that body . . .
would have kept my sight, my hearing, all my senses in a position as

cramped and uncomfortable (even if I had stretched out my legs) as that of Cardinal La Balue in the cage in which he could neither stand nor sit? It is our noticing them that puts things in a room, our growing used to them that takes them away again and clears a space for us. Space there was none for me in my bedroom (mine in name only) at Balbec; it was full of things which did not know me, which flung back at me the distrustful glance I cast at them. . . . I kept raising my eyes—which the things in my room in Paris disturbed no more than did my eyelids themselves, for they were merely extensions of my organs, an enlargement of myself— towards the high ceiling of this belvedere . . . and deep down in that region . . . where we experience the quality of smells, almost in the very heart of my inmost self, the scent of flowering grasses next launched its offensive against my last feeble line of trenches. . . . Having no world, no room, no body now that was not menaced by the enemies thronging round me, penetrated to the very bones by fever, I was alone, and longed to die. (*Remembrance,* 1:717–18)[18]

Something central has been given up in this passage from Proust; we are deep into pathos rather than canniness. Drawing on imagery of medieval torture and Renaissance battle, Proust sequesters Marcel in nothing more menacing than an unfamiliar summer hotel room at the beach. Yet all these terms have lost their traditional valence.[19] Subject, object, space, and time have become disturbingly interpenetrating domains, revealing a complex of unmanageable interdependences far removed from the Enlightenment contract. Rational scrutiny—disengaged, orientational—here cedes to internal beleaguerment: *res cogitans* no longer takes the measure of *res extensa.* Consciousness in Proust is no coherent strategist, parsing reality ever more effectively, tracking the movement of objects in space and time. Rather, consciousness experiences the very body it inhabits as an alienated "mass of sensations" ("conscious" body, not "physical" body: the latter is inaccessible, one's own in name only). The unfamiliar room sets off, within Marcel, an SOS of unassuageable distress. In conventional spatial/temporal terms such as any nineteenth-century realist novel would use to access the subject here, nothing of note is happening to Marcel. Yet he feels as though he is dying. Proust's wager, throughout the *Recherche,* is that the consequent analysis—severe neurosis—will inaugurate rather than terminate readerly reflection.

Neurosis: Proust shows this, as Freud did, to be endemic to the human drama, rather than a state of affairs reserved for some defective subgroup. Proust has no need of the category of repression to make sense of neurosis;

the mere experience of space and time is sufficient. Finding itself unprepared (always unprepared) in a new setting, consciousness operates reactively, in both senses of the term. Uninstrumental and maladaptive, consciousness remains attached to the familiarity of its prior setting. It wants to return, it faces backward. There is no "room" inside Marcel for the present Balbec room to enter: an earlier Paris room, its dimensions faithfully habituated and inscribed, still configures his interiority and cries out against being displaced. Neurosis is the inability of consciousness to avoid hearing, deep within, an earlier pact of subject/space/time cry out against being displaced. A precious mutual arrangement is under assault. This displacing activity—the very stuff of realist fiction, the journey of self-making as a subject moves across a range of space/times—appears in the *Recherche* as torture, uprooting. José Ortega y Gasset claims that Proust registers a new distance between self and the world, but it is more accurate to say that, by thinking self, space, and time as *interdependent* terms, Proust registers an unstanchable bleeding of self into world, world into self. Postimpressionist painting conceived this interpenetration of subject and world earlier and more dramatically than modern fiction did. As Umberto Boccioni put it in his "Technical Manifesto," "our bodies penetrate the sofas upon which we sit, and the sofas penetrate our bodies. The motor bus rushes into the house which it passes" (cited in Kern, 197).

At its most benign, Proust represents sublimely the penetration of others into oneself, like the grandmother's entry into Marcel's Balbec hotel room, allowing him to breathe again: "Then my grandmother came in, and to the expansion of my restricted heart there opened at once an infinity of space" (1:718). Her entry reconfigures his external space by spiritualizing it, domesticating it through her familiar love. Proust shows the spatial dimension of this dynamic by having the revived Marcel seek to embrace her heart itself, yet—"like a man who tries to fasten his tie in front of a glass and forgets that the end which he sees reflected is not on the side to which he raises his hand" (1:718)—able to reach no further than her cheeks. Together, grandmother and grandson transform their hotel rooms into two chambers of a shared heart, her taps on the intervening wall decoded by him as signals of her acknowledging spirit, the material wall separating them transformed into an intersubjective membrane. Such penetrability operates in Proust more typically, however, as vertigo, hemorrhage: the misalliances of an apperceptive subject taken by surprise, out of phase with invasive events occurring in present space and time.

Misalliances: how much of the tragicomedy of the *Recherche* depends on getting external space wrong, and this less for lack of Cartesian resources

than because there is something awry at the heart of the human's engagement with others (subjects and objects) in space? Sent to his bedroom, Marcel schemes feverishly to escape, for if where one is for that very reason a
prison, then where one is not becomes charged with value. Marcel fantasizes over the dining room he is forbidden to enter: "where . . . the ice
itself—with burned nuts in it—and the fingerbowls seemed to me to be
concealing pleasures that were baleful and of a mortal sadness because
Mama was tasting of them while I was far away" (1:32). His daily dining
room! Rooms in Proust emerge as nothing in themselves (a premise at
which a realist like Balzac would shudder); all commerce with them is
shaped by the subject's own investments. To get out of the room one is in,
and into the room one is out of: how this motive fuels the dynamic of
Proustian social life, not to speak of Proustian sexual life.[20] Its reverse—to
get out of the rooms one wanders in, and more deeply into the single
"room" truly one's own (one's immaterial subjectivity)—fuels no less the
dynamic of Proustian recovery.

The plight of the Proustian subject in space goes beyond either neurotic
attachment to a former space or unmanageable penetration by—or mistak-
ing of—what lies outside. Perhaps the deeper spatial menace is to the body
itself—a body intrinsically ill designed to prosper in space (as though outer
space were what it actually is: outer space). This condition usually remains
veiled until the onset of illness. Here is Marcel reflecting on his grandmother, just after she has suffered a little stroke:

> Yes, it might have been said that a few minutes earlier, while I was looking
> for a cab, my grandmother was resting on a bench in the Avenue Gabriel.
> . . . But would it have been really true? A bench, in order to maintain its
> position at the side of an avenue—although it may also be subject to certain
> conditions of equilibrium—has no need of energy. But in order for a living
> being to be stable, even when supported by a bench or in a carriage, there
> must be a tension of forces which we do not ordinarily perceive, any more
> than we perceive (because its action is multi-dimensional) atmospheric
> pressure. Perhaps if a vacuum were created within us and we were left to
> bear the pressure of the air, we should feel, in the moment that preceded
> our extinction, the terrible weight which there was now nothing else to
> neutralise. Similarly, when the abyss of sickness and death opens up within
> us, and we have nothing left to oppose to the tumult with which the world
> and our own body rush upon us, then to sustain even the thought of our
> muscles, even the shudder that pierces us to the marrow, then even to keep
> ourselves still, in what we ordinarily regard as no more than the simple

negative position of a thing, demands, if one wants one's head to remain
erect and one's demeanor calm, an expense of vital energy and becomes the
object of an exhausting struggle. (2:325–26)

Newton provides, with his gravitational theory of forces, all the terms we
need to make sense of the mechanics of this passage, yet the somatic disorder it describes has no parallel, to my knowledge, in any premodernist
novel. It is as though the threat to human coherence that we associate with
modern physics supervenes upon an earlier gravitational model; and we
see, in Marcel's grandmother, Eddington's schema of swarming electrons,
now granted their human-unmaking power. The human body has lost its
solidity, becoming "spongy," hole-filled, inhuman. Proust shows us, as no
Western novelist did before, the expense of energy required to keep still.
(What premodernist novelist was ever concerned with the literal struggle
to keep still? James's drama of Isabel Archer's staring into the fire, late at
night, "motionlessly seeing," registers such motionlessness figuratively.
She is to recognize, in these sustained hours of immobility, what her later
actions must be, the path they need to take. The grandmother's path goes
somewhere else altogether.) The notion of a nonhuman field of force has
been present in the Western scheme of things ever since Galileo and Newton, yet kept by humanist insistence from the precincts of the embodied
subject—at least in the realm of literature—until the emergence of modernist practice. Here, the compact of the unitary Enlightenment subject's
negotiation with space—mobile, free-standing, appropriative—shatters.
Marcel's grandmother ceases to be a singular entity—a vital coherence of
subparts—and becomes instead a congeries of weakening resources, a
doomed target upon a field of forces shaped impersonally to annihilate
her. *Res cogitans* is implacably undone by the force of *res extensa.* "She"
implodes into a something brutalized by both the alien world and her own
no less alien body. The writer's imagination here is, we could say, subatomic, except that, unlike the arid, mid-twentieth-century "nouveau
roman," which made a career out of reducing the subject to its physical
substratum, Proust's text never deviates from the pathos of the grandmother's gathering extinction, even as it concedes the thing-dynamic to
which she is condemned.

   Emma in a room, K. in a room, Marcel in a room: I have tried to show
that a paradigm shift occurs when, exiting from a nineteenth-century text
that still (darkly) honors the Enlightenment contract of protagonists in
lawful commerce with Newtonian space and time, we examine two twentieth-century ones that do not. In Flaubertian realism subjects proceed as

we have learned to expect them to—recognizably moving and being moved by others—which is why there is room in such novels for plot and character development. ("The project of modernity," as Friedland and Boden put it, "has always pointed toward tomorrow" [in Giddens, 10], and no one has ever yearned more for tomorrow than Emma.) In Kafkan and Proustian modernism, however, this commonsensical frame of expectations dissolves; with its dissolution comes the end of character development. These texts are drawn to vertigo and trauma, centered on blockage rather than maturation as conceived under the sign of realism. ("Art brings to light," Adorno writes gnomically, "what is infantile in the ideal of being grown up" [*Aesthetic,* 43].) Freud is this literature's supreme mapmaker, for he knew that the human psyche does not experience space and time in the ways that classical science proclaimed—as objective frames, lawfully operative, detached from the subject-dramas occurring within their midst. Rather, he saw, in human prehistory as well as in the return of the repressed, a scandalous confusion between events occurring in here and those occurring out there. He knew that we obscurely project upon current objects the vestigial lineaments of earlier ones, that the space we actually occupy is furrowed by time and warped by desire—apparently lawful but always potentially uncanny. In such knowing he was not alone. As critics have shown, other thinkers at the turn of the century were repudiating Cartesian dualism, recognizing spatial perception to be "permeated with emotions, facts with values, the objects of sensation with the coloring of all that we have experienced in the past."[21] I turn now to my third modernist creatively invested in the revocation of the subject's pact with familiar space and time, Faulkner.

"PERHAPS LOOKING SAW ONCE, FASTER THAN THOUGHT": FAULKNERIAN UNCANNY

Once again, the scene involves a man entering a room—Joe Christmas rushing from the dancehall to Bobbie's room, thinking to elope with her:

> He knocked. There was a light in her room, and another at the end of the hall, as he had expected; and voices from beyond the curtained windows too. . . . He knocked again, louder, putting his hand on the knob, shaking it, pressing his face against the curtained glass in the front door. The voices ceased. . . . He knocked again . . . he was still knocking when the door . . . fled suddenly and silently from under his rapping hand. He was already

stepping across the threshold as if he were attached to the door, when Max emerged from behind it, blocking it. He was completely dressed, even to the hat. "Well, well, well," he said. His voice was not loud, and it was almost as if he had drawn Joe swiftly into the hall and shut the door and locked it before Joe knew that he was inside. Yet his voice held again that ambiguous quality, that quality hearty and completely empty . . . like a shell, like something he carried before his face and watched Joe through it . . ."Here's Romeo at last," he said. "The Beale Street Playboy." Then he spoke a little louder. . . ."Come in and meet the folks."

Joe was already moving toward the door which he knew, very nearly running again, if he had ever actually stopped. . . . suddenly he saw the blonde woman standing in the hall at the rear. He had not seen her emerge into the hall at all, yet it was empty when he entered. And then suddenly she was standing there. She was dressed, in a dark skirt, and she held a hat in her hand. And just beyond an open dark door beside him was a pile of luggage, several bags. Perhaps he did not see them. Or perhaps looking saw once, faster than thought *I didn't think she would have that many* Perhaps he thought then for the first time that they had nothing to travel in, thinking *How can I carry all those* But he did not pause, already turning toward the door which he knew. It was only as he put his hand on the door that he became aware of complete silence beyond it, a silence which he at eighteen knew that it would take more than one person to make. But he did not pause; perhaps he was not even aware that the hall was empty again, that the blonde woman had vanished again without his having seen or heard her move.

He opened the door. He was running now; that is, as a man might run far ahead of himself and his knowing in the act of stopping stock still. The waitress sat on the bed as he had seen her sitting so many times. She wore the dark dress and the hat, as he had expected, known. . . . And in the same instant he saw the second man. He had never seen the man before. But he did not realise this now. It was only later that he remembered that, and remembered the piled luggage in the dark room . . . [22]

This is not Kafka's boardinghouse room where you perceive only inadequately who is there, nor is it Proust's hotel room where unhabituated objects threaten to suffocate you, yet the subject-space contract operative in realism is no less fundamentally revoked. What in the Kafkan encounter emerges as anxiety, and in the Proustian one as anguish, registers in Faulkner as velocity and incomprehension. Joe is not traveling at the speed of Eddington's atoms, but he is moving at more than human speed—faster than thought can keep up with—and he runs pell-mell into disaster. Nothing in this space—which nevertheless he thought to be perfectly familiar—answers to his expectations. The door opens suddenly, pulling Joe as of its own accord, and Max emerges, dressed for a purpose Joe is too rushed to worry about not understanding. Max's words, with their racist barb, are likewise incomprehensible, but Joe cannot attend to them, is moving too fast to register anything accurately. The blonde woman appears and disappears, jerkily, the representation of her movement aligned with Joe's heaving sensory apparatus rather than with her own deliberations. Joe's consciousness may be intentional in the philosophic sense, but it lacks intention in any other sense. He is unbearably unfurnished. In this definitive moment of his life—Joe's fifteen years on the road follow hard on this traumatic encounter—he can get nothing straight, just registers, cameralike, the incomprehensible data coming at him. Why are they dressed this way? How can he carry all those bags? Who is this stranger?

He does not so much think these questions as become, fleetingly, penetrated by them one after the other, like events on a speeding movie reel, each one just short of enough repetitions to permit coherent representation. The entire scene is punctuated with "perhaps"; the narrative act refuses to sort out Joe's spatial/temporal experience, to reduce it to retrospective epistemological order. (Retrospective arrangement in Faulkner tends to be ideological rather than accurate.) When the encounter is over he is on the floor, abandoned and bleeding profusely: he has learned nothing. His final moment will repeat this one: again flat out on the floor, castrated and with his life pouring out of him, still having learned nothing. *Light in August* is fiercely nonpedagogic. Again, the film analogy is pertinent: the sound and fury of experience exploding upon the subject (in the subject) in the form of unmasterable encounters, at a pace faster than thought can digest. Consciousness, despite Cartesian and Kantian guarantees of accountability, is a defective resource for mapping these spatial/temporal events.

Such kaleidoscopic urgency does not command all of Faulkner's representational registers, though I have no hesitation in claiming this as his most compelling one. *Go Down, Moses,* written some ten years later, shares a measure of the abrasive shock coiling in Joe's narrative moments; but it more insistently replaces Joe Christmas's errancy with Ike McCaslin's development. Point for point, Joe's misread spaces become Ike's tutelary spaces. The wilderness yields its orientational richness, gradually, coyfully, to its patient lover. Ike finally encounters, at its center, his beloved bear; and they will engage in their fatal embrace, yielding a legacy good almost for a lifetime. By contrast, Joe Christmas lacks cultural furnishing. No cultural space yields him alignment (he is pure intrusiveness); this unfurnished state makes him one of Faulkner's memorable modernist subjects.

THE MODERNIST SHOCK OF NONIDENTITY

What are we to make of this modernist attention to the subject's spatial distress? What is at stake in the ways in which Kafka, Proust, and Faulkner sabotage the realist model of confusion gradually overcome and orientation achieved? K.'s bureaucratic career in the Bank, Marcel's incapacity to find vocation (indeed to grow up at all, prior to the last two hundred pages of a thirty-five-hundred-page novel), Joe's mangled and mangling relation to the governing ideologies of his culture (a brutal mix of Calvinism, racism, and sexism): all three trajectories suggest that the drama of spirituality does not occur *there*. Narratives invested in instrumental reason and aligned with its secular embodiment—ever-expansive Western capitalism—intimate all too clearly that the subject's engagement with the object-as-known has degenerated into an engagement with the object-as-commodity—the object as mere counter in a schema of acquisition. This all too familiar scenario is one that modernist fiction not only will not endorse but will not even imitate.[23]

Such refusal arises in overlapping quarters, including philosophers (Henri Bergson and F. H. Bradley, Friedrich Nietzsche before them) who read the Enlightenment-descended model for the subject's relation to the object—indeed to the "other" more broadly—as missing a spiritual dimension. (Such a model misses as well the unsystematizable density of our actual traffic with objects and others in the world.) Michael Taussig puts the case against instrumental Cartesian man in extreme form: "this disenchanted [world] is home to a self-enclosed and somewhat paranoid, possessive, individualized sense of self severed from and dominant over a dead and nonspiritualized nature, a self built antimimetically on the notion of work as an instrumental relation to the world within a system wherein that self ideally incorporates into itself wealth, property, citizenship, and of course 'sense-data,' all necessarily quantifiable so as to pass muster at the gates of new definitions of Truth as Accountability."[24] Even heavily discounted, this description remains disturbingly recognizable as the downside of realist empowerment. If so, then—as with the Ptolemaic system in astronomy—better perhaps, Copernicus-like, to jettison it altogether than craft another complicit modulation while leaving the framework intact.

Modernist refusal to recycle the story of acquisition rejects neither the subject nor the object, but reconfigures both, by reconceiving their relationship at moments of unprepared encounter. As the business-as-usual contract between knowing subject and knowable object collapses, this fiction follows the fallout in all its vectors: K.'s displacement, the grandmother's unrecognizability, Christmas's disorientation, to name three instances. I can perhaps best suggest the stakes of these modernist procedures by drawing on the critical enterprise of Theodor Adorno.

Adorno argues (in *Negative Dialectics*) that both the subject and the object are self-contradictory rather than self-identical (as in the Enlightenment schema and the capitalist ideology and bourgeois worldview it underwrites). Subject and object are not naturally destined for each other as, in such different ways, is claimed by both science and advertising.[25] Rather, Adorno understands subject and object to be indispensable concepts that have become mystified, deformed by the ongoing history of capitalist implantation. (This history is, of course, the history of the West.) Probing beneath the object-as-commodity—the object "destined" for subject-acquisition—Adorno finds the object as signaling the labor of those who produced it, the object as revealing (in its constructedness) a complex social history of ideology and exploitation.

Adorno approaches the fissured subject by way of the fundamental Marxist tenet that "Society precedes the subject" (*Negative,* 126): thus a subject unknowingly shaped in alignment with larger ideological discourses. The arduous task of thought is to unmask the ideology sanctioning the subject as natural knower/possessor of objects. For Adorno, the subject starts out self-blinded, a socially mediated "work" in need of interpretation—not an unmediated "nature" that can be posited as self-presence.[26] The structural connection to Freudian thought is patent: we carry inside us, unknowing, social arrangements not our own. Even though Adorno is as little interested in infantile desires as Freud is in unmasking ideology, both refuse the unified and self-knowing subject of realism.

Freud and Adorno are thus among our greatest theorists for understanding the shocks and discontinuities that mark modernist aesthetic form: "Scars of damage and disruption are the modern's seal of authenticity; by their means, art desperately negates the closed confines of the ever-same; explosion is one of its invariants" (*Aesthetic,* 23). At explosive moments, indeed *only* at such moments, the socially sutured subject ruptures, opening up to a new kind of diagnostic: "the modern is myth turned against itself; the timelessness of myth becomes the catastrophic instant that destroys temporal continuity" (23). Put otherwise, unless space and time actually "go wrong," as they do in modernism, the myth of ongoing subjective orientation—of business as usual, even if moralized—is likely to remain intact.

For Adorno, the subject—however blind to its own social constructedness—remains capable of self-enlightenment, and thus of a demystified grasp upon the object as well. Adorno speaks of this precious subject-object relation as "discrimination." "[D]iscrimination['s] . . . postulate of a capacity to experience the object," he insists, "provides a haven for the mimetic element of knowledge, for the element of elective affinity between the knower and the known. In the total process of enlightenment this element gradually crumbles. But it cannot vanish completely if the process is not to annul itself. . . . If this moment were extinguished altogether, it would be flatly incomprehensible that a subject can know an object; the unleashed rationality would be irrational" (*Negative,* 44–45).[27]

Let us generalize these claims. The trouble-making moments in the work of Kafka, Proust, and Faulkner—the moments when the subject's strategies of knowledge and power over the object founder—function as the work's diagnostic center, the locus of its spiritual energy. The representation not of resolution but of crisis is the work's project: "The artwork is related to the world by the principle that contrasts it with the world, and that is the same principle by which spirit organized the world" (*Aesthetic,* 7). What such work articulates is not the harmony of existing social practices but the Utopian promise of what does not yet exist: "the fact that artworks exist signals the possibility of the nonexisting. The reality of the artwork testifies to the possibility of the possible" (*Aesthetic,* 132). It follows that modernist fiction—in which the subject's relation to itself and to the world begins mystified, in need of reinterpretation—is going to be unavoidably difficult. Its representational strategy necessarily torpedoes the procedures of realism, while at the same time testifying to the pathos of this undoing.

Finally, as Adorno recognized, we respond to such art otherwise than we respond to realism, glimpsing in the jagged modern work "a stage of consciousness in which the I no longer has its happiness in its interests, or, ultimately, in its reproduction" (*Aesthetic,* 346). The central moment in the reader's experience of these troubled works is a sort of interior shattering: "Shudder [the shock of the modernist aesthetic experience] is radically opposed to the conventional idea of experience, provides no particular satisfaction for the I, which, shaken, perceives its own limitedness and finitude" (*Aesthetic,* 245). Shudder rather than pleasure: this harsh term captures the aggression such work levies upon its reader as it stages its disorienting encounters, the assault it must launch if it would reach and thaw the frozen sea within.[28] It remains but to suggest—briefly here, at greater length in part 3—how postmodern representations of the subject in space tend to reject precisely these modernist premises.

TOWARD THE POSTMODERN WAKE OF REPRESENTATION

The telling postmodern stance is the abandonment of anything "out there" as reliably knowable (and therefore credibly representable): the end of epistemology, and therefore of plot (except as irony)—no more "really." As Robert Siegle puts it, "Postmodernism is the resumption of rhetoric in the wake of representation."[29] In this wake subject is severed from a mappable world. Insofar as subjects are radically incapable of knowing objects or others, then—to reprise Adorno—the resultant "unleashed rationality would be irrational." Such irrational rationality characterizes much of the post-Nietzschean strand of nonreferentiality—in the wake of representation—prominent in postmodern thought, both continental and analytic. Here is W. V. O. Quine on how little the subject can know:

> Epistemology . . . simply falls into place as a chapter of psychology. . . . It studies a natural phenomenon, viz. a physical human subject. This human subject is accorded a certain experimentally controlled input—certain patterns of irradiation in assorted frequencies, for instance—and in the fullness of time the subject delivers as output a description of the three-dimensional external world and its history. The relation between the meager input and the torrential output is a relation that we are prompted to study . . . in order to see . . . in what ways one's theory of nature transcends any available evidence.[30]

The Eddington scenario cited earlier here assumes its postmodern dimensions. In a domain of speeding atoms and irradiation frequencies, what kind of effrontery is required to claim that we are capable of accurately mapping the world? Richard Rorty presses home the implications of an outer space disdainful of our terms of reference, wondering "if we could ever become reconciled to the idea that most of reality is indifferent to our descriptions of it, and that the human subject is created by the use of a vocabulary rather than being adequately or inadequately expressed in a vocabulary."[31] Rorty praises modernist art for its courage to take on this indifference: "For it somehow became possible," he claims, "toward the end of the nineteenth century, to take the activity of redescription more lightly than it had ever been taken before. It became possible to juggle several descriptions of the same event without asking which one was right— to see redescription as a tool rather than a claim to have discovered essence" (*Contingency,* 39).

Rorty's claim of "lightness" misses the anxiety that befalls the subject suddenly immersed in uncanny space and rendered unknowing. That anxiety has been my topic—an anxiety at the heart of much modernist fiction and the source of its gravity. But his generalization applies to a good deal of modern art. Even more succinctly, it announces the arrival of a postmodern fiction of vocabularies, a fiction in the wake of representation. In thus jettisoning the project of coming to know the object, it implies one final reconfiguration: the erasure of the subject.[32] For how can there be a subject still operative in that scene of ceaseless atoms and irradiation? Henry Sussman sees the art of our time finally arriving at Rorty's "plain of indifference": "The literature of postmodernism thus toys with the fictive conventions by which each character claims a uniqueness of essence and purpose."[33] I end this analysis of the subject in space with the twentieth-century writer perhaps most obsessed with the end, Samuel Beckett. Here is Molloy, the last of my characters to find himself in an unfamiliar room:

> I woke up in a bed, in my skin. . . . I went to the door. Locked. To the window. Barred. . . . What is there left to try when you have tried the door and the window? The chimney perhaps. I looked for my clothes. I found a light switch and switched it on. No result. What a story! . . . I found my crutches, against an easy chair. It may seem strange that I was able to go through the motions I have described without their help. I find it strange. You don't remember immediately who you are, when you wake. On a chair I found a white chamber pot with a roll of toilet paper in it. Nothing was being left to chance. . . . My beard was missing, when I felt for it with anguished hand. They had shaved me, they had shorn me of my scant beard. How had my sleep withstood such liberties? . . . To this question I found a number of replies. But I did not know which of them was right. Perhaps they were all wrong. . . . such as it was they had docked my beard. Perhaps they had dyed it too, I had no proof they had not. . . . If they had come and told me I was to be sacrificed at sunrise I would not have been taken aback. . . . I said, If only your poor mother could see you now. I am no enemy of the commonplace. She seemed far away, my mother, far away from me, and yet I was a little closer to her than the night before, if my reckoning was accurate. But was it? If I was in the right town, I had made progress. But was I? . . . I must

have fallen asleep, for all of a sudden there was the moon, a huge moon framed in the window. Two bars divided it in three segments, of which the middle remained constant, while little by little the right gained what the left lost. For the moon was moving from left to right, or the room was moving from right to left, or both together perhaps, or both were moving from left to right, but the room not so fast as the moon, or from right to left, but the moon not so fast as the room. But can one speak of right and left in such circumstances? That movements of an extreme complexity were taking place seemed certain.[34]

Beckett's postmodern passage wryly reveals how a subject that cannot grasp objects cannot function—and in this incapacity starts to become unrecognizable as a subject. Indeed, without recognizable objects in familiar space/time there are no recognizable subjects: the terms are interdependent. Descartes's *homo mensura*—nimbly recyclable for two centuries of realist fiction, besieged with anxiety in modernist fiction of uncanny encounters—takes his last bow here in perhaps the only guise remaining: parody. The drama of appropriate measurement reduces to a strategy of how to suck sixteen stones in correct order, even as it reappears in Hamm's urgent command to Clov (in *Endgame*) to move his wheelchair to the center of the room, the center! K.'s bewilderment, Marcel's anguish, Joe's vertigo—these emotional crises signaling revocation of the subject's anaclitic contract with space—resurface in Beckett as a peculiar linguistic comedy, in which not just the Proustian ordeal of sleep but the larger Western plot of coming to know, of the spatial/temporal return to the mother, to origins, makes its appearance as one of the unbelievable stories we tell ourselves. If there is such a thing as a "we" to tell them. Molloy gazes upon a moon caught up in Newtonian motion yet beyond measure, a moon hopelessly alienated from the subject gazing upon it. Kafka's "give it up!" has been taken to heart; project comes to exhaustion. Exhaustion, rather than the energy of the uncanny (the anxiety of a disorienting encounter), throbs as the base note here, the state of being reduced to knowing only what the words know: nothing.

Inasmuch as words cannot know anything—only subjects can—much postmodern fiction runs the risk, in abandoning the subject who would know, of confining itself to a scene of exhaustion. Are there alternatives to knowing other than not-knowing? Is *acknowledging*—in which one's encounter with the other refuses mastery or a reduction of the other to an economy of the same—one of them? Perhaps it is the postcolonial, not the postmodern, that may suggest how to reinvigorate the narrative act, to reconceive possibility within it. Perhaps the postcolonial, drawing on non-Newtonian cultural resources—evading thus the rise and fall of Enlightenment's knowing subject—beckons with a different subject/space/time dynamic. But for Ursula to walk out of Macondo and come upon the civilization José Arcadio vainly sought, for the butterflies to preside over Meme's lovemaking in the aromatic baths, for Remedios the Beautiful to rise from the earth and ascend beyond the clouds, flicking away Newton's laws of gravity as she does so—for space and time to orchestrate a scene of human possibility again—there must at least be an Ursula, a José Arcadio, a Meme, and a Remedios the Beautiful. More critically, there must be a Macondo: a premise of community put under pressure not only by the irresistible spread of global capitalism, but also by the conclusion of *One Hundred Years of Solitude* itself. Non-Western cultures, it seems, knew (perhaps still know) how to imagine this drama of a subject in nonappropriative space and nonprogressive time. Even from within the nightmare of our own culture a Beloved can be sprung free from Enlightenment fiat, come back to haunt our alienating norms of the subject in space/time. Hope, plenty of hope, as Kafka might say, but how to make this a hope for us?

CHAPTER SIX

Unbound Time

Proust, Kafka, Faulkner

TIME'S SEIZURE AND DISPLAY: PROUST

"WHAT WAS ABOUT TO HAPPEN WAS A DIFFERENT EVENT"

Time in Proust: has any critic *not* written on this topic? From the beginning, time has been recognized as Proust's distinctive theme (the first and last words of the huge novel both contain "time" ["temps"] in them). Samuel Beckett's *Proust* (1931) explored the inhuman force of Proustian time in diagnostic terms no subsequent critic has bettered. Julia Kristeva's *Proust and the Sense of Time* (1993) confirms that, some sixty years later, "time" remains the royal road into the Proustian project. So much has this been the central approach that some impressive readers of Proust—Gilles Deleuze and Vincent Descombes, to name two—have labored to debunk the role of time in Proust. For Deleuze, Proust's novel is fundamentally about learning (*apprentissage*); for Descombes, it is a novelistic critique of the philosophic idealism underlying the primacy of subjective time. Yet one of Proust's most sophisticated critics, Gérard Genette, has devoted a booklength study to the unconventional logic of Proust's representation of time. In what follows, I concur with Genette that to access the richest dimensions of the Proustian text, one must attend to its deployment of time. Like Genette again, one must attend *formally*. The conceded limit of Genette's analysis, however, is that it is formal alone. By considering Proustian formal arrangements as a departure from those normative in realism, I seek to suggest some of the nonformal investments as well: "Art perceived strictly aesthetically," Adorno writes, "is art aesthetically mis-perceived" (*Aesthetic,* 6). How and why does the Proustian text so deform traditional models for narrating time? We begin with a representative Proustian moment.[1]

> Near the church we met Legrandin coming toward us with the same lady, whom he was escorting to her carriage. He brushed past us, and did not interrupt what he was saying to her, but gave us, out of the corner of his blue eye, a little sign which began and ended, so to speak, inside his eyelids and which, as it did not involve the least movement of his facial muscles, man-aged to pass quite unperceived by the lady; but, striving to compensate by the intensity of his feelings for the somewhat restricted field in which they had to find expression, he made that blue chink which was set apart for us sparkle with all the zest of an affability that went far beyond mere playful-ness, almost touched the border-line of roguery; he subtilised the refine-ments of good-fellowship into a wink of connivance, a hint, a hidden meaning, a secret understanding, all the mysteries of complicity, and finally elevated his assurances of friendship to the level of protestations of affection, even of a declaration of love, lighting up for us alone, with a secret and lan-guid flame invisible to the chatelaine, an enamoured pupil in a countenance of ice. (1:136–37)

Although the structure here is realistic—a protagonist describing/analyz-ing what he sees in familiar space—Proust's deployment of it is not. No realist novel can afford to *stay this long* with such modest thematic material. Insofar as a realist novel might risk description swollen to this extent, its plot-bearing potential would have to be correspondingly portentous. James gives us (in *Portrait of a Lady*) Osmond's face in the finest detail, just as Balzac presents (in *Père Goriot*) a cornucopia of material minutiae that together represent the Pension Vauquer. In both cases we know that the thematic charge wrought in these carefully narrated details will eventually surface, revealing either the deeper motives of a character or the larger bearing of setting upon subject behavior. (Think of Krook's lingeringly described besmeared face: the denouement of *Bleak House* lurks within that description, awaiting its moment of arrival.) Put more generally, per-ceptual details in realist texts are either plot-pregnant or kept to a (reason-able) minimum. But Legrandin bears only slightly on the career of Marcel.

Noting the plot vacuity of this intense portrait, Vincent Descombes writes, "But this was not yet for a society novel. It was more like a piece written in the style of the moral portrait, or 'Character.'"[2] Indeed, it is not novelistic, yet the seventeenth-century category of "portrait moral" scants the *perceptual* insistence of the passage, as well as—more striking yet—its over-the-top brio. What "they see" soon passes beyond what anyone could see. Style becomes vision; the Legrandin-ness of Legrandin emerges within the frame of a single physical description. All this occurs in merely a moment of perception, but—to repeat—a moment absent from realist narrative. Precisely because realist narrative depends on plot to unpack later what is latent in a moment occurring now, the realist moment is correspondingly lean, serviceable, disciplined to the requirements of that future becoming. By contrast, this *is* Legrandin, all of him in concentrated form. His future appearances merely repeat (they do not unpack in plot time) what is given in this single, hypnotic moment. Another way to say this is: Proust's Legrandin, undestined for the developments that an Austen or Dickens or Tolstoy might have in mind for him, is *unplotted*.[3]

Unplotted in time: this is a condition of the novelistic power of Proust's portraits (we see such static intensity in other memorable portraits as well—those of Charlus, Saint-Loup, Léonie, Françoise, Mme. Verdurin, Bloch). But unplottedness in another of its senses—our not knowing what comes next—can be, for Marcel as character rather than narrator, a condition of menace. Marcel's problem with time surges into view whenever the *moment* arrives unplotted. Unless it has been prepared by what came before (harnessed within the regime of habit), the moment opens into unaligned "thrownness" (as Martin Heidegger might put it). Marcel's most vividly anticipated moments collapse on themselves (exit from imagination's scenario) whenever they actually arrive. Here he is finally about to be introduced to the much-fantasized Albertine: "Elstir was about to call me. This was not at all the way in which I had so often, on the beach, in my bedroom, imagined myself making the acquaintance of these girls. What was about to happen was a different event, for which I was not prepared. I recognised in it neither my desire nor its object. I regretted almost that I had come out with Elstir" (1:915). Comically, after looking away in an indifference that is both feigned and momentarily real, when Marcel turns to meet Albertine and the other girls, they are already departing without having been introduced! The subject's state of "presence" in a moment like this approaches a sort of abstracted emptiness; he turns blank. Compared with any realist protagonist, Marcel lacks canniness, has no capacity to negotiate actual doings in space and time.

When he later manages, with some help, to meet Albertine at Elstir's, the moment ceases to follow imagination's script. In entering the condition of enactment, it becomes so radically unfocused as to exit from representability.

Rather than give us—as any realist novelist *must* give us—some of their maiden conversation (necessarily pertinent for future plot development), Proust provides not a word that they say to each other, noting instead Marcel's sudden boredom when in her presence ("even when I knew it to be her, I gave her no thought" [1:931]), and resuming narration only when Albertine has departed again. Marcel concedes that the long-sought introduction gave him a certain pleasure, yet demurs crucially: "But so far as the pleasure was concerned, I was naturally not conscious of it until some time later, when, back at the hotel room, and in my room alone, I had become myself again. Pleasure in this respect is like photography. What we take, in the presence of the beloved object, is merely a negative, which we develop later" (1:932). Until developed later (a motif to which I shall return), experience in the present moment is—nothing. Unplotted, it lacks all qualities and contours. The subject is "in" it as in a fog.

There is one more form of the present moment perhaps worse—at any rate more painful—than either of those discussed. These are the moments that occur when what was anxiously sought has been found, and materially domesticated. Albertine sequestered in Marcel's Paris apartment bifurcates, as it were, into two: a literal Albertine (all too boringly present), and a phantasmatic Albertine, everywhere in space and time but here and now. "[B]y nature I have always been more open to the world of potentiality than to the world of contingent reality" (3:16), Marcel recognizes. His obsession with what may be, and what may have been, disfigures his moments of presence, turning them into scenes of imprisonment and anxiety for him and Albertine both. He is painfully aware that his desire for Albertine transforms her into a being of flight ("*un être de fuite*"): "To understand the emotions which they [beings of flight] arouse . . . we must realise that they are not immobile but in motion, and add to their person a sign corresponding to that which in physics denotes speed" (3:86–87).[4] Speed: as no realist novelist ever proposes, Proust registers that when others enter the field of our desire, they cease to be locatable in a present composed of here and now, but rather transform into entities in motion—engaged in a spatial/temporal flight away from our desiring gaze.[5]

These are some of the moments that the Proustian text chooses to represent. Let us note briefly other events that would be de rigueur in a schema of realist representation but that the *Recherche* sees fit to omit. First, there are Marcel's duels over the Dreyfus affair, referred to at least twice (2:368, 631) but never recounted. Even Flaubert, who knew that duels were the material of an earlier kind of narrative, consecrates (ferociously comic) space to Frédéric's duel in *Sentimental Education*. Proust omits Marcel's duel as irrelevant, and if one asks why, a shorthand answer might be: "irrelevant because Marcel is not *like* any figure on a realist canvas." (I mean "like" in an ontological rather than a psychological sense; it is his kind of being, not his character, that is different.) In any event, this omission is hardly noticed by the reader, given what else gets omitted in the *Recherche.* Consider, for example, the narrative treatment of Gisèle, one of the girls at Balbec whose provocative gestures Marcel immediately finds irresistible. For the next five pages he fantasizes over all the spatial/temporal details requisite for launching an affair with her, including the "dark corner" of the train to Paris she is to take, and where he plans to meet her and begin their liaison. Thereafter we read: "Within the next few days, in spite of the reluctance that Albertine had shown to introduce me to them, I knew all the little band of that first afternoon (except Gisèle, whom, owing to a prolonged delay at the level crossing by the station and a change in the time-table, I had not succeeded in meeting on the train, which had left some minutes before I arrived, and to whom in any case I never gave another thought)" (1:951). Killed off in a parenthesis! Gisèle exists for Marcel, no less than Martha Clifford for Bloom in *Ulysses,* only as a figure for fantasy, in no need of further plotting. Such figures neither intersect with the deeper career of the protagonist nor have pertinent spatial/temporal lives of their own. In Proustian narrative, unlike realism, none of their actual moves need be provided.

A few more examples will suffice. After the laborious lead-up to Marcel's momentous decision to marry Albertine ("I absolutely must marry Albertine" [2:1169] are the closing words of *Cities of the Plain,* culminating some four hundred pages of reflection), the next volume, *The Prisoner,* opens with Marcel in an unidentified bedroom. A page later we read: "When I reflect now that, on our return from Balbec, Albertine had come to live in Paris under the same roof as myself, that she had abandoned the idea of going on a cruise . . ." (3:2). Since the material details of her getting there—what he said, how she responded, her hesitations, her decision, her packing her bags—are (within the logic of this novel) irrelevant, they are granted no representation. Which means: the sense of how people actualize their identity by purposively engaging things in space and time—that larger Newtonian protocol of entities encountering each other and reacting in singular, measurable ways—no longer applies.[6] A concern for such verisimilitude is absent throughout the *Recherche;* Albertine needs only to *be* in Marcel's apartment. Put otherwise, Proust's representational model is not invested in the illusion of embodied beings moving coherently on a lawful spatial/temporal canvas. Within his model, things tend to happen in a long-dilated present.[7] We do not see them "become," within a developmental pattern that might coordinate the relation of here to there, of past to present to future.

Nor does Proust's model for representing Marcel in present time share realism's insistence on linking events involving others to the character of the protagonist, illuminating the latter through the former (what I explored in realism as "familiarizing the subject"). Consider this minor example. Charlus, after goading the Verdurins repeatedly, finally gets his comeuppance; he is publicly humiliated at a soirée at their house. Marcel worries about the gathering calamity—"the thought of the sufferings that were in store for M. de Charlus was intolerable to me"—and then we read: "I would have liked to warn him, but did not know how to do so" (3:294). Why does Marcel not know how? The answer, again, is not psychological (we know he has fought duels, is not lacking in courage), but ontological. Marcel is not *there* in the capacity of one sharing the social scene. The status of his narrative being is other. He is present as a lens upon a social dynamic that he scrutinizes without interrupting, one that he does not (in any plotted way) cohabit. Let me clarify by way of an example from realism's *War and Peace*. If we think of Pierre's unanticipated rescue of a child from the burning house in Moscow—a rescue that registers Pierre's unthinking inclusion within the social compact—we glimpse that the supremely unplotted figure in the *Recherche* is Marcel himself. I shall explore further, in the next chapter, the logic underwriting Marcel's (un)representability. Let me close this analysis of the Proustian subject in time by simply noting that the enigma of how Albertine gets into Marcel's house pales to nothing next to the enigma of how Marcel becomes an old man. In a novel that gives several thousand pages to his youth, with the final two hundred going to his last years, some thirty years are narratively missing: try staging *that* in realism.

"THE STRANGER WHO DOES NOT BELONG TO THE HOUSE"

We have examined several forms of unbound temporality in Proust: the prolonged moment of unplotted portraiture, the vacant moment of sheer presence, the menacing moment haunted by an unspecified past, an uncontrollable future. In all these cases the Proustian text revokes the bread-and-butter assumptions of a realist model for representing the subject in time. The moment is lingered over too long for plot purposes, the moment turns blank and plot-useless, the moment (in the field of desire) becomes charged with an anxiety of before and after. Put otherwise, the present moment in

Proust is, for all subjective purposes, a defective structure—revealing, indeed, *"l'imperfection incurable dans l'essence même du présent"* (cited in Benjamin, *Illuminations,* 203). Though the reasons have little to do with unacted desires, Marcel is no more able than Freud's patients to "do" anything progressive with time as it passes. If we turn now to how Proust configures Freud's second temporal category—the time of trauma—we shall find a significantly different problematic, fueled less by repression than by primordial lack. Reduced to merely himself, the subject fails to cohere, yet no compact sought as a remedy for aloneness is unassailable. Prior to all compacts, *lack* threatens the subject's insertion in the insecure field of space, time, and others. Put otherwise, lack reasserts itself whenever the anaclitic frame (within which we experience the world outside ourselves as familiar, reliable, breast-sponsored) ruptures. Perhaps Proust's most moving instance of this dynamic occurs when Marcel, anxious about his grandmother's health, comes upon her unannounced. The passage is long but needs to be quoted in its entirety:

> Alas, it was this phantom that I saw when, entering the drawing-room before my grandmother had been told of my return, I found her there reading. I was in the room, or rather I was not yet in the room since she was not aware of my presence, and, like a woman whom one surprises at a piece of needlework which she will hurriedly put aside if anyone comes in, she was absorbed in thoughts which she had never allowed to be seen by me. Of myself—thanks to that privilege which does not last but which gives one, during the brief moment of return, the faculty of being suddenly the spectator of one's own absence—there was present only the witness, the observer, in travelling coat and hat, the stranger who does not belong to the house, the photographer who has called to take a photograph of places which one will never see again. The process that automatically occurred in my eyes when I caught sight of my grandmother was indeed a photograph. We never see the people who are dear to us save in the animated system, the perpetual motion of our incessant love for them, which before allowing the images that their faces present to reach us, seizes them in its vortex and flings them back upon the idea that we have always had of them, makes them adhere to it, coincide with it. How, since into the forehead and the cheeks of my grandmother I had been accustomed to read all the most delicate, the most permanent qualities of her mind, how, since every habitual glance is an act of necromancy, each face that we love a mirror of the past, how could I have failed to overlook what had become dulled and changed in her, seeing that in the most trivial spectacles of our daily life, our eyes, charged with thought, neglect, as

would a classical tragedy, every image that does not contribute to the action of the play and retain only those that may help to make its purpose intelligible. But if, instead of our eyes, it should happen to be a purely physical object, a photographic plate, that has watched the action, then what we see, in the courtyard of the Institute, for example, instead of the dignified emergence of an Academician who is trying to hail a cab, will be his tottering steps, his precautions to avoid falling on his back, the parabola of his fall, as though he were drunk or the ground covered in ice. So it is when some cruel trick of chance prevents our intelligent and pious tenderness from coming forward in time to hide from our eyes what they ought never to behold, when it is forestalled by our eyes, and they, arriving first in the field and having it to themselves, set to work mechanically, like films, and show us, in place of the beloved person who has long ago ceased to exist but whose death our tenderness has always hitherto kept concealed from us, the new person whom a hundred times daily it has clothed with a loving and mendacious likeness. And—like a sick man who, not having looked at his own reflexion for a long time, and regularly composing the features which he never sees in accordance with the ideal image of himself that he carries in his mind, recoils on catching sight in the glass, in the middle of an arid desert of a face, of the sloping pink protuberance of a nose as huge as one of the pyramids of Egypt—I, for whom my grandmother was still myself, I who had never seen her save in my own soul, always in the same place in the past, through the transparency of contiguous and overlapping memories, suddenly, in our drawing-room which formed part of a new world, that of time, that which is inhabited by the strangers of whom we say "He's begun to age a good deal," for the first time and for a moment only, since she vanished very quickly, I saw, sitting on the sofa beneath the lamp, red-faced, heavy and vulgar, sick, vacant, letting her slightly crazed eyes wander over a book, a dejected old woman whom I did not know. (*The Guermantes Way,* 2:141–43)

Freud understands trauma as a breaching of the psyche's defenses sufficiently violent to unleash unmanageable distress. The psychic system, suddenly overwhelmed, fails to reorder itself, thus revealing how progressive time is dependent on the functioning of the intentional ego. As the ego loses its resourcefulness, so movement in time loses its linearity. One enters, as it were, a state of fibrillation; purposive behavior ceases. Sometimes, however, psychic trauma may erupt long after the material "event" occurred, in which case a later interpretive frame transforms something originally benign into something now traumatic. In either case, time goes awry, and behavior in the present ceases to be functional. Proustian trauma arises otherwise. It involves a sudden and unbearable recognition of one's actual temporal conditions, rather than dysfunctional behavior within them. In the space of a single moment, Marcel sees something traumatizing: what does he see?

First, he sees that seeing itself is reciprocal (a shared pact rather than a private resource), and therefore without guarantee, liable to collapse. All his former seeings of his grandmother have been unknowingly conditioned upon a reciprocal seeing-back that underwrote their value—exactly what Benjamin describes in another context as "aura" (the blessed capacity of artworks to return our gaze). Her inestimable value resides in this mutual seeing; he remains Marcel so long as she remains his grandmother. But her physical insertion in space and time makes her, at the same time, a being continuously altering and materially unreachable—a situation repressed by the needs of sanity itself, but unfortunately revealed in this untoward moment. Looking at her not looking at him, he discovers himself as "the spectator of [his] own absence." Literally, he is not there in her field of vision; more deeply, he is *not there* unless sanctioned by her field of vision. Uncorroborated, he gazes at his own absence. Becoming "the stranger who does not belong to the house," he is suddenly confronted, as it were, with "the blackened breast" of one who has up till now unfailingly nourished him. Insofar as all oriented human being depends upon the unthinking sponsorship of others, Marcel momentarily ceases to be. Need it be said that no realist novel entertains these quietly terrifying notions, that no realist novel fails to deliver the drama of coherent individuation? If, as Adorno proposed, modernist art "brings to light what is infantile in the ideal of being grown up" (*Aesthetic,* 43), Proust reveals what is grown up in thinking through the aporias of subjective interdependency.

"How could I have failed to overlook . . . ?" Marcel asks, and we remember by contrast K.'s suddenly distressful "How could he have failed to notice that?" In the Kafka example, space suddenly becomes opaque, closed to subjective mastery. In the Proust example, time—no longer repressed—lurches into view, complicating what has seemed to be only a familiar entity in space. Marcel realizes that for the longest time now he has not been seeing his actual grandmother. He has been "overlooking" her as though his commerce with her in space were time-free; but a photographic lens is ruthlessly time-focused, intent on the present. The pathos of the passage resides in the fact that it takes her not seeing him for him to see her, for once, as she is. There is no iterative becoming here, no cozy continuity of being-in-time. Rather, there is a convulsive alteration, lasting a moment only; then the curtain drops again. She appears once more as what she used to be. The disinterested camera, capturing only what is actually there, registers (in Proust's model) the world as seen without a self, intolerably up-to-date. About this photographic model I shall have more to say, but for now let me make explicit what is implicit here: that the inhumanity of this disinterested gaze is potentially Marcel's as well, the camera merely an alibi.

Marcel speaks elsewhere, when thinking of objects transfigured by their connection with his beloved Gilberte, of the "infrared" perspective that comes with love, a privileging subjective lens absent from all disinterested camera perspectives. Yet this scene of *depriviledging* is a no less powerful instance of "infrared." The unfurnished grandmother appears with unmatchable distinctness here, bathed in the estranging and disfiguring medium of time. To see her like this is to recognize all human being in space as continuously time-marked, and to realize that the normal time-coefficient for such seeing is long out-of-date, the act of seeing "an act of necromancy." The newspaper Georg sees his father reading is unrecognizable; the grandmother in this room is no less so. The passage speaks of "a new world, that of time," which is "inhabited by strangers." Though Proust uses the phrase *"êtres de fuite"* only for beings in the field of desire, we grasp here its larger resonance. A stranger, his grandmother is being whisked away from him in time, no less than her body will later be (faculty by faculty) taken from her during her illness. In time there are only decomposing strangers headed for unspeakable destinations. The passage's ultimate message is *unknowing,* "a dejected old woman whom I did not know." "Infrared" announces thus the menace of Proustian trauma, in which what bursts forth is not the return of the repressed but the rupture of the time-annealing intersubjective compact.[8] The present breaks through—it breaches—and all is disfigured. Marcel sees that, unknowing, he has all along been seeing the past in place of the present. In this moment he becomes a stranger—to the loved one, to himself—for the new seeing (the past *as* past, the present *as* present) is not bearable (and mercifully not there for long: Proustian subjects falsify time as they falsify space, necessarily, involuntarily, continually). Thus undone, it is Marcel who emerges as "the stranger who does not belong to the house."

The psychic operation in Proustian trauma is eviction from the familiar—a forced relinquishment of the maternal breast.[9] The passage insistently reminds us that, as the pact is mutual, the damage done to her registers in him. The analogies offered—the tottering academician, the sick man—point to a male subject. Indeed, the sick man whose strategies consist in eluding awareness of his own illness figures Marcel more deeply, perpetually buoyed by the reciprocal love of mother and grandmother, ignoring his irreversible physical passage through time. Deprived of his outdated, supportive mirror, he is forced to see himself in uncanny fashion, to catch up with himself: the nose as huge as a pyramid weirdly intimating the momentarily emergent, detested Jew in Proust himself—the Jew otherwise concealed, or projected outward upon Swann, Bloch, others.[10] Such glimpses, however they differ from each other, imply the same collapse—a falling back upon one's always inadequate personal resources, a return to incurable lack. Whether it be Saniette brutally ejected from the Verdurin circle, Swann later evicted from the same circle, or Charlus yet later expelled from that circle, all scenes of collapse rehearse the original ejection of Marcel from his mother's kiss, his mother's breast, his mother's womb. Against such primordial lack—renewed in the undoing of all our factitious pacts with time—what answering model for the subject's temporal passage can the *Recherche* propose?

"FOR WE REALIZE OUR NATURES ONLY IN THE COURSE OF TIME"

An attempt to answer the question just posed takes us to the dimension of time that we analyzed earlier, first in realist, then in Freudian terms: recognition, deferral, recovery. Nowhere does Proust more resemble Freud than in his insistence that the time we need to know about is time past—a time that is gone but, given the "incurable imperfection" at its heart, that was never (in its unfolding) possessed as presence. We encountered above the richest figure Proust offers for understanding this labor upon an opaque past: the work of developing photographs. In that instance, the figure was metaphoric. Marcel could not know whether his meeting Albertine was pleasurable until later, once he had a chance (alone) to "develop" its elements for their value. Earlier, however, Marcel had encountered the dynamic of photo development more literally. His grandmother, during that first visit to Balbec, had uncharacteristically let him know of her anticipated pleasure in Saint-Loup's offer to photograph her. Detecting vanity, Marcel, through "a few sarcastic and wounding words calculated to neutralise [her] pleasure" (1:844), managed to remove the expression of joy from her face, as Saint-Loup took the picture. Later that week, finding her hotel door inexplicably closed to him, for reasons he imagined as either "resentment" or "indifference," he waited without response for her acknowledging taps on the wall and cried himself to sleep. End of scene.

Years thereafter, long after her death and at an interval of a thousand pages, Marcel returns to the same Balbec hotel room. Bending down to remove his boots, he is suddenly invaded by her presence. She removed his boots before, and his making the same gesture brings her before him, exactly as she was. For the first time—inasmuch as the grandmother undergoing bodily extinction, earlier, seemed a stranger to him—he realizes she has died. Now, relentlessly, the "photo" taken earlier starts to develop. He learns (later, as one always learns: later) that she was already mortally ill and that the anticipated joy in that picture was for him alone; it was to be a posthumous reminder of their bond. More, Françoise and the hotel manager both reveal now, in a relentlessly unaware manner, how greatly she suffered during that first visit, this told in such a way as to say: but of course, *everyone* knew she was dying—everyone but Marcel. The "photo" continues to develop. His mother comes to join him at Balbec, and on seeing her face he now recognizes what has been there all along but invisible to him: "I realised with horror what she must be suffering. For the first time I understood that the blank, tearless gaze (because of which Françoise had little pity for her) that she had worn since my grandmother's death was fixed on that incomprehensible contradiction between memory and non-existence" (2:796). Deferral indeed: years after her bodily death, Marcel's grandmother returns as she actually was—and now can die as she actually was—for her grandson. Likewise, thanks to his now recognizing what he merely "saw" earlier—thanks to his developing the photo—he reads in his mother's ravaged face what only a kindred orientation can make visible.

Proust drives home the temporality of vision as *after-vision,* as a recognizing—once one possesses the interpretive key—that the tired woman on the bus in need of a seat is pregnant, or that the man making strange, woman-like gestures is a man-woman. We recognize not in the moment of seeing, but when—only when—we later get the key that allows us to decode. Because recognition is coded, because it is a function of our hermeneutic relation to phenomena, understanding is a culturally mediated act driven by deferral. Put otherwise, the ratio of what we do and do not understand within present experience is, for Proust as for no realist novelist, scandalous. The fog obscuring presence—Proust's awareness of how radically unequipped we are to grasp what is at stake in it as we undergo it—ensures that, without *later,* there can be no understanding of *earlier.*[11]

Famously, the last volume of the *Recherche* concludes on the triumphant note of later understanding of earlier events. The process of such understanding is that of art itself, and Deleuze has rightly pointed to the violence lodged in Proustian recognition. Given that we are creatures supremely adroit at deceiving ourselves—creatures actuated by motives we disown, as

well as incapable of measuring the stakes of our own present experiences—
we must arduously read against the grain if we would attain to truth.
Whatever comes easy, Proust never tires of saying, is not our own but the
property of the ambient culture.[12] Developing the true picture requires
negativing its apparent meaning: "Sometimes the script from which I deci-
phered Albertine's lies . . . needed simply to be read backwards" (3:85). Our
own lies are harder to decipher. Just as locating genuine sexual identity in
Proust often requires inverting what is proposed—finding the "invert"—
so accessing our own motives may mean "the abolition of all that we have
set most store by, all that in our solitude, in our feverish projects of letters
and schemes, has been the substance of our passionate dialogue with ourselves" (3:926). What is this but revisiting our own "photographic dark-
room encumbered with innumerable negatives" (3:931) and struggling
painfully to bring them to the light?

And yet, and yet. The lacunae in Proustian time cannot be filled, the
eviction repaired. The book's celebratory proposition—that "Real life, life
at last laid bare and illuminated . . . is literature" (3:931)—uneasily suggests
the converse of its proclamation. Such life is real only insofar as it gets converted into literature. It cannot be made real on its own terms; its own
terms are irremediably impoverished, inescapable as well. Yet Proust
claims that, in joining a forgotten moment with a present one, we not only
recover the lost one but access something even rarer: "a fragment of time in
the pure state" (3:905). The being that enjoys experience thus—both as it
was and as it is—is said to find therein "its sustenance and delight": home,
finally, the breast returned.

But a darker, and stronger, revelation of time's all-dispersing power
comes later in the text, in the "dance of death" that occurs all during the
final Guermantes party. Gazing upon the gap between these players' age
and their performance—the drama of their out-of-date behavior revealing
a terminal *unknowing*—Marcel registers time as anything but celestial sustenance: "These were puppets bathed in the immaterial colours of the
years, puppets which exteriorised Time, Time which by Habit is made
invisible and to become visible seeks bodies, which wherever it finds it
seizes, to display its magic lantern upon them" (3:964). So illuminated, so
deformed, these figures emerge as strangers to Marcel, and what is worse,
to themselves. No one knows anybody, anything. Not that he is much better off. Repeatedly addressed as an old man at this party, Marcel finally
comes upon perhaps the most insidiously startling insight in all of the
Recherche: "that adolescents who survive for a sufficient number of years
are the material out of which life makes old men" (3:969).

The faculty for recovery of the past—memory—is simultaneously the faculty that subverts recovery. As in Freud's model, Proust thinks of normal memory as radically defective; the assumption of "the unconscious" virtually mandates the corresponding assumption of consciousness as unreliable. True remembering consists in the recovery of what was never consciously attended to at the time. Again, Freud: "becoming conscious and leaving behind a memory-trace are processes incompatible with each other within one and the same system" (*Beyond,* in *SE,* 18:225). Any memory known to consciousness is—for that very reason—impure, revised by one's defenses and projects for pragmatic purposes. Only unaccessed "memory-traces" take one truly back in time. But if our past was lived "unknowingly" then, what is actually occurring when we access it "knowingly" now? As a former present, it was opaque; as a spiritually recovered present, it becomes transparent. In what sense can a moment divided between these two takes upon it be said to be the same?[13] As Kafka might say of such recovery—yes, plenty of recovery: but not for us. What is recovered is not what we were.

Finally, we might ponder further Proust's most radiant claim—that poets of the past have erred in situating paradise in front of us: "Yes: if, owing to the work of oblivion, the returning memory can throw no bridge, form no connecting link between itself and the present minute . . . if it keeps its distance . . . for this very reason it causes us suddenly to breathe a new air, an air which is new precisely because we have breathed it in the past, that purer air which the poets have vainly tried to situate in paradise and which could induce so profound a sensation of renewal only if it had been breathed before, since the true paradises are the paradises that we have lost" (3:903). I have sought to show why, despite the intoxicating sense of recovery, the air of these two moments can never coincide. Recovery is inseparable from invention. More, while Proust perspicaciously recognizes that our models of paradise arise from earlier fantasies (however we situate them in the future), the very lyricism of the phrasing invites us to forget the darker temporal equation glimpsed at the grandmother's return: "I knew that if I ever did extract some truth from life, it could only be from such an impression [that contradiction of survival and annihilation] and from none other, an impression . . . which had neither been traced by my intelligence nor attenuated by my pusillanimity, but which death itself, the sudden revelation of death, striking like a thunderbolt, had carved within me, along a supernatural and inhuman graph, in a double and mysterious furrow" (2:787).

I spoke earlier of trauma in Proust as the experience of inalterable eviction, and here the bearing of that eviction gets its name: death. Death is the mother of beauty, for Proust as for Wallace Stevens. Death is what our irremediable discontinuity in time never ceases to reference, it is what comes before, during, and after all attempts to generate home. The grandmother must die before she can be recovered as alive. All experience—if it would enter its immortal condition of time recovered (*temps retrouvé*)—must first relinquish to the past its carcass of actuality. "For we realize our own nature only in the course of time" (3:386), Proust writes; the stress is on "only." We are creatures only (irremediably) in time; our realizations are necessarily partial, enabled and delimited by immersion in time. No novelist has shown better than Proust how thorough-going that immersion is, how vexed yet indispensable one's belated attempt to understand, and repair, the blindness of the past must be. If we would grasp the stakes of this project in reverse time, the theoretician is Freud, but the poet is Eliot:

> And last, the rending pain of re-enactment
> Of all that you have done, and been; the shame
> Of motives late revealed, and the awareness
> Of things ill done and done to others' harm
> Which once you took for exercise of virtue.
> Then fools' approval stings, and honour stains.
> From wrong to wrong the exasperated spirit
> Proceeds, unless restored by that refining fire
> Where you must move in measure, like a dancer.
> (*Four Quartets*)

A man spending his remaining time to write the book that must (if anything can) justify his ill-spent life, a book whose title loosely translates as "making up for lost time," a necessary yet impossible return to a past whose terms are new, whose access requires both ordeal by fire and movement "in measure like a dancer": such paradise, if paradise it be, is time-immersed, death-encircled. Its clearing can be reached (if at all) only by way of purgatory.[14]

"FLIES STRUGGLING AWAY FROM THE FLYPAPER": A REPORT ON KAFKAN TIME

It happens all at once, often at the beginning; a momentous report is under way: "Someone must have traduced Joseph K., for without having done anything wrong he was arrested one fine morning." "As Gregor Samsa

awoke one morning from uneasy dreams he found himself suddenly transformed in his bed into a gigantic insect."[15] "I [a country doctor] was in
great perplexity; I had to start on an urgent journey; a seriously ill patient
was waiting for me in a village ten miles off . . ." These three well-known
openings report quandaries that will receive not an iota of resolution; the
donnée announced at the outset is fatal.[16]

There will be motion after such announcement, but not progress.
Kafka registers this primordially. He takes the stance of the body we
regard as definitive of homo sapiens itself—the transition from the animal's horizontal motion along the ground to the human's vertical motion
in the air—and, in "The Metamorphosis," inverts it: "he [Gregor] fell
down with a little cry upon all his numerous legs. Hardly was he down
when he experienced for the first time this morning a sense of physical
comfort; his legs had firm ground under them . . ." (84). Finally at ease, in
pure reversal of Freud's broadly shared anthropological schema of development, in which the animal, fatefully rising into the air, achieves human
status. For Freud, this is the moment in prehistory when the genitals get
exposed and thus need to be concealed, when anal attraction undergoes
repression, when body smells become shameful. Commenting on this
stance of lifted nose and lifted body as producing humanity by distancing
it from animality, Freud writes to Wilhelm Fliess in 1897: "'he turns up
his nose' = he regards himself as something particularly noble" (cited in
Sulloway, 200). Gregor, we recall, samples the various "half-decayed"
edibles set out for him by his sister, then goes unerringly for the most dis-
gusting cheese: his nose decidedly turned down rather than up. It gets
worse in time.

Echoing Walter Benjamin's oft-cited warning about the two ways of
misreading Kafka's works ("one is to interpret them naturally, the other is
the supernatural interpretation" [*Illuminations,* 127]), there are two ways
of misreading the opening sentence of *The Trial.* The first is to believe one
is reading third-personal realism and thus to trust the narrative voice
(someone did in fact traduce Joseph K., and we will in time find out who
and why). The second is to believe one is reading first-personal modernism and thus to distrust the narrative voice (he *says* he was traduced
but we suspect he lies, and will in time discover why). Both ways produce
cogent interpretations. Both likewise miss the intrinsic instability of that
voice's reference, its bid for readerly trust joined with its betrayal of such
trust—a bid and a betrayal inseparable from the text's peculiar deployment of the subject in space/time. One finishes the book exactly as one
began, in confusion. The immediate response to reading Kafka is likely to

be frustration tinged with anger: reading is not supposed to be like this.[17] The idea of progress—which means a prospering in time—is a constituent premise of reading itself. We must *learn* to read, and reading carries the same fundamental promise that learning carries: "pay attention and you will benefit." The attentive reading of serious writing is one of our most cherished liberal activities for making time make sense and reward our investment. Who does not assume that, for a small price—a little bit of reading time—a well-chosen text may pay off handsomely, yielding a great deal of insight?[18]

Joseph K. gets nowhere, nor do we as we seek to understand him. Two of the Freudian categories for time that we explored separately in Proust— shock and trauma—seem in Kafka to join inseparably. Something implacable has occurred; it stops the protagonist in his tracks, immediately, permanently. Kafka foregrounds this subversion of progress by way of the intermittent struggle between K. as would-be successful banker and his competitive rival, the Assistant Manager. The latter appears to us (and to K.) as a mobile figure of pure ambition, his every gesture charged with professional calculation, obsession to rise to the top. His motives—a time-measurable, successful career—are as transparent as K.'s are opaque. Whenever we as readers become frustrated with K.'s incompetence vis-à-vis the Assistant Manager, we fall into the trap of wanting K. to succeed, to "get over it" in order to "get on with it." The Bank figures as that institutional form of life in which (as the Assistant Manager all but says) time is money. Kafka teasingly allows us, if we want, to "invest" in it.

The same dynamic operates when the Manufacturer presses K. for approval of his plans: "K. had actually followed the man's argument quite closely in its early stages—the thought of such an important piece of business had its attractions for him too—but unfortunately not for long; he had soon ceased to listen and merely nodded now and then as the manufacturer's claims waxed in enthusiasm, until in the end he forgot to show even that much interest and confined himself to staring at the other's bald head bent over the papers and asking himself when the fellow would begin to realize that all his eloquence was being wasted" (130). Staring at a businessman's bald head instead of listening to him urge his project: K.'s stance toward time shifts from projective-cohesive to vacuously phenomenological. He sees without hearing or thinking. Oddly like Melville's Bartleby, but without politely declaring (without even knowing) that "he would prefer not to," K. is no longer (in any purposive way) *present*. Whatever has hit in that opening "announcement" is traumatic; the normalcy (the projectivity) of time is its abiding casualty.

Time under arrest: one way to clarify this temporal disfiguring in *The Trial* is to examine the various legal options that Titorelli proposes for K.'s dilemma—definite acquittal, ostensible acquittal, and indefinite postponement. Of these three procedures, only the first permits healthy resumption of time—the possibility of getting on with one's life, getting the trial into one's past—and this is the procedure Titorelli cannot influence. Indeed, this pathway seems decidedly mythical; "such acquittals are said to have occurred . . . they can be believed but they cannot be proved" (154). The remaining two options share a continued arresting of time: either a getting clear that is ostensible only (always to be renewed), or a postponement of trial that is rescindable at any subsequent moment. In the midst of such abiding nonresolution, Kafka lends his own legal training to his narrator's rhetoric, thus generating, sentence by sentence, page by page, the illusion of progressive orientation within the unchanging muck: "It was not to be gainsaid that these methods could achieve for the moment surprisingly favorable results for the accused, on which the petty lawyers prided themselves, spreading them out as a lure for new clients, but they had no effect on the further progress of the case, or only a bad effect. Nothing was of any real value but respectable personal connections with the higher officials, that was to say higher officials of subordinate rank, naturally" (117). Such rhetoric delights in fine logical distinctions, telling markers of improvement, signals of authoritative orientation ("it was not to be gainsaid"). Some results are known to be favorable, some abusive strategies are confidently rebuked ("but they had no effect"), all this preparing for what will make genuine headway (the "real value" of interventions by "higher officials"). The passage closes in the casual form of a slipknot (recurrent in Kafka): such "higher officials" are, "naturally," further instances of lower ones. Much ratiocination, no advance. All lawyers in *The Trial* are—by definition, if one is able to encounter them—pettifogging lawyers. Kafka's critics have studied the logical character of his "lawyerly" rhetoric—its insistence on *aber* clauses, on the elaboration of reversals, refinements, corrections. Horst Steinmetz (drawing on Herman Uyttersprot) generalizes as follows: "Given facts are reflected on, hypotheses are won out of them, hypotheses are in turn explained into facts, out of which again hypotheses are derived. . . . Every known fact . . . often appears in a bright veil of doubt, every hypothesis, on the other hand, contains something of the rigor of certainty" (cited in Robbins, 83).

The "rigor of certainty": what is "law" itself but the promise that, given sufficiently rigorous procedures, justice can be achieved? The premise of "law" is that social muck, however extensive, is open to mapping and adjudication—that arrest, however sudden, will yield to justification. The realm of "law" is that of human behavior mapped, rationally, into rights and responsibilities, permissible and impermissible actions. This is a signature project of Enlightenment: a human ordering—founded on individual liberty—as cogent and answerable to reason as Newton's calculus-mapped, physical world. More, "law" (like reading) assumes the "cash value" of time. Both law and reading rely on the continuing pertinence of texts written over time—texts still available, requiring study and requiting it in the measure that they permit pertinent juxtapositions, telling comparisons, rigorous distinctions. A world with laws, like a world with books more generally—like, ultimately, a world of shared language—presupposes a knowable past as orientation for present enterprises: a record of adjudicated former experiences that allows the present to be clarified and the future to be pursued. Laws, books, and language more generally are *media* that enable the rational flourishing of human being over time. They serve to mediate human life in time, to make it orderly (repeatable) enough to warrant projects, the activity of projecting. But in a narrative where law books are filled with pornographic pictures, where paintings are representationally delusive, where lawyers are all pettifoggers, where the offense is undiscoverable, and where the incessant deployment of rational language obtains neither clarification nor results—in such a muck-filled world the subject's efforts avail nothing: "Into his [K.'s] mind came a recollection of flies struggling away from the flypaper till their little legs were torn off" (225).[19]

Time passes in these narratives, without anyone getting anywhere. Time becomes a parenthesis, possibly a lifelong parenthesis. As with the heart analogy I proposed for Proustian time, time here "beats" in a rhythm of fibrillation. One is still alive, still breathing, still anxious, but halted; a crucial inner mechanism—what one might call the "time-processor"—has gone awry.[20] Consider Block reading his scriptures—"He never got past the same pages all day and he was following the lines with his fingers" (194)—or listening to Huld and Leni abuse him verbally in "a well-rehearsed dialogue which had been often repeated and would be often repeated and only for Block would never lose its novelty" (193). Such time passes as the repetition of an obscure ritual, its foreclosure reiterated; only *for Block* does it unfold as always novel. Perhaps this is the fiendish dimension of Kafkan time. Although it never goes anywhere, it also never *familiarly* repeats itself. In it one never "comes home." The erasure of anaclisis from the Kafkan canvas is so thorough, so minutely engrained into the textual rhythm, that one hardly notices it happening. But one registers its consequence: the unfailing detachment of the narrative in its temporal movement—no rises or falls, few expectations or disappointments. In their place one finds only the subject's blank-because-unfurnished coolness as the unprepared-for arrives, again and again.

Gregor awakes and ponders, reasonably, how he might get his giant-insect body out of bed and then to the office without being too late. The country doctor is awakened by an unknown patient and rushes into the night, on horses he did not know were in his stable, at the probable price of his maid's virginity, all this fleeting through his mind unprocessed, unauthenticated. K. enters foreign buildings, climbs to a fifth-floor entry, and is ushered in by an unknown woman as though he were expected. Speeches occur without context, unknown others listen and sometimes applaud; later K. sees they are wearing unfamiliar badges.[21] He returns, and the woman who let him in now starts to make love to him, but this is interrupted by a bandy-legged "student" who carries her off. His uncle visits him (looking like no one's uncle: all is unfamiliar in his appearance, speech, and gestures); they go to a lawyer's office where the female servant likewise seduces K. (or does he seduce her?) on the floor of the room just on the other side of the lawyer who is still talking to K.'s uncle. I have rehearsed only a small portion of the diachronic procedure of *The Trial*. Nothing that occurs is prepared for by what occurred earlier: none of this has happened before or will happen again. Time lacks anaclitic familiarity. Wherever this is going, it is not to the mother's breast.

In *The Castle* the same procedure is perhaps even more insistently operative. As David Ellison writes, "narrative closure is impossible in a novel whose framing devices are continuously exceeded by the negative unravelling energy of the episodes they contain" (156). Night and day seem to blur into each other in this later novel. The Castle itself—seemingly near in the novel's opening sentence ("It was late in the evening when K. arrived" [3])—is of course unreachable. In its place are numerous, dreamlike, substitute spaces—inns, carriages, barrooms, classrooms (with K. and Frieda undressed as the students arrive: what could be more oneiric?), bedrooms, rooms off corridors. The unfinished book ends with K. involved in an intense, unclear argument with the landlady, about clothes . . . In the course of time Frieda becomes Olga, Olga becomes Pepi: interchangeable not characterologically but structurally—unknowable, talking figures K. meets, listens to, may make love to. None of them recalls Proust's Albertine as an "*être de fuite*" in the field of Marcel's desire, inasmuch as K.'s own relation to each is momentary only, never more deeply etched. They are what he meets when he moves, and they can neither arrest his movement nor aid in its resolution. Authority in Kafka seems to be insistently male. Eroticized women may sleep with or arouse men in power (Leni, Frieda, Amalia), but they themselves lack power, lack even an understanding of power. Men in power, by contrast, tend to lack erotic charge: overworked figures of writing, bureaucratic servants of the written word (the *files*)— when would they have time for sexual distraction?[22]

Perhaps the ultimate instance of unpreparedness occurs late in the novel, when—despairing of reaching Klamm—K. doggedly seeks an interview with Erlanger instead, and finds: an unknown Castle bureaucrat named Bürgel. This latter cannot be shut up, even claims to be prepared to offer K. the keys of the kingdom: "one must show . . . how the applicant [K.] . . . can, however, now, if he wants to, Land-Surveyor, dominate everything and to that end has to do nothing but . . . put forward his plea, for which fulfillment is already waiting" (349–50). Finally arrived, it seems, but no, K. apologizes for being—just at this moment—helplessly overcome by the need to sleep. To which Bürgel replies: "No, you don't need to apologize for being sleepy, why should you? One's physical energies last only to a certain limit. Who can help the fact that precisely this limit is significant in other ways too? No, nobody can help it. That is how the world itself corrects the deviations in its course and maintains the balance" (351). Sleep: the mark of human contingency, the rebuke of human will, the daily need no one can command (and whose uncommandableness Kafka suffered from his entire life). Beings who are merely human, who require daily something as humiliating to their larger pretenses as body-horizontal sleep, will, at best, make it to the Castle office where a Bürgel awaits them, and will be put to sleep by his all-promising chatter.

Kindred, perhaps, is the apparently all-resolving parable of "Before the Law" in the penultimate chapter of *The Trial*. Scripture, for once in Kafka, is not only available but remembered and pronounceable; K. quietly listens.[23] What would serve in any realist text as a resolution dispelling prior difficulties functions here, however, as a resolution announcing further difficulties. As K. and the priest inconclusively argue for pages over the meaning of the parable, its promise of enlightenment retreats. Eventually, "[h]e was too tired to survey all the conclusions arising from the story, and the trains of thought into which it was leading him were unfamiliar. . . . The simple story had lost its clear outline" (220–21). The principle of deferral, as we have seen extensively in both Freud and Proust, invokes, precisely, the emergence of a "clear outline" from materials earlier unmapped (or erroneously mapped). Yet deferred knowledge—the very motor of meaning-making in time—remains scrupulously absent from the typical

Kafka text. The present seethes, here as in Kierkegaard, with its unbound capacity for menace. As opposed to all realist procedures, one has no clue as to what comes next.

What, for example, would any realist novel make of Kafka's way of narrating Fraülein Bürstner? Let us consider first the superficial offenses to realism wrought into the details of K.'s initial meeting with her. He enters her apartment late at night; he watches fascinated as she—apparently innocent of sexual motives—"slowly caressed her hip" (26); he engages in a bizarre psychodrama of rearranging her furniture and replaying the scene with the inspector, calling out his own name in a "long drawn-out shout" (27); he urges her to "have it announced that I assaulted you" (28); he seizes her, kissing her first on the lips and "then all over the face, like some thirsty animal lapping greedily at a spring of long-sought fresh water" (29), the kiss finishing "on the neck, right on the throat" (29). We learn, as he leaves her, that he does not know her first name. All of this is "wrong" for realism—it is not thus that any protagonist meets his possible love interest—and indeed the scene cannot be imagined in any novel by Austen or Dickens, Balzac or Stendhal, Tolstoy or Dostoevsky. In their work, *encountering others in space and time* does not occur thus. Yet these remain Kafka's superficial offenses to realism. The deeper offense is that K.'s initial meeting with Bürstner is his only meeting with her. None of the realist writers mentioned above commits this atrocity: to introduce the probable love interest on page 25 and then not to have her reappear.[24] Such lacunae make the grounding logic of realist temporality leap into view: life takes on significance as it moves forward in time. It does so through the telling lens supplied by deepened relations with others. Others shed indispensable light on the protagonist; love stories illuminate the lovers. (Even Marcel is illuminated by his failed relations with Gilberte and Albertine.) Bürstner *has* to come back, so that—through her penetration to his depths—K. can discover who he is, we can discover who he is. Freud characterized this essential process of self-discovery through time as "working through" (a strenuous activity that requires identifying the influential role of others in the subject's obscured selfhood). Rather than return Bürstner to K.'s narrative for such purposes, Kafka replaces her. The washerwoman, Montag, Leni—each follows Bürstner, impenetrable, all of them contingent rather than essential for letting us learn the one thing needful: who K. is.

Not to know K. is not to know Kafka, as any realist protocols understand knowing. In refusing the clarification that comes with deferred resolution, in keeping the reader locked in the affective flatness of mere sequential happening (however fatal), Kafka undoes the promise of beginnings themselves. Beginnings take on their inaugural character only when they receive the retrospective emotional luster of an appropriate ending—an ending other than "'Like a dog!' he said; it was as if the shame of it must outlive him" (229). In both *The Trial* and *The Castle* K. emerges not as the beginning letter of a name we shall eventually complete, recognizing it to be either Kafka or not-Kafka. His name remains incomplete, even as so much of Kafka's work remains—accidentally? unavoidably?—incomplete. Yet K. is essentially what we have of Kafka. If we would know more than this, we must come to know *otherwise,* we must proceed on a path of unknowing.

"TEMPORARY": THE PATHOS OF FAULKNERIAN TIME

"IT'S NOT EVEN TIME UNTIL IT WAS"

Proust's unbound and unorientational moment, Kafka's moment of affectless surprise: next to these, Faulkner's moment registers as a locus of vertigo, anguish, and belatedness.[25] It is saturated in trauma and longing. One discovers oneself in the wrong time (a claim as pertinent for Faulkner as for his most salient protagonists); the time one would know is past before one has properly recognized it *as* time. Late in *The Town* (1957) in a passage that feels suggestively autobiographical, the narrator broods over the temporality of his Yoknapatawpha County, musing: "Because the tragedy of life is, it must be premature, inconclusive and inconcludable, in order to be life; it must be before itself, in advance of itself, to have been at all."[26] Life participates, at its core, in temporal dissonance; the time of being cannot coincide with the time of knowing.

I draw on this 1957 passage about *presence* as beyond accommodation (no less so than in Kierkegaard or Kafka) in order to analyze Faulkner's remarkable apprenticeship: his learning anew, between 1928 and 1930, how to "write time." Inasmuch as this period (embracing three experimental novels) lasts a scant three years, the quote from *The Town* is, suggestively, not "in advance of itself" but belated. For Faulkner's later fiction tends to become, at least with respect to its models for narrating time, more traditional—humanistic—when juxtaposed with the earlier modernist masterpieces. This reversion in formal procedures, as we shall see, virtually sabotages his attempt to reprise the savage *Sanctuary* (1931) within the retrospective mode of *Requiem for a Nun* (1951). The early novels that memorably deliver his portraits of time-distressed subjectivity (Benjy, Quentin,

Temple, Vardaman, to name four) also powerfully undermine the formal premises of realism, in order to convey time's refractoriness, its resistance to human desire. The pain Faulkner is after—the pain of being time-deranged—is inexpressible within realist protocols. The Faulknerian subject of these fictions suffers by being caught up in another scene; he is simultaneously somewhere else in space and time. "It must be before itself, in advance of itself, to have been at all"—or, as Mr. Compson puts it, "It's not even time until it was."

Time's hostility to human projects is a recurrent theme of modernist literature in general, but it is one thing to thematize it and another to register time's assault at the level of narrative form itself. Faulkner's beginning novels still "do" time's damage thematically rather than formally. Donald Mahan and Bayard Sartoris are unquestionably time-wounded figures—traumatized—but Faulkner narrates them within a rhetoric not itself time-dislocated. Thus they emerge mainly as figures of inscrutability. Innovative forms appear only when Faulkner's rhetoric of subjectivity enters, so to speak, the force field of fractured time, resulting in dislocations that are simultaneously psychic and narrative.

That force field has no purchase on realist models of representation. The subject of realism, as we have recurrently argued, is rendered as sufficiently self-gathered in the present to pursue the projects that make up realist plot. That is realism's Enlightenment birthright: the bestowal of project upon every (white male) subject. From the beginning Faulkner refuses this culturally furnished subject—look again at Donald Mahan—but Faulkner does not yet know how, as it were, to make an unfurnished subject speak. Is it any surprise that the conceptual model of mind that will allow Faulkner to "open up" damaged subjects is the one coming into power at the same time as Faulkner himself: psychoanalysis? Faulkner joins Freud in realizing that, to articulate a Donald Mahan, one will have to read him backward in time, see him splayed *across* time rather than gathered *in* time. Faulkner sees, no less than Freud did, that the projective Cartesian subject screens a more troubled subject—caught up in unfulfilled desire and unnegotiated wound, and therefore in great part absent from himself at any given present moment: in a word, a traumatized subject. Indeed, psychoanalysis understands inarticulate desire and unresolved damage to underwrite the subject's opacity in the present, exactly as Enlightenment realism understands self-awareness and future projects to underwrite the subject's legibility in the present.[27] For Faulkner as for Freud, psychic life is fraught with turmoil because it remains traumatically attached to events "on another scene."

Put more generally, modernist emphasis on unnegotiated desire and damage transforms the subject's experience of time from a productive present to a dysfunctional one. By contrast, the irresistible fantasy secured by realist representation comes into focus as the illusion of subjectivity amply sufficient to itself, bathed in the aura of discrete and (so to speak) extensible presence. It is not accidental that realism dies hard, indeed, seems immortal. To the extent that we are condemned to experience our identity in passing time as uncohered—as uncentered, unknowing—we are not likely to relinquish realism's confirming narrative of (achievable) center and consequent self-knowledge. The power of Faulkner's breakthrough novels resides in his learning how to word the subject's anguished experience of presence as unnegotiated wound and desire—a here-and-now under siege by a spectral there-and-then. I test this claim by attending to how Faulkner narrates the subject in space/time as he moves from *Flags in the Dust* to *The Sound and the Fury, Sanctuary,* and *As I Lay Dying.*

We begin with the relatively traditional rhetoric of *Flags.* Here is young Bayard Sartoris, wounded and asleep, watched over by Narcissa. His agon erupts swiftly:

> He made an indescribable sound, and she turned her head quickly and saw his body straining terrifically in its cast, and his clenched hands and the snarl of his teeth beneath his lifted lip, and as she sat blanched and incapable of further movement he made the sound again. His breath hissed between his teeth and he screamed, a wordless sound that sank into a steady violence of profanity; and when she rose at last and stood over him with her hands against her mouth, his body relaxed and from beneath his sweating brow he watched her with wide intent eyes in which terror lurked, and mad, cold fury, and questioning despair.[28]

Narrated in the syntax and vocabulary of realist objectivity, this scene scrupulously locates the reader within a coherent spatial/temporal frame, yet stumbles on the threadbareness of predictable formulae. Bayard's sound is "indescribable," for Faulkner can "describe" it only from a perspective securely anchored in a later time frame—that of a detached realist narrator looking back at someone else's illness. Faulkner uses Narcissa to provide physical cues for how to read Bayard's otherwise inexpressible inner torment: his terrific straining, her "blanched" paralysis echoing his "clenched" paralysis, his hissing breath and wordless scream. As after an orgasm, his body relaxes after this climactic release, yet Faulkner can articulate what is going on *inside* Bayard only through familiar nouns like "terror," "fury," and "despair." This could be Joseph Conrad relying on the same slightly fustian vocabulary to deliver Jim's torment. Both writers understand that their target (the traumatized psyche) is "unspeakable," but neither knows (Conrad never, Faulkner not yet) that it is "unspeakable" only within realism's norms for representing the subject as a cohered being in present time and space.

Faulkner departs from such norms in the narrative disjunctions of his next three novels, but *Flags in the Dust*—however expansive a quarry of *thematic* materials it provides for the writer Faulkner will become—remains formally conventional. It can articulate Bayard's trauma only indirectly, through scenes of transgressive speed, rather than directly, through a new vocabulary and syntax that might yield the subjective quick and temporal strangeness of such pain. *Flags* is reduced to gesturing toward Bayard's distress (the passage cited is a familiar cameo), yet even so we gather something of what is at stake. Bayard is caught up in trauma—the anguishing afterlife of events that occurred earlier, elsewhere. He is on that other stage, overtaken, penetrated. Something unspeakable that happened in the war holds him prisoner still. The closest Faulkner comes to unlocking his wounded interiority is to describe it as ruptured "with ghosts of a thing high-pitched as a hysteria" (134). Faulkner never returns to this "thing high-pitched" as it first occurred; he focuses on its traumatic aftereffects, later. Bayard attracts Faulkner to the extent that he is absent here and now, beyond therapeutic recovery. Intensity of portrait and dysfunction of character go hand in hand, but Faulkner has not yet figured out how to craft the prose that—in yoking then with now, there with here—will dance their fusion. In Quentin Compson he figures it out.

> *I have committed incest I said Father it was I it was not Dalton Ames* And when he put Dalton Ames. Dalton Ames. Dalton Ames. When he put the pistol in my hand I didn't. That's why I didn't. He would be there and she would and I would. Dalton Ames. Dalton Ames. Dalton Ames. If we could have just done something so dreadful and Father said That's sad too people cannot do anything that dreadful they cannot do anything very dreadful at all they cannot even remember tomorrow what seemed dreadful today and I said, You can shirk all things and he said, Ah can you. And I will look down and see my murmuring bones and the deep water like wind, like a roof of wind, and after a long time they cannot distinguish even bones upon the lonely and inviolate sand. Until on the day when He says Rise only the flat-iron would come floating up. It's not when you realise that nothing can help you—religion, pride, anything—it's when you realise that you dont

need any aid. Dalton Ames. Dalton Ames. Dalton Ames. If I could have
been his mother lying with open body lifted laughing, holding his father
with my hand refraining, seeing, watching him die before he lived. *One
minute she was standing in the door*[29]

To find his way into Quentin thus, Faulkner has had to rupture the syntax
of realism's knowing subject in space/time. Realist narrative—secured by
means of a later (always unspecified) point of reference from which a forward-moving, past-tense discourse can be launched—tirelessly sutures its
materials into the linear decorum of subject, verb, and predicate. Such a
syntax, still operative in the *Flags* passage, uses its own temporal distance to
represent the subject as a discrete doer performing his discrete deed: a little
parable of agency in familiar space/time. All of which is absent here:
Quentin's phrases either lack verbs or mix them up indiscriminately—
present perfect, past, conditional, conditional perfect, present, future. The
nineteenth-century tools for realist representation that Faulkner inherited
could register the subject only as a something seen from a certain distance
and therefore stable, self-contained, gathered into presence, in black and
white. By contrast, he knew that it was a something moved and moving,
penetrated by absence, hurtling through space and time—a locus of desire
and damage—and in color.

To articulate that color, Faulkner had to rearrange the positioning of the
subject in space, time, and the field of the other.[30] Perhaps most of all, he
had to get himself out of the picture (had to remove his temporally removed
narrator). He had to articulate—yet as though it were happening without
his narrator telling it—the subject careening between discontinuous spaces
and times, immersed in the force field of absent others. The coherence of
space in this passage disappears (the reader is swallowed up in Quentin's
place-shifting interiority). Space in Quentin's chapter is, so to speak, represented seismically rather than rationally, moving from the fight with Dalton
Ames to the one with Gerald Bland in a single line. The representation of
time is even more aggressively deranged. The Dalton Ames moment, the
Caddy at the door moment, and the moment with his father are here
pressed together while remaining apart—not fused but confused. Time's
cleanly forward motion (perhaps the deepest assumption our sanity requires
and that realism blessedly supplies) is eclipsed. Finally, the presence of
absent others inside the self is clamorous beyond pacifying. Quentin's mind
is a defective transformer through which incompatible human voices pass
like so many electric charges. He is a figure composed of screaming texts,
some spoken, some read, some fantasized, none assimilated, none forgotten.

In Quentin Compson Faulkner produces perhaps his most memorable instance of the human subject as "premature, inconclusive and inconcludable": a figure caught in multiple times and splayed out into multiple spaces, penetrated by multiple others.

I turn to Temple Drake in *Sanctuary*.

> "Then I said That wont do. I ought to be a man. So I was an old man, with a long white beard, and then the little black man got littler and littler and I was saying Now. You see now. I'm a man now. Then I thought about being a man, and as soon as I thought it, it happened. It made a kind of plopping sound, like blowing a little rubber tube wrong-side outward. It felt cold, like the inside of your mouth when you hold it open. I could feel it, and I lay right still to keep from laughing about how surprised he was going to be. I could feel the jerking going inside my knickers ahead of his hand and me lying there trying not to laugh about how surprised and mad he was going to be in a minute."[31]

Perhaps because *Sanctuary* was first conceived with a larger public in mind, Faulkner writes it in more or less classic realist form. Most of its scenes respect realist protocols for "doing" the subject in space/time as a coherent and objective sequencing. All the sentences in the passage cited would diagram properly. Yet the passage remains inconceivable within the rhetorical premises of *Flags in the Dust*. Rather than clothing Temple's agon in "indescribable" terror, "cold fury," and "questioning despair," Faulkner dispenses with narratorial mediation and words Temple's wound as though from within. Removing that narrator safely distanced in space and time, Faulkner gets us to encounter Temple's wound itself; he has learned how to make *it* speak. The narrative that Temple's wound speaks both articulates and conceals the assault on her. We see everything materially relevant—the cold corncob, the invaded body, the jerking flesh—but we see this as she has phantasmatically reconfigured it in order to endure it, in the crazy, cross-gendered scenario her defenses have summoned into being for psychic survival. The passage is phenomenological rather than Newtonian. She has fantasized herself onto another scene. Faulkner's prose registers less what is done to Temple than what she does with what is done to her— a doing on her part that is verbal alone, because no escape from Popeye is possible. Popeye coopts material reality as present torture; she absents herself by fleeing into fantasy. The poetry of this passage is the poetry of Temple's outraged (Freud would say "breached") system of psychic defenses. Narrating the assault as a breaching of her defenses, Faulkner puts us in touch with Temple's naked core. We seem to hear her psyche speak. What it speaks is the here/not-here, now/not-now of her unbearable wound and impossible desire.

I turn to Vardaman in *As I Lay Dying*.

> And so if Cash nails the box up, she is not a rabbit. And so if she is not a rabbit I couldn't breathe in the crib and Cash is going to nail it up. And so if she lets him it is not her. I know. I was there. I saw when it did not be her. I saw. They think it is and Cash is going to nail it up.
>
> It was not her because it was laying right yonder in the dirt. And now it's all chopped up. I chopped it up. It's laying in the kitchen in the bleeding pan, waiting to be cooked and et. Then it wasn't and she was, and now it is and she wasn't. And tomorrow it will be cooked and et and she will be him and pa and Cash and Dewey Dell and there wont be anything in the box and so she can breathe. It was laying right yonder on the ground. I can get Vernon. He was there and he seen it, and with both of us it will be and then it will not be.[32]

It is commonplace to derive *As I Day Dying* from *The Sound and the Fury,* but if Vardaman emerges from Benjy, he shares no less with Temple Drake. Her self-transformation into an old man in order to avoid annihilation as merely herself echoes Vardaman's transforming of Addie into something else—anything else—in order to avert her annihilation as merely herself. In both characters Faulkner dramatizes the plasticity of the psyche under duress—a plasticity that can be articulated only when fantasy is allowed to command the scene of representation and release it from realism's fidelity to what is physically occurring in objective space, linear time. Fantasy soars wherever it wants—into a rabbit, into a fish—yet the wildness of its flight is grounded in the immobility of its referent: Addie Bundren is being put into a coffin and then into the earth. Vardaman embodies desire as impossibility. Immersed in the field of the other, his own being is secured by his mother's: to lose her is to lose himself. The desperate transferences he plunges through in order to resecure her, to reroute her by springing her from that to-be-nailed and suffocating coffin, conclude in a line that no reader ever forgets: "My mother is a fish" (54). Is there any purer expression of impossible desire in literature (of human being *in flight* and *as flight*) than those five words of Vardaman?

"Death," Mr. Compson tells Quentin, is "only a state in which the others are left" (*Sound,* 50). Vardaman is frantic at being "left," and Faulkner shows us the present moment not as realism construes it—a life-supportive frame, individual-centered—but rather as modernism construes it: a death-dealing, individual-dissolving frame ("Excrement Father said like sweating" [*Sound,* 49]), a medium inside and outside us that is always passing, being evacuated as we move through it. Vardaman cannot tolerate the wounds it brings in its wake.[33] As with Temple, Faulkner emphasizes less the thing itself that "abrupts" upon the subject than the strange psychic poetry with which it is/is not borne—the fantastic not-here, not-now we mentally construe when we cannot bear to be here and now. We the living are the ones who experience death; and Faulkner's prose attends, no less than Proust's, to what interior resources protect us from having to know this—our defenses, with their poignant swerves of misrecognition. By the time he has written *As I Lay Dying,* Faulkner knows how to word this ordeal in which the subject's illusion of sufficiency in present time shatters. Here is Addie Bundren:

> And when I knew that I had Cash, I knew that living was terrible and that this was the answer to it. That was when I learned that words are no good; that words don't ever fit even what they are trying to say at. When he was born I knew that motherhood was invented by someone who had to have a word for it because the ones that had the children didn't care whether there was a word for it or not. I knew that fear was invented by someone that had never had the fear; pride, who never had the pride. I knew that it had been, not that they had dirty noses, but that we had had to use one another by words like spiders dangling by their mouths from a beam, swinging and twisting and never touching, and that only through the blows of the switch could my blood and their blood flow as one stream. (115–16)

The writer of this passage knows that realism's premise of a gathered subject sustained in present space and time is a convention that collapses under pressure. He knows that conventional language is the medium we use to swaddle and domesticate the outrage inflicted on us by our being in time, the resource we draw on to maintain the illusion of self-presence and guard against the incessancy of death. Thus he recognizes that conventional language is the enemy he must selectively befriend in order to outwit. Insofar as the "abruption" of the real is wordlessly unpreparable, and its impact traumatic—fracturing the subject into a then that still clamors, a now turned hollow, an elsewhere in irresoluble tension with one's being here—then the only words that matter will be those that, descending to the earth, track this devastation. He realizes, as well, that we are born virgin in more ways than sexual, and that the spatial/temporal world's assault upon our virginal self-sameness enters as an aggression of the body, *"the citadel of the central I-am's private own,"* as Rosa Coldfield puts it.[34] Desire and damage register perhaps most deeply in Faulkner's fiction as the psyche's song of resistance to the penetration of its embodied borders.

Violation is of course Faulkner's signature theme as early as *Soldiers' Pay.* But it is only in the three novels that follow *Flags in the Dust* that he invents his modernist rhetoric for registering time-as-assault. In these novels he gets past the words that swing and twist and never touch, finding his way into the words that wound, trading assault for assault. Indeed, he generates an arsenal of modernist rhetorical strategies—selective use of italics, ungrammatical fragments of pain, unedited substitution fantasies, vertiginous condensations of space and time. These strategies work to express the penetration of self by other and to locate violation where it touches down, upon the outraged body/mind. Desire and damage coil together there, fueling the subject's psychic defenses for rerouting or just enduring the "premature, inconclusive and inconcludable" abruption that is life in time.

"UNAPPEASED AND PEREGRINE"

Faulkner's career differs most from those of Proust and Kafka, perhaps, in the restless proliferation of narrative experiments that mark its various stages. Proust's huge novel is syntactically and thematically consistent during a protracted period of time that outlasts his own life (the last volumes of the *Recherche* appearing posthumously). Kafka's published writings hardly amount to two hundred pages; it is difficult to speak of significant shifts in topic or form. For both writers, the years of publication do not exceed a single decade (in effect, the same years—1912–22—although Proust's lesser writings begin to appear in the 1890s). Faulkner, by contrast, enjoys (or suffers) a thirty-five-year history of fiction writing—a career that has been parsed by way of a number of developmental paradigms. Inasmuch as my focus is on Faulkner's modernist strategies for representing time, I turn now to a brief meditation on what happens when his work exits from the modernist protocols for representing the subject in space/time. My aim is diagnostic; I wish to show in what ways a thematic *return* (to *Sanctuary*'s protagonist, Temple Drake) is subverted by a formal *departure* (from *Sanctuary*'s mode of representing her).

My argument risks sounding perverse. I propose that *Requiem for a Nun* (1951) is to *Sanctuary* (1931) not as solution to problem—moralized recovery after nihilistic fall—but rather as problem to solution. For *Sanctuary* produces, despite its apparent shattering of all cultural truisms, a kind of truth nevertheless, to which *Requiem*'s retrospective commitment aspires, but which the later text cannot produce: the truth of Temple's somatic, time-and-space-disabled being. This truth appears in/as a violation that proceeds through her body, *"the citadel of the central I-am's private own"* (*Absalom,* 115). It matters not what lies or deceptions *Sanctuary*'s Temple may think or speak; her assaulted body does not lie. Indeed Faulkner's text "confesses" that body with an interrogating rigor that a medieval inquisitor might well envy.[35] Let us consider this pair of examples from *Sanctuary:*

> She felt herself flying through the air, carrying a numbing shock upon her shoulder and a picture of two men peering from the fringe of cane at the roadside. She scrambled to her feet, her head reverted, and saw them step into the road. . . . Still running her bones turned to water and she fell flat on her face, still running. (205)
>
> She could hear silence in a thick rustling as he moved toward her through it, thrusting it aside, and she began to say Something is going to happen to me. She was saying it to the old man with the yellow clots for eyes. "Something is happening to me!" she screamed at him, sitting in his chair in the sunlight. . . . "I told you it was!" she screamed, voiding the words like hot silent bubbles into the bright silence about them until he turned his head and the two phlegm-clots above her where she lay tossing on the rough, sunny boards. "I told you! I told you all the time!" (250)

Although two people are in that car, Faulkner's text accesses (and makes the reader access) only the female body flying through the air. The prose represents her as gravitationally unhinged (Newton's laws apparently suspended), her mind so shocked as to lose its housing within her own body. Relentlessly, she is being temporally and spatially discoordinated: unable to control her movement, unable to guess what comes next. In the second passage, she appears unable to think as well. The rape "abrupts" into Faulkner's prose as a "something" dreaded "all along," whose impact on her she can acknowledge only by sidestepping it, hurling it at Pap. Faulkner inserts Temple into a spatial/temporal frame so unrecognizable—so far from all that she has known, anaclitically, as home or college—that her fragile integrity disintegrates. The text dilates on the pieces in disarray, the body out of mental/moral harness, the speech in confusion or halted altogether: this is the truth of *Sanctuary*'s Temple Drake.

Throughout the novel, she is undergoing rape. Jerked, gripped, lifted, entered, she ceases to be an intentional ego moving in purposive time, unified under the name of Temple Drake. Rather than an organ for speaking, her mouth reduces to human matter, opening and closing soundlessly, leaving a half-masticated piece of sandwich unswallowed on her tongue. Like Benjy wailing incoherently, like Rider unable to swallow the food or drink he stuffs into his mouth, Temple seems almost literally to lose her body and her mind. Most characters in this novel fail any moral test we might propose for them, but only Temple is not only found ethically defective (a sustainable shortcoming after all) but somatically invaded, infantilized. Unable to move from Popeye, Temple moves anyway—Faulkner records as no other writer can the second-by-second moves one makes when one cannot move—but it avails her nothing. In these terrifying moments, no guiding behavioral signals are being received by the mind; she is at the other extreme of canniness. Temple appears here as purely what can happen to her body—a poor bare forked animal, the thing itself. What does it mean for us to be asked to take this as a necessary truth?

I suggest that Faulkner seeks to show us, in the space-and-time-ravaged Temple, that the embodied human being, sufficiently aggressed, gives the lie to every normative model of cultural furnishing, especially those circulating around the male dream of female virginity. "Seem like that the most hardest blood of all to get—" (280), Miss Reba's maid says, trying to scrub away the telltale sign of Temple's first intercourse. The hardest blood to get, with the deepest truth to reveal: as though this shocking attack upon a culture's array of ideological furnishings would lay bare the thing itself. The memorable moments of *Sanctuary* do just this corrosive work, producing epiphanies of unaccommodation.[36] If, however, all language is culture-funded—a premise that all three modernist writers in this study in different ways reject—then even epiphanies that seem to touch down on bedrock are in fact mediated. If there is no such thing as pure encounter, one might well ask: what ideological stances remain intact in *Sanctuary*, protected from exposure by the very collapse of other ideological stances? I am not sure how to answer that question, although I believe it is the right one to ask. At the least, a text imaging its concealed truth as "the most hardest blood of all to get" is embedded in an undeclared gender politics. The blood to be let is that of a woman; the questing figures who would discover the secret lodged in her spilled blood are male. Her body houses the secret; only they can resolve it. (Faulkner does not deliberately couch the quest in *Sanctuary* in these terms, though a later take on his novel certainly might.) His revelatory Temple emerges as a being undone in a moment (a sequence of discontinuous moments) marked by shock. The novel is wholly undidactic.

Twenty years later the writer returns to the same materials, and in the very figure of *return* we see something of Freud's and Proust's deeper investment in recovery. One returns to know more. An "I" was there earlier, that "I" suffered but did not see; now, years later, the "I" can return and make sense of what it earlier suffered. Freudian psychoanalysis draws on this premise as the very motor of its program. Proust's work likewise privileges this project of return, seeking—by way of "working through"—to recover what was missed the first time. Indeed, *Requiem* engages in a treble program of return: an outer narrative of return to the founding of Jefferson in the Mississippi hinterland, an inner narrative of return to the time of Temple's disastrous events (eight years earlier), and a metanarrative of return, on Faulkner's part, to a novel completed (yet somehow incomplete) some twenty years earlier. To succeed, however, all these returns rely upon a realist—rather than a modernist—sense of time as a transparent medium (Newton thought of it as an invisible ether), open to successful remounting. All of them invest in the transfiguring power of recall as recovery. This model of the subject in time is perhaps the dearest we know; it motivates the oldest aesthetics of the West—that of Aristotle's *Poetics*—in which the concealed truths of the past painfully come to light, producing recognition and catharsis. *Requiem for a Nun* is in search of such catharsis. Gavin, Gowan, and the Governor surround Temple, posing question after question as so many dialogic leads for her to follow in her quest for the hidden truth of her past.

The outer narrative we shall not discuss here, except to say that it surrounds Temple's story as a sort of mythic becoming (punctuated by foundational moments we are invited to take as unforgettable) of the community of Jefferson. With respect to the inner narrative, time seems likewise potentially benign. Eight years have passed since that fatal event at Frenchman's Bend, eight years in which Temple might catch up to herself and decipher the script of her own becoming. This would be classic catharsis, in which the self-blinding wound of an earlier time submits to therapeutic recognition.

Such a model of time—a continuum of interwoven years accessible to the reflective mind—differs, however, from *Sanctuary*'s model of time: the explosion of unbearable moments. "Something is happening to me," *Sanctuary*'s Temple registers in shock; she does not know what that "something" is, cannot see a second ahead. Time in *Sanctuary* is nightmarishly opaque, "abrupting" as an assault of moments. The shapeless future is already upon Temple, beyond predication yet presaged since her earliest cultural training: "I told you! I told you all the time!" *Requiem,* by contrast, uses its comprehensive time frame to return, deliberately, to the past, so as to review it and recognize that "The past is never dead. It's not even past."[37] Not dead, this past, on being revisited, is expected—as in Proust— to yield a new and deeper meaning. The overseeing spirit here, the guide for Faulkner's quest for later and darker epiphanies, is T.S. Eliot of *Four Quartets:* "We had the experience but missed the meaning / And approach to the meaning restores the experience / In a different form, beyond any meaning / We can assign to happiness." This retrospective project fuels Faulkner's second attempt to confess Temple Drake.

The project misfires, for a couple of reasons. One is that second Temple is body-(re)constituted in ways that make her incompatible with first Temple. *Requiem's* Temple is somatically whole, not just because an actress in a sutured body is to play her(this part of the novel is in theatrical form), but also because she addresses herself as a gathered, integral being who was given her choices and (within an implicitly realist model of iden- tity) failed them:

> So I saw the murder, or anyway the shadow of it, and the man took me to Memphis, and I know that too, I had two legs and I could see, and I could have simply screamed up the main street of any of the little towns we passed, just as I could have walked away from the car after Gow—we ran it into the tree . . . (567)
>
> Because I still had the two arms and legs and eyes [Temple is revisiting her stay at Reba's whorehouse]; I could have climbed down the rainspout at any time, the only difference being that I didn't. (569)

Temple's truth in *Sanctuary* was inscribed on an assaulted body that ceased spectacularly to obey her and her culture's sanctions. *Requiem's* Temple, coming later, enjoys a different relation to her body. Moreover, second Temple accesses first Temple's body not as it was experienced in earlier moments of crisis, but from a distant temporal perspective. But this order- producing retrospect changes the experience itself, cohering and imbuing it with moral norms and their betrayal. Second Temple has eyes to see with, legs to run with, a mouth to use for effective resistance. First Tem- ple's dispossessed body, silently reassembled in the intervening time, per- mits second Temple to ask repeatedly: what kept me from doing the right thing? This is revision, not return and recovery.[38] It is what Proust calls *forgetting,* the fictitious rewriting of the past that constitutes (conscious) remembering. And something appears now that never surfaced the first time around: moral recrimination. *Requiem* is afloat in it.

The second reason the project misfires is that second Temple is mind-transformed as well.[39] She has become an avid reader and writer in the intervening years, can quote Hemingway and Shakespeare, and has more than passing acquaintance with Faulkner's other works. She is also an achieved letter writer, resembling thus the figure who was in *Sanctuary* her ostensible opposite, Narcissa Benbow. She is now thoroughly furnished, enabled by her culture's training. Such unthinkingly assumed enabling disables any attempt to recognize—and thus to confess—her earlier avatar. The original devastation, despite an orgy of revisiting, eludes recognition, remains traumatic. No catharsis occurs; Temple is reduced at the end to a state of despair. "Tomorrow and tomorrow and tomorrow—" she murmurs, to which Gavin, without missing a beat, supplies the continuation: "—he will wreck the car again against the wrong tree, in the wrong place, and you will have to forgive him again, for the next eight years until he can wreck the car again in the wrong place, against the wrong tree—" (611). Depressed, she wonders repeatedly: "But now it can go on, tomorrow and tomorrow and tomorrow, forever and forever and forever—" (614).[40]

We know how much those lines from *Macbeth* meant to Faulkner, for they tersely convey the modernist sense of time out of control, unfructifying, that suffuses *The Sound and the Fury.* Here, rather than illuminate the darkness of temporal disorder, they may serve a bleaker purpose yet. For *Requiem* formally yearns (as the early novels do not) for the repose that comes with putting past wounds to rest; it would resolve its traumas in time. Its title and retrospective moves tell us this; it is a song in search of repose. But in this *Requiem* no repose is to be found.

Might the stalemate that emerges shed a disturbing light on more than Temple? Is it too much to suggest that, behind the frustrated Temple, we glimpse her baffled author—both of them trapped in a model of time that promised to bring insight by way of return to the past? "Unappeased and peregrine" (to quote Eliot's *Four Quartets* again), the later Faulkner revisits—like his protagonist—his earlier modernist crises, retells his earlier stories through the mouths of others, sets up structures of retrospection that might permit cathartic recognition. None comes. It seems, rather, that the early masterpieces that mocked time—dismantling realist protocols of cause followed by effect, idea by reality, wound by healing—have yielded place to later works that, though seeking everything from time, time itself mocks. With no catharsis in sight, no confession that might bring repose, no relation to earlier performances that might probe them at their hidden and generative core, *Requiem* (like *A Fable* three years later) displays all unintentionally the pathos of a subject stranded in the present moment and *talking* (louder and longer and with increasing frustration), in search of a truth that his youth repudiated and that his age is dying for.[41]

ABOUT TIME

Early in this chapter I asked: How and why does the Proustian text deform traditional models of time? I have sought, with respect to the practice of all three novelists, to show how. The question of why has been broached as well, and that question drives much of the next chapter. But it is about time to take it up now as well. The central issue is *unknowing*, an unknowing often crafted so as to transpire on two stages simultaneously—that of the protagonists experiencing misrecognition or shock, and that of the reader encountering these texts. It has long been a truism (but not often probed) that one has trouble reading modernist literature. More precisely, one has trouble reading it the first time around. Further readings, later in time, uncover organizing patterns at first unrecognizable—which means, among other things, that the recalcitrant modernist text is itself, deliberately, *about time*. Better, it is *about time as trouble the first time around*. Which is, of course, how we actually experience time: as Rilke puts it in *The Notebooks of Malte Laurids Brigge,* "There are no classes in life for beginners, it is always the most difficult that is asked of one right away."[42]

All three writers access characters at moments when their self-unknowing is spectacularly on display. Legrandin (or Saint-Loup or Charlus or Bloch) appears on the Proustian canvas as lacking the interpretive key to his own moves—lacking this but not missing it. Thus a moment isolated and placed under slow-motion analysis—the typical move of the *Recherche*—reveals a fraudulent being, one immured in effective defenses, lost to his own motives in time. Perhaps more disturbingly, Marcel is no less incapable of reading his own immersion in time. His coming upon his grandmother unaware shows, startlingly, how his very love for her has fixed her in a role that is years out of date. But if she is out of date, so is he, for his love—however sincere—is also strategic. It is his way of stabilizing himself by relying on her knowing/endorsing him in advance. The entire compact shatters at an unwanted moment of discovery. Knowing—on a Newtonian model of error-free recognition—becomes unknowing. Despite the illusion of stability, he and his grandmother are both in free flight, in time's perpetual motion—the two of them almost inconceivably joined and dissevered, spiritually bonded and materially estranged.

None of this unfolds as realism, for it forfeits the Cartesian premise of *res cogitans,* an independent entity capable (through clear and distinct reasoning) of accurately mapping others in space and time. Proustian time is not a transparent medium within which one can take oneself for granted, as one engages in one's projects. Or, put better, one can do this, one does do this, and the labor of the Proustian text is to reveal its terminal inauthenticity. Terminal in the sense of permanent nonarrival: one cannot arrive in Proust (as Tom Jones, Clarissa Harlowe, Elizabeth Bennet, Julien Sorel, Emma Bovary, Rodion Raskolnikov, and Merton Densher all arrive at their inner and outer destinations). But one can, Proust proposes, go back—find out where one has been, even who one has been. In all this we find a sustained rebuke of bourgeois plotting, of instrumental, progressive, acquisitive careerism—indeed, an undermining of Enlightenment-inspired *projecting* (attempted, failed, revised) that constitutes the main business of European realism for over two hundred years. If human being is, more deeply, something other than *res cogitans*—if its situation is something other than the epistemological mandate of the realist plot—what might that something other be? Let us begin by saying that it involves a profoundly different sense of one's relation to self and others in space and time. Within a modernist model, a more extensive weave of reciprocities and interdependencies is required for human being to *be* at all. As I shall analyze in the next chapter, Marcel—the central figure in the *Recherche*—is represented less as a projective character than as a revelatory lens on that extensive weave.

What would Kafkan realism look like (if one could for a moment fantasize it)? I suspect it would center on the unfolding career of the Assistant Manager in *The Trial.* This figure—centered in his ceaseless ambition to rise to the top of his career ladder, unquestioning as to the ends that motivate his effort (focused wholly on the means of arrival)—has no trouble with space, time, or others. His compact is unshakable; in Freudian terms, there can be no breaching of his defenses. Spiritually empty, he effectively embodies his culture's materialist norms, and (if asked) he would say to K. what the chief clerk says to a suddenly recalcitrant Gregor-turned-giant-insect: "this is not the season of the year for a business boom, of course, we admit that, but a season of the year for doing no business at all, that does not exist, Mr. Samsa, must not exist" (*Metamorphosis,* 77–78). Time as money is the uninterrogated convention within which worldly projects are pursued, attained, failed, or revised. One fine day he will die, but the Assistant Manager will not experience his death until then. His world makes sense, it has a plot, that plot is realism.

As all readers of Kafka know, nothing in his texts happens this way. In the terms operative in my study, the anaclitic premise of familiarity is erased. In place of the Assistant Manager, who is culturally constructed so as to be immune to surprise (every moment of his pathway is lighted by habit), we find figures like Georg and Gregor and K. Although they themselves are unsurprising (how many of them long to become Assistant Managers!), their pathway suddenly becomes a thicket of surprises. Nothing is any longer what it was; even an innocent (previously inventoried) bank storeroom can now house a lurid scene of whipper and victims. It is as though an all-transforming report had been issued offstage, terminating the successful deployment of habit, career, project. Canniness no longer applies. The new dispensation is unspeakable, unwritable. As Benjamin says, Kafka's parables "do not modestly lie at the feet of the doctrine. . . . Though apparently reduced to submission, they unexpectedly raise a mighty paw against it" (*Illuminations,* 144). His parables represent not tradition, which is the communal ordering of behavior in time in its benign form, but rather "a sickness of tradition" (143). More, the subjects caught up in such sickness react not as Doctor Rieux does in Camus's *La peste*—in a mode of organized resistance against the malady descending upon them all—but rather as unknowingly coopted elements in a larger and unappeasable malaise. As Adorno puts it, Kafka's "mute battlecry against myth is: not to resist" (*Prisms,* 264). The subject is here envisaged not as Camus's resourceful (realist) warrior against evil but as an obscure participant in a more comprehensive disorder—one in which the very (Enlightenment) idea of the subject no longer operates. No one here knows why or wherefore. Why Kafka himself might so labor at thus annulling familiar orientations is the central question of the next chapter.

As for Faulkner, he seems to have taken seriously Nietzsche's remark (which he undoubtedly never read): "I'm afraid we are not rid of God because we still have faith in grammar."[43] Between *Flags in the Dust* and *As I Lay Dying* a writerly transformation takes place. Faulkner rids himself (as needed) of the god that is grammar, inventing an entire rhetoric for saying trauma—for wording psyches under assault and immersed in space/time in ways unpremeditated by Newtonian realism. The subject splits asunder, lives incoherently a scene occurring then and now. Faulknerian stream of consciousness savages the decorum of realism's gathered subject-verb-predicate; the reader is hurled unprepared into the melee that is the text. (I still remember reading *As I Lay Dying* for the first time, on a train in France in 1962, and turning resignedly from the last page to the first again. I had, it seemed, understood nothing.) Though

Faulkner's texts are soaked in Southern tradition—if you remove the vignettes of Southern history from Faulkner's work (at any point in his career), very little remains—this tradition appears in his great novels as irradiated, denatured, suffocating. Protestant belief is figured in Doc Hines and Mr. McEachern, virginity is enshrined in the punitive hypochondria of Mrs. Compson, familial cohesion is dramatized as the bizarre—indeed insane—doings of the Bundrens. And this is not even to discuss his culture's race relations. Faulkner saw, and invented formal ways of conveying, a dysfunctional Southern culture at the end of its belief system. Realism—whose protocols assume the continuity of cultural norms (norms open to tweaking as a protagonist moves orientationally in familiar space/time)—was useless for his purposes. Put otherwise, realism is congenitally *friendly* to its reader: it presupposes a shared, already (or at least almost) viable world. It is of limited help if, as a writer, you want to make (and to report on) a great deal of trouble.

I return then to time as trouble. The abiding appeal of realist fiction is that it represents the subject's trouble in time as manageable and awaiting resolution. Trouble is mounted in realism so as to be surmounted; it is a distracting turbulence presented in order to be pacified—like dark clouds in a weather mandated as sunny. I do not want to exaggerate realism's good humor; Tolstoy's *Anna Karenina* is unsurpassably tragic realism. But realism's insistence on *capacitating* its protagonists remains constitutive of the genre. Realism typically chooses (this is why Georg Lukács admired it) protagonists sufficiently resourceful to dramatize the deepest (but negotiable) problems agitating the ambient culture. Realism remains recognizable and—in its very procedures—reasonable. Finally, its Enlightenment conviction that individuality is the priceless condition of humanity, that individuals negotiate their own lives against a complex social backdrop that is neither intolerable nor inalterable, disposes realism toward moralized dramas of individual success and failure. These are stories with undying appeal, if only because they soothe—often in richly unobvious ways—the anxiety their readers otherwise obscurely suffer from: that life is not actually like that. Given Sartre's "live or tell," realism chooses "tell" and works to make it look like "live."

In a number of courageous ways modernism chooses "live," and its quite different work is cut out for it. For how can you write ("tell") "live" without turning "live" into "tell"? Ultimately you cannot, but the heroism of my three writers—a heroism regarded as naïve and rarely attempted by postmodern followers—resides in their innovative attempts to do so. Most notably for this study, they brought the trouble of time into their narrative forms. For the truth is, we are not knowing in time in the ways realism continuously proposes. Realism is constitutively unwilling to do justice, precisely, to such trouble. The larger part of our actual experience is uninsured by knowing. Our lives unfold in an unending present that becomes, willy-nilly, opaque whenever it escapes the grooves of habit or expectation. In reality we learn slowly in time, by dint of many repetitions. For many aspects of our lives, we cease, after a certain point, to learn at all. Who is wise in love? Who even becomes wise in love? The Duchesse de Guermantes, seeing poor Swann distraught over Odette, tells her husband how absurd she finds it that "a man of his intelligence should let himself suffer for a woman of that sort" (1:373). To which the narrator adds: she spoke this "with the wisdom invariably shown by people who, not being in love themselves, feel that a clever man should only be unhappy about a person who is worth his while; which is rather like being astonished that anyone should condescend to die of cholera at the bidding of so insignificant a creature as the common bacillus" (1:373). Error in Proust is serious, often permanent.

Realism is friendly not least because the space/time it represents is already inventoried. The scales are loaded: the figure/ground model operating in realism is distorted in favor of the figure. (Would we still believe, to the extent that we do, in the coherence of personal identity if we did not have hundreds of years of realist novels telling us: it exists, it really does?) Kafka's terrain, by contrast, does not allow one to be smart, perhaps not even to remain oneself. The figure/ground ratio—however fantastic his narratives—may actually shift toward a truer concession of the unmapped in our experience of space, time, and others. His protagonists encounter only unresolvable troubles. (Kafka has no interest in the sine qua non of realism: resourceful human will.) Likewise in Faulkner: his first protagonist, Donald Mahan, wounded beyond healing, returns after World War I to a South altered beyond repair. Faulkner seems to find his own writerly self only by descending into a sort of distress for which no resolution is imagined. Benjy, Quentin, and Jason are supreme embodiments of trouble in time that no subsequent learning can dispel. As I shall explore more fully in the next chapter, Faulkner must become "not-I" to become Faulkner at all.

The primordial conviction underlying realism's representational norms—that we come to know more in time—is under assault in these three modernist writers. Proust, of course, seeks wisdom (and, in ways significantly detached from novelist plotting, he delivers wisdom), but this is hardly the same as recovering one's past self. More, no reader feels "plot-wise" (canny about how to move around in Proustian time) while reading the *Recherche*. Mme. Saint-Loup of the Overture is also (we learn later) Gilberte, even as Mme. des Laumes is also Oriane, the Duchesse de Guermantes; no less, Marcel's lady in pink turns out to be Swann's Odette; this list is quite edited. The narrator's take on each figure in the *Recherche* respects the limited perspective presently operating.

In Kafka there is no past to recover; his figures are, so to speak, time-lobotomized. K.'s mother and niece are unrepresentable, and his uncle appears out of nowhere, no trace of familiarity clinging to him. Poor Georg's past (his old friend in Russia) lasts only until his father removes it from him ("You have no friend in Saint Petersburg. . . . How could you have a friend out there!" [*Metamorphosis,* 57]). Now is cut off from then, and thus cut off as well from what is to come—unless what is to come is merely a full (fatal) delivery of what is already here.

For Faulkner, the idea of a deeper return is mocked by the unedifying repetitions that punctuate time in *The Sound and the Fury* ("each in its ordered place"—Benjy's static, empty view of the statue of the Confederate soldier, once again being circled from right to left—concludes this novel that goes nowhere). Likewise, *Requiem for a Nun* can bring no resolution to the devastation unleashed in *Sanctuary*. The retrospective figures, no matter how yearningly invested in past avatars, find nothing in time's mirror. Like Marcel made absent by his grandmother's not seeing him, like Freud uncannily disconcerted by the aged gentleman in the mirror, later Faulkner accesses early Faulkner only in the mode of nonrecognition. The moment uncontrolled, trauma unabated, recovery a groundless fiction: if these are the temporal conditions of *unknowing,* what possible knowledge in ongoing time? And if not knowledge, what alternative to it?

CHAPTER SEVEN

Subject and/as Other

Kafka, Proust, Faulkner

"HERE I AM" II

The two previous chapters have argued that the meaning of "here I am" changes significantly within the representational schema of modernist fiction. Space and time, "here" and "now," no longer function as detached, lawful frames within which the Enlightenment drama of a subject coming to know unfolds. In such conditions, the subject himself—"I"—alters as well. A microscopic and ceaseless traffic among all three terms—subject, space, time—replaces the more easily manageable figure/ground polarity implicit in the drama of the singular Cartesian subject. (In Levinas's terms, "The word *I* means *here I am,* answering for everything and for everyone" [*Otherwise,* 114].) In the former model, a foregrounded *res cogitans* moves through doubt and learns to gauge accurately a backgrounded *res extensa.* By contrast, modernism's representational schema draws on quite different tenets that might be loosely gathered together as phenomenological.

Since my study is literary, not philosophical, I shall only sketch some basic phenomenological tenets. A range of late-nineteenth- and early-twentieth-century Western thinkers (Bradley, Bergson, Franz Brentano, and Edmund Husserl among them) were engaged in reconceptualizing the embodied subject's way of inhabiting and registering the exterior world. Oversimplifying, one may say that in their work, individual consciousness appears less as the separate subjective lens through which a Hume would despair of arriving at lawful objective conclusions, and more as the participatory "field" within which world-apprehension continuously occurs. Consciousness and the world pre-engage each other, primordially, producing in individuals the experience of a life-world. Husserl claims that our minds never grasp "the matter straight out," but rather how things "'appear.' For this reason, they are called 'phenomena,' and their most general essential character is to exist as the 'consciousness-of' or 'appearance-of' the specific things."[1] With Heidegger's publication of *Being and Time* (1927), phenomenology emerges (and for the next two decades remains) as a major current in European philosophy, marking the existentialist thought of Gabriel Marcel, Maurice Merleau-Ponty, Levinas, and Sartre.

As in my earlier discussion of Freud, I make no claim as to influence. (It is likely that, apart from Proust's knowing some of Bergson's work, none of my novelists read these philosophers.) Rather, I seek to disengage some common intuitions that shape my writers' representational strategies, and one leaps into view. In modernist fictional practice things tend (more aggressively than in realism) to enter representation as perceived or "intended" by consciousness. Of course, Enlightenment thought also understands the subject's grasp on the object as phenomenal alone, but subject and object—an immaterial *res cogitans* and a material *res extensa*—remain oppositional terms. By contrast, phenomenology stresses the mental framing of world-perception so as to bond inseparably subject and object; subject and world are "hard-wired" into each other.

As Merleau-Ponty puts it, this is, *pace* Descartes, "a philosophy for which the world is always 'already there' before reflection begins—as an inalienable presence."[2] I am always inserted in the world; all my analyses of it are affected by that preobjective insertion.[3] Merleau-Ponty again: "It is because it is a preobjective view that being-in-the-world can be distinguished from every third person process, from every modality of the *res extensa,* as from every *cogitatio,* from every first person form of knowledge—and that it can effect the union of the 'psychic' and the 'physiological.' . . . We must therefore avoid saying that our body is *in* space, or *in* time. It *inhabits* space and time."[4] "Here I am," in phenomenologically oriented modernist fiction, means not that a separate "I" happens to find itself in space and time, but that the (embodied) "I" cannot be responsibly thought apart from the space and time it always inhabits.[5] Such inhabiting may be a cohabiting yet, as Proust shows, a cohabiting that no human being can afford for long to confront. Some of the things that happen to human being in space and time will not bear thinking on. In this cohabiting, a certain subset of *res extensa*—one's body—gets reconceptualized as the inalienable grounding of *res cogitans:* not alien body but *lived* body. As Heidegger puts it in his study of Nietzsche, "we do not 'have' a body; rather, we are 'bodily'" (as cited in Welton, 124).[6] With a different set of assumptions, Freud arrived at a similar view. The body "speaks" the being, speaks it more revealingly, often, than the mind. We have had occasion, in the two previous chapters, to attend to all three novelists' extensive attention to the body as symptom, gauge, problem; we shall press this body analysis further below. Suffice it to say for now that, among the single-sentence definitions of modernist fiction one might propose, the following is not the worst: Modernist fiction takes the body *as such* as an inexhaustibly revealing problematic.

"Here I am," an incarnate being moving in space/time. In realism, the subject's capacity for movement is taken for granted; the narrative focuses instead on the various projects of *res cogitans.* In phenomenologically inflected fiction, however, the details of the embodied subject's life-world—an array of orientational arrangements prior to, more intimate than, the pursuit of projects—become richly pertinent. These writers are more likely to attend to the elemental world-furnishing that makes human being possible. Heidegger writes: "When we speak of man and space, it sounds as though man stood on one side, space on the other. Yet space is not something that faces man. . . . Spaces, and with them space as such— 'space'—are always provided for already within the stay of mortals. . . . To say that mortals *are* is to say that *in dwelling* they persist through spaces by virtue of their stay among things and locations."[7]

Levinas understands this primordial insertion of embodied being into familiar space/time as enjoyment itself—that unthinking orientational confidence that I have been calling throughout this study anaclitic. Levinas writes:

> Dwelling is the very mode of *maintaining oneself* . . . as the body that . . . holds *itself* up and *can.* . . . The "at home" is not a container but a site where *I can,* where, dependent on a reality that is other, I am, despite this dependence or thanks to it, free. It is enough to walk, to *do,* in order to grasp anything, to take. . . . The site, a medium, affords means. Everything is here, everything belongs to me. . . . The possibility of possessing, that is, of suspending the very alterity of what is only at first other, and other relative to me, is the *way* of the same. I am at home with myself in the world because it offers itself to or resists possession.[8]

If this extensive passage seems somehow familiar in its claims—however unfamiliar its vocabulary—it means that it reprises an assumption about the subject in space/time so embedded in realist protocols that it escapes thought: the assumption that human being is *at home* there. Taken for granted and therefore unspoken in an Enlightenment model, that assumption gets articulated—put into thought—in twentieth-century phenomenology, allowing us to see writ large the anaclitic dimensions of our pact with space/time.

Yet a crucial difference emerges in the later schema. In undoing the separation between free-standing subject, on the one hand, and entities in space/time, on the other, the phenomenological model binds *subject, space,* and *time* as radically interdependent terms. No embodied subjects without immersion in space/time; no absolute space/time indifferent to embodied subjects. The terms are now wholly correlative.

If subject/space/time are bonded as mutually inseparable, however, the possibility of the bond's *rupture* becomes fraught with a distress unimaginable in realism. In Enlightenment thought neither such a pact nor its rupture is readily conceivable. By contrast—and this is the point I have been working toward—much *modernist philosophy and fiction engage this intimate, moment-by-moment pact ("here I am") by way of exploring the fallout of its rupture.* The shattering of the subject/space/time bond is the signature event in the fiction we have been examining. Levinas has already let us see how this scenario of at-home-ness—furnishedness—sustains itself by converting the alterity of the other into dimensions of the same. What is modernist shock if not the arrival (what Faulkner calls in *Absalom* the "abruption") of unconvertible alterity?

Before resuming analysis of the assaulted modernist subject, let us stay with Levinas's terms a bit longer. Although his concern is philosophical rather than literary, he identifies the spatial/temporal logic that drives progressive realist motion. The wayfaring subject, engaging a set of suspended obstacles (alterity), eventually manages to negotiate these obstacles, converting them into a continuation of the same. In so doing, he returns home. In these terms, realism is the infinitely rewritable story of Ulysses making his way through alterity as he heads back to Ithaca. This drama of turning other into self—of coming to possess it as knowledge, as challenge met and resolved—is, as I argued in part 1, the Ur-narrative of Western realist fiction and Enlightenment philosophy.

In identifying the logic of realism's subject-drama, Levinas grasps the "perversion" of time (Brooks's term) at the heart of realist representation:

Representation is the force of such an illusion and of such forgettings. Representation is a pure present. The positing of a pure present without even

tangential ties with time is the marvel of representation. It is a void of time.
. . . To be sure the I who conducts his thoughts *becomes* (or more exactly ages)
in time. . . . But this becoming in time does not appear on the plane of representation. . . . Every anteriority of the given is reducible to the instantaneity of
thought and, simultaneous with it, arises in the present. . . . To represent is
not only to render present "anew"; it is to reduce to the present an actual perception which flows on. (*Totality*, 125, 127; emphasis in the original)[9]

The passage is remarkably suggestive. To represent one's former experience is to present (make present) a picture of one's past rather than to
reveal oneself as marked by that past. Realist representational protocols—
using the past tense consistently to render previous experience as "clear
and distinct," as present, now, to the consciousness of protagonist and
reader—reproduce that previous experience as a seemingly pure present.[10]
The effect of time's passage is effaced. Realism is shaped so as to enable the
subject to elude recognition of any disfiguring mark of time upon the
scene of representation. (Hence it takes shock, assault, for Marcel to see
that his representation of his grandmother is *in time,* is *timed,* is *out of
date.*) The past event, as narrated in realism, appears clean, discrete,
bounded. It is re-present-ed to consciousness as a wholeness. Finally, Levinas characterizes not just the spatial/temporal logic of realist representation, but its seductiveness as well:

[We are dealing with] an experience always anticipated and consented to. . . .
The given enters into a thought which . . . invests it with its own project, and
thus exercises mastery over it. What affects a consciousness presents itself at
a distance from the first . . . is represented, does not knock without announcing itself, leaves, across the interval of space and time, the leisure necessary
for a welcome. What is realized in and by intentional consciousness offers
itself to protention and diverges from itself in retention, so as to be, across
the divergency, identified and possessed. This play in being is consciousness
itself: presence to self through a distance, which is both loss of self and recovery in truth. (*Otherwise,* 101–2)

Attended to with sufficient care, this knotty description reveals the spatio-
temporality of realist plot as an approaching and unfolding of experiences
anticipated, consented to, accommodated, eventually mastered. Knock,
knock: who's there? Realism informs us who, maintains the good man-
ners of announcing the intrusion in advance and providing time for it to
be appropriately welcomed. The other then enters the field of intentional

consciousness as something partly recognizable in advance (it permits pro-tention), as well as something rewardingly recognized later as slightly dif-ferent (its retention in consciousness is corrective). The other—its alterity thus managed over the time of encounter—is thereby "identified and pos-sessed," becoming, for the subject thus encountering it, an event in the career of the same. This game of the subject's loss and recovery—of con-sciousness at first inadequate to its encounters but eventually adequate to them—enacts the spatio-temporality that "grounds" identity: to lose and then to recover oneself by engaging others in objective space and ongoing time just *is* identity. Time—within the anaclitic realm of realism—is the medium in which, encountering others, we (re)become ourselves.

I have entered into this (perilous) discussion of phenomenology because Enlightenment philosophy—be it idealist or empirical—is typically unpre-pared to analyze the teeming world-traffic that occurs at this microscopic level of "here I am." Its epistemological project is focused elsewhere. To recognize what is at stake when this obscure traffic goes awry and orienta-tion *fails,* I have briefly drawn from the work of Heidegger, Merleau-Ponty, and Levinas. Despite his insistence on human furnishing, even Heidegger concedes that orientation may fail. "In anxiety, we say, 'one feels ill at ease [*es ist einem unheimlich*].' . . . We can get no hold on things. In the slipping away of beings only this 'no hold on things' comes over us and remains."[11] *Unheimlich:* the reverse of canniness, of the "I can" of inten-tional identity. David Krell glosses this negative liability in Heidegger as follows: "Such intricate contexts of meaning—which are usually implicit in our activities and become visible only when something goes wrong, when the hammer breaks or the bulb burns out—constitute what Heideg-ger calls 'world'" ("General Introduction," *Heidegger: Basic Writings,* 20).

The broken hammer, the burned-out bulb, the interrupted enjoyment of a "world": when our subject/space/time contract shatters, "here I am" shifts from capacitation to arrest, from orientation to errance and obses-sion. "Obsession traverses consciousness countercurrentwise," Levinas writes, "is inscribed in consciousness as something foreign, a disequilib-rium, a delirium. . . . In the form of an ego, anachronously *delayed* behind its present moment, and unable to recuperate this delay—that is, in the form of an ego unable to conceive what is 'touching' it, the ascendency of the other is exercised upon the same to the point of interrupting it, leaving it speechless" (*Otherwise,* 101; emphasis in the original). Space here becomes opaque (I cannot name what is "touching" me), time loses its re-presenta-tional docility (I cannot catch up with what is marking me and will not release me). Such a subject has exited from the soothing familiarity that

Levinas calls "the disappearance of what could shock" (*Totality*, 124). This is the subject who claims our attention in the work of Kafka, Proust, and Faulkner. Wherever he is going, it is not to Ithaca. His distress registers an unknowing penetrated by anxiety, an unpreparedness fraught with fear and trembling. A frozen sea is being made to thaw. How might this disabling at the same time imply an annunciation?

ONESELF IN THE ACCUSATIVE FORM: KAFKAN SUBJECTIVITY

Otherwise than being: this is both the title of Levinas's most provocative work and the condition of subjectivity in Kafka. *Being* unfolds, as Heidegger, Merleau-Ponty, and others propose, as the drama of an intentional I. The premise of "I" assumes, as the existentialist psychologist Rollo May has claimed, "the I of I can."[12] In my projects—my intentional commerce with the world—I access and confirm my "I." What interrupts the I-program and launches a state of affairs "otherwise than being"? For Kafka, as for Levinas, the answer (though not the motives fueling it) is the same: *accusation*. Accused, I am no longer I but me. Latin grammar elegantly makes the point: when "I" ceases to be subject, and becomes instead object, it enters the accusative case, as "me." "Someone must have traduced Joseph K." (1): as object of an unknown subject ("someone"), he has been dispossessed of project, arrested, "me'd."[13]

"Me" differs from "I" by being inserted into a social frame that comes before "I." "I" converts to "me" in responding to others who inaugurate, who call me. In Kafka, the "I" suddenly converted to "me" (read interrogatively: "me?") never succeeds in identifying the other "I" who issues the call. Yet without that call there is no narrative at all. The Kafkan narrative unfolds as response to events or arrangements prior to narration. This is Kafka's terrifying temporality. I am accused as "me" before I can properly exercise my "I." In this tiny pronominal arrangement Kafka inverts the Declaration of Independence and the liberal judicial system that are the pride of Enlightenment. So long as "I" retains precedence, "I" is a figure of entitlement, endowed with rights, deemed innocent until proven guilty. Emergence from "self-incurred tutelage" (Kant's phrase) serves as "I's" inalienable project.

In Kafka the egotistical impertinence, so to speak, of this stance reveals itself (think of Joseph K. flamboyantly arguing his case, unaware of the identity of either his audience or his crime). In the ambient scheme of things I am unknowing, preinserted into situations that never asked my permission first, marked by complicities to which I never intentionally gave my name. My prehistory is longer and darker than my history. If lucky, I can escape knowing about this prehistory, though the imaginaries of Kafka and Faulkner share a commitment to reconnecting the "I" with "that Porto Rico or Haiti or wherever it was we all came from but none of us ever lived in" (*Absalom,* 246): that place before "I," the place of "me." In that place I am accused.

Freud knows what I am accused of, for his enterprise is devoted to interpreting the array of symptoms that speak my guilt outside the medium of words. I am guilty of repressed desires, intolerable wishes, and this because—once again prior to the formation of my "I"—my infantile being was awash in now-taboo behaviors, monstrous in its wants and moves. Though this malaise involves others (especially my parents), it is essentially the trouble I incurred by being born. Freud's therapy seeks to make manageable the vicissitudinous pathway the infantile "me" has to tread in its arduous and ineluctable project of maturing into an "I." For Freud, I must learn to reconfigure guilt as illness; his aim is not to make me innocent but to make me well enough to function.

Levinas, likewise, knows what I am accused of, but his answer does not resemble Freud's. I suffer from the radical limitation attaching to personal identity itself, to my "I"-ness. The other accuses me of this injustice; his face tells me that my enjoyment battens on his penury. Gazing upon his face, I come upon myself, horrifyingly, as "oneself in the accusative form, before appearing in the said proper to knowing as the bearer of a name" (*Otherwise,* 106). Prenamed, presaid, I am found out in my unpreparedness, a "no one, clothed with purely borrowed being, which masks its nameless singularity by conferring on it a role" (106). I discover my self to be "an inequality with itself, a deficit in being, a passivity . . . not offering itself to memory" (107). Memory of who I am—that re-presentational system so empowering for the intentional ego's march through time—fails me. Suddenly, "here I am." Yet this dispossession is also a launching. For if I owe the other all, more than I can possibly repay, he is silent and it is I who read his indicting presence thus: "It is an assignation to answer without evasions, which assigns the self to be a self" (106). His face calls to me, assigns me. In responding to that call as me, I become I. I assume my identity not through any set of traits already mine, but through my suddenly acquiring "the uniqueness of someone summoned" (194 n. 9).

A deficit in being, a nameless singularity, a passivity unenlightened by memory, a summoning: the dimensions of Levinasian accusation so powerfully resemble those of Kafkan accusation that one becomes (against one's better judgment) hopeful for more light. Here is Joseph K. being called:

> But it was no congregation the priest was addressing, the words were unambiguous and inescapable, he was calling out: "Joseph K.!"
>
> K. paused and stared at the ground before him. For the moment he was still free, he could continue on his way and vanish. . . . It would simply indicate that he had not understood the call, or that he had understood it and did not care. But if he were to turn round he would be caught, for that would amount to an admission that he had understood it very well, that he was really the person addressed, and that he was ready to obey. (209)

Kafka's difference disturbingly manifests itself here. To answer Levinas's call of the other is to enter the ethical life, as to answer the call Kierkegaard's Abraham receives from God is to enter the spiritual life. But to answer the call K. receives—to say "here I am"—is to assent to annihilation.[14] He has been called by a power to which no institutional name can be attached, called to self-immolation. Although this deeper call might replace the corrupt and superficial one of the Bank, the meaning of its depth remains inscrutable. The cited passage may be saturated in the language of understanding, of distinguishing between surfaces and depths, calls and codes; yet the call remains (like K.'s response to it) opaque.

As critics have noted, K.'s words and gestures are, from the beginning, opaque, irreducible to a single set of intentions:

> "I'd better get Frau Grubach—" said K., as if wrenching himself away from the two men (though they were standing at quite a distance from him), and making as if to go out. (3)
>
> K. was surprised, at least he was surprised considering the warders' point of view, that they had sent him to his room and left him alone there, where he had abundant opportunities to take his life. Though at the same time he also asked himself, looking at it from his own point of view, what possible ground he could have to do so. (8)
>
> "It must be a black coat," they said. Thereupon K. flung the coat on the floor and said—he did not himself know in what sense he meant the words—"But this isn't the capital charge yet." (9)[15]

As if: the Kafka text recurrently cites K.'s gestures toward "another scene" of significance, even as he remains scrupulously blank as to their portent. These gestures are never clarified. As if wrenching himself away—but not really. Half of Kafka's critics fall into the trap (identified by Benjamin) of filling in the really, and saying why. But we cannot know why, even as we cannot ignore the telltale gesture inviting us to figure out why. In like manner, one could unify that second passage by arguing that K. is (atypically) imagining the case against him held by others though not by himself. Yes, possibly, but the sequence seems to intimate something more, by its way of opening with "K. was surprised" and then going (in a sort of bad-faith explanatory way) to a mitigating, later-supplied logic of others' point of view. He does think his own suicide, exactly as he wonders why he should think his suicide.

The third passage is perhaps the most confusing, for it puts us in the presence of a verbal event inconceivable in realism: a strong claim, followed by denial of responsibility for it. (Levinas would be scandalized. The call, in his ethical world, is the force that humanizes even as it confounds identity; in Kafka it merely confounds.) No literature of project can afford this scandal of a claim simultaneously asserted and emptied of intention. The scandal is less at the level of logic than at that of subject coherence: how can we engage a figure who claims but does not know why he claims? The assertion remains, but whom is it coming from? His motives are, in Heisenbergian terms, undecidable: "The term 'not decided' is by no means equivalent to the term not known. Not known would mean that the atom is really left or right, only we do not know where it is. But not decided indicates a different situation, expressible only by a complementary statement" (*Physics and Philosophy,* cited in Schleifer, 18).

K.'s undecidability, however, escapes even the framing imposed by Heisenbergian complementarity—as though he were always (though unpredictably) locatable in the one stance or the other. His mindset is not locatable at all, for any unifying purposes. More, we are equally far from the cohering that a Freudian solution—reading his denial as repression—might offer. K. lacks the characterological complexity that invites Freudian depth readings. Such a reading would falsely restore some of the anaclitic dimension that is missing here. Not just space and time, in Kafka's world, are unfamiliar, but the subject is too. The unfamiliarity is radical; nothing that follows will domesticate it. Kafka is the supreme writer of sequences that promise—without ever managing—to make familiar what was posited earlier.

Sequence in Kafka enacts a temporality foreign to project resolution. The consequences that arrive have nothing to do with the "I" of "I can." Figures of lack, each of his protagonists is brought upon the scene to reveal, in endlessly differing ways, what cannot be done. If realism invokes arrest so as to deepen the stakes of release and arrival, Kafkan modernism invokes the fantasy of release and arrival in order to deepen the stakes of arrest. We realize, at a certain point of our reading, that we are not going to get anywhere; where we are is *where we are.* The point of Kafka's arrests seems not to be their resolution; nothing in his world gets better in time. Rather than plot, then, in which a subject encounters obstacles and comes to terms with them—a sequence that treats time as a medium for the becoming of selfhood—Kafkan narrative proceeds otherwise. Rather than develop, it repeats (but not in the realist form that allows recognition the second time around). Rather than deliver an arrival in time, it delivers doublings in space. Let us call this a fiction of obscurely resonant trouble.

"The Judgment" (as has been widely recognized) launches Kafka's fictional enterprise. Georg Bendemann appears here and now ("here I am"), on the first page; what remains to be seen, fatally, is *where he is.* This involves less a plotting of his possibilities than a revealing of his impossibilities. He is/is not his bachelor Russian friend who left home and is prospering/failing. He is/is not the fiancé who in marrying will reproduce the family. Most of all, he is/is not the father whose seed created him and whose word will uncreate him. These other identities, simultaneously who he is and who he is not, are in irreconcilable tension with each other. To marry is to betray the friend; to leave or to marry is to betray the father; to die (in the event, a lesser offense) is to exit unbetraying from a scene of betrayals. Were this a plot, he would sort out his obstacles; instead, his obstacles sort him out. He is revealed to be not–Georg Bendemann (though there was no one else he could become).

Under his father's attack Georg first loses his memory: "At this moment he recalled this long-forgotten resolve [to avoid being "surprised by any indirect attack"] and forgot it again, like a man drawing a short thread through the eye of a needle" (*Metamorphosis,* 60). Then he loses his friend: "he knows everything a hundred times better than you do yourself," Georg's father says; "in his left hand he crumples your letters unopened while in his right hand he holds up my letters to read through!" (62). Then he loses ownership of his voice. His father thunders, "He knows everything a thousand times better!" to which Georg responds, "'Ten thousand times!' . . . to make fun of his father, but in his mouth the words turned into deadly earnest" (62). Unremembering, unfriended, unvoiced—Georg now can only speak his father—he is finally uncreated. Bursting with filial love, he hurls himself off the bridge in obedience to his father's death sentence. The last line of the story—"At this moment an unending stream of traffic was just going over the bridge" (63)—echoes, in the German word for traffic (*Verkehr*), the act of intercourse by which he was conceived.[16] The reversal is complete: first, from birth to adolescence to manhood; then, backward, through forgetting, unfriending, unvoicing, and finally unconceiving. He is, if you will, un-can-ed.

To be thus spatially doubled, mirrored in the others—as K. is doubled by the Assistant Manager, Block, the man from the country—is for the Kafkan subject to cease to have a singular identity that unfolds in time. (One notes the unorientational flatness of K.'s identity as son to mother, nephew to uncle, uncle to niece—familial relations that normally guide subjecthood down that temporal path, based on the mother's breast, that we are calling anaclitic.) What kind of identity—exited from becoming, cut off from the projects that might give it focus—here emerges?

Levinas gives us a disturbing idea of it: "The more I return to myself, the more I divest myself, under the traumatic effect of persecution [by the other], of my freedom as a constituted, willful, imperialist subject, the more I discover myself to be responsible; the more just I am, the more guilty I am. I am 'in myself' through the others. The psyche is the other in the same, without alienating the same" (*Otherwise,* 112). Imperialist will, the "I can" underlying all self-projecting, would fund my separate identity. The call of the other shatters this illusion of separateness, turns me into "oneself in the accusative form," posits my responsibility to the other within me as the core of myself. The ethical psyche, in Levinas's thought, teeters on the verge of incoherence. Primordially innocent and guilty at the same time, it functions as an openness prior to the "I," responsible for every ill it did not commit but has not cared for. Even this harsh clarification is lacking in Kafka (although, for this reader at least, it sheds light on the premise that K.'s guilt—whatever it may be—is somehow compatible with his innocence). The other that calls on the Kafkan protagonist seems to be composed in equal measures, so to speak, of almighty God and of Kafka's abusive father. What would it mean to be called guilty toward and by such an other? Even Levinas grants that our guilt toward others is a justifiable charge only if we make the accusation ourselves: "in me alone innocence can be accused without absurdity. To accuse the innocence of another, to ask of the other more than he owes, is criminal" (*Otherwise,* 195 n. 18).

Finally, though Levinas may shed light on the Kafkan text, his thought cannot ethicalize it. Nothing can ethicalize Kafka, because he writes not an ethos but an endless pathos—a passivity in which "I" is a "me" who is entered rather than an "I" who enters—without return, without homecoming. You cannot strenuously read him and find his other domesticated into your same. Surely his work matters most in its underweaving of being itself, in its manner (in Levinas's words) "of presenting one's passivity as an underside without a right side" (*Otherwise,* 106).

His animal stories show (in ways unpremeditated by Darwin or Freud) the animal lurking in the human, yet unavailing. How the apes would laugh were they to gaze upon the painfully learned "self-controlled movement" (*Metamorphosis,* 177) that we insist on calling human freedom. Human is to animal in Kafka neither as solution to a problem (the royal road of Enlightenment thinking, the motor of its plots), nor as problem to a solution (the desperate path attempted by a D. H. Lawrence or a Henry Miller), but rather as wry and inalterable stalemate: jackals juxtaposed with Arabs, the have of each exquisitely appearing as the other's have-not.

Likewise, when we come away from the whirlwind of movement that is "A Country Doctor," we conclude nothing about the (plottable) potential of human subjects. Awakened in the dead of night, this poor protagonist is summoned upon an adventure taking him everywhere but home, meeting in others not potential versions of the same, but rather encountering in their very substitutability his own emergent undoing—a self-shattering in which he is both innocent and guilty. We end by glimpsing the constructedness, at once precious and fraught, of identity itself. In Adorno's words, "It is thus that aesthetic experience . . . breaks through the spell of obstinate self-preservation; it is the model of a stage of consciousness in which the I no longer has its happiness in its interests, or, ultimately, in its reproduction" (*Aesthetic,* 346). What makes such an othering of selfhood valuable?

NATIVE OF AN UNKNOWN COUNTRY: PROUSTIAN SUBJECTIVITY

That the Kafkan text centers on a shattering of ego is easy to see, hard to explain. By contrast, the Proustian text labors mightily toward the opposite effect: to reconstitute the unity of ego, to reconnect the native subject with the (unknowingly abandoned) homeland of his soul. Such soul unity is achieved in the generativity of art itself: a stance most fully articulated during an afternoon at the Verdurins. There, Marcel first hears Vinteuil's septet:

> The impression conveyed by these Vinteuil phrases was different from any other, as though, in spite of the conclusions to which science seems to point, the individual did exist. . . . for then Vinteuil, striving to do something new, interrogated himself, with all the power of his creative energy, reached down to his essential self at those depths where, whatever be the question

asked, it is in the same accent, that is to say its own, that it replies. . . . [I]t is indeed a unique accent, an unmistakable voice, to which in spite of themselves those great singers that original composers are rise and return, and which is a proof of the irreducibly individual existence of the soul. . . . Each artist seems thus to be the native of an unknown country, which he himself has forgotten. (3:257–58)

The idealism wrought into this paean is patent, and Vincent Descombes has analyzed a couple of its debatable assumptions: the achievable univocity of the work of art, the normally fractured (but through art unifiable) individuality of the soul (what Descombes calls the "myth of interiority"), articulable only in a language that each of us must learn to utter for himself. Rather than pursue, like Descombes, a programmatic deconstruction of such idealism, I want to show something else: the text's own sabotaging of these claims of achieved individuality—its strenuous decoupling of "natives" from their "country," its investment in the subject not as native and singular but as unknowing and plural.

Let us begin with the familiar cameo of Mlle. Vinteuil and her lesbian friend, eavesdropped on by Marcel, some years after M. Vinteuil's death. The scene is memorable. Divided beyond healing between daughterly modesty ("a shy and suppliant maiden") and lesbian desire ("a rough and swaggering trooper"), Mlle. Vinteuil engages in an elaborate ritual of inauthentic moves. Prior to her lover's entry into the house, she places her father's photograph on a nearby table, so that when their embrace commences, it will be readily at hand—though not apparently by her doing. As for the embrace, she hungers for it, and is ashamed to want it, in equal measure; her gestures are consistently false. Pretending to close the shutters, she answers her friend's retort with "But it's too tiresome! People will see us," followed by "When I say 'see us,' I mean, of course, see us reading. It's so tiresome to think that whatever trivial little thing you do someone may be overlooking you" (1:176). Her lover replies "And what if they are?" in a practiced (and anticipated) cynical tone, but still the embrace is withheld: Mlle. Vinteuil's "sensitive and scrupulous heart was ignorant of the words that ought to flow spontaneously from her lips to match the scene for which her eager senses clamored" (1:176).

After reciting another rehearsed phrase for precipitating matters, the friend suddenly kisses Mlle. Vinteuil on the breast, the two women chase each other about the room "squealing like a pair of amorous fowls" (1:177), and—the moment now arrived—Mlle. Vinteuil points to the portrait of her father, saying, "I can't think who can have put it there" (1:177). Overhearing this, Marcel remembers how, in visits made to her father long ago, M. Vinteuil had similarly excused the "inexplicable" presence of his sheets of music, a move allowing him to receive—without seeming to ask for—his guests' admiration for his work. The scene gathers intensity: "This photograph was evidently in regular use for ritual profanations, for the friend replied in words which were clearly a liturgical response: 'Let him stay there. . . . D'you think he'd start whining . . . if he saw you now with the window open, the ugly old monkey?'" At which point she ritually threatens to spit on the photograph, is disingenuously rebuffed by Mlle. Vinteuil, then carries out her threat/promise. The love-making commences; the window and shutters are finally closed.

"Someone may be overlooking," Mlle. Vinteuil complains. Rarely, indeed, was a scene more populated with unseen and invisible overlookers. (How many of the *Recherche*'s memorable vignettes would we have to give up if all scenes of eavesdropping were removed?) Overlooking, Marcel describes a ritual of bad faith, centered on a young woman hopelessly riven by, unaware of, conflicting motives. It takes the overlooker, Marcel, to tell us what is at stake: "Sadists of Mlle Vinteuil's sort are creatures so purely sentimental . . . that even sensual pleasure appears to them as something bad. . . . And when they allow themselves for a moment to enjoy it they endeavor to impersonate . . . the wicked, and to make their partners do likewise, in order to gain the momentary illusion of having escaped beyond the control of their own gentle and scrupulous natures into the inhuman world of pleasure" (1:179). Not wicked, she tries to appear wicked; not spontaneous, she recites a rehearsed script of rising desire.

Though seeking to humiliate her father, she places him (by repetition of his gesture with the sheet of music) all the more irremovably in the scene. Marcel emphasizes her mannerisms, facial features, and even her blue eyes, as so many heirlooms announcing the spectral presence of the father she would escape. Indeed, the scene is so narrated that two males (the dead M. Vinteuil and the concealed Marcel) provide shaping lenses for understanding two females (Mlle. Vinteuil and her friend), both rendered as objects under scrutiny, lost to their own motives. Marcel's installation of an oedipal narrative preempts Mlle. Vinteuil's attempt at lesbian escape ("into the inhuman world of pleasure"), making her identity double, contradictory. The scene becomes, perforce, one of unaccommodated remembering, of failed forgetting. Ritual predominates in the form of their rehearsed script of desire, as a result of Marcel's relentless recall of what Mlle. Vinteuil herself repeats without recognizing. He cues us to what we henceforth register as a scene of dysfunction and distress, almost of traumatic repetitions.

After two more pages of intensive analysis, the scene terminates thus: "Perhaps she would not have thought of evil as a state so rare, so abnormal, so exotic, one in which it was so refreshing to sojourn, had she been able to discern in herself, as in everyone else, that indifference to the sufferings one causes which, whatever other names one gives to it, is the most terrible and lasting form of cruelty" (1:180). Oneself in the accusative form: Mlle. Vinteuil appears in this vignette (as elsewhere in the text) objectified, analyzed, contradictory, seen as she cannot see herself. The accusation is gentle, indeed forgiving, yet it absents her from her "I" no less than Kafkan accusation dispossesses his protagonists of their "I." This closing sentence of the vignette carries such vintage Proustian wisdom that Mlle. Vinteuil virtually disappears into it, transformed into an exemplum of the narrator's larger insight.

Having completed thus its business with the "Méséglise way," the text departs for the "Guermantes way." But if we linger a bit longer, some interesting questions emerge. The world of pleasure is characterized as "inhuman," and the deepest form of cruelty is identified as "indifference." Our first question might be: what in the Proustian imaginary insists on coupling these notions—on suggesting that pleasure itself is inhuman inasmuch as it necessarily entails the cruelty of forgetting absent others? The second question would be: how does Marcel's imposing an oedipal scenario upon a lesbian one reengage the time-laden issue (explored above) of neurosis? Both questions probe the discontinuous Proustian subject in space/time.

Sexual pleasure is fantasized as an ecstatic entry into sheer incarnate presence, an "inhuman" escape from one's bondage to a past history of space and time and others. Such release is figured as free of memory (read: loyalty to absent others)—an eclipse at once desired and abjured. (I say "fantasized" because actual sexual experience in Proust, if we take the Albertine scenes to be representative, unfolds as a depressing amalgam of awkwardness, anxiety, and boredom: memory-fraught rather than memory-free.) We grasp the inverse relation of release and neurosis when we recall that the Proustian text glosses neurosis as the subject's incapacity to ignore the call of an earlier self in a prior space/time pleading to be retained—"the plaints of the most humble elements of the self which are about to disappear" (1:722). "The inhuman world of pleasure"—which would be orgasmic and purely present—beckons as both liberation and treachery. Erotic movement toward current others in space and time is figured not as normal development but as obscure betrayal of prior commitments (including, in this case, a daughter's lesbian betrayal of her heterosexual father).

Something in Proust knows, of course, that the betrayal of the past that we call *forgetting* is health itself. Furthermore, subsequent recovery of the past requires having earlier forgotten it and moved on. Nevertheless, something else in Proust scrutinizes subject-experience with an "infrared" intensity that searches and finds, precisely, what was forgotten (by others) and brings it back into play. If, therefore, Mlle. Vinteuil is insistently held to a parental/oedipal dynamic that overcodes lesbian escape and guarantees her self-blindness in time, the neurotic dysfunction that results may belong not so much to her as to the narrative imaginary that is accessing her. Whose neurosis operates here?

Finally, if this portrait of Mlle. Vinteuil attends to a few all-revealing minutes of her behavior, its genesis as a portrait requires a much greater passage of time. Its analytic coherence is unobtainable without this sustained incubation period. The vignette begins by announcing that it is from an "impression which I received at Montjouvain, some years later, an impression which at the time remained obscure to me, that there arose, long afterwards, the notion I was to form of sadism" (1:173). *She* is the unknowing participant in a momentary experience that *he* has had untold time to ponder, digest, and master. The vignette emphasizes his temporal privilege. "And yet I have since reflected . . ." (1:178), Marcel thinks, having come to recognize (over time) that, even in blaspheming her father's memory, Mlle. Vinteuil obscurely reveals her kindred "goodness of heart" (1:178).

A pervasive narrative logic is here embedded. Like all embodied characters in this text, Mlle. Vinteuil must take on accusative form if her onlooker, Marcel, is to assume nominative (better would be "pronominative") form. She must be visible and self-divided object to his invisible and self-cohered subject. More, it is precisely scenes like this one that establish Marcel's coherence and authority as subject/narrator. His achieved knowing requires a scrupulously unnarrated temporal continuum, just as her self-fissured unknowing must be situated within a narrated, revelatory moment. *In* the moment, he is no wiser than she is.

Let us test this claim by turning to one of the text's radiant moments of time turned into wisdom: Elstir's confession to Marcel that he used to be known, indeed, not as (the noble painter) Elstir, but as (the pretentious fop) Biche:

> "There is no man," he [Elstir] began, "however wise, who has not at some period of his youth said things, or lived a life, the memory of which is so unpleasant to him that he would gladly expunge it. And yet he ought not entirely to regret it, because he cannot be certain that he has indeed become

a wise man . . . unless he has passed through all the fatuous or unwholesome incarnations by which that ultimate stage must be preceded. . . . We do not receive wisdom, we must discover it for ourselves, after a journey through the wilderness which no one else can make for us, which no one can spare us, for our wisdom is the point of view from which we come at last to regard the world." (1:923–24)

That last sentence reappears predictably in studies published on Proust, for nothing else sums up better the arduous, yet generous, path toward self-enlightenment that the *Recherche* espouses. Less often cited is what immediately follows Elstir's peroration: "Meanwhile we had reached his door. I was disappointed at not having met the girls" (1:924). Not a word of outward response or inward meditation on the painter's outpouring of wisdom; it is as though Marcel did not even *hear* him. As Elstir says, each of us has to do it for ourselves, yet for Marcel to follow up Elstir's eloquence with complete indifference is almost shocking, like a moment of cognitive dissonance.[17]

Such dissonance (such subjective discontinuity in ongoing time) occurs elsewhere too. After Marcel has painfully thought his way into the hopelessness signaled by Gilberte's actual behavior—a hopelessness he elsewhere has managed not to recognize—he realizes that her feeling for him is "indifference": "it was I alone who loved" (1:446). Unified insight, finally! But the next sentence (which ends the entire subsection) reads: "And so, as from the very next day . . . I would ask Gilberte to terminate our old friendship and to join me in laying the foundations of a new one" (1:447). Unified insight, never. One may be reminded of the ending of "Swann in Love," in which, after two hundred pages of minutely recorded suffering over Odette, Swann comes to his senses and realizes: "To think that I've wasted years of my life, that I've longed to die, that I've experienced my greatest love, for a woman who didn't appeal to me, who wasn't even my type!" (1:415). After which, at a later moment that Proust sublimely leaves unnarrated, he marries her. What logic of subjective discontinuity operates in this text?

To this question a couple of answers may be proposed. The first would be: the embodied subject in a particularized space/time differs, crucially, from the meditative subject abstracted from the immediate scene. It is easier to rise into wisdom if one is given the time to "have since reflected . . ." Elstir encompasses it memorably in his speech to Marcel, while the latter, uncharacteristically caught up in a strategic here/now, merely thinks: where are those girls? If the Proustian narrator is supremely reflective, the conditions permitting such wisdom are clear: his disembodiment in specific space and time. Invisible as narrator, he tends to be no less unrepresented—*physically*—as character. We do not *see* Marcel (who can describe him?). We do not know his age, his look, or even his name (in the sense of our seeing others using his name and him responding to them). Put otherwise, Marcel is largely *unaccused*. Only vaguely en-spaced, en-timed, he is allowed to remain unplotted, freed from the contradictoriness of being that comes with the searching representation of one's behavior. In place of an embodied character named Marcel and rendered visible within particularizing scenes with others, Proust gives us—as Marcel—a mobile sensorium, a reflective mind, and an unfailing double: the narrator.

He is "at" the great social scenes of the novel—the endless dinners and parties, replete with the guests' microscopically detailed clothing and gestures and speeches—only spectrally, interpretively. (One remembers the scene of Charlus's humiliation. As a good friend, Marcel knows it is coming, wants to prevent it, cannot do so. He cannot because he is not there as others are there.) Attention to any number of scenes would reveal what it is like, in Proust, to be there. I shall draw only on Proust's exquisite rendering of the Princesse des Laumes's late entry into Mme. de Saint-Euverte's party: four pages describing her gestures of false modesty, her uncertainty as to how to respond outwardly to the unfamiliar music being played (a problem resolved by her beating time "for a few bars with her fan, but, so as not to forfeit her independence, against the rhythm" [1:361]), her mockery of Mme. de Gallardon, and her put-down of the latter's taking the liberty of calling her by her first name: "'Oriane' (at once Mme des Laumes looked with amused astonishment towards an invisible third person, whom she seemed to call to witness that she had never authorised Mme de Gallardon to use her Christian name)" (1:363). This is oneself in the accusative: Oriane is wholly there, richly duplicitous, displayed in ways she herself cannot know. We rarely envisage Marcel in similar fashion.

In this book of over thirty-five hundred pages, I can think of only a few times when he is intimately addressed. One occurs in *The Captive,* when we learn that Albertine, often on awakening, would say: "'My——' or 'My darling——' followed by my Christian name, which, if we give the narrator the same name as the author of this book, would be 'My Marcel,' or 'My darling Marcel'" (3:69). Coyness can hardly go further. The book elegantly bends itself out of shape—distancing itself from the narrator by inventing, for the moment, *another* narrator—so as to keep this young man nameless insofar as he is actually present in the scene. It is this second narrator who supplies (at his spatial/temporal distance) the pertinent information, and even so in a subjunctive manner.

An earlier instance is no less revealing. Gilberte, at a certain moment while playing with Marcel in the Tuileries, proposes that they call each other by their first names, then actually says his name (though Proust does not textualize the saying). Afterwards Marcel thinks: "I distinguished the impression of having been held for a moment in her mouth, myself, naked, without any of the social attributes which belonged equally to her other playmates and, when she used my surname, to my parents, accessories of which her lips . . . had the air of stripping, of divesting me, like the skin from a fruit of which one can swallow only the pulp, while her glance, adapting itself to the same new degree of intimacy as her speech, fell on me also more directly and testified to the consciousness, the pleasure, even the gratitude that it felt by accompanying itself with a smile" (1:439).

Naked, stripped, divested, swallowed: this is Marcel in the accusative form, held immovable in the grip of her gaze and voice. It is an atypical and disturbing moment, emphatically here and now, as though to be thus addressed as me (me?) were to be bodily menaced.

Her seeming to place him, as he puts it, in her throat recalls the scene just thirteen pages earlier, in which a related utterance takes Marcel, so to speak, by the throat. Hearing from his parents that his intensely fantasized trip to Venice is actually going to take place in two weeks, Marcel is "raised to a sort of ecstasy . . . divesting myself, as of a shell that served no purpose, of the air in my own room which surrounded me, I replaced it by an equal quantity of Venetian air . . . I felt myself undergoing a miraculous disincarnation, which was at once accompanied by that vague desire to vomit which one feels when one has developed a very sore throat" (1:426–27). Seriously ill, he takes to his bed; Venice is "absolutely out of the question" (1:427). Is it too much to suggest that *actualization in a scene of desire*—the embodying of identity in a subjectively desired encounter that will unfold as an objective here and now—registers in Marcel as suffocation, illness, or (as in the Albertine kiss scenes) vertigo? In these two instances the anxiety of an inescapable predicatedness locates in the throat. Gilberte's or his, it matters not which: the throat, as the voice-carrying organ negotiating one's dual identity as specified body and free-floating mind, registers the same menace. Physical actualization threatens to break into the protected space of fantasy. Finally, we should note that, despite the anxiety wrought into his metaphors, Gilberte's addressing him still leaves Marcel relatively disembodied. Only *her* speech, pleasure, and smile are available to representation.

To state the issue in the larger terms of my study, why is Marcel insistently unplotted? Why would representing him as embodied, en-timed, and en-spaced thwart the project of the *Recherche?* I return to the question posed above—what logic of cognitive dissonance, of subjective discontinuity, operates here?—and suggest now a second answer. Marcel can give what he must give to this narrative—can escape the self-contradiction that sustained representation in space and time inevitably brings with it—only if he remains free of accusation. Liberated from narrated becoming, he is available for richer usages, indeed for the richest. Not required to become anyone, he can be *potentially* everyone. Such potentiality allows Proust to register—in Marcel alone—less the contradictoriness of being than its fabulous plasticity. Unaccused, he is free even to accuse himself, without our thus accusing him. This narrative strategy accounts for the extraordinary undefensiveness of the Proustian text.

Upon first seeing Gilberte he responds: "I loved her; I was sorry not to have had the time and the inspiration to insult her, to hurt her, to force her to keep some memory of me. I thought her so beautiful that I should have liked to be able to retrace my steps so as to shake my fist at her and shout, 'I think you're hideous, grotesque; how I loathe you!'" (1:155). We do not expect this response from him, and perhaps the text could not risk proposing it if he were emplotted. This truth of feeling stays, so to speak, liberal—more broadly illuminating—so long as it is not forced to do plot-work and become either the dark reality of Marcel's nature or the obstacle he learns in time to overcome.

Consider as well this later moment, from *The Captive:* "To be harsh and deceitful to the person whom we love is so natural! If the interest that we show towards other people does not prevent us from being gentle towards them and complying with their wishes, it is because our interest is not sincere. Other people leave us indifferent, and indifference does not prompt us to unkindness" (3:106). Casually said, terrifyingly true: Proust's text, in innumerable instances, reaches its reader through the sheer power of its unplotted insights into the darker intricacies of human behavior. Put into plot service, the insight articulated here must needs turn damaging, its range reduced to the local instance. Proust is out for larger game than the story of Marcel's life. To reach this game requires a double logic of the subject, one that permits plasticity without falling into contradiction.

Marcel as no one, as potentially everyone: the Proustian text takes this anodyne abstraction and fleshes it out compellingly. Marcel is/is not every major character in the book. The opening drama of the good-night kiss tells us that he is, permanently, his mother's child. He cannot outgrow her and thus prevent his all-shaping experience with her from shadowing—deforming—later love relations. (He will never escape into "the inhuman world of pleasure.") Freud would recognize the priority of the parent as the normal burden shadowing everyone's later love life, but Proust finds in this dilemma a different drama. He does not give us a plot that makes Albertine a troubling version of Mamma, but focuses rather—mainly through the grandmother—on the anguish of our housing, internally, the others who matter to us.

Proust tirelessly reveals that the two careers of these others—their dual reality as both inside us and outside us—cannot coincide. Although this huge novel has often been called solipsistic, it is almost Levinasian in its awareness that the others we contain in ourselves are not actually convertible into dimensions of our sameness. What are the moments of shock in Proust but the recognition that she remains other—terminally other—despite my absolute absorption of her into myself? Rather than realism's reassuring conversion of others into dimensions of myself—producing an adventure of the same by turning the other into the other *as known*—Proust writes the pathos of our incapacity to assimilate others who nevertheless lodge within the very sanctuary of our sameness.

This pathos, pressed further, arises from what I earlier called lack: the Proustian dilemma in which, thanks to our radical inadequacy as merely ourselves, we require, but cannot reach, others. *Méconnaissance*—the absorptive misapprehending of others—is constitutive of our identity. We cannot exist except as figures in an intersubjective field doomed to misrecognition. It is lack that spurs the insight cited above about our harshness to those we love; lack that funds Proust's awareness that love is also torment, however indispensable to human being. Were we not needy, we would cease to be exploratory, identificatory, interested beings. (We would surely not write.) We are interest*ing* only because we are interest*ed* (think of Legrandin and Charlus from this perspective). None of this is possible in a solipsistic text. There is all the difference between not needing others and not being able to get them right.

Proust explores this lack not in terms of a plot, but through the text's rendering of Marcel as incessantly invested in—and by—the being of others. Sometimes this investment is declared—as with his mother and grandmother, Gilberte and Albertine—but it is no less operative more broadly, and undeclared. He is Léonie in having Albertine not enter his bedroom until rung for, he is Saint-Loup and Charlus in his undeclared homosexuality, he is Bloch in his self-hating Judaism. The "is" in these claims is not predicative in the sense of traits that a plot will later reveal to be his own. Rather, endlessly penetrable and projective, he is in and out of all these others, possessed by them yet unpossessing.

Sometimes the undeclaredness all but announces its own artifice, as when Marcel submits Bloch to twelve consecutive pages of persiflage in *Within a Budding Grove* (1:793–804). In the midst of this relentless attack, Marcel reminds us that "I bore him no ill-will . . . for I had inherited from my mother and grand-mother their incapacity for rancour even against far worse offenders, and their habit of never condemning anyone" (1:801). This disclaimer looks like simple bad faith, unless we consider as well the following sentences, inserted in the very middle of the character assassination: "And to the bad habit of speaking about oneself and one's defects there must be added . . . that habit of denouncing in other people defects precisely analogous to our own. For it is always of those defects that one speaks, as though it were a way of speaking about oneself indirectly, thus adding to the pleasure of absolving oneself that of confession. Moreover it seems that our attention, always attracted by what is characteristic of ourselves, notices it more than anything else in other people" (1:798). Who is talking about whom? Is complicity with Bloch being denied, or intimated?

Intimation rather than declaration: Marcel learns at Balbec that Charlus will never reveal his motives upon simply being asked, and likewise the Proustian text intimates rather than emplots its most telling interconnections.[18] These interconnections imply a model of subjectivity that is discontinuous, at any given moment only partial. "We realize our own natures only in the course of time" (*On ne se réalise que successivement*). We do not essentialize as unified natives of an unknown country. Vinteuil, Bergotte, and Elstir all reveal, over time, multiple and contradictory identities. Marcel is inextricably complicit in others not reducible to himself.

I close this analysis of Proustian subjectivity as othered by making the claim in its strong form: Marcel is textually possible *because* he is/is not the narrator of the *Recherche,* even as the narrator is/is not Marcel (Proust). His textual identity is unfixed, necessarily double: old and young, wise and foolish, engaged and disengaged. We can unify these dualities into a time-enabled resolution only by turning this text into the kind of novel it brilliantly refuses to be.[19] "*Les unes dans les autres,*" Proust claimed as his guiding method for composing the book. The reader is to see, in each thing that appears, all those other things it resembles, yet without converting their otherness into aspects of its sameness. *Les unes dans les autres:* the subject and/as other.

NOT I: FAULKNERIAN SUBJECTIVITY

> *"he was not a being, an entity, he was a commonwealth"*
> Absalom, Absalom!

Quentin Compson was not always so "extensive." As we explored earlier, *The Sound and the Fury* is content to access Quentin, so to speak, from within himself—but himself as out of control, *in extremis*: "thinking I was I was not who was not was not who" (*Sound*, 108). In the epigraph from *Absalom*, by contrast, Faulkner figures him as a something that exceeds the dimensions of discrete being itself. Both phrasings articulate a Quentin incapable of assuming the function assigned to all realist protagonists—emplotment. The mind of Quentin I has no room for projects; his interior space is filled to bursting with memory, fantasy, and obsession. In producing Quentin II, in *Absalom*, Faulkner clears him of such inner turmoil. But this is only to prepare him to carry out purposes even more distant from the intentionality of a personal plot. I analyze later the ways in which a Quentin thus dysfunctional serves Faulkner—as K. serves Kafka and Marcel serves Proust—less for characterological development than as a lens permitting a diagnostic take upon troubles larger than his own. Faulkner joins Proust and Kafka in deploying a central protagonist in such ways as to make *what he does* subordinate to the larger ramifications of *where he is*. For now, though, let us unpack further the stakes of Faulkner's rewriting his protagonists' interiority, his subverting the sanctity of their *"central I-Am's private own"* (*Absalom*, 115; emphasis in the original).

As we know, it took Faulkner three prior novels before he "learned" how to write a Benjy or a Quentin Compson. Faulkner's earlier fiction is still invested in the narrative of "I." We can now further explore, not how he invented a new rhetoric for articulating damaged subjectivity, but why he might have wanted to do so. Why would a writer suddenly desire to elude (in himself, his protagonists, and his readers) a rehearsal of the story of "I"? The simplest answer may have to do with Faulkner's need to call into deeper question than realism *can* the propriety of the subject's insertion within the social—a need so pressing that it catalyzes a new rhetoric for representing human being in (socialized) space/time. In Adorno's words, "Identity is the primal category of ideology." All ideology—which is to say all socially sponsored paradigms of individual identity—strives toward the suturing of "I." Louis Althusser has famously argued that there is no subjectivity without ideological alignment, even as there would be no ideology without subjects who orient themselves by entering it. My capacity to center my "I" is enabled by stances embodied in (groups of) others—parents, friends, others belonging to the same race, gender, class, country—stances offered (sometimes insisted) that I variously refuse, internalize, and revise. In so doing, over time, I become I.

As I argued above, realism is dedicated to becoming "I" over time–a becoming full of trial and adventure. Trial especially; realist fiction regularly submits my becoming "I" to pressures that either ratify it or mandate change. For Elizabeth, David, Dorothea, and Densher: Darcy must replace Wickham; Agnes, Dora; Ladislaw, Casaubon; and Milly, Kate. The story of becoming "I" proceeds on four assumptions: (1) that time progresses in orderly fashion and that I can remount it; (2) that over time I can come to know others around me and make better choices; (3) that I achieve, eventually, ideological alignment; and (4) that I register others who enter my orbit as intelligible dimensions of myself. None of this is true of Faulkner's Benjy or Quentin Compson, his Temple Drake or Darl Bundren, his Joe Christmas or Thomas Sutpen.

Refusal to deliver the "I"-narrative reconfigures the novel's capacity for resolution, and in so doing revises as well the call on the reader's judgment. For judgment is the reason-fueled, Enlightenment-driven activity centrally invoked in realism: judgment based on knowing. Realism aspires to ever finer judgments; its plots are made up of bad judgments superseded by better ones. It presses forward, toward increasingly resourceful subject orientations. For these plots to function, the above assumptions must operate: the capacity to remount time, to know others objectively, to achieve ideological alignment, and to undergo one's experience in such a way as to confirm one's identity. In realism the facts of the case emerge in time, earlier misassessments get revised, the subject's viable social orientation comes—however painfully—into focus.

In assuming that I can come to know others accurately and judge them accordingly, something further is in play—a fantasy of detachment, completion, and innocence. In judging, I seem to secure a certain distance from what I judge: I attend more to "the other seen as it really is," than to myself in the act of assessing it. I have achieved knowledge of what I judge and am done with it. This stance of fantasized detachment simultaneously enacts my innocence: I imagine myself free(d). Levinas: "If freedom denotes the mode of remaining the same in the midst of the other, knowledge [the knowing of another on my terms] . . . contains the ultimate sense of freedom" (*Totality*, 45). In judging, I cease to see the intricacy with which I shape and share the scene I see, cease to note the other's unremitting and reciprocal hold upon me. That we judge critically every day of our

lives, that judging is perhaps our chief psychic defense for keeping ourselves clear of what might otherwise enter us, has led Elias Canetti to write:
"No special knowledge is thought necessary [for judgment]; those who
have the capacity to abstain from judgment can be counted on the fingers
of one hand. Judgment is a disease and one of the most widespread; hardly
anyone is immune from it."[20]

Faulkner's great work shares with modernist fiction more generally a
refusal to indulge in the fatuity, so to speak, of a judgment-centered stance
toward its materials. If reason-governed "trial" is a central activity fueling
realism—a careful trying of the materials over time, to get them (and thus
oneself in relation to them) into finer focus enabling judgment—then it is
telling that perhaps the most famous modernist novel turns "trial" on its
head. Kafka's *Trial* enacts, as Adorno says, "the trial of a trial." This time a
genuine trial though: a trial of the subject's capacity to map, judge, and
master the object. Joseph K. learns no more about his trial, at novel's end,
than he knew when it began. Likewise, Joyce's Bloom learns nothing in his
twenty-four hours, Mann's Castorp passes his seven years atop the mountain as in a heady, yet personally weightless parenthesis, Proust's Marcel is
stuck for several thousand pages in a fluid time zone somewhere between
childhood and early manhood. These novels refuse, like Faulkner's, to
grant their protagonists the ever more accurate judgments of their world
that constitute maturation. For such modernists, the underlying drama of
the subject that countless realist novels deploy—yet another story of the "I"
of "I can"—has revealed a parochialism at once myopic and imperial. This
well-worn story of Ulysses heading home remains enclosed within a self-
protectiveness incompatible with the trial of spirit itself. It is closed to fear
and trembling, it does not dream of thawing the frozen sea within, it is too
attached to self-sameness to take such chances. Such adherence to the "I"
remains—in Levinas's terms—"the guide and guarantee of the whole spiritual adventure of being. But this is why this adventure is no adventure"
(*Otherwise*, 99).

Against such a background Faulkner forges a rhetoric of "not I" in *The
Sound and the Fury*. The noncontradictory narrator who tells his three earlier novels disappears into the immediacy of Benjy, Quentin, and Jason.
Faulkner has to become "not I," one surmises, because he has realized that
any voice he assumes as "I" is enabled and inflected by the judgments of his
ambient culture, is the furnished voice of a citizen of that culture. The wisdom and authority he can articulate in his own voice are, willy-nilly,
Southern wisdom and authority—the voice (however qualified) of the
white master. (Under the sway of Gavin Stevens, he will later grant great

swatches of text to the blandishments of this voice.) But in his finest work he undertakes a different task: not to *speak* Southern wisdom and authority at all, but rather to put them under an unparalleled diagnostic stress. In *The Sound and the Fury* he first succeeds in staging the clash and tension of his characters' stances, while himself remaining silent.

He ceases to be a narrative *voice* and emerges as a *stylistic performance*. The distinction is critical, for "performance" accommodates writerly identity differently than "one's own voice" does. Performance allows the writer Faulkner to *be* what his fiction *does*. It is *style*, in the largest sense, that delivers artistic Faulkner from the grip of biographical Faulkner. No overarching writerly identity—sustained in time—is at issue. The identity-revealing time in a schema of performativity is present time.

Indeed, if Joe Christmas could understand his own identity as past-inflected but *present-enacted* performance rather than as the timeless (yet unknown) essence of inherited blood, if he could accommodate his sense of self to the moment-by-moment enacting of self that his creator actually depicts, he would—cease to be Joe Christmas. "I got some nigger blood in me," he tells Bobbie; "you're what?" she responds (*Light*, 543). In turning attribute ("some nigger blood") into essence ("you're what?"), her reply recapitulates the race neurosis of the South. Identity is posited as singular and inalterable essence. It is deranging him that he is not sure who he is— i.e., who he was born as and must die as. Faulkner leaves *that* identity blank while showing, page after page, his performative one. Occurring in the moving present moment, outside the reach of any idiom of fatality or the "Player," performance enacts what Faulkner called (in *As I Lay Dying*) the speechless "real" that remains "on the ground," beneath the insistent word fables that rise into the air. What is said about Christmas— nigger/rapist/murderer—are overarching fictions that rise into the air, an airy unreality that will nevertheless mandate his death. Communal judgment is based on word fables, narratives of an essence either timeless or sutured over time, predigested, murderous. Christmas must become communally identified, posited as a full "I," before he can be killed. Out of the gap between such communal fables of unreality and the speechless real erupting in the present Faulkner generates his fiction of "not I."

Communal fables of unreality—the shared and speakable—require the assumptions posited above: that time proceeds in orderly fashion; that over time we come to know others objectively; that individual identity enters into ideological alignment; that selfhood is a function of experiences in space/time converted into a narrative of sustainable sameness. It becomes clear—in the developmental plot of realism—who is white, who is black, who is innocent, who is guilty. Communal fables of unreality supply the bread and butter of realism, a fiction of essences disclosed (over time) in their fullness and offered up for knowledge and judgment. Faulkner's great work, by contrast, makes the reader unknow that story. By centering not on a maturation of judgment over time but on the violence (mental and physical) of unharnessed moments, these novels privilege astonishment rather than familiar sequence. They deliver a diagnostic X-ray of a culture's abiding troubles rather than pretend to solve those troubles plotwise, by means of some consoling fable of unreality. In such work the standard figure/ground of realism—the swollen significance of the foregrounded individual agent, the shrunken (contributory) role of everything that is backgrounded—gets reconfigured. The subject remains foregrounded, yes, but he is no longer in control of the machinery. Faulkner writes no Ulyssean return to Ithaca achieved in orderly time and space; he engages in no pedagogic fables of unreality (uplift in its various forms). His best fiction is shaped to render the speechless real that remains on the ground.

Why does this desire to speak the speechless, this attempt to thaw the frozen deep, require *stylistic* innovation? I can perhaps best address that question by drawing on the work of Michel de Certeau. Examining the resources available to city dwellers within an inalterable cityscape, de Certeau distinguishes (in *The Practice of Everyday Life*) between *strategy* and *tactics*. De Certeau uses the distinction to characterize disempowered city dwellers' constrained yet precious arena of agency. If they had power, they would reshape the city's pathways. Lacking power, they practice the city's already-laid-down pathways, but they practice them *unpredictably*, in ways unpremeditated by the city fathers. *Strategy* may be defined, then, as the procedures of those who own space and can (re)shape it, while *tactics* refer to the responsive, straitened procedures of those who do not own, who instead poach on others' already shaped space. (Those with a full "I" concoct strategies; those hemmed in, reduced to "me" status, engage in tactics. Black signifying is a tactic, not a strategy. Tactics are the weapons of those powerless to change the plot but able to get one to see differently what that plot might mean.)

Let me generalize de Certeau's pertinence for understanding modernist experimentation. In Faulkner's work, as in modernism more generally, *style* enacts the writer's opposition to his culture's normative stories by way of *tactics* rather than *strategy*. *Style* is the life-blood of modernist *tactics*, even as *plot* is the fulcrum of realist *strategy*. Realist plot proposes, in its incremental way, to reshape reality by selectively allowing individual will to engage the real and (in a modest measure) to correct its abuses. Realist plot presupposes the power of the subject effectively to reckon—and reckon with—the social structure she or he lives within: hence Faulkner's scorn for its progressive pretenses. Modernist style refuses this story of reform, by reconfiguring the very figure/ground (subject/world) contract, thus conceding social ills their staying power, indeed their gravity. Its oppositional move occurs elsewhere, in its unprecedented formal diagnosis of a social reality it does not pretend—as art—to reshape.[21]

One goes to the three novelists under study here—as one goes to Joyce or Woolf or Mann or Musil–less for a new *plot* than for diagnostic insight into what the familiar one kept from the scene of representation. This diagnostic insight—arguably the most precious element in modernist fiction—is wrought into the text's *style*, its experimental form. Art's most compelling critique resides in its form: As Adorno said, "[R]eal denunciation is probably only a capacity of form, which is overlooked by a social aesthetic that believes in themes" (*Aesthetic*, 230). In reading modernist texts we are sprung free from plots of denouement and immersed instead in the formally interwoven play of echoing motifs—an immersion both immediately astonishing and cumulatively diagnostic. The modernist text's aim is less to resolve than to *awaken*, even as *Absalom, Absalom!* awakens us to the astonishingly repercussive emotional reality and fallout of the South's defeat some seventy years earlier. No consoling Tara here, no "figured out South," just a stylistically delivered diagnosis—implicit and subjunctive rather than declarative and judgmental—of the interwoven dimensions of a collapse not yet (not even now) recovered from.

Lukács was the first to indict modernist style as an evasion of social responsibility. His indictment is instructive because, like much current critique of modernism, it assumes generic standards of realism (focused on plot and character resolved in time and open to judgment). It took Adorno to show how Kafka's representational contortions enact—rather than ignore—unmastered social pressures deforming the urban subject. In like manner, the Faulkner text is compelling insofar as it articulates the modernist pathos of radiating damage rather than the realist ethos of gathered resolution. It has little interest in the canniness of "I can."[22] Quentin's last words in *Absalom, Absalom!* conclude the book only by *not* resolving its plot, and this because Quentin—like his author—is inescapably in and out of a scene he must but cannot master and hence judge.

The act of judgment, at its core, assuages an anxiety of our being in time itself, an anxiety about knowing what others in the world outside us mean: finally, now, once and for all. By contrast, Faulknerian style stages the hemorrhaging of prejudgment in the unanticipated and uncontrollable moment; it stages unknowing as an assault on the known. Faulkner's modernist style—his restless syntax and discontinuous sequences—registers time's disorienting power, not time mastered into noncontradictory significance and offered up for judgment. Faulkner's style lets him (and his fiction) not know and not judge, lets the fiction set up, by way of gathering juxtapositions and differed/deferred information, emergent patterns of dysfunction whose repercussions and permutations he sees—and lets us see—but does not pretend to see beyond. Such seeing achieves something perhaps finer than judgment based on knowledge. It converts into structural resource the blindness inherent in *all* present moments of seeing. Faulkner's greatest fiction articulates the caughtness of human judgment in time itself—rather than the fantasy of outwitting time that fuels judgment in its dismissive phase.

I have been exploring "not I" as the subject-position motivating Faulknerian stylistic innovation. I conclude by seeing "not I" as also the pathos of Faulknerian character. Although the Quentin of *Absalom* has been granted syntactic coherence, he nevertheless emerges in that later novel—in a more intricate way—as, yet again, a figure of stalemate. Pondering, in the mid-1930s, the wrecked Quentin of *The Sound and the Fury*, Faulkner seems to have grasped that his very depletedness, on the plot model of realism, would permit a different kind of serviceability. Quentin is 100 percent dead, plot-extinguished: what role can he play *now*? Of the many ghosts resurrected in *Absalom*, the most resonant is Quentin himself. Resurrected, not characterologically transformed: this is the same Quentin—still headed for his suicide, unresolved, plotless—but now available (suggestively like K. and Marcel) for the modernist task of diagnostic insight.

His own story over, no longer an "I," he is made to serve as an endlessly passive and available (read: open to assault) "me": "not a being, an entity, he was a commonwealth" (*Absalom,* 9). Executed like Joseph K. (but before the narrative even begins), invested—like Marcel—in all that he narrates as the prehistory within which he originated, Quentin is/is not Rosa's nephew, Sutpen's offspring, Bon and Henry's spectral third brother, Judith's (Caddy's) doomed fraternal lover. *Les unes dans les autres,* Faulkner-style. Being a mere Compson (sufficient to drive him to suicide in the earlier novel) is not confusing enough, in this most identificatory of Faulkner's novels. The opening pages' rhetoric inaugurates the con-fusing of poor Quentin's "here I am" into a miasmal mass, immeasurable and all-contaminating, made up of him and Rosa and the Sutpens, of Jefferson and Cambridge and the Caribbean and New Orleans, of now (1909–10) and

1865 and 1833 and 1808 . . . Quentin descends into his inescapable cultural history and its foreclosed future ("I am older at twenty than a lot of people who have died" [301]). In his demise Faulkner suggests that the *"maelstrom of unbearable reality"* (120, emphasis in the original) bears, not on the doings of one Quentin Compson, but on the crucifixion, at once deserved and undeserved, of the American South. The only subject appropriate for this undertaking is one already terminally othered.

PART 3

Beyond Knowing

Postmodern and Postcolonial Flights from Gravity

CHAPTER EIGHT

Adventures in Hyperspace

MEDITATING ON BLACKOUT

As I begin, on August 18, 2003, to consider how postmodern representational strategies differ from those of modernism, it seems appropriate to cite, not Lyotard, Fredric Jameson, Linda Hutcheon, David Harvey, or some other postmodern guru, but today's *International Herald Tribune*. (I write these words from Paris.) Four days ago an inexplicable power blackout brought to an immediate halt the normal lives of fifty million Americans and Canadians living within eight hundred miles of Lake Erie. "The grid" shut down. As James Glanz writes:

> The grid is the invisible circulatory system of the things humanity relies on, more and more, to let it operate untethered, free of the older mechanical world of rotary phones and strangely shaped keys made of polished brass. Portable phones, electronic hotel locks and Palm Pilots have replaced those vestiges of a clunkier age, creating an illusion of wireless mobility. In the process, people are becoming ever more dependent on the systole and diastole of the grid.
>
> And the grid is always there, humming with electronic life.
>
> Except during blackouts . . . (1)[1]

"Beyond knowing," I have entitled a central problematic of a postmodern fiction that tends to inscribe itself within the force field of a global and unimaginable grid. How does such a problematic differ from both the drama of knowing (my chapters on realism) and the drama of unknowing (my chapters on modernism)? Realist fiction, as we know, centers on a protagonist's achieving orientation. One begins clueless or misinformed; one learns to interpret clues, become better informed.

This generic story of "coming to know" (the bread and butter of Western fiction, regardless of era) turns untellable in the experimental, modernist fiction of Proust, Kafka, and Faulkner. Untellable, but not unsought: the errant Marcel, the arrested K. and metamorphosed Gregor, the stymied Quentin and confounded Joe—each attempts, unsuccessfully, to inhabit his territory effectively. But in the postmodern fiction I explore, the project of knowing appears not so much unachievable as irrelevant. These protagonists tend to locate in a fictional territory unamenable to orientation. The narrative of orientation, by contrast, adheres to an Enlightenment belief in mappable correspondence between one who would know and what is to be known. Belief, not proof: as Thomas Nagel skeptically puts it in his discussion of Cartesian assumptions, "Descartes's god is a personification of the fit between ourselves and the world for which we have no explanation but which is necessary for thought to yield knowledge."[2]

Suppose that this correspondence model (what Rorty calls the "mirror of nature") ceased to compel belief, and that the project of objective knowing was viewed with radical skepticism. Suppose that, given our immersion within an incessant array of technological practices that power multinational capitalism and constitute globalization, our relation to the real outside us has lost spatial/temporal specificity and exited from representability.[3] What might it mean to say that individuals no longer find themselves in a concrete here and now permitting a reliable take on their world?

Fredric Jameson argues, in "Cognitive Mapping," that subjective orientation and objective reality, in the era of later-twentieth-century global capitalism, have become incompatible notions. No correspondence between them obtains. We have reached "a situation in which we can say that if the individual experience is authentic, then it cannot be true; and that if a scientific or cognitive model of the same content is true, then it escapes individual experience."[4] Jameson sees the representational problem as both aesthetic and economic. He speaks of "the intensification of communications technology to the point at which capital transfers today abolish space and time, virtually instantaneously effectuated across national spaces," producing "new and unrepresentable symptoms in late-capitalist life" (260).[5] Elsewhere, calling this vertiginous realm where we currently live "hyperspace," Jameson concedes that "we do not yet possess the perceptual equipment to match this new hyperspace . . . in part because our perceptual habits were formed in that older kind of space I have called the space of high modernism" ("Postmodernism," in *Reader,* 219). Unrepresentable: no perceptual terms yet available for delineating "where we are." But to be unable to imagine "where we are" erases the pertinence and gravity of "here I am." By contrast with postmodern unrepresentability, modernist writers were eager to describe their space of unknowing as a shattered realist paradigm. "These fragments I have shored against my ruin" ("The Waste Land") rehearses a recognizable Eliotic refrain of order turned ironic, collapsed into shards.

Let us return to the blackout of August 14. My daughter Katherine experienced it in New York City, at virtually the same moment it began somewhere in that energy belt surrounding Lake Erie. But how could she work into her imagination of lived space/time an event whose cause was unknown and whose origin was hundreds of miles away? A speeding car or airplane, as Faulkner starkly reveals, can wreak havoc as it collides with earlier modes of life proceeding at slower speeds. We (especially we modernists) know how to represent such a collision. We can narrate or photograph it; it is a discrete, visualizable event. But "the grid," unlike the airplane, is not simply operative here and moving fast, it is simultaneously operative there and enabling movement at an indescribable velocity. It involves a kind of power we have trouble troping into spatial/temporal familiarity; anaclitic terms no longer apply.

This power's resistance to our images of space/time is doubled by its undoing of our assumptions about mass as well. The elements in the grid are so small as to be virtually weightless. (Who has not registered with awe—and perhaps a touch of vertigo—the increasing lightness of electronic technology? the way that each new generation of camera and cordless and palm pilot is lighter than preceding ones, the phenomenon, on removing the cover of one of these new objects, of seeing almost . . . *nothing?*) Gravity itself seems under attack. The gravity that underwrote Newton's science and realism's fiction attaches not just to individual objects but to our myth of matter itself. Gravity seems inseparable from matter's dignity, its abiding self-sameness. I suggest that the price that objects (including the most precious one, the embodied human being) tend to pay for their "lightness of being" in much postmodern fiction is the loss of identity-bestowing gravity.[6]

To explore these different stances toward the subject's locus in space/time, consider the opening sentences from a modernist and a postmodern novel:

Someone must have traduced Joseph K., for without having done anything
wrong he was arrested one fine morning. (Kafka, *The Trial*)

In a sense, I am Jacob Horner. (John Barth, *The End of the Road*)

Both openings disturb, but not in the same manner. The Kafka sentence
sets a trap that is never to be resolved. We will not learn whether someone
did, or did not, traduce Joseph K. But we do know, from that sentence, that
K.'s struggle will be with others who intrude into his space and time. We
know that something "arresting" happened this ("fine") morning, his thir-
tieth birthday. We know that his bedroom has been invaded by strangers
and that a moral dilemma (apparently no wrongdoing, yet arrest) has
begun. A commonsensical figure/ground scenario continues to be
invoked—self different from others, private space different from public
space, innocence different from guilt—even as this figure/ground norm
seems no longer to function.

In the terms of my argument, K. (and with him the reader) is suddenly
being pressed to *unknow* a set of social norms so familiar as to constitute
common sense itself. A system of primordial assumptions is entering *trial*.
The idea of "trial" is the motor of Kafka's novel, even as it undergirds liberal Western society. "The distinction between the true and the false,"
Perry Anderson writes, "is the ineliminable premise of any rational knowledge. Its central site is evidence."[7] I claimed, in the chapters above, that *The
Trial* is a scandalous text; I do not wish to soften that claim now. But its
scandal never escapes the frame of an interpretive dilemma that we could
characterize as lack of demonstrable evidence, known motive, and specified crime. In other words, a scandal of *unknowing:* we are positioned to
understand how it is supposed to work, but it will not work that way.

Though apparently milder, the postmodern sentence—"In a sense, I am
Jacob Horner"—is more destabilizing. The disturbed arena at first seems
more restricted—just a possible gap between "I" and my name, Jacob
Horner—but the shock waves go further. We are far from a Defoe-like
incognito (Moll Flanders's real name is not Moll Flanders). No name could
denote Horner's identity because Horner has none to denote; identity here
is only "in a sense identity." Inside Jacob Horner is nothing identifiable
(his job is accidental, his relation to others accidental, his gestures and feelings learned and arbitrary). He has no discrete, self-identifying gravity (he
cannot die).[8] But he is cunning enough to talk Rennie Morgan into eavesdropping on her all-American husband, Joe. Rennie demurs: "Real people
aren't any different when they're alone. . . . What you see is authentic."

"Horseshit," Horner replies. "Nobody's authentic. Let's look."[9] What they see is Joe Morgan in front of the mirror antically rehearsing the authoritative gestures that support his all-American role, then rushing back to his writing desk, "his tongue gripped purposefully between his lips at the side of his mouth . . . masturbating and picking his nose at the same time. I believe he also hummed a sprightly tune in rhythm with his work" (70–71).

The gap between public performance and private discovery at first seems telling here, yet no spatial binary operates, in terms of which Joe Morgan—in either of his roles, flag waving or masturbating—might be authentic. (The "sprightly tune" Joe hums sabotages any attempt to code his masturbating and nose picking as his deeper reality. Further glimpses could reveal other Joes, ad infinitum.) If every enactment of human being is an arbitrary performance, a mask that conceals nothing deeper beneath, then this apparently revelatory scene hardly constitutes evidence. As the "Doctor" explains to Horner, it is all a matter of masks: "Don't think there's anything behind them: *ego* means *I,* and *I* means *ego,* and the ego by definition is a mask. . . . If you sometimes have the feeling that your mask is *insincere*—impossible word!—it's only because one of your masks is incompatible with another" (90).

Kafka's Joseph K. does not know where he is; the reader's "trial" in engaging that novel is to wonder, increasingly, whether K. knows who he is. But Barth's "in a sense Jacob Horner" neither does nor does not know who he is (a case of knowing or unknowing); there is no "who he is" not to know (a case of beyond-knowing). He has no specific gravity. We could not say of him, as Kierkegaard has Abraham say of himself: "here I am." This three-word statement meets the minimal requirement for trial of any sort: a genuine subject ("I") who can be present ("am") in space and time ("here"). As Locke saw over three centuries ago, personhood is about accountability. By contrast, nothing that we see of Jacob Horner, private or public, *could* count as evidence. In Anderson's terms, we are in postmodern limbo, where, since the notion of "evidence" has lost its bearing, there can be no trial. Nothing can be *tried*—an activity that affects subjectivity in ways at once spatial (involving objects that enter our ken and, once approached and analyzed, reveal something pertinent) and temporal (involving projects that we launch and that, in the course of time, prove to be fruitful or not). "Evidence" and "trial" belong to a vocabulary of the developmental subject in space/time, a lexicon whose viability enables realist fiction, whose dysfunction launches much modernist fiction, and whose irrelevance characterizes a good deal of postmodern fiction.

When space no longer yields settings that could ground subjectivity, when time no longer permits experience that could enlighten subjectivity, is it any wonder that subjects no longer house specific gravity? It is time to test these claims, by a series of comparisons between modernist and postmodern texts. I begin anecdotally, with Faulkner and Pynchon.

A DIFFERENCE OF PENISES

In 1999 the annual Faulkner and Yoknapatawpha Conference sought to explore the intersection of Faulkner and postmodernism. I spoke at this conference, but I shall say nothing here about my paper. The connections variously proposed between Faulkner and postmodern paradigms that succeeded him tended to be brittle and (in my view) unpersuasive. One proposed connection, however, seemed to me so insistently misguided that it "worked" on me, highlighting (all unintentionally) Faulkner's modernist orientation.

The speaker's topic was Faulkner and Pynchon, focusing on resemblances between *Absalom, Absalom!* and *Gravity's Rainbow.* As the talk continued, the list of proposed traits in common grew, and increasingly something seemed awry—as in that picture with the caption: "What's wrong with this picture?" At a certain moment in the lecture, I got a glimmer of what was wrong. Drawing on the fact that, in *Absalom,* Sutpen's progeny fail to re-produce him—his reproductive power turns foreign to his own design—the speaker made the connection with how, in *Gravity's Rainbow,* Slothrop's penis follows a trajectory likewise alien to his design(s). Thanks to twentieth-century microtechnology (weightlessness counts here), a certain "Mystery Stimulus" scientifically attached to the infant Slothrop's penis allows him to be monitored by unnamed governmental agencies. *Gravity's Rainbow* goes on to do wonderful things with Slothrop's coopted member, but I remained arrested by the deeper difference undermining this surface resemblance: Slothrop's penis and Sutpen's are nonnegotiably unlike each other. I knew this immediately, but not what it portended.

One difference is that Sutpen's penis (the physical organ itself) cannot be isolated within the representational strategy operative in *Absalom, Absalom!* Its power or impotence is of course crucial to the dynastic design Faulkner is exploring, but there can be no question of textually "detaching" it and exploiting it for domestic or foreign powers. This is not an issue of propriety, of what may or may not be said. Rather, Sutpen remains an embodied figure of focused will and failure of will; his internal contradictions (and he has them aplenty) play themselves out within a unified corporeal schema. His penis is both unspeakable and unspeakably his own. That he begets (the perhaps not-white) Charles Bon with that penis speaks not to the political cooptability of body parts but rather to the scandalous race logic determining (in the U.S. South, but not in Haiti) that the (perhaps not-white) Eulalia Bon is unsuitable as wife and mother.

Unlike Sutpen, Slothrop is represented (like others in *Gravity's Rainbow*) as possessing only a modicum in the way of developed identity—little specific gravity. Obviously fabricated by his creator for particular functions (his name calls attention to this), Slothrop's body is available for social and textual dismantling and reconstitution. No problem, while doing this, for Pynchon to coopt and alienate Slothrop's penis from Slothrop's own organizing regime of personhood. (The technology making this seem plausible, just emerging in the 1960s, is becoming commonplace now, at the beginning of the twenty-first century.) Within the textual world of *Gravity's Rainbow*, Slothrop (thanks to his rescriptable member) can become "organically" aligned within political organizations utterly alien to his sense of who he is. Engineered so as to be somatically foreign to himself, but unaware of this, he is, for much of the novel, both Slothrop and not-Slothrop. (One cannot imagine Sutpen body-engineered into an ideological alignment utterly alien to his own consciousness.)[10] Pynchon makes use of Slothrop by wiring into him, puppetlike, the subject-overriding codes that organize the conspiratorial world of *Gravity's Rainbow*. A crucial result is that Slothrop is smaller, less agential, than Sutpen.

He is smaller in the sense that Pynchon's textual universe requires a large number of necessarily small players in order to operate at all (this game mandates a roster of dozens, if not hundreds). The only large player in *Gravity's Rainbow* is the unrepresentable "grid" itself. The numerous small players circulate along interpenetrating orbits, and Pynchon's genius is to coordinate and motivate/mystify these interpenetrations. In so doing, he bypasses the drama of individual subjective becoming. For this strategy to succeed, here as in the less ambitious but equally brilliant *V*, a good deal of geographic space is required (Pynchon's novels tend to cover lots of territory) and a number of unintegrated time frames. With respect to the representation of subjectivity, one stance, especially, must be kept at bay. This stance, as insistently refused by Pynchon's text as it is mandated by Faulkner's, is the soliciting of identifications.

Sutpen is large because he accommodates (as does Charles Bon) intense narratorial and readerly identifications. Take away the premise of identification—of finding oneself emotionally caught up in the dynamics of a drama not one's own—and one loses not only the representational strategy of *Absalom, Absalom!* (a novel teeming with identificatory narrators). One loses as well the designed impact of much modernist fiction. *The Trial* has room for only one identification—ours with K.—but that one is indispensable for the work to "work." One could say the same with respect to Gregor, to Georg, even to the ape in "Report to an Academy." These texts, however bizarre, insist on putting the reader *there,* inside the skin of their protagonist. One cannot read *A la Recherche du temps perdu* without identifying, massively, with the thought and feeling processes of Marcel, even as his own narrative is memorably punctuated by his anguished identifications with his mother and grandmother. Every reader who cares for *The Sound and the Fury* becomes immersed, at a level deeper than anticipated, in the incurable pathos of Benjy and Quentin.

The soliciting of identifications is perhaps the fundamental activity at work in the modernist fiction under study here. Proust, Kafka, and Faulkner variously realized that the plight of unknowing is capable of moving the reader at a level more intimate, more disturbingly faithful to one's actual experience in time, and more diagnostically revealing than the myriad stories of knowing that fill the shelves of realist fiction. Capable of moving the reader: for all these writers, the phenomenon of being moved by another's plight is foregrounded so as to *matter.* Although the novelist Evelyn Scott claimed, over seventy years ago, that Benjy's distress (in *The Sound and the Fury*) compels us as no drama of well-adjusted protagonists does, modernism's larger invocation of readerly identifications is still insufficiently explored. It may require postmodernism's seemingly generic rebuke of identification for us to begin to recognize what was at issue in modernism's investment in this stance.

At a minimum, at issue is the plight of characters with specific gravity—characters whose inner lives and outer dilemmas are shaped to intersect imaginatively with the problems and possibilities of others attending to them, both within and outside the fictions themselves. Everything about the crafting of these novels testifies to identification as a *value.* It is no accident that modernist fiction invented stream of consciousness: a representational technique as foreign to earlier realism as it is to later postmodernism. What is stream of consciousness if not a mode for representing characters' consciousness (their specific gravity) flowing—apparently unedited— through a time that feels like the genuine present? Unlike the gathered and composed subjectivity of realist protagonists (figures capable of knowing), equally unlike the stylized and reified subjectivity of the Slothrops of postmodern fiction (figures diminished by the coded language that speaks them, thus fixed and seen around, incapable of development), stream of consciousness is subjectivity dramatized as ongoing thought and feeling, in process rather than control, caught up in the state of unknowing.[11]

The argument of these six paragraphs was not available to me as I listened to that Faulkner-Pynchon lecture a number of years ago. All I knew then was that a telling difference in fictional procedures was being ignored. When I questioned the speaker immediately after the lecture, I got no concession that there was anything to discuss. Persevering with my questions (all this was taking place in public), I suddenly remembered that moment in Jameson's first major essay on postmodernism when he contrasts E. L. Doctorow's *Ragtime* with the earlier *Book of Daniel.* This is Doctorow's transition, Jameson argues, from a seemingly authentic rhetoric of modernist anguish to a coded one of postmodern pastiche. Daniel and his circle versus the cast of figures in *Ragtime:* these two groups of characters are written in different rhetorics. The "Daniel rhetoric" invites identification (it seems to speak the real), thus generating Daniel as a figure with specific gravity. By contrast, the rhetoric of *Ragtime,* as Jameson puts it, "operates powerfully and systematically to reify all those characters [historical and invented alike] and to make it impossible for us to receive their representation without the prior interception of already-acquired knowledge or doxa" (207). They come to us as figures-in-discourse, openly coded, offered up more for reflection than identification. They access their own interiority in an already commodified language that announces itself *as* language.[12] At my stammered version of this claim the speaker slightly relented. I went away knowing I had to figure out (as I have sought to do in the foregoing pages) what was wrong with that picture.

Moving now to a sequence of more sustained comparisons—all of them focused on the modeling of the subject in space and time—I seek to illuminate the most salient tendential differences between the earlier and the later practices ("tendential" because the highly selective subset of texts under consideration permits no claim for hard and fast distinctions between modernist and postmodern stances). We begin with Rilke's *Notebooks of Malte Laurids Brigge* (1910) and Calvino's *Invisible Cities* (1972).

CHAPTER NINE

Urban Nightmare and City Dreams

Rilke and Calvino

"IT IS ALL BROKEN UP INSIDE ME"

There is but one city in *The Notebooks of Malte Laurids Brigge*—Paris—and it appears unlivable: thus Malte's opening words, "So, then people do come here in order to live; I would sooner have thought one died here" (13). In a haunting, notebook-fragmented, stream-of-consciousness rhetoric, the young Malte Laurids Brigge rehearses his ongoing disorientation. Having fled the aristocratic estates of his childhood, Malte can make no connection between their (past) cohesion and Paris's (present) confusion.[1] The city continually aggresses him: "Electric street-cars rage ringing through my room. Automobiles run their way over me. A door slams. Somewhere a window-pane falls clattering. Then suddenly a dull, muffled noise from the other side, within the house. Someone is climbing the stairs. Coming, coming incessantly. Is there, there for a long time, then passes by. And again the street. A girl screams: Ah tais-toi, je ne veux plus. An electric car races up excitedly, then away, away over everything" (14). A paranoid attentiveness fills this passage. Malte's sensibility records not the wholeness of entities but their assaultive edges—the detached pane, the muffled roar, the noise of steps being climbed, the girl's isolated scream. Space has become the setting for the sensation of being invaded; objects refuse to keep their distance.

The abiding assurance of Newtonian space—that it serves to separate objects—is here revoked. As Richard Swinburne describes the prephenomenological model, "No two material objects can have the same primary place at the same temporal instant."[2] But the streetcar outside is unbearably inside; the car on the street repeatedly runs him over.[3] Malte registers as a figure of exacerbated nerves, driven by a quicksilver sensorium outside the representational norms of realism's assurance of gathered, free-standing subjectivity. Such a balance was secured (in part at least) by an Enlightenment model of space as both (overtly) subject-neutral and (covertly) subject-manageable. (Witness the sanity-preserving barrier between home and office regularly installed in representations of Victorian culture, and so insidiously removed from Kafka's urban space). Malte can neither familiarize this city nor escape its otherness, he can only be penetrated by it.

Immured in a Parisian space that offers no stabilizing ceremonies, Malte starts to conceptualize time as a nonlinear medium hostile to maturation. He is suddenly overcome by childhood memories not worked through, more frightening than ever:

> I am lying in my bed, five flights up, and my day . . . is like a dial without hands. As a thing long lost lies one morning in its old place . . . fresher almost than at the time of its loss . . . so here and there on my coverlet lie lost things out of my childhood and are as new. All forgotten fears are there again.
>
> The fear that a small, woolen thread that sticks out of the hem of my blanket may be hard, hard and sharp like a steel needle; the fear that this little button on my night-shirt may be bigger than my head, big and heavy; the fear that this crumb of bread now falling from my bed may arrive glassy and shattered on the floor, and the burdensome worry lest at that really everything will be broken . . . the fear that some number may begin to grow in my brain until there is no room for it inside me . . . and the fear that I might not be able to say anything because everything is beyond utterance . . . I asked for my childhood and it has come back . . . it has been useless to grow older. (60–61)

The passage virtually choreographs a darkly modernist program of subject/ space/time. Time ceases to permit progress, all that seemed overcome (or at least put behind) returns more ominous than ever, objects lose their self-sameness and their immobile other-locatedness, threatening with the possibility of approach and assault (sharper, larger, more lacerating, more suffocating). The fear of madness returns, which perhaps screens a more abiding fear: that, to articulate such experience, Malte will have to cease being Malte. He has neither language nor syntax for saying what he is on the verge of becoming. His experience in no way matches realism's developmental subject in familiar space/time. Wisdom is not a reward of passing time: "it has been useless to grow older." Or, as Malte's mother puts it, "There are no classes in life for beginners; it is always the most difficult that is asked of one right away" (80).

Unknowing: one would know, but cannot. The hardest is asked of us from the beginning. Time no longer unfolds pedagogically: beginnings that lead satisfyingly to middles and then to ends. The task of representing such incoherence spurs modernism's innovative and dislocating forms. Modernism refuses to make time "easy," to supply, in advance, the coherence that present experience will obtain only later, when re-cognized. Caught up in a city-space that disorients, immersed in a temporality that "fibrillates" rather than advances, Malte sees, in others around him, doubles of his own mounting incoherence. By contrast, consider how, on all the city streets of Dickens's and Dostoevsky's novels, there is no one the protagonist *can* meet who does not eventually contribute to his or her development. But Malte sees, on the streets of Paris, a woman with her face in her hands, and the face sticking to the hands when she attempts to raise it. He sees a man inside a *crêmerie* undergoing a fatal interior event—cerebral hemorrhage? aneurysm? He sees a man on the street desperately, elaborately, trying to manage an inhuman energy ransacking his body. I cite this last hypnotic vignette at some length:

> But then I perceived . . . that in this person's busy hands there were two movements: one a rapid, secret movement, with which he covertly flipped the collar up, and that other movement, elaborate, prolonged, as if exaggeratedly spelled out, which was meant to put it down. This observation disconcerted me so much that two minutes passed before I realized that in the man's neck, behind his hunched-up overcoat and the nervous activity of his hands, was the same horrible, bi-syllabic hopping which had just left his legs. From that moment I was bound to him. I understood that this hopping impulse was wandering about his body, trying to break out here and there. . . . I forgot to mention that he carried a stick. . . . And, in his searching anxiety, the idea had occurred to him of holding this stick against his back, at first with one of his hands (for who knew what the other might yet be needed for?) right along his spine, pressing it firmly into the small of his back . . . I knew that as he walked and made ceaseless efforts to appear indifferent and absentminded, that awful jerking was accumulating in his body; in me, too, was the anxiety with which he felt it growing and growing, and I saw how he clung to his stick, when the jolting began inside him. The expression of his hands then became so severe and unrelenting that I placed

all my hope in his will, which was bound to be strong. But what could a will do here. . . . His will had given way at two points, and the concession had left behind in the obsessed muscles a gentle, enticing stimulation and this compelling two-beat rhythm. . . . He turned his head slightly, and his gaze wavered over sky, houses and water, without grasping anything. And then he gave in. His stick had gone, he stretched out his arms as if to take off and fly, and there broke out of him a sort of elemental force that bent him forward and dragged him back and made him nod and bow, flinging dance-force out of him in among the crowd. For already many people were around him, and I saw him no more. (64–66)

Need one say that no realist novelist represents someone's bodily behavior in this manner and at this length? Dostoevsky choreographs every second of Raskolnikov's movement in the pawnbroker's apartment as he commits/botches the murder, but such registration of the body's second-by-second gestures is nothing if not pedagogic. No reader exits from that scene without learning that Raskolnikov's feverishly willed act is abusing his essential being, and that his spiritual identity suffers accordingly. By contrast, Malte records the amoral, unplotted release of monstrous bodily energies. The vignette is a Cartesian nightmare of *res extensa* taking its revenge on *res cogitans*. There is nothing salutary here, nothing to be learned from this terrifying dance, everything to be feared.

Indeed, the larger Enlightenment narrative turns away from such vignettes. When Locke wishes to distinguish human will from compelled matter, he goes precisely to St. Vitus dance: "Convulsive motions agitate his legs, so that though he wills it ever so much, he cannot by any power of his mind stop their motion, (as in that odd disease called *chorea sancti viti*), but he is perpetually dancing; he is not at liberty in this action, but under as much necessity of moving, as a stone that falls, or a tennis-ball struck with a racket" (*Essay,* 2.15.8). A human being stripped of agency reduces to mere Newtonian matter: "but what could a will do here"? Rilke choreographs a recognizable human portrait, but one gone radically defective, in which the ravaged body slips every tattered disciplinary control urged by the unavailing mind. The whole thing unfurls in slow motion: a singular subject's minutely detailed moves in specified space and time. We see him—unique, mesmerizing, scandalous. As with the defaced woman and the dying man, Malte identifies involuntarily with this figure, and through Malte's identification comes the reader's.

This vignette of inhuman energy routing the programs of human reason crystallizes Malte's modernist project: how to escape the order-producing conventions of his previous education, access his unspeakable core, yet not go under? Imagining within himself a dying man's tachycardial gusts of consciousness—"Yes, he knew that he was now withdrawing from everything: not merely from human beings" (51)—Malte sees the man defend (his idea of) himself no longer (just as the hopping man "gave in"), and he wonders what it would be for him as well to yield all: "For a while yet I can write all this down and express it. But there will come a day when my hand will be far from me. . . . But this time I shall be written. I am the impression that will change" (52). Self-unknowing finally, but perhaps transfiguration as well: the promiscuously detached hands that have haunted Malte throughout his Paris experience here return in the figure of his own hands, now far from him and no longer his—hands that might write himself for once authentically (however outrageously), outside familiar terms.

"ALL ARE ONLY ASSUMPTIONS"

In place of Rilke's Paris—singular, real, nightmarish—Calvino's *Invisible Cities* produces fifty-five cities of human fantasy, each differing from the others, all meant to tease the reader out of thought. The frame of these travels is an intermittent, spatially and temporally unspecified set of imagined interchanges between Marco Polo and Kublai Khan. The latter's kingdom includes these cities (and more); they are ostensibly his yet he has actually visited none of them. The former's native city is an absent Venice against which he reads every city he describes as foreign and fabulous. Both men thus access these conjured cities as sites of translation: places mediated by words, their coherence dependent on their difference from other places known and encountered. Marco tells his master to make room for them all, "not because they are all equally real, but because all are only assumptions."[4]

Rilkean singularity is absent—and with it, specific gravity. Each city has its appeal in its divergence from the others, all of them word constructs, "only assumptions." It is tempting to think of this bewitching text as, among other things, a fantasia premised on Saussurean linguistics. For Saussure, as for Calvino, language is primarily nonreferential—an internal system of "empty differences" in which sounds and ideas take on their value by way of their difference from other sounds and ideas. The intrinsic protocols of the system trump in importance any referential use it might have. These are, correspondingly, cities without reference to the real, visitable only in Calvino's prose.

More, if Rilke's city is predicated as a pre-existing reality hostile to any of Malte's projects, Calvino's cities are in sync with the subjective stances of those who inhabit them. The charm of these verbal cityscapes inheres in the imaginative fusion of subject/space/time configured in each of them. A couple of examples (no single one would do) from the book's opening will have to suffice:

CITIES AND MEMORY 1

Leaving there and proceeding for three days toward the east, you reach Diomira, a city with sixty silver domes, bronze statues of all the gods, streets paved with lead, a crystal theater, a golden cock that crows each morning on a tower. All these beauties will already be familiar to the visitor who has seen them also in other cities. But the special quality of this city for the man who arrives there on a September evening, when the days are growing shorter and the multicolored lamps are lighted all at once at the doors of the food stalls and from a terrace a woman's voice cries ooh!, is that he feels envy toward those who now believe they have once before lived an evening identical to this and who think they were happy, that time. (7)

CITIES AND MEMORY 2

When a man rides a long time through wild regions he feels the desire for a city. Finally he comes to Isidora, a city where the buildings have spiral staircases encrusted with spiral seashells, where perfect telescopes and violins are made, where the foreigner hesitating between two women always encounters a third, where cockfights degenerate into bloody brawls among the bettors. He was thinking of all these things when he desired a city. Isidora, therefore, is the city of his dreams: with one difference. The dreamed-of city contained him as a young man; he arrives at Isidora in his old age. In the square there is the wall where the old men sit and watch the young go by; he is seated in a row with them. Desires are already memories. (8)

Imaginative fusion: the subject encountering these fantasy spaces is wrought into their logic, though the logic is hardly sentimental. Both vignettes move toward an Escherian disappearing act, in which the substantiality of the desiring subject seems to collapse in upon itself, thanks to a trick of passing time and elusive space. The apparent present-tense immediacy of "you reach" (in the first vignette) dissolves, as "you" morphs, as it were, into that spectral congregation of those who (believe they) have earlier experienced what "you" are now experiencing, and who "think they were happy, that time." (But, by implication, they were not? Were to forget later that they were not? Were, as in both of these scenarios, to experience the essential mockery of desire itself, caught up in absence and by definition unrealizable?)

Both vignettes, indeed all the vignettes in *Invisible Cities,* are emphatically *written:* we would never confuse them with the stream-of-consciousness journal entries of a Malte seeking, at the moment, to figure things out in a language we are to take as "really his." More, these vignettes are written in that elevated lexicon that Roland Barthes calls Literature: they serenely announce to us, through syntax and vocabulary, that the sequences to be narrated enact not the haphazard immediacies of life but the mediated arabesques of Literature. To return to Jameson's description of the rhetoric of *Ragtime,* such sentences announce their literary provenance, operating "powerfully and systematically to reify all those characters and to make it impossible for us to receive their representation without the prior interception of already-acquired knowledge or doxa." Adding to this sense of the nonreferentiality of Calvino's prose is the recurrence of phrases like "it is said," "it is rumored," "they say." Such phrases are charged with representing the territory of multiple, atemporal, and nonspatial "assumptions": cities of words. (Not, however, that the vignettes thereby lack definition; each city swiftly emerges into imaginative view, a complex of characteristics as shapely as they are lacking in spatial/temporal reference.)

One will not have failed to notice the 1 and the 2 that follow these citations from "Cities and Memory," signaling a larger organizational system. *Invisible Cities* is structured with a rigor rarely found in fiction: there are nine parts to this novel (if we call it a novel), of which the first and the last comprise ten vignettes apiece. The seven (middle) parts are composed of five vignettes apiece; each vignette is assigned its topic; each topic precedes (and succeeds) another topic according to an undeviating sequential pattern. The ten vignettes of part 1 include four on "Cities and Memory," three on "Cities and Desire," two on "Cities and Signs," and one on "Thin Cities." Part 2 follows suit by way of a fifth vignette on "Cities and Memories," a fourth on "Cities and Desire," a third on "Cities and Signs," a second on "Thin Cities," and a final vignette inaugurating a new topic ("Trading Cities"), yielding a structure of repetitions that unfolds as 5, 4, 3, 2, 1. Parts 3 through 8 reenact this structure without variation, issuing into a final part 9 whose ten vignettes ensure that every topic introduced will have been satisfyingly rehearsed five times.

One notices, as well, the casual "Orientalism" that runs throughout *Invisible Cities.* Perhaps Literature is unlikely to give us anything other than a "literary" lexicon of "the Orient." At any event Calvino's text delights in scenarios of domes, statues, precious metals, nubile girls, camels, caravans, tankards, temples, bracelets (these items all taken from vignettes in part 1). Or perhaps one should say that the very designation of Literature annuls the charge of mystified vocabulary, for Calvino's text—unlike the discursive practice of "Orientalism"—never urges us to take the verbal for the real.[5]

The deployment of gender shadows the text no less than its languorous "Oriental" lexicon. Every city is feminine (the names of fifty-two of them have the feminine ending "a," while nineteen have women's names). More, the voyager (like the reader) is inevitably figured as male—traveler, adventurer, the subject par excellence—even as the exotic delights and deceptions he is to encounter are predictably troped as women (alluring cities that function as elusive spaces of memory and desire, static yet chimerical). In making these critical remarks, however, I remember Jameson's warning that "we do not yet possess the perceptual equipment to match this new hyperspace" (*Reader,* 219). Does Calvino's overt refusal of referentiality clear his text of such vulgar charges as sexism or "Orientalism"? Be that as it may, I cannot see what Utopian possibilities might lurk within vignettes that, however fabulous, remind us of (gendered and cultural) arrangements only too familiar.[6] (Or is the question of "Utopian possibilities" likewise irrelevant in this postmodern context?)

I have suggested that the Pynchon text is wary of invoking readerly identification. That wariness operates here as well; these vignettes tease the mind, but the subjects and objects they deploy are hard to remember, swiftly replaced by others, discontinuous. Markedly omitted from *Invisible Cities* is any possibility of shock. (Even the monsters one meets in Calvino lack the wounding force of Rilke's deformed Parisians. Instead one encounters a literarily certified bestiary of unreal creatures: "sphinxes, griffons, chimeras, dragons, hircocervi, harpies, hydras, unicorns, basilisks" [160].) You (as traveler, as reader) cannot come up against anything penetrative. Rilke's phrase for Malte's sharp-edged damaging memories ("it is all broken up inside me" [30]) is inconceivable here. No one in *Invisible Cities* has discrete, private memories; no one has sustained interiority in which such memories might roil. There are in this elegant text no shards that wound. By contrast, Rilke's text of shock and unknowing requires Malte's immersion within a spatial/temporal manifold of objects (and other subjects) that refuse to (re)confirm his identity.

More, the *Notebooks* make clear that in the absence of confirmatory others, there is no confirmable self. Personal identity is nonnegotiably reciprocal. It requires "cooperation," even as knowing is reciprocal, dependent on viable correspondence between knower and known. Is it any surprise that, in *Invisible Cities*'s array of settings that are all merely "assumptions," the subject engaging these settings (usually a free-floating "you") is likewise emptied of substance? A central realist condition of *to be* is to be located in a specified space/time filled with specific objects and others. In the absence of that condition, in a postmodern landscape where whimsically revocable arrangements replace the discrete orientations that permit *encounter,* subjects tend to become thinner and lighter, assumptions without gravity.

Let us pursue this subject/space/time configuration further. One of the provocative topics of *Invisible Cities* is the noncoincidence of a place with its name. "Irene," for example, is a city utterly different, once inside it, than it appears to those at a distance (possessing of the city only its name)—a paradox on which the Khan expects Marco to shed some light:

> But Marco cannot do this: he has not succeeded in discovering which is the city that those of the plateau call Irene. For that matter, it is of slight importance: if you saw it, standing in its midst, it would be a different city; Irene is a name for a city in the distance, and if you approach, it changes. . . . There is the city where you arrive for the first time; and there is another city which you leave never to return. Each deserves a different name; perhaps I have already spoken of Irene under other names; perhaps I have spoken only of Irene. (124–25)

Again, an Escher-like effect occurs; one finishes the vignette with a slip-knottish feeling that Irene has evaporated into an elusive mindscape. The unreliability of place-names emerges—the ways in which places change once one has gone past their name and come to know them, even as they change again once one has left them, not to return. The passage ends deep in meditation.

At this juncture it may be instructive briefly to compare Proust's and Calvino's ways of representing the subject's encounter with the object. No less than Calvino, Proust is invested in the gap between our actual encounter with something outside ourselves, on the one hand, and the fantasy terms by which we access it prior to encounter, on the other. One vignette will stand in for countless others. When Swann is about to kiss the long-pursued Odette for the first time, he hesitates for a moment, thinking: "He had wanted to leave time for his mind to catch up with him, to recognise the dream which it had so long cherished and to assist at its realisation. . . . Perhaps, too, he was fixing upon the face of an Odette not yet possessed, nor even kissed by him, which he was seeing for the last time, the comprehensive gaze with which, on the day of his departure, a traveller hopes to bear away with him in memory a landscape he is leaving forever" (1:255).

The essential motif is the same: the fantasized encounter versus the realized one, the subject's ever-altering relation to objects and others. But whereas this tension is for Calvino, so to speak, intransitive—permitting the vignette to conclude in pure meditation—in Proust it leads to the tragicomedy of Swann's relationship with Odette. Unlike the postmodernists who come after, Proust endows with specific gravity the figures in this unmasterable game of encounter. Unlike the realists who come before, Proust reads its dynamic as incorrigibly lopsided, unamenable to improvement. Condemned to see Odette from within his own altering optic, Swann will marry this unsuitable woman and suffer for it. He lives the epistemological conundrum (misprision of the other, the bleeding of subjects into the objects they engage) as unknowing rather than as wisdom.

Finally, we might consider the status of oppositional motifs in Calvino's cities. Recurrently, his cities reveal an organizing contradiction at their conceptual core. Marozia is in fact "two cities: one of the rat, one of the swallow" (154). The rat city is infernal, an affair of carnage, sewers, and tombs. The swallow city is celestial, an affair of summer flights. The charm of the vignette lies in its ways of negotiating this opposition: "Marozia consists of two cities, the rat's and the swallow's; both change with time, but their relationship does not change; the second is the one about to free itself from the first" (155). City space, in this vignette, loses its discrete time-bound character, accommodating instead cyclical oppositions and dissolving, so to speak, into the timelessness of parable.

I conclude my analysis of Calvino with Penthesilea, a city whose identity is even more difficult to define than that of Irene or Marozia. For Penthesilea does not hover between contradictory understandings; rather, you cannot know, spatially, whether you are in it or out of it: "You have given up trying to understand whether, hidden in some sac or wrinkle of these dilapidated surroundings there exists a Penthesilea the visitor can recognize and remember, or whether Penthesilea is only the outskirts of itself. The question that now begins to gnaw at your mind is more anguished: outside Penthesilea does an outside exist?" (157–58). If one were tempted to say that the lexicon of such vignettes has little to do with the contemporary power grid of global capitalism, the figuring of Penthesilea's (non)borders might give pause. For the uselessness of markers is gestured toward in disturbingly similar ways. Space turns unimaginable (and what is a city without spatial confines?), becoming an inside for which there may be no outside: a conundrum no subject is ever summoned to negotiate.

Such oppositional, indeed Escherian, figuring of identity, joined with
the collapse of basic thought-enabling binaries, is far from modernism's
wrenching attack upon the premises of unified identity. The fractures so
insistent in modernist practice emerge as diagnostic (though not didactic):
Malte's mirrored plight in the fate of the de-faced woman and the hopping man, Marcel's echo in the range of characters—homosexual, Jew,
snob, hypochondriac—who surround him, Georg's fatal splitting into
friend/lover/son, K.'s simultaneous identity as prosecutor and victim,
Benjy and Quentin and Jason's narratives as inseparable, unintegratable
perspectives on a single Compson drama not narratable as such. These undoings operate in the service of a diagnostic unknowing, a coming to
unknow what one thought one knew, to split and pluralize what one has
taken as single or sutured, so as to bring into view (for us, not for the characters) the discontinuous and deterritorialized world in which the characters actually live. In a word, to limn their state of crisis.

Crisis is hardly a term to associate with *Invisible Cities*.[7] Subject/
space/time take on a different configuration, suavely enervated, discharged
of historicity, and answering to Henry Sussman's characterization of postmodern tendencies: "The past is no longer an origin, a time more authentic
than others because a greater degree of intimacy once prevailed there. It is,
rather, a relative position along an indifferent continuum—one might say a
tedium—of time" (177). Objects freed of the specificity of space and the
differential of time cease to engage the free-floating subjects all around
them. As Adorno knew, these terms take on value only so long as they
maintain their tensile interrelationship in the form of an encounter: "The
objectivity of truth really demands the subject. Once cut off from the subject, it becomes the victim of sheer subjectivity" (*Against Epistemology: A
Metacritique,* cited in Anderson, 54). Such loss of coordinates leads, in
Calvino, to a series (but perhaps also a tedium?) of gorgeous, weightless
flights. How a condition of "beyond knowing" might become compatible
with crisis, finding its way back into a politics of "terrible unquiet fuss,"[8] is
an issue we confront in the next modernist/postmodern contrast—between
Forster's *A Passage to India* and Rushdie's *The Satanic Verses.*

CHAPTER TEN

Passage and Passing

Forster and Rushdie

To what extent can subjects at home in one culture's norms for inhabiting space and time accommodate subjects aligned within another culture's model of space and time? At what point does the project of passage between cultures encounter such turbulence as to suffer defeat, or to eventuate in the undoing of the subject itself (the collapse of sustainable interiority)? Both questions put pressure on the guiding notion of my study: subjectivity as a set of norms for negotiating space and time. Furthermore, they highlight fundamental tensions between a postmodern and a postcolonial conception of the subject. For postcolonial thought, the capacity of Western and non-Western subjects to achieve passage into each other's cultural norms—to translate the other's norms viably, beyond stereotype—tends to trump other issues, so great is the need to develop this capacity. But for postmodern thought (invested in acute problematics of Western subjectivity itself), the agent of such passage—the *subject*—has perhaps become a passing notion.[1]

The postmodern writers under scrutiny in this study, at any rate, remain intent on dismantling a first-world assumption of free-standing, free-moving subjectivity. Extending modernist strategies for rebuking Enlightenment overconfidence, their postmodern texts subvert even more starkly the narrative of the sovereign subject coming to know. Yet, such an aesthetics of subversion, however deserved, is singularly ill suited for articulating third-world aspirations.[2] Without a minimally viable notion of the subject, it is hard to conceive of a politics of social transformation; the erasure of agency condemns in advance any possibility of coming to terms with the other. The work of Pynchon, Don DeLillo, and Calvino, among others, represents the incapacity of individuals not only to alter the social fabric, but even (in the former two cases) to grasp its salient contours. (In Calvino, a single idiom for writing self and world guarantees not that the subject's encounter with the object misfires, but that it never takes place.) The "grid" operates a global set of power relays (or an array of imaginary cities) unresponsive to individual trajectories.

A postcolonial project of social change can neither passively accept nor casually dismiss the postmodern attack on the knowing subject. In this discussion and the next, I attend to Rushdie's, Gabriel García Márquez's, and Morrison's attempts to rewrite the individual subject (to free that figure from failed Enlightenment premises, without falling into postmodern indifference). I consider as well their effort to reconceive the underlying stances—market oriented, instrumental, implicitly or explicitly colonizing—that fuel first-world social arrangements. (This latter dimension of their work would be its Utopian reach.)[3] For early-twentieth-century Forster, however, writing in the heyday of Western colonialism yet grasping the logic of its exploitation of the other, the need and the impossibility of conceiving subjective passage between British Empire and Indian subjection are equally palpable. His hesitant modernism, still attached to realist protocols, encounters in *A Passage to India* (1924) its Waterloo.

Forster's novel and Rushdie's *Satanic Verses* (1987) both get bent out of shape in their attempt to imagine resolution for first-world/third-world encounters. But bent out of shape differently—and in ways that expose to different ends the limitations of realism's representational protocols. Without question, the realist subject has long and honorably served as a site for addressing social abuse. Yet that subject's tendency to transform otherness into a version of the same remains its constituent blind spot. Should such a subject really attempt to "see India," outside all Western preconceptions, it must come a cropper. *A Passage to India* registers this aporia of the subject so patently, so immovably, as to sabotage the entire liberal project. Seeking, and failing, to achieve genuine passage, the novel collapses upon itself, producing an autumnal mood of stalemate and longing.

"WE MUST EXCLUDE SOMEONE FROM OUR GATHERING"

We might begin this analysis of collapse by recalling some minimal requirements of the Enlightenment model. For his part, Forster grasps that the incapacity to tolerate the other (as other) that fuels Western subjectivity mandates, in a colonial context, an exclusionary dynamic: "We must exclude someone from our gathering, or we shall be left with nothing," the narrator muses.[4] We know ourselves by what we exclude, and this "we" is plural, group-shaped; such is the enabling premise of ideology itself. If the other cannot be transformed into a version of the same, it must be cast out, as not-us. As Pierre Macherey writes, "Like a planet revolving round an absent sun, an ideology is made of what it does not mention."[5] Made of what it does not mention, ideology achieves group coherence by abjecting its other outside the group's constituent borders. If the act of excluding others is definitive, in both senses, of individual (but group-secured) identity, how could individuals pass beyond their (group's) borders and yet retain coherence?

Within Forster's novel of empire, the desire to pass beyond specifically offends two interrelated colonial norms—those for regulating the identity of British *nation* and *gender*. Significantly, the text opens on a scene of relaxed, reclining Muslims males, smoking and drinking and talking, teasing and affirming each other, bound together by a communal Muslim identity whose limits, nevertheless, they deplore. They lack friendship with their British colonizers, they would pass from bureaucratic arrangements into intimacy. Pressed harder, this opening scene allows us to glimpse the larger dilemma of desire operating throughout *Passage to India:* how can British-Indian relations escape the self-other constraints imposed by British empire, into friendship among equals? More dangerously, how can male-male relations pass beyond British heterosexual norms into a shared space of bodily intimacy?

Two revisionary projects—for reconceiving nation and manhood—are at stake. Perhaps because these projects are so fraught (the first all but inalterable, the second all but unspeakable), Forster displaces them both onto a female register: the attempt, by a pair of British women, to pass beyond the barriers separating them from their Indian counterparts.[6] Indeed, Forster's simultaneous desire for and fear of such passage motivate the text's conflicted narrative stance—in equal measure sympathetic and punitive—toward Mrs. Moore and Adela. The text levies its violence first upon Mrs. Moore (aging her, then killing her off), and then more emphatically upon Adela (penetrating her body with cactus quills, staring gazes, and a fantasy/foreign penis).

Passage of all sorts proved easier in Forster's earlier, realist novels, not least because realism is precommitted to championing the liberation of resourceful subjects in familiar space/time, their eventual passage into other (domesticatable) territories. The telos of realist plot is the release, in the course of time, of such individuals from ideological fetters (a release permitting them to "become themselves" while remaining, at a deeper level, unchanged, still inscribed within the culture's shaping norms). At any rate, no individual release pursued in Forster's earlier, liberal texts seems to be impossible.[7] Only in *Passage* does Forster engage a critique of realism for which realism has no answer: the premise that ideology, always coming from "out there" (it is socially composed), is nevertheless constitutive of "in here" (our interiority itself but a negotiation of stances deriving from the social). Unanswerable because this critique, in its radical form, dispossesses the individual of individuality. There is, suddenly, no private realm richer, freer, more flexible than the public realm that makes it possible. No human space exists that might permit a self-making cleanly emancipated from ideological framing. Realist protestations notwithstanding, if one were to erase from subjectivity every ideological trace, one would discover that—no sustainable identity remains at all. In making this unwanted discovery Forster reaches the limits of where even angels may safely tread. Divesting its two female protagonists of their ideological furnishing, *Passage* exposes them to a mind-numbing distress in which individual resource no longer avails. The admirable Mrs. Moore reduces to a dying and inarticulate body; the intrepid Adela, emptied of agency, reduces to a bewildered and bewildering problem for others.

What desire fuels these women's (collapsed) projects? The shorthand answer is the desire "to see India"—to befriend and accommodate what is genuinely foreign in it, but without losing their own self-sameness. Writ large, this specular project is the liberal premise underwriting realist fiction: that experience enlarges self-hood, that it is pedagogic and profitable to see the world, that doing so develops one's individual resources, that one can come to know the other without departing from the same. Mrs. Moore and Adela both assume this as a personal project, innocent of larger social investments and obstacles. At a larger level, the desire "to see India" undergirds a burgeoning tourist industry enabled by the commodification of a foreign culture's icons: so many purchasable items (or stereotyped itineraries) that promise to pass the culture's otherness onto/into the consuming British subject—and to do so pleasantly![8] Forster's first two realist novels endorse the allure of this travel project; Italy is inexhaustibly pedagogic for repressed British males and females. (It is no accident that a considerable film enterprise has battened on the potential wrought into these travel novels—their promise to deliver a foreign culture's otherness into the purview of paying subjects/customers who are not, themselves, required to change.)

At a political level, the belief that one is able "to see India" is more portentous yet, underwriting British colonialism's centuries-old conviction that Britain has indeed "seen India" both steady and whole, has understood her possibilities and limitations better than she herself has—a view that rewrites Indian otherness in terms of British instrumental priorities. This immovable colonial stance blocks the sensitive male longing to pass over into an encounter with Indianness, as well as the project of the two traveling women. At the deepest epistemic level, to employ Foucault's appropriate term, the desire "to see India" rehearses a classic premise of Western epistemology: that the centered subject—the British I/eye—can measure/comprehend/negotiate the object it beholds, even an object the size of India. No matter how foreign the object, the centered subject presumes a detached, and accurate, purchase on what it sees. It need not alter, inside, in order to see responsibly, outside. All levels of this specular plot "to see India" depend for their success upon commodifying or stereotyping Indian otherness into Western configurations: a procedure that leaves the seer unchanged, and India's otherness unknown.

Forster knows that this specular plot is ill conceived and destined to fail. Either the British colonists will brutalize and reify India in order to manage it, or the errant British subject who does pass into a space of genuine Indianness will lose all functional identity. Forster thus uses the Marabar caves to stage the collapse of his realist plot of individual development. Drawing on modernist techniques, he places his intrepid subjects in a space they cannot map, and in a time that loses its progressive character. Echoing Plato's cave (that other challenge to the individual's epistemological overconfidence), the scene at Marabar turns suddenly modernist, becoming the epicenter of the novel's implosions, the moment at which a gathering mystery (the novel's awareness that what is precious about India is beyond policing or commodification) reaches crisis and deflates into a muddle (the state in which the attempt to pass over has necessarily failed). After the Marabar fiasco, the earlier ideological barriers of nation and gender—although thoroughly deconstructed—begin to be comically, depressingly, reasserted.

Passage ceases, during the Marabar crisis, to deploy a realist narrative of fine-grained personal relations within manageable space/time. The text enters territory never broached before by Forster (familiar to us, though, by way of Freud, Proust, Kafka, Rilke, and Faulkner): encounters that undo the doer, shattering a lifetime of learned expectations and revealing one's precious worldview to be nothing more than "poor little talkative Christianity" (166)—not truth, just words pretentiously claiming to be truth. Forster puts behind him once and for all the realist plot of enabling individual journeys. The text cannot map Marabar blur; nuances of sight are replaced by brutalities of touch. A core realist assumption—that of embodied subjects sustaining their difference from, and knowledge of, a field of familiarizable others, *seeing* them—ceases to operate. Mrs. Moore and Adela never do know what they press against in those caves, nor where the event takes place (the caves are indistinguishable), nor even if it is an event. Deprived of personal furnishings (which are revealed, as in no other Forster novel, to be impersonal ideological coordinates that orient group thought and behavior), the women are given only two options, both sterile: either return to standard (British) identity that collapses their precious illusion of personal uniqueness (Adela's withdrawal into domestic spinsterhood), or undergo a speechless falling away from human culture into inhuman nature, from individual identity to mere bodiness, destined for death (Mrs. Moore's speechless crack-up). Suddenly, there is nothing more (nothing personal) the subject knows to *say*—a silence binding on both women and, it turns out, on their creator as well.

A Passage to India reveals that there is no coherent selfhood without group-shaped distinctions that furnish identity by othering what cannot be accommodated. Put otherwise, Forster's sustained attention to the reach of British colonialism allowed him finally to glimpse the *politics* of subject development: a politics that is (despite its liberal individualist vocabulary) always group-enabled, never innocent. In *Passage*'s trial, the abjecting fury of colonial ideology itself—its attempt to resecure Adela's self-narrative within an us-against-them colonial script—is tried and found guilty. With no other plot in sight, however—or with the other plots that can be imagined leading toward inadmissible passages saturated in shame—the novel resignedly concludes by shrinking back into its ill-fitting borders of nation and gender norms. Aziz, Fielding, and Adela each reduce to more conventional type: Aziz's Muslim traits "Indianize" as he withdraws from British encounters and retreats to the Hindu hinterland, the wanderer Fielding becomes a safely masculinized British functionary (even marrying to prove this), and the defeated Adela returns to a shabby life as old-maid-schoolteacher in the suburbs of London. Forster's last novel thus closes in wistful defeat, its incapacity to imagine passage testifying to a surrender at once gendered (the writer remaining in his closet), political (the two nations locked in colonial abusiveness), and narrative (the shift to modernist shock and the torpedoing of realist assumptions signaling the end of fiction writing). A modernist "ouboum" shuts down Forster's career as a novelist, intimating a crisis of sensemaking that his available narrative options are powerless to resolve.

"NONE OF US ARE *LIKE THIS*"

Rushdie has other narrative options. His 1987 text opens with a scene that, in a sense, the Forster text dreams of but cannot write: two men in suggestive embrace, plummeting in free fall, passing beyond conventional restraints. By contrast, Forster, writing only what he believes can happen within a familiar spatial/temporal frame, cannot write this scene. Forster cannot disavow Newtonian laws of gravity—the ways in which, on a correspondence model of knower to known, subject-object relations occur in space and time. But Rushdie's representational strategy is not bound by Newtonian realism: his embracing pair is allowed to tumble 29,002 feet into the English Channel without shattering (to draw on modernism's privileged term for vulnerability, casually dismissed here).

To fall over five miles into the sea below, without being hurt, exacts its price however. The Rushdie text, like Pynchon's discussed above, rescripts the human body at the cost of representing the reality of human pain—pain credible enough to elicit abiding readerly identification. (The larger issue, as with Pynchon, is identification itself.) I cannot prove this, but I suspect that the dignity and pathos of human pain are the province of realism, and no less powerfully (but more narrowly) of modernism. No postmodern novel can represent pain of the unforgettable sort that Anna Karenina suffers, or that Quentin Compson undergoes—not to mention the pain of Rilke's Malte or Forster's Adela. Pain has its full value only within a representational schema premised on the singular gravity of human subjects and their dilemmas. There is, of course, nothing optimistic about Rushdie's sense of the human scene, but there is a determination—at once aesthetic and political—to write outside the Newtonian frame of realism, as well as outside the arrests and shocks of modernism. An enormous representational asset of realism and modernism—the resonance of discrete pressures impinging painfully (and in modernism inalterably) on the subject—is being thus yielded up. What is being obtained in its stead?

In lieu of Forster's narrative that replaces realist development only with modernist arrest, Rushdie's text delights in recombinatory moves. As much as Pynchon, he parades a huge cast of (mainly small) characters, incessantly varying his settings and injecting new motifs into his pages. (Dickens's text is calm by comparison, for realist protocols keep Dickensian invention in check, requiring at least passing obedience to the Newtonian censor.) Rushdie's protagonists, Gibreel and Chamcha, are themselves experts in negotiating recombinatory moves. As successful actors, both are adept at performing roles they manage not to interiorize, moving at ease among passing sets—instrumental cruisers who profit from their travels. In Rushdie, high culture and pop culture, liturgy and songs and ads, the sacred and the profane, theology and theologicals: everything august encounters its low-life other, becomes hybrid.

Do we perhaps recognize—in the in-your-face, commodity-filled, camera-posed, performance-scripted world of Rushdie's excessive text—Jameson's postmodern space? "The new space," Jameson writes, "involves the suppression of distance (in the sense of Benjamin's aura) and the relentless saturation of any remaining voids and empty places, to the point where the postmodern body . . . is now exposed to a perceptual barrage of immediacy from which all sheltering layers and intervening mediations have been removed" ("Cognitive Mapping," in *Reader,* 280). All is heterogenous and up-close: surface, citation, image, commodity—no object maintains the depth, distance, discreteness, and specific gravity required for *aura.* This teeming canvas seems thus to imitate the soulless, boundary-trashing traffic of global capitalism. There can be no question of stilling this traffic into the form of a reliable map; rather, Rushdie attends to its transformative capacities.

Capitalist invention and recycling are here proposed as prior to, generative of, what used to be regarded as the fixed and unfabricated real. A linguistic enterprise attuned to such transformations will be less interested in respecting traditional (Newtonian) paradigms than in contesting any claim by Authority (for Rushdie: Islamic) that truth is unchanging and impervious to language, once and for all revealed by Holy Writ. As any object can be reinvented or simulated, so any discourse—launched into the recycling machine of culture and politics—can be rewritten. (Holy Writ is not given in its entirety once and once only, but is (re)produced over time, continually engaged in contestation.) The correspondence model—where carefully chosen words seem to imitate familiar nonverbal realities—loses its purchase; Rushdie fills his representational stage with scenes whose spatial/temporal coordinates would be taboo on Newtonian terms.

Rushdie's language delights in a contemporary hybridity (thanks to postcolonial two-way traffic) that was unimaginable in Forster's day. Travel to and from India, in the early twentieth century, was costly and time-consuming, not to mention arduous enough to be counterrecommended (during certain seasons) for females. The English language of that period likewise retained much of its national character as a securely bordered territory. In Forster's India, English is not hybrid but binary: either native or foreign. No foreigner in *Passage* hears or speaks English like a native; witness Aziz's misunderstanding of Fielding's casual throwaway phrases. In small as at large *Passage* reveals the stubbornness of colonial binaries. By contrast, Rushdie deploys an English elasticized by countless border crossings—a medium at once native-and-foreign. There are no natives, hence no foreigners, in *The Satanic Verses*. Virtually every page deploys the recombinatory, postcolonial forms of an English transformed by an empire that has learned to talk back. Here is Chamcha's mother reacting to her son's recently acquired British fastidiousness:

> "See how well he complains," Nasreen teased him in front of his father. "About everything he has such big-big criticisms, the fans are fixed too loosely to the roof and will fall to slice our heads off in our sleep, he says, and the food is too fattening, why don't we cook some things without frying, he wants to know, the top-floor balconies are unsafe and the paint is peeled, why can't we take pride in our surroundings, isn't it, and the garden is over- grown, we are just junglee people, he thinks so, and look how coarse our movies are, now he doesn't enjoy, and so much disease you can't even drink water from the tap, my god, he really got an education, husband, our little Sallu, England-returned, and talking so fine and all."[9]

Within this recombinatory context (try imagining *that* passage in *Pas- sage*) let us return to Forsterian impasse. The opaque, modernist event in the Marabar caves that torpedoes the realist principle of binary exclusion (of this being self-affirmingly not that) occurs in the middle of the novel. Like a black hole within which character and motive lose the exclusive borders that make them identifiable and purposive, entry into the caves subverts the women's future plotting. Or, to reverse the image, it is as though the sun whose absence ideology mandates should make an unwanted appearance. In the light it suddenly sheds, all gesture stands nakedly revealed in the provincial ideological webbing that licenses it: ide- ology outed and suddenly embarrassingly obvious. Christianity becomes "poor little talkative Christianity," the British Empire becomes—the British Empire: mere words, naked power.

In the light of this exposure, Forster could either adopt a modernist proj- ect of traumatic undoings, or he could cease to write (realist fiction). He chose the latter option, and we might speculate further as to why. Forster- ian narrative is at heart a realistic enterprise—tirelessly epistemological, committed to knowing better and mapping more wisely the world outside the voyaging subject. The authority of Forster's narrative voice testifies to this consensual project of getting it better, getting it right, and getting us to agree on its rightness—an intimate voice that measures and corrects. When his protagonists do not succeed in "seeing India," his incapacity to make good on that failure (to see past their blindness) seems literally to lead to his silence. The world is still out there, and it must still be a singular, objective whole. In order to establish an accurate correspondence between subject and object, one needs mapping instruments beyond anything he possesses as a novelist. The epistemological project collapses under the pressures imposed by a colonial situation, yet, within a realist frame of assumptions, it remains the only project appropriate to narrative.

Rushdie's postmodern text, by contrast, has little interest in epistemology. No Newtonian gravity grounds and legitimates the contours of his worldview. He knows that the world is not simply out there as a set of real objects open to mapping. It obeys no spatial/temporal pieties and is certainly not a singular whole. More, there exist no instruments available for getting it right. Instead, the world is ceaselessly being (re)produced, woven of heterogenous realities that operate according to their own dis-cursive/behavioral logic. Places and things no longer have specific grav-ity; Forster's clinging to the dignity of (non-man-made) geography in *Passage* has no Rushdian counterpart. The London of *The Satanic Verses* is constructed rather than pregiven—Ellowen Deeowen (city of letters) rather than London (city of the fact)—a site for conflicting belief-and-behavior systems. When Rushdie does turn to geography, he gives us the fabulous: a survived fall of 29,002 feet into the English Channel, a desire to tropicalize the English weather. In like manner, for Rushdie there could never have been a majestically non-man-made Islam that, under pressure, risks collapsing into "poor little talkative Islam." His text accesses Islam in the first place as a constructed human phenomenon, a political/religious enterprise employing persuasion (and if need be, force), negotiating its own discontinuous descent in time and engaged in battle with competing belief systems.

The priority of social processes over individual essences may shed light on why Rushdie's protagonists tend to appear as rescriptable outlines—sites where transforming events occur—rather than as fixed Forsterian subjects with specific gravity. Rushdian narrative can make Gibreel and Chamcha live and move only by submitting them to conditions that would require Forsterian narrative to abandon them. They must become ideologically incoherent—no longer viable subjects, but rather hybrid amalgamations (indeed monsters) who have been assaulted and recomposed by competing discursive realities. We must then revisit Gibreel and Chamcha's status as actors who perform roles without being affected by them—postmodern cruisers, à la Jacob Horner, who move profitably and instrumentally through a world of simulacra.

At its deepest level, *The Satanic Verses* is committed to dismantling such privileged subjective trajectories. Both of Rushdie's protagonists are already walking contradictions waiting to implode—Gibreel the atheist who plays divinity in the "theologicals," Chamcha the native who would become more British than the British. Rushdie can use these protagonists, as Pynchon could use Slothrop, only by recombining their parts without asking permission of their will. In the midst of an English phrase, Chamcha's Indian slang breaks out; in the midst of acting (for film) the role of the prophet, Gibreel is spiritually entered and transformed. By savaging the contours of his protagonists' proposed coherence, by insisting on transformations that bypass their shaping will and reveal, beneath, the hybrid culture's deforming pressures, Rushdie dramatizes the challenge to subjectivity at the heart of *The Satanic Verses*. One cannot pass through the zone of such turbulence—such "terrible unquiet fuss"—and remain oneself. "None of us are *like this*" (65; emphasis in the original), Chamcha thinks—articulating a situation that spurs Rushdie's pen as it would have paralyzed Forster's. Gibreel is catapulted into the religious vision his professional life has profitably feigned; Chamcha becomes the bestial outsider his pilgrimage to London was shaped to elude.

"The trouble with you," Pamela tells Chamcha, "is that you still think of normality as being normal" (280). Otto Bone puts it equally trenchantly: "'the most dangerous of all the lies we are fed in our lives' [is] the idea of the continuum" (295). The forces shaping his life, Chamcha realizes in horror, "wanted nothing to do with his pathetic personality" (9). Normality, continuity, personality: these assumptions that serve as the very foundation of Western common sense—they make possible the realist priority of the knowing subject—are cast aside. In their place emerges a fictional domain operating on a different figure/ground model: "they have the power of description" and—bombarded—"we succumb to the pictures they construct" (168). *They* shape *us:* the realist priority turned on its head. If Rushdie's migratory protagonists do not go crazy, burst their identity-borders by encountering alterities stronger than their own fragile self-sameness, he has no postcolonial novel. In Forster by contrast, a certain kind of craziness—hitting a certain wall of subject incoherence—means the end of narratability. But Rushdie does not dilate, as Rilke does, upon the inner dimensions of subject collapse. He has no interest in a novel so unsociable that only one character moving in present-tense time is granted a credible name. Rather, Rushdie is after a political resonance that Rilke's modernist aesthetics refused. He wants lots of names, he wants even to name names. It is precisely this political energy that lands Rushdie, and his book, in so much "terrible unquiet fuss"—exposing him to the turbulence of a larger postcolonial condition in which there can be no return to the security of privileged subjectivity, managed exclusions.

Homi Bhabha writes, "The non-synchronous temporality of global and national cultures opens up a cultural space . . . where the negotiation of incommensurable differences creates a tension peculiar to borderline existences."[10] Borderline existences become incommensurate with themselves: this is the dark side of Bhabha's insight taken to its limit, as well as the subject dilemma of *The Satanic Verses*. Neither Gibreel nor Chamcha can subjectify—can make his own—the belief and behavioral contradictions Rushdie settles on them. He will not allow their passage to translate, to cohere into subject sense. "Irradiated by history, radioactive with history and politics," ousted by their author into a spatial/temporal frame they cannot domesticate, Gibreel and Chamcha transmogrify rather than develop.[11] Postcolonial trajectories are neither shaped to the questing subject (realism's project), nor restricted to that subject's interior collapse (modernism's project). As a minor character says, "I mean, in these days, character isn't destiny any more. Economics is destiny. Ideology is destiny. Bombs are destiny. What does a famine, a gas chamber, a grenade care how you lived your life?" (432).

As the novel moves toward conclusion, a determination to savage subjective coherence turns, oddly, into a desire to salvage such coherence. Rushdie backs away from his earlier verbal fireworks. (The novel that begins as Joyce, Sara Suleri has remarked, finishes as Dickens, ending with Gibreel's suicide and Chamcha's return to home and father, seeking reconciliation.) Gibreel's failure to organize the messages invading him into viable subjectivity eventually drives him into something close to classic schizophrenia. This is hardly Gilles Deleuze and Félix Guattari's sexy, postmodern schizophrenia that promises a way out from the Freudian paradigm of fixed, oedipal subjectivity, but rather the sign of shattered being.

The final chapter represents the hybrid protagonists as singular individuals moving through linear time, in search of resolution. "Now you can stop acting at last" (534), Zeeny tells Chamcha, on learning that he is no longer to be called Saladin but, gravely enough, his given name, Salahuddin. Stop acting: what can this advice mean in a postsubjective, lavishly simulative text like Rushdie's? Increasingly, Rushdie makes his text shrink (as Forster made his shrink) toward the narrow realist choices of subject collapse or subject coherence. The episode of Chamcha's homecoming and his father's death is bathed in a moving monologic style—a death as realistic-resonant as the earlier deaths of both protagonists' parents was postmodern-casual (extinctions that occur in the space of a paragraph, chicken-bone suffocations or fatal strokes). A text that first played with death (staging a miraculous survival from a plane explosion in midair) now takes death as ultimatum, *the* serious event revealing the gravity of our finite condition. (The most beautiful sentence in the book—"The world, somebody wrote, is the place we prove real by dying in it" [533]—testifies to such textual reorientation.)

These later moves complicate the book's earlier mockery of grave matters, allowing us to glimpse Rushdie's more inextricable relation to the Eastern and Western cultures that hold him fast and loose. "Incommensurable differences," Bhabha wrote. As son of both Voltaire and Mohammed, does Rushdie incoherently embody, along with his protagonists, an unsubjectifiable "tension peculiar to borderline existences"—lives exposed to the "terrible unquiet fuss" disfiguring contemporary postcolonial life outside the whale? Whatever the case, *The Satanic Verses* succeeds in representing a teeming, metastatic world—its secular and sacred elements morphing before our eyes: a world whose dynamic "grid" eludes the map of any subject's knowing.

I have called *The Satanic Verses* "postcolonial," and I do not renege on the term. Yet Rushdie's fictional world is no less invested in a range of assumptions we might consider "postmodern." Returning to the tension between these two terms may serve to indicate twin pressures acting upon Rushdie's imagination. On the one hand, there is his sophisticated Western awareness that the reach of multinational capitalism disqualifies any urge to speak, at this juncture of history, of a third-world space securely other, free of Western commodification. (Whose imagination is more alert to the reach of commodification than Rushdie's?) This Rushdie, writing from the heart of the metropolis, can out-ironize postmodern ironists: there is no limit to the truth claims in which he does not believe.

On the other hand, Rushdie has taken over—as though they were invented with him in mind—third-world techniques enabling Latin American magic realism (techniques inspired by folkloric narratives arising far from the metropolis), and made them his own. His writerly identity is inconceivable outside these techniques. A representational strategy enlarged by the premises of magic realism permits him not just to weave into his fiction heterogenous materials from Indian (and other) folklore. More important, it does for Rushdie what the Western inheritance (in all its phases: realist, modernist, postmodernist) seems unable to do: it accommodates his fierce political energies. Freed thus of the oppressive common sense associated with realism's representational regime (its insistence on the familiar), he frees himself as well from modernism's austere insistence on the collapse of that regime. In so doing, Rushdie reconfigures the *subject/space/time* contract itself, producing a narrative that delights in transfiguration, that delights in bad taste as well. Mid-century Latin American fictional techniques encourage the latent Rabelais (but also the Indian bad boy, the protocol buster) in Rushdie, guiding his swerve from a British fictional legacy only too likely to intimidate a brilliant young migrant making his way to frosty Cambridge in the early 1960s.

There remains one final comparison in this analysis of modernist and postmodern/postcolonial procedures. To conclude my argument, I return to Faulkner and move outward, to two contemporary, postcolonial writers— Gabriel García Márquez and Toni Morrison—both creatively marked by his work, yet revealingly clear of the tragic stance at the heart of his fiction. How do the representational tenets of magic realism enable these two writers to free their work from modernist arrest? What different configurations of the subject in space/time do they set in motion? The more-than-Western array of strategies they put into play engenders a subject/space/time manifold that is neither "knowing" nor "unknowing," but "beyond knowing." Such strategies make possible, as perhaps no Newton-descended procedure can, a narrative canvas shimmering with Utopian possibilities.

CHAPTER ELEVEN

Arrest and Release

Faulkner, García Márquez, Morrison

TRAGIC LOOMING

The moment in *Absalom, Absalom!* is unforgettable: Judith Sutpen—an "unwived widow"—coming up to Grandmother Compson in the middle of Jefferson and offering her the murdered Charles Bon's love letter, telling her to keep it or destroy it, as she wishes, saying, "it cant matter, you know that, or the Ones that set up the loom would have arranged things a little better, and yet it must matter because you keep on trying" (105).[1] This vignette crystallizes the patriarchal Old South's incapacity to acknowledge (some of) its subjects' endeavors. It "cant matter" because of how the "Ones" in control have set up the loom. The larger dilemma of arrest common to Faulkner and other modernist writers is that, for their protagonists, the loom of Western norms for individual fulfillment no longer functions.

In Faulkner such dysfunction, as I explore in greater detail in this chapter, is inseparable from the Old South's patriarchal privileging of white male planters. In Kafka's texts, by contrast, class and race differentiation is minimal, if not invisible; the stumbling protagonist is typically male. The malaise that has invaded the Kafka world, it may be more pertinent to say, attaches to the collapse of sanity-producing bourgeois norms themselves— a collapse that the texts seem to represent as, in equal measure, devastating and necessary. In any event, Kafka's texts never suggest an alternative arrangement to those that have collapsed. As for Proust, issues of class clearly trump those of race and gender as social materials receiving the writer's critical attention. But Proust attends to class hierarchy less in order to highlight resultant social inequalities than to expose the inauthentic grounds of superiority it appears to provide—grounds discreetly assumed by the aristocracy, tirelessly asserted by the bourgeoisie.

Common to all three writers—however different the stances they take toward it—is the collapse of a normative social loom. That loom, enabling individual progress through objective (yet cooperative) space and time, is perhaps the signature assumption of what I am calling the standard Western plot. Functioning so smoothly in realism that one hardly hears it humming, it becomes dysfunctional in modernism. So dysfunctional, I wish to argue now, that insofar as postcolonial writers seek to tell a different story, they must deploy a different set of representational procedures. If Faulkner's modernist protocols differ from prior realist ones, they differ no less from later postcolonial protocols—the latter embodied, for my purposes, in the work of García Márquez and Toni Morrison. To reprise in epitome the stakes of the realist arrangement: space and time are understood (since the Enlightenment) to be linear, lawful, and orientational; the subject moving through them is the Lockean individual entitled to life, liberty, and the pursuit of happiness.[2] Let us consider further why Faulkner must trash this story.

Judith's "loom" figures the warp and woof of subject movement through social space and time. "Social" because human beings never encounter space and time in unmediated fashion, as mere conditions of nature. Rather, cultures *design* the space and time their subjects experience, arranging normative pathways through them—pathways that, in Faulkner's work as elsewhere in Western fiction, are insistently patriarchal. When these sanctioned pathways fail the subject moving through them, identity shatters; Judith's "arrest" resonates throughout Faulkner's fiction. Donald Mahan paralyzed, Bayard Sartoris traumatized, Benjy and Quentin Compson moving urgently, yet without progress—these figures are followed in *Absalom* by Henry and Rosa and Wash and Sutpen himself, all of them assaulted by something incomprehensible, thinking "*I kaint have heard what I know I heard*" (*Absalom,* 238; emphasis in the original). The list could be extended; it goes beyond Faulkner. "History is what hurts," Jameson has cryptically written.[3] History eventually brings to bear, on the social structures shaped to accommodate reality (but shaped—as in patriarchy—selectively, inadequately, unjustly), the crushing weight of what has remained unaccommodated. The form of that hurting in modernism is arrest, a paralyzing moment in which the progressive subject comes up against the social loom's inadequacy and becomes unfurnished. In dramatizing such fallout, much modernist fiction enacts the assault of history upon the prevailing ideology's selective narratives for managing the real. Where but in a modernist novel could the concluding words so purely interrogate patriarchal norms as "*I don't I don't! I don't hate it! I don't hate it!*" (*Absalom,* 311; emphasis in the original)?

An examination of a single "career" in *Absalom,* that of Charles Bon's son, opens up the spatial/temporal dimensions of Faulknerian arrest. This child is born in a New Orleans in which he "could neither have heard nor yet recognised the term 'nigger,' who even had no word for it in the tongue he knew who had been born and grown up in a padded silken vacuum . . . where pigmentation had no more moral value than the silk walls and the scent and the rose-colored candle shades" (*Absalom,* 165). Abruptly he is seized by Clytie and transported—without explanation or even a shared language—to a northern Mississippi where the literal space he inhabits has altered seismically, beyond assimilation:

> the few garments (the rags of the silk and broadcloth in which he had arrived, the harsh jeans and homespun which the two women bought and made for him, he accepting them with no thanks, no comment, accepting his garret room with no thanks, no comment, asking for and making no alteration in its spartan arrangements that they knew of until that second year when he was fourteen and one of them, Clytie or Judith, found hidden beneath his mattress the shard of broken mirror: and who to know what hours of amazed and tearless grief he might have spent before it, examining himself in the delicate and outgrown tatters in which he perhaps could not even remember himself, with quiet and incredulous incomprehension) hanging behind a curtain contrived of a piece of old carpet nailed across a corner. (165)

Recognizing yourself in a mirror: Lacan has bewitched a generation of critics into seeing, there in miniature, the installation of Western culture within the not-yet-subject. The infant sees in the mirror a sutured and mobile image of who he is to be. The image proposes an unattainable imaginary wholeness that spurs the infant toward self-realization within a social framework he would make his own. The mother's eyes confirm the infant's desire and launch the forward-moving progress through time that, for Lacan, is simultaneously alienation and "maturity." Either way, the physics of the scene organizes space as a mirroring frame in which the infant projects his desire-fueled image of himself-to-be. The drama is projective, its genre is realism, its telos is patriarchal.[4]

Bon's son's mirror operates in reverse. It shows him the chasm between what he was and what he is. Each present item of clothing reads as the despoliation of a former item of clothing. His New Orleans–furnished body has been intolerably displaced by his Mississippi-furnished body, none of this his own choice. As in Lacan, this is an identity-launching moment, but it inaugurates not a centering but an implosion. Charles Etienne de St. Valery Bon materializes as a culturally impossible being, torn between here and there, now and then. He lacks ideological resources that might resolve this tearing. Puritan northern Mississippi and Catholic New Orleans, the jagged racist present and the harmonious race-neutral past, share him equally and incoherently.

His solution to these incompatible cultural markings is to combine them as crucifixion. Identity, as often in Faulkner, operates as the embodied and conflicted enactment of social coding; and Bon's son's body is worse than a palimpsest—it is a contradictory social scripting that permits no erasures.[5] One needs an infrared light to read the black man in this white man, but he makes it easy by guaranteeing, through premeditated acts of violence, that he be recognized as both at once. Performing white and black codes with unfailing accuracy, he chooses for a wife the kind of black woman that white and black alike will decode (for different reasons) as scandalous. Abreast of the nuances of every cultural code that entraps him, he naturalizes nothing, learns nothing, projects nothing except trouble upon black and white alike. Viewed from the pedagogic stance that guides realist maturation, he is—like Joe Christmas—a figure of nightmarish negativity.

Faulkner "says" Charles Etienne's torment by jamming his motion in the socially configured time and space available to him. Unwilling to suture a factitious self in northern Mississippi's cohesive time (to get on with life by passing as white or settling for black), the young man fractures in scandal time, transforms any event where he appears into a spectacle of violence. No time can further him, no space accommodate him, no mores fit him; his clothes are wrong before they become bloodied as well. He does not so much communicate through language as strike through gesture. Time, space, mores, clothes, and language function as social resources for subject development only so long as there is a minimal ideological consensus. If one asks why Charles Etienne seems to epitomize modernist crisis, one could say that he exposes his culture's racial narratives as warring ideologies. His experience takes shape as an unfurnishing.

When Walter Benjamin spoke of wisdom as "the epic side of truth," he meant that the older, prenovelistic narratives of the West furnished wisdom to their audience by drawing upon a shared understanding of experience that gave value to subjects' movement through social time and space.[6] Benjamin claimed that post-Enlightenment narratives emphasize less the sharing of experiential wisdom than the stimulus of new information (the "novel" in the novel)—produced for individual consumption. "Time" in the novel, he argued, segments into ever-smaller instrumental units, ceasing to accommodate the longer rhythms required for communally nourished lives. Benjamin captured, presciently, the alienation and brittleness lurking within the form of a liberal bourgeois genre that has become incapable—in its privileging of individual fulfillment—of portraying the social as an enabling fabric of shared norms.

But as my previous reading of realist fiction suggests, the soulless alienation implicit in the "ego-logy" of these texts is countered by a Kantian ethics centered in the family/familiar. Flaubertian dyspepsia toward cultural norms is not a routine nineteenth-century novelistic condition; the subject's passage through space/time does not typically reduce (in realist fiction) to mere instrumentality, let alone absurdity.[7] By the time of late-nineteenth-century naturalism and early-twentieth-century modernism, however, the Benjaminian diagnosis is harder to rebut. The "time" dynamic he identifies, now further exacerbated, tends to split into the brittle extremes of either inauthentic habit or unassimilable shock. Disappeared is the wisdom that once lay between them and bound the individual's momentary events into larger social meaning. What is *Absalom, Absalom!*—as epitomized in the career of Charles Bon's son—but the abruption of shock upon habit, the real upon ideology's selective version of it, with no viable space in between?

Charles Etienne's dilemma, at once traumatic and traumatizing, inverts the masterplot of Western realism. It torpedoes realism's continuous time and manageable space, realism's subject as (eventually) mapper, shaper, and owner. To make the point more concrete: Margaret Mitchell's *Gone With the Wind* differs from *Absalom, Absalom!* in precisely these ways. Whereas Mitchell's Civil War unfolds as a bounded event mapped according to how it accommodates or frustrates individual projects, Faulkner's Civil War resists coherent narration—remaining monstrously possessed of a half-life still disorienting its twentieth-century narrators in 1909–10, even its twentieth-century author in 1935. Sutpen's Hundred burns and Quentin hates/does not hate the South. Tara remains and Scarlett knows that tomorrow is another day. The modernist text shows the decentered subject careening outside the furnished paths of space and time: ideology shattered. The realist text shows the subject bloody but unbowed, wiser for her travails, her will redirected rather than undone: project revised and thus intact.

It is one thing to grant *Absalom*'s procedural difference from realist fictions that precede it, and another to insist on its procedural difference from
postcolonial ones that follow it. In fact, one of the vibrant strands of current cultural studies is bent upon revisiting narratives of the U.S. South by
way of their hemispheric kinship with narratives of that other South, Latin
America.[8] A number of scholars have paired Faulkner with his Latin
American counterparts, not least because those counterparts have recognized his enabling influence. More, Faulkner's modernism is crucial in this
recognition, for his experimental modes invited—through their reconfiguring of the pact of subject, space, and time—a Latin American rethinking
of problem and possibility (of why, and even more how, one might tell the
standard story *otherwise*), outside the procedures of Western realism.[9] This
pairing, however, reveals differences as telling as the resemblances, as
becomes evident if we compare Faulkner with the postcolonial writer most
often linked with him: García Márquez.[10]

The major similarities are already well established, and they revolve
around a broadly shared "history that hurts": imaginative chroniclers of
minoritized cultures dominated by larger ones (the U.S. South by the
North, Latin America by the United States); writers who have experienced
and conveyed the bitter taste of economic and cultural defeat (as opposed to
the seemingly resistless material progress of the non-Southern United
States); novelists creatively suspicious of the ideology lurking in authorized
versions of history (Benjamin's claim that history is written by the victors,
not the vanquished); figures with firsthand and troubling familiarity with
the colonial dimensions of their own culture (Faulkner's polarized whites
and blacks, Latin America's subtler array of whites, blacks, Indians, and
mixed-race figures); and therefore writers aware that Southern subjects
may live a relation to space, time, and the other quite different from the
instrumental, will-centered models proposed by Enlightenment-nourished
realism. More than any of his modernist peers, Faulkner "spoke" to García
Márquez, his work revealing how much reality was omitted (or deformed)
by the ideology shaping realism's linear narratives.

Yet Faulkner's representational forms differ crucially from García
Márquez's in their ways of engaging the subject in space/time. However
fiercely Faulkner jams the progressive-acquisitive, patriarchal plot, he does
not replace it. Long-standing Western premises—involving individuals
proclaiming "life, liberty, and the pursuit of happiness," committed to
mapping subjects and objects in lawful space and time, invested in discern-
ing the real from within the welter of appearances—shape his practice at a
level deeper than choice. He does not escape a Western novelistic history

invested in the project of *coming to know*. When consensus about the objectively real begins to dissolve, modernist fictions do not so much change course as obsess over the quandary such slippage brings, the impossibility of getting the object right. They still honor, if only by way of the negative, an Enlightenment correspondence model aligning the signs of representation with the dimensions of the real.[11]

Incompatible versions of—lenses upon—the real propel Faulkner's fictions of tragic encounter, motivating the arrest, vertigo, and anguish that are their hallmark. The negativing shadow of Flaubert, Thomas Hardy, and Conrad (all prototragic writers alienated from the acquisitive, bourgeois subject-object pact, even as they share realist norms for representing subject motion through lawful space/time) lies heavy upon Faulkner. Such precursors share with him a sense of the selective and unacceptable logic of the patriarchal loom, producing fictions—in this respect like his—in which the errant subject either fails to know or cannot bear what is finally known. García Márquez is culturally positioned otherwise in relation to this extensive Western history and its hegemonic fictional forms. To be sure, his work cannot avoid the colonizing incursions abetted by Enlightenment rationalism. But, drawing on native folkloric traditions, it can repudiate (in ways Faulkner could not permit himself) the representational form most authorized by the West: realism.

DESIRE GRAPHED IN ITS GRANDEUR

García Márquez's difference can be briefly illustrated by seeing what misprisions occur when one thinks of both writers as subscribing to the same model of the subject in space/time. On the kinship of *Absalom, Absalom!* and *One Hundred Years of Solitude,* Lois Zamora writes: "Each [Thomas Sutpen and José Arcadio Buendía] is hoping to forget his past and begin history again, for both are convinced that in a world without a past, the future can be molded to their historical design. As stubborn and strong as they are in holding to their visions of historical renewal, they learn that the moral burdens of the past are not so easily sloughed off" (35).

All true for Faulkner's novel, but while each detail may be plausible for García Márquez's novel, the ensemble is profoundly misleading, virtually a misrecognition of the latter text's genre. José Arcadio Buendía is not broodingly psychologized as Sutpen is, nor does *One Hundred Years of Solitude* unfold as a heavily moralized rebuke of the first Buendía's sinful design. Time does not weigh on subjectivity in the same way in both writers.

Charles Bon does indeed embody the "moral burdens of the past" that Faulkner makes Sutpen reencounter, but Prudencio Aguilar? He is more a colorful piece of a many-generational history than the all-revealing index of its failed design. Zamora's terms for assessment ("Hoping to forget," "visions of historical renewal," and most concisely that verb "learn") draw on a vocabulary appropriate to resolution in time (realism) or to such resolution shattered (modernism), but inapplicable to the steamroller energy of unfolding character-and-event—the subject/space/time compact—that flourishes in *One Hundred Years of Solitude*. Zamora's Western model of time and space as lawfully charged, continuous domains in which the subjective drama arrives inevitably at maturation or collapse is blind to the Utopian swerves, the muscular renewals that characterize each Buendía's unique self-enactment upon the familial/historical stage.[12]

It is not surprising, then, that the hubris-rebuking Charles Etienne has no counterpart in this supreme text of García Márquez. No one in *One Hundred Years of Solitude* (until the final Buendía) anguishes over who, when, and where he is; they operate for the most part on a stage beyond the problematic of knowing.[13] No existential crises, no epistemological quandary (no "what happened?": we know exactly what happened), no vertigo within time and space: plenty of solitude, but no alienation. Macondo is a culture increasingly invaded from without, but it *furnishes* those within. To be, for the Buendías, is to move securely within time, space, and identity. What other family in twentieth-century literature is so surely in possession of themselves as the Buendías?

To be, for this novel, is to be emphatically narrated. The word "perhaps" occurs, so far as I can tell, only twice in the entire narration of *One Hundred Years of Solitude*. (Think how that epistemologically laden word modulates the narratives of Mr. Compson and Quentin and Shreve.) As García Márquez's narrator is in possession of his materials, so his characters are in possession of their cultural roles, playing them out unhesitatingly until their death. José Arcadio Buendía, his two sons, Ursula, Amaranta and Rebeca, Arcadio and his two sons, Aureliano Secundo's offspring (José Arcadio and Meme and Amaranta Ursula), then the last Aureliano: does anyone really have difficulty telling them apart? They share and repeat family traits, of course, but each with his or her own memorable (unique yet culturally understandable) accents.

They thus elude the central agon of Faulknerian tragedy that Judith knew so well: that of *others who are in the way*. From Locke's pursuit of individual happiness, to Tolstoy's sentencing Anna to death, to Faulkner's unworkable loom, to Sartre's *"l'enfer, c'est les autres,"* Western narrative has obsessed over the encounter between individual project and social constraint.[14] By contrast, García Márquez's Buendías wear their communal history as orientation, not confinement. Their omnipresent culture—their "Macondan-ness": unthinking self-acceptance, relatedness to other Buendías present, past, and to come, membership in a shared community and spontaneous desire to defend this—is the nourishing ground of resources they draw on to be distinctively themselves. Knowing unthinkingly who they are (read: where, when, and with whom they are), they avoid self-doubt. This accounts for the stunning authority of their behavior: José Arcadio Buendía's search for the philosopher's stone, José Arcadio's earth-shattering intercourse, Colonel Aureliano's thirty-two uprisings, Rebeca's dirt eating, Amaranta's weaving of her shroud, Meme's courtship and silent suffering.

Their being at ease in their setting allows them to perform, in full, what is in them to perform—figuring for us what we might perform if we were wholly aligned within culturally coherent space and time. Unlike the pathos of García Márquez's earlier negatived Colonel, none of these characters' interior resources is hoarded or wasted or stymied. To demonstrate this on a minor note, consider the "Elephant." She is a sublime eater not for Western competitive reasons ("be the number one best eater"), but because "a person who had all matters of conscience in perfect shape should be able to eat until overcome by fatigue."[15] Why not? Ideally aligned body accommodates spirit through effortless expansion, not by soul-driven, punitive correction. (Try to compute that in Cartesian terms!)

That same note of unconstrained being sounds in Remedios the Beauty's rising into the air when it is time for her to depart. Read in numerous ingeniously allegorical ways, this event may yield more as an imaginative figuring of what can occur when the embodied human being is perfectly oriented in space and time. Why not? The opposite of Charles Etienne, Remedios performs, completely, what is in her to perform; this is a performing that releases her. "I am fire and air, my other elements I give to baser life," Shakespeare's Cleopatra proclaims, but her final performance is hard-won, loss-driven, tragically self-destroying because self-transcending—a performance constrained by warring ideologies. Remedios rises into the air as Remedios, not as a transcending of Remedios, not as an escape from Remedios's conditions. The book thus joins its realistic and its fabulous doings by aligning its people within a folklore-provided weave of personally appropriate doings that appeal to the reader as unforgettable realities.[16] Through such doings these characters appear to be virtually hardwired with identity—identity as plenitude rather than lack.

I do not forget the bitterness that can suffuse them—Amaranta and her shroud, Rebeca in her solitude, Colonel Aureliano and his fishes—and Rey Chow has properly warned against idealizing the Other as if it were "essentially . . . beyond the contradictions that constitute our own historical place."[17] The point here is that García Márquez is deploying a representational technique that expresses, not the idealized, but the possible. Such a "possible" is freed from the sentimentality attaching to any pretense that the idealized has become the real. Rather, García Márquez's techniques allow him to represent the "possible" as though it were the real, yet without seeking to persuade us that it *is* the real. (The text's fabulous doings repeatedly "remind" us that we are in the territory of desire.) This distinction is subtle but crucial. It is not that the setting of Macondo rewards (in some instrumental fashion) the Buendías but that, by providing space for their moves, it textualizes—lets us see by way of metaphor—their possibilities. He thus writes, more purely than any other novelist I know of, a fiction charged with moments of Utopian imagination.[18]

"Can a person marry his own aunt?" a startled Aureliano José asks a passing soldier, and he is told: "He not only can do that, but we're fighting this war against the priests so that a person can marry his own mother" (163). Why not? *One Hundred Years of Solitude* recognizes that children want to mate with their mothers—that plenitude is the full embrace of the mother, the ultimate providing of space/time (of *home*) to the desiring subject, that everything else is substitute—and it delineates a native culture that releases this desire by half screening it. It is not hard to see that Pilar and Petra and Amaranta are mother substitutes. Not that the book lacks a sense of taboo—its hundred years of doings will come to term through the breaking of a taboo—but it is unlike *Absalom, Absalom!* (and Faulkner's father-haunted fictions more generally) in that the No of the father governs the conclusion, but not everything that happens in between. A cornucopia of happenings occurs in between—all of them crystalline—and this is possible only because the cultural imaginary operative here envisages the desiring subject moving through a space and time configured as in sync with Utopian desire. No Cartesian instrumentality, no bourgeois rationalizing of means and ends, no patriarchal design of inheritable goods: no Western plotting.[19]

This generosity toward what can happen extends beyond the representation of incest and into that of miscegenation. It is the Western patriarchal edict of racial purity that confounds Faulkner's Charles Etienne. In a racist culture where he must be this or that but not conceivably both, he has only two options—passing (never a temptation for Faulkner's figures) or self-crucifixion. By contrast, as Alejo Carpentier saw decades ago, "America, a continent of symbiosis, mutations, vibrations, *mestizaje,* has always been baroque [and has thereby generated in its subjects] the awareness of being Other, of being new . . . of being a *criollo.*"[20] "The awareness of being other," the desire to marry your aunt: both situations are as acknowledgeable in García Márquez's capacious Macondo as they are scandalous in Faulkner's boundary-obsessive South.

The butterflies orchestrate Meme's lovemaking not because García Márquez is sentimental enough to want us to believe things actually happen like this but because, within his folklore-nourished representational schema, the natural world is in sync with Buendían energies—"in sync" not in the saccharine sense of "actually support," but in the neutral sense of "imaginatively aligned with": in sync so that, by way of metaphor, we can *see* what such relationality would look like (if it existed). In Michel Foucault's terms, the Buendías inhabit a culture organized—as he claims premodern Western culture was likewise based—in terms of *resemblances.* All the elements that make their appearance, human and natural, seem related, as though they came into being with each other in mind, cohabited a common frame.[21]

The deaths in this novel—José Arcadio Buendía's, Arcadio's, Colonel Aureliano's, Amaranta's, José Arcadio's—are unforgettable because, accented personally, they emerge from within the being who is to die. "In the course of modern times," Benjamin writes, "dying has been pushed further and further out of the perceptual world of the living" (*Illuminations,* 93–94). In the modern bourgeois world, he goes on to say, one dies a standard death issued by sanatoria and hospitals. Not so in García Márquez's novel, in which we die as ourselves, eventually going elsewhere, but capable of returning if need be. Death is here a dimension of ineffaceable human being, not—as the Enlightenment/scientific tradition has insisted for over three hundred years—its permanent extinction. Put otherwise, folk cultures around the globe encountered and found narrative terms for death long before Western science took on the task. Recurrently in their view, death is a chapter in the common human drama, not the end of the book.[22]

The genre enacted in *One Hundred Years of Solitude* is of course magic realism. The energies shaping that genre's procedures are no less political than aesthetic. Magic realism's swerve from realism operates, as Kumkum Sangari and others have argued, as a critical revision *of* realism.[23] This is critically charged reseeing, not sentimental escape from seeing. "Metaphor is turned into *event,*" Sangari writes, "precisely so that it will *not* be read *as* event, but folded back into metaphor as disturbing, resonant image."[24] Metaphor shows, Utopianly, what is missing in the real. In Amaryll Chanady's terms, magic realism "challenges realistic representation in order to introduce *poiesis* into *mimesis*." The correspondence model fueling both realism (positively) and modernism (negatively) is eclipsed.[25]

In Faulkner, by contrast, *poiesis* cannot be granted precedence over *mimesis;* correspondence with the real retains narrative priority. (If the real cannot be known authoritatively, it enters narrative perspectivally, speculatively.) Given the Newton-descended commitment to knowing and respecting the real (in all its gravity) that Faulkner inherits from realism, given as well realism's (white, male) plot of inheritances and acquisitions, of progressive ownership of one's place (and others) in space and time—given, finally, the disastrous Southern history to which this plot corresponds—Faulkner's available swerve is, not to write another plot, but to *jam* the inherited one. His creative response to a two-hundred-year-old narrative tradition focused on such familiar acquisitions is arrest, vertigo, collapse of projective motion. In all of this, the loom set up for guiding questing subjects' movement through space and time remains immovably in place. Thomas Sutpen's patriarchal design may be doomed before he even conceives of it, but he aspires to no other plot. Rather than reconfigure his culture's arrangements, Faulkner shows, with ceaseless repercussion, how and why and to whom those arrangements do their damage. Mocking the poignant energies of "must matter," "cant matter" guarantees the tragic thrust of his fiction, registering the inescapable "hurt" that history levies upon a subject's attempts to operate a bankrupt plot. The "might-have-been" his wounded people dream of may be "more true than truth," but it remains unreal, imaginable only in the idiom of what was not.

García Márquez does not jam the representational loom; he *reconfigures* it. Sangari writes: "The power of Márquez's narratives lies in the insistent pressure of freedom as the absent horizon—which is neither predictable nor inevitable. . . . This may be an absent freedom, but it is not an abstract freedom: it is precisely that which is made present and possible by its absence—the lives people have never lived *because* of the lives they are forced to live or have chosen to live. That which is desired and that which exists, the sense of abundance and the sense of waste, are dialectically related" (176). Free of Newton's legacy, enriched by a folk culture's capacious vision of collective human being, García Márquez recovers Utopian images of human possibility. The Buendía lives he portrays do not escape the pressures of colonial history, but his prose is oriented—as no prose of realism can afford to be—toward the graphing of human desire in its actual grandeur. Desire emerges here as plenitude rather than lack. In such a fiction of sufficiency—liberated from Western realism's insistence on knowing ("but was it really like that?")—García Márquez rewrites Faulkner's "might-have-been" as "what might be," upon a canvas wherein the human figure is once again furnished with self-enacting moves within communal time and space. Fiction written according to the logic of this other loom allows us to recognize, by positive rather than negative silhouette, the cost of all our waste, and the need to become what we potentially are.[26]

I have discussed Faulkner and García Márquez as instances of how the representational practices of modernism and postcolonialism respond to a damaging Western loom. Broadly speaking, the patriarchal arrangements that selectively shape this loom seemed adequate for two centuries of Enlightenment-based realism. However disastrous these arrangements appear to Western writers by the end of the nineteenth century, even an experimentalist like Faulkner cannot write a fiction that would fly by such nets. By contrast, García Márquez's third-world relation to the West—his brutal and vertiginous Latin American history, his folkloric cultural inheritance—permits a creative distance from first-world canonical procedures. Refusing the Newtonian premises of Western realism, he positions himself to write otherwise. More, he has before him an array of modernist practices (the most important of which is Faulkner's) that, in jamming the patriarchal loom, help point the way toward his (and other postcolonialists') reconfiguring of it.

"THE GRACE THEY COULD IMAGINE"

Toni Morrison enters this discussion as a postcolonial writer whose ways of narrating the damage her people suffer from patriarchal paradigms are enabled, suggestively, by the prior practice of both Faulkner and García Márquez.[27] There is hardly a single-line influence from Faulkner to García-Márquez or from García-Márquez to Morrison. Rather, she *joins* García-Márquez, even as she comes after him, as a writer intent upon escaping some of the Enlightenment-based protocols still binding the Faulknerian text. This analysis attends to the figuring of arrest in both Faulkner's and Morrison's careers, before turning to Morrison's increasingly nonrealistic strategies for representing release. The pertinent issue is no longer Faulkner's tragic stance toward the immovable Western "loom"—the ideological model guiding the subject's moves through space and time—but rather the release implicit in Morrison's provocative phrase from *Beloved:*

"the grace they could imagine."[28] How, given the paralyzing injury American whites have inflicted on American blacks for over three hundred years, might grace and release—an emancipatory reconceiving of the subject in space/time—be yet imagined? What untapped plotlines outside the mandate of a progressive realism traditionally blind to black resource (a resource rarely taking the form of achieved will) are open to narration? As Morrison puts it in *Paradise,* looking at her endangered women from the perspective of weapons trained upon them and about to fire, "In that holy hollow between sighting and following through, could grace slip through at all?"[29]

Faulkner's protagonist supremely incapable of negotiating the Western loom is the unfurnished idiot Benjy Compson.[30] Here is the opening of *The Sound and the Fury:*

> Through the fence, between the curling flower spaces, I could see them hitting. They were coming to where the flag was and I went along the fence. Luster was hunting in the grass by the flower tree. They took the flag out, and they were hitting. . . . Then they went on, and I went along the fence. Luster came away from the flower tree and we went along the fence and they stopped and we stopped and I looked through the fence while Luster was hunting in the grass.
>
> "Here, caddie." He hit. They went away across the pasture. I held to the fence and watched them going away.
>
> "Listen at you, now." Luster said. "Aint you something, thirty three years old, going on that way. After I done went all the way to town to buy you that cake. Hush up that moaning. Aint you going to help me find that quarter so I can go to the show tonight?" (3)

Through the fence: Benjy on the other side of that fence, hemmed in, defective, speechless; a game of golf described by one who has no idea what it means, and who thinks it is taking place on a pasture; a golfer's casual command ("Here, caddie") that triggers inexplicably an outburst of tears in Benjy. This passage stages an idiot's continuous disorientation. He cannot know why people do what they do, lacks any sense for his culture's projects, makes nothing happen. He is dysfunctional—ideology-deprived, without canniness—as no realist protagonist can be. Since he cannot master language, he thinks a golf caddie refers to his sister Caddy, and he weeps because she is not there. Since he has no understanding of time, he thinks what was once his pasture is still his pasture (though golfers play on it). Incapable of negotiating space and time, plotless, he is still waiting by the fence for Caddy (gone these past eighteen years) to come home.

This passage, like the larger text, registers spatial/temporal disorientation on a scale inconceivable in realism. Faulkner's narrative refuses to "see past" the sound and fury of Benjy's uncomprehending, though the Reverend Shegog does provide, in the novel's closing Easter sermon, a figure for Benjy's plight—in the image and aftermath of the crucified Christ: "O blind sinner! Breddren, I tells you; sistuhn, I says to you, when de Lawd did turn His mighty face, say, Aint gwine overload heaven! I can see de widowed God shet His do" (184–85). "Aint gwine overload heaven": Benjy emerges as heaven's orphan, his innocence unaccommodated, his plight incurable. All paths in the novel circulate about this unfurnished child. In his lack one reads the larger incapacity of an inbred, incompetent, disoriented Southern white culture at the end of its belief system. The forms of progress Faulkner knows of are unendorsable; the kind of progress he could endorse is unimaginable. The widowed God has shut his door; Faulkner is not about to try to open it.[31]

As he continues his career, Faulkner's gaze widens, and he begins to identify the cultural coordinates for such dysfunction. In the turmoil of *Light in August*'s Joe Christmas and of *Absalom, Absalom!*'s Thomas Sutpen he presents a stunning diagnosis of Southern self-wounding. These are canvases in which white and black share the most intimate spaces (even as white cannot bear to know this sharing), in which male and female, landed and sharecropper, Mississippi Puritan and New Orleans sensualist live each other's lives, breathe each other's breaths. However spacious, Faulkner's world is suffocating—lacking shared racial, gender, and class norms in which these opposed figures can fruitfully imagine or encounter each other, and thus issuing into cries of outrage and disbelief. The patriarchal loom mangles rather than orients, "the strings are all in one another's way" (*Absalom*, 101); none of this can be righted. Hightower in *Light in August* (like Quentin and Shreve in *Absalom, Absalom!*) cannot alter the outcome, but he does take the measure of his culture's insistence on crucifixion. Hightower glimpses "a more inextricable" compositeness, amalgamating the opposed "faces" in his story, all striving "in turn to free themselves one from the other" (763), yet (in a figure related to that of the death-dealing loom) inseparably bound upon the same wheel of torture. His Southern culture cannot imagine its own grace—an incapacity silhouetted against Faulkner's most perspicacious narrators' capacity to grasp the need for it but not to bring it into being. The pathos of the might-have-been calls out unceasingly, but heaven's door remains shut.

Toni Morrison's career opens, as Faulkner's did, on the crucifixion of an unfurnished child. *The Bluest Eye* begins by acknowledging the abused and

sacrificed Pecola Breedlove—dead before the narrative gets under way.
Like her parents, Pecola lacked the homegrown resources of a native black
culture, yearning instead for the commodified white icons of Shirley Temple dolls and impossible blue eyes. All three Breedloves are culturally
unfurnished, focused upon a meretricious grace imagined by and for
whites, thus "always wrong to the light," as Robert Frost put it, "so never
seeing / Deeper down in the well."[32] Morrison's later novels provide a
range of attempts to see "deeper down in the well," to refuse the disorientation and madness to which a preoccupation with the Western patriarchal
loom leads. It is not that the widowed God has shut his door, but that the
Breedlove family are looking for it in the wrong place, fantasizing others'
grace rather than imagining the possibilities of their own. The creative
turn—the black cultural refurnishing—occurs in *Sula.*

  Sula records simultaneously Morrison's exit from the realist fiction of
black victimization and her taking possession (in her own way) of some of
the resources of Latin American magic realism. Not García Márquez's non-
Newtonian events—in which the "scientificity" of the represented world is
suspended—but rather a deployment of events that are possible yet simultaneously fabulous: the appearance of the indistinguishable Deweys, the
drowning of Chicken Little, the burnings of Plum and Hannah. Her practice here departs from realist norms in ways that Faulknerian modernism
never does (his characters' weirdest behavior, like that of the Bundrens
throughout *As I Lay Dying,* is always, so to speak, statistically credible, if
only because they pass through a human landscape of normal and scandalized others).[33] Morrison's departures lead somewhere else, past individual or
family eccentricity. That elsewhere is a vividly delineated, non-middle-class,
black folk culture whose narratives she draws on with increasing power:
"We are very practical people, very down-to-earth, even shrewd people. But
within that practicality we also accepted what I suppose could be called
superstition and magic, which is another way of knowing things."[34] Such
black folklore, quietly refusing Newtonian givens, harbors instead non-
Western narratives for understanding life outside the instrumental register
of subjects mapping and mastering objects in lawful space and time.

  In different ways all of her texts after *Sula* testify to the postcolonial task
that Morrison calls "the reclamation of the history of black people in this
country" (Gates and Appiah, 418). She writes: "There is a confrontation
between old values of the tribe and new urban values. It's confusing. There
has to be a mode to do what the music did for blacks, what we used to be
able to do with each other in private and in that civilization that existed
underneath the white civilizations" (371). Spoken nine years before the

publication of *Jazz,* these words are prescient; the narrative arc they inti-mate has little to do with instrumental progress. Tribe, enchantment, music, a civilization beneath a civilization—the traditions she would make contact with are black: the staying power of the matriarchal black family and the tissue of shared beliefs and behaviors that make up a community; the dignity-enabling roots of black families as these go back to nineteenth-century records and then further back to folk myths of flying men and swamp women; the survival of black people even during the depredations of slavery, thanks to their mutual dependencies and inventiveness, their fragmented yet still viable grasp upon an African heritage that predated the Middle Passage; and finally the irresistible music with which they colo-nized New York of the 1920s into a series of interlocking neighborhoods at once intimate and dangerous.

If *Sula* is Morrison's breakthrough novel—her exit from realist victim-ization—*Beloved* reveals where this departure can take her, perhaps most suggestively in the figure of Beloved herself. Perfectly clear, perfectly mys-terious, this character embodies a prodigious undertaking: a crazed and abused black girl who believes Sethe to be her mother, Sethe's murdered daughter come back from the dead and seeking both the maternal embrace and the infant's revenge, and finally the symbolic embodiment of all those shipwrecked and injured slaves whose voices were never recorded, whose silenced cries began with the nightmare of the Middle Passage. How radi-antly different this overdetermined figure is from either Charles Etienne or Pecola. Equally damaged (and by the same murderous racism), Beloved is yet not alienated—arrested—but instead a carrier of precious, otherwise irretrievable racial memories, an umbilical connection to an unspeakable past that will continue to inflict damage until, somehow, it gets spoken. This is a speaking that neither the bright logic of realism nor the dark logic of modernism can deliver; both logics are Western and remain attached to Newton.[35] Listening to the sounds outside the door of 124, Stamp Paid hears—folklorically—more than realism concedes can be heard between heaven and earth: "he believed he knew who spoke them. The people of the broken necks, of fire-cooked blood and black girls who had lost their ribbons. What a roaring" (181). "This is not a story to pass on" (275), for it retrieves, through the returned figure of Beloved, too much damage to acknowledge and keep on living. "So they forgot her. . . . Sometimes the photograph of a close friend or relative—looked at too long—shifts, and something more familiar than the dear face itself moves there. They can touch it if they like, but don't, because they know things will never be the same if they do" (275).

The drowned girl who lost her ribbon, the suicidal Pecola who wanted blue eyes, Sethe's undone infant, the murdered Dorcas in *Jazz:* all figures for the unfurnished orphan child, all figures of dysfunction within a patriarchal frame, yet becoming something other than figures of mere dispossession. Morrison is learning how to say their significance outside a model of individual achievement. The loss is turning into gain, the dispossession into richness, within a black folkloric schema steeped in non-Western values. The returned Beloved is priceless even as she is heartbreaking, and Joe Trace muses in *Jazz* that "when [Adam] left Eden, he left a rich man. Not only did he have Eve, but he had the taste of the first apple in his mouth for the rest of his life. . . . To bite it down, bite it down. Hear the crunch and let the red peeling break his heart."[36] The broken heart figures in *Jazz* as a kind of wealth unrelated to ideological integrity or attainment, one that you cannot conceive as a "project" but must experience instead, one that neither realism nor modernism is prepared to articulate.[37] This novel signals Morrison's return to damaged lives as uniquely capacious—lives that must be narrated in new ways that do not merely report the damage. "Something is missing there [in that negative register]," *Jazz*'s narrator muses; "Something rogue. Something else you have to figure in before you can figure it out" (228).[38] Figuring it in—letting her readers see the resource implied by the deprivation (the Grace in Gigi, the Consolation in Connie)—accounts for Morrison's setting up in *Paradise* a new loom where metaphor reconfigures event and where fatal damage yields to the grace she can imagine.

Morrison begins by granting the full damage done to her thrown-away women gathered together in the Convent. In responsible realism or modernism they would be out for the count. But she has other plans for them, choosing, like García Márquez, to delineate not the constraining details of the given but rather the yeasty ones of desire, beginning with the magic of a maternal care embodied first in "mother," then in Connie, and finally in the generative capacity that flourishes anew in each of the orphan girls secure in her retreat. So generative that Mavis's dead children come back to a strange half-life within the Convent's womblike walls—not seeking revenge like Beloved but chirping with pleasure. As though the difference between life and death were a permeable membrane and not an uncrossable barrier, the Convent bestows upon its women an elasticity beyond the appearance/reality binary that confines realism and haunts modernism. Readers do not know whether the women are killed or wounded by the attack of Ruby men, whether their final reappearance in their old haunts is merely imagined or a real event, whether the last locale in the novel is or is not Paradise. The authority of the prose is not invested in such mastery of *knowing*. Morrison places us, at novel's end, deep within what in Faulkner's mimetic world would be a might-have-been, yet is presented here as real.

"Don't you want the world to be something more than what it is?" (208) Violet asks Felice at the end of *Jazz*, and in these later novels Morrison intimates to the reader that the world is always more than what fidelity to Newtonian givens shows it to be. Breaking with the authority of such a model, she supplies that dimension beyond the demonstrably real, figuring in a "something rogue," as when Connie is visited by a mysterious friend: "Suddenly he was next to her without having moved. . . . Not six inches from her face, he removed his tall hat. Fresh tea-colored hair came tumbling down, cascading over his shoulders and down his back. He took off his glasses then and winked, a slow seductive movement of a lid. His eyes, she saw, were as round and green as new apples" (252). Is he real? fictive? Does it matter? Epistemological questions are as beside the point here as in the magic realism of *One Hundred Years of Solitude*. All one knows is that this "friend" supplements the real, shows what is missing, completes the scenario of human desire. At Connie's final moment—"'You're back,' she says, and smiles" (289) at her former lover Deacon, even as his brother Steward shoots her between the eyes—does one know whether she is addressing the flesh-and-blood Deacon or her mysterious spirit Friend? Whether she is actually dead or not? Does it matter?

"Don't separate God from His elements. He created it all" (244), Lone advised Connie. Opposing realms cohabit; as in other postcolonial texts, the dead come back to life. "Stepping in," Lone calls this gift of resuscitation, as she urges Connie to draw on her native/God-given resources to breathe life back into the dead body of Soane's child. Connie does, and his life returns. "Stepping in" is Morrison's rogue move, the making of the world more than what it is, the figuring in of what is uncannily necessary if one would figure it out, seeing the world as it might look according to another loom. That move is steeped in mystery, yet utterly quotidian. Richard and Anna glimpse, at the end of *Paradise*, a closed door (or is it an open window?), and they think: "what would happen if you entered? What would be on the other side? What on earth would it be? What on earth?" (305). As with that shimmering photograph at the end of *Beloved*, if one dares to enter, if one "steps in" and sees more than Newton's optics allow to be seen, all will be changed—though no one can say in advance how. What can be said is that the change will be here and now, both given and imagined—partially wrought out there and wholly to be sustained in

here. The transfigured space will be the home one thought one knew, not
an exotic elsewhere, for the afterlife is but an ever-present dimension of
the present one—what the present one looks like in visionary mode, when
all the lights are on.[39] "Now they will rest," Morrison writes as the last line
of her novel, "before shouldering the endless work they were created to do
down here in Paradise" (318).

However the modernist Faulkner longs for sanctuary (the closest his fiction gets to Paradise), his deepest conviction is that it is not here, not now,
not ours. The pathos of his history-haunted fiction is that the grace it lumi-
nously imagines is unavailable to any of his white characters in this dispensation, but rather the mark and measure of their loss. No vision of a
might-have-been can undo damage that is done, refurbish an ideological
fabric tattered beyond repair. The widowed God has shut his door: aint
gwine overload heaven. For reasons that have been gathering for centuries,
the loom of Western patriarchy—its privileged design for white males
moving acquisitively through space and time—begets not fulfillment but,
in a culture filled with others who are both disowned and one's own, disaster. No one knows better than Faulkner how intricately the resultant "cant
matter" trumps human desire's unceasing "must matter."

How might one see beyond such collapse, into the Utopian territory (not
yet realized but compellingly imaginable) of a non-Newtonian world
where human being might flourish in culturally refurnished space/time,
outside the patriarchal mandate? How might one forge a representational
model in which "must matter" would stand up to "cant matter," without
pretending that "cant matter" does not intrude with all the weight of the
Western colonial legacy? These are the unsentimental questions of much
postcolonial fiction, and I have sought to show their reach in the practice of
García-Márquez and Morrison, as well as why the modernist Faulkner
cannot find his way into this territory.

Refusing the individualizing projects of realism, going beyond the
arrest and alienation of modernism, drawing on non-Western, folkloric
tropes, their work envisages new ways of setting up the loom. In their representational schema, the arrest of the real is accompanied by the release
of desire. For both García Márquez and Morrison, yet in such different
ways, the world is always more, potentially other, than what it is. Of
course History remains what hurts, its alienating force undeniable; the
gorgeous cosmos of Macondo ends by being "wiped out by the wind and
exiled from the memory of men" (*One Hundred,* 422). But history in *One
Hundred Years of Solitude* shares the scene with desire, such that the novel
stubbornly refuses to succumb to its own final sentence, instead staying in

the mind as a luminous reservoir of images of what we might be like if we were both free and at home. As for Morrison, the grace she can imagine is that Paradise (a word she wanted spelled with little *p*) has never been overloaded, never been shut off from us, never been easy, never been anywhere but here.

Conclusion

Acknowledging—Modernism's Weak Messianic Power

> The country of Narrative, that dark territory
> Which spells out our stories in sentences,
> Which gives them an end and a beginning.
> CHARLES WRIGHT, "APPALACHIAN FAREWELL"

"THE COUNTRY OF NARRATIVE"

Opening his poem "Appalachian Farewell" with the clause "If night is our last address," Charles Wright lets us glimpse, through the echo of "that dark territory," narrative's constituent relation with death. Yet, he intimates, narrative fashions "farewell" into something more than loss and departure. End-driven, narrative arises from our unceasing journey toward death, our need to make sense of passing. Acknowledging that dual sense of an end—as extinction, as purpose—it conceives beginnings. The end as purpose, though concealed, is all-motivating and actually comes first. That is the "spell" produced by "spell[ing] our stories in sentences," suturing our passage through time by wording it—what Peter Brooks calls narrative's perversion of time. Realism invests massively in such "spells," inventing a rhetoric in which subjects seem to encounter time and space freshly, progressively, moving toward purposes both unforeseen and appropriate.

Postmodernism, by contrast, seems intent on withholding any "spelling" that would pretend to transcend the deathliness of our being in time. As Lyotard puts it, "The postmodern would be . . . that which denies itself the solace of good forms, the consensus of a taste which would make it possible to share collectively the nostalgia for the unattainable" (81). In such postmodern narrative we do not cross from our space into the space of the other, we do not surmount time and secure identity within time's passage, by way of intact memory and unifying recognitions. Or rather, such passage and surmounting, when they do occur, tend to be delivered in a rhetoric announcing its own fictiveness, its status as "conversation" rather than an attempt to say the real. "Live or tell," Sartre insisted. Go forward, unpredicated, or backward, end-supplied. Realism reassuringly passes off the latter in the guise of the former, while postmodernism insists on their separation.

What of modernism? How does it negotiate that "dark territory"—the death that stalks and founds "the country of Narrative"? I end my book by returning to modernism—to where we have been—rather than speculate further on where we have arrived, or might be headed. I prefer not to promote some linear metanarrative of Western fiction itself—some structure that would align realism, modernism, and postmodernism as steps in a necessary sequence of progress or decline. Such a sequence, triangulated into Significance, would simplify the stubborn realities motivating and sustaining each of these "moments"—by proposing a dialectical schema that transcends the contingencies, the discontinuities, wrought into time's passage. As Bakhtin writes, "Take a dialogue and remove the voices . . . remove the intonations . . . carve out abstract concepts and judgments from living words and responses, cram everything into one abstract consciousness—and that's how you get dialectics" (*Speech,* 147). This study is invested less in dialectics—in limning the future fictional practice that a history of past ones might seem to mandate—than in construing better, retrospectively, what one of those past practices, modernism, was most about. The temporality of my argument, as in modernism itself, is backward, returning to the "dark territory" of the dead.

"Knowing" sutures the subject by coming into possession of the object over space and time; it is future-oriented. "Beyond knowing" tends to insist that no objects out there are disinterestedly knowable, and that any talk of objective mapping and mastery is either mistaken or malicious—an affair of the police. "Unknowing," however, may proceed by way of a different dynamic: an *acknowledging* irreducible to knowing. Levinas's emphasis upon the other (his claim upon my being), Bakhtin's focus on dialogic (language's escape from the progressive mastery of dialectic), and Benjamin's attempt to understand language as "nonsensuous similarity" (words' inexplicable capacity for "aura," their purchase on something other than other words—on the nonverbal real): all these stances envisage the representation of the subject in space, time, and the field of the other as a drama of social *encounter* rather than a latently solipsistic one of knowing or an openly solipsistic one of beyond knowing.

Art-language presses, by way of its formal energies, toward social encounter outside the protocols of objective knowledge or logical argument: "Art requires philosophy," Adorno writes, "which interprets it in order to say what it is unable to say, whereas art is only able to say it by not saying it" (*Aesthetic,* 72). Fiction's way of saying the subject's imbrication in the social is a resonant not-saying; "in artworks nothing is literal, least of all their words; spirit is their ether" (*Aesthetic,* 87). Rather than representing such imbrication as already familiar experience, modernist artworks violently decompose it (and sometimes Utopianly recompose it).[1] K.'s bedroom invaded by the warders, Marcel seeing his grandmother not see him, Hightower envisaging Christmas's face on a wheel of inextricable compositeness: these are—for the reader—diagnostic moments of encounter. Though Adorno speaks of art in general, he seems to have especially in mind the revelatory contortions of modernist form: an art that neither re-presents the social in familiar ways nor abandons it as beyond representation.

Fiction's way of not-saying the world is no less resonantly a saying, a *wording.* It proceeds as though through a primordial belief, however vestigial, in a magic of mimesis seeded in words themselves. What creative writer has not struggled to get the work's verbal form somehow—indirectly, impossibly—to mimic the nonverbal experience that is its material? Walter Benjamin's insistence on the mimetic faculty as supremely present in language itself—the flash of similarity between words and what they reference—reveals his lifelong attempt to get past Weber's Enlightenment model of the knowing subject inserted in a "disenchanted world." Inheriting the modern worldview of language-as-arbitrary and the world as masterable-but-alien, Benjamin chafed at his inheritance, sought to reenchant the subject's relation to the world. He wanted to apprehend the world qualitatively (indeed, religiously), to encounter it in the form of "an unmutilated experience" (Jürgen Habermas's term).

Benjamin knew that such experience could be grasped—fleetingly, Utopianly—only from within the precincts of a commodity-saturated setting. Even the lowliest commodity harbors an unfulfilled dream of liberation; the meanest newspaper article might release surprise.[2] Rejecting a Barthesian prison-house of language, in which the writer is enjoined to use words to "inexpress the expressible" (Barthes's phrase for breaking down language into its dead/deadly codes), Benjamin insists on language as a repository of potent yet scrambled correspondences, a latent connection with others—with the dead. "To read what was never written" (*Reflections,* 336): so Benjamin glosses those ancient acts of imagination—reading from entrails, stars, or dances—by which one crosses over, mimetically, to what is not oneself.

One crosses into the territory of the dead. "The past carries with it a temporal index by which it is referred to redemption," Benjamin writes: "There is a secret agreement between past generations and the present one" (*Illuminations*, 254). Genuine critique is rescue work, a return to the words of the dead that penetrates beyond surface resolution and recognizes—in a flash of "profane illumination"—their unresolved charge, their unanswered call.[3] Though gone, the dead await us (in both senses of the verb). Is this perhaps the deepest belief animating our reading and writing—that it can put us in touch with those who have died, as well as with those who will live after we ourselves are dead? Our traffic in language is never merely personal. "Quests for my own word," Bakhtin writes, "are in fact quests for a word that is not my own, a word that is more than myself" (*Speech*, 149). Produced socially—the Trojan horse within me—the language that lets me articulate myself is not my own. It articulates me within a field of fellow language users (living and dead), whom it likewise articulates.

Creaturely myself, inconceivable without the enabling priority of others, I owe those others an unpayable debt. Paul Ricoeur writes: "As soon as the idea of a debt to the dead, to people of flesh and blood to whom something really happened in the past, stops giving documentary research its highest end, history loses its meaning."[4] Indebtedness to the dead resonates in the dual meanings of the verb *render*. To render is to represent—the definitive activity of narrative itself—and also to return something to others. No return without a something represented to return. "In this term 'to render,'" Ricoeur writes, "I see the desire to 'render its due' to what is and to what was" (152). If to render is to go from now to then, it is no less to go from me to you.

"AND YOU ARE——?"

I opened my chapter on the modernist subject, as I opened this book itself (the beginning of the Kierkegaard chapter), with the haunting words from Genesis: "Here I am." To what am I already, unknowingly, exposed? What others' calls upon me has my utterance itself acknowledged, even as I cannot know in advance either who those others are or the bearing of their calls? All I know is they are there and approaching me. The reverse of the Cartesian cogito, Abraham's trial—echoed by the modernist trials explored above—entails the risk of one's being within an unanticipated field of others.

In *Absalom, Absalom!* "here I am"—Quentin's unsought availability to the entire Sutpen narrative—reaches its apogee when he enters the once proud, now dilapidated Sutpen's Hundred and, pressed by Rosa, climbs to the bedroom off the upper hall. There he discovers the last piece of the puzzle, the dying Henry Sutpen, to whom, bewildered, he poses the question: "*And you are*——?" (306; emphasis in the original).[5] He gets in response not an explanation but only a name—"Henry Sutpen"—and perhaps the form of his question has already intimated (to us, if not to him) not to expect more. His question is that of identity itself: the question realism confidently answers by never posing, being posed here such that the blankness following the words (——) shrouds them in darkness. In *Absalom,* as more broadly in the work of Proust, Kafka, and Faulkner, the issue of subject identity is launched thus in the interrogative mode, inseparable from the blankness of——whether this be the full name of K. (unprovided, unprovidable) or the full name of Marcel (never pronounced, intimated only a few times in over thirty-five hundred pages). Identity emerges here, as it rarely does in realism, as a question launched in the field of the other.

The answer Quentin receives to his question brings no resolution. Leaving Sutpen's Hundred that night, Quentin does not convert his encounter with the dying Henry Sutpen into the fabric of his own identity: "outside the house now, breathing deep and fast now . . . finding that he was about to run, thinking quietly, 'Jesus, Jesus, Jesus,' breathing fast and hard of the dark dead furnace-breath of air" (305). Lying in bed later, "sweating still, panting . . . it was all the same, there was no difference: waking or sleeping he walked down that upper hall . . ." (306). Meeting the other does not take him Ulysses-like homeward. His home transforms into a not-home in which he no longer sleeps, "thinking 'Nevermore of peace. Nevermore of peace'" (307). This encounter propels him, in fear and trembling, to an elsewhere that has no name, unless it be the haunted South itself.

And you are——? Suppose the question were serious, suppose that "you are" is in question, suppose that *you are in question.* Modernism's courageous project is to put its reader's "here I am" in question. This project is wrought into the labor of its formal inventiveness, its refusal to serve as a mirror for confirming what we already know of ourselves. Adorno sees that the unfamiliarity of the artwork carries its spiritual charge: "it is in art's enigmaticalness, not its meanings, that spirit is manifest" (*Aesthetic,* 127). More fully, "The artwork is related to the world by the principle that contrasts it with the world, and that is the same principle by which spirit organized the world" (*Aesthetic,* 7). If art would reach the frozen sea within its reader, it *must* be at first unfamiliar. It must rupture realism's standard adventure of consciousness converting its obstacles into dimensions of the same. For the sake of a deeper acknowledging, it must interrupt our apparent knowing. We who engage it are to experience our identity (however briefly) as unfamiliar, as a something socially inflected according to premises we have mistaken for nature: "Art completes knowledge with what is excluded from knowledge and thereby once again impairs its character as knowledge" (Adorno, *Aesthetic,* 54). For the reader to access the shaping and interrogative play of spirit within unfamiliar forms takes more *time* than readers typically like to bestow. By refusing swiftly to *render,* such art calls into question the reader's instrumental stance toward time itself.[6] For that reason alone, modernist works will forever lack a huge audience.

The diagnostic potential within such art is latent rather than immediate, and its illumination is valuable only insofar as it issues from a prior and sustained experience of readerly blankness (——). Proust writes recurrently of the time and effort needed to penetrate unfamiliar art forms: "No doubt they [Marcel's great-aunts] regarded aesthetic merits as material objects which an unclouded vision could not fail to discern, without one's needing to nurture equivalents of them and let them slowly ripen in one's own heart" (1:160). What we find out about ourselves without lengthy, painful self-investigation, he claims (and here he could be Freud), is not ours. If we would know, we must endure—spend some time in—the darkness of unknowing, must relinquish our canniness in order actually to see ourselves in the field of space and time and others, in "infrared." Objects encountered in such acts of seeing escape our grasp. In Levinas's terms, "a being is in a relation with what it cannot absorb, with what it cannot, in the etymological sense of the term, comprehend" (*Totality,* 80). Comprehending as a sort of primordial grasping and converting to our own utility— what all prehensile creatures are supposedly equipped to do—fails in this fiction. Unseen others are in the room. Or, as in Forster's *Passage to India,* upon entering a dark and unmapped space, one is suddenly, maddeningly, touched by others whom one does not see, will never know, and cannot keep at a distance. One is accused; Mrs. Moore will die of this accusation.

Accusation, disempowerment, distress: my study of modernist fiction has centered on these states, and I have recurrently asked, what can be the good of such disabling? It is time to frame some answers. "I don't think one realises how very discrete (in the mathematical sense) one's existence is," John Maynard Keynes once remarked.[7] One's existence as discrete, indeed infinitesimal within the immeasurable field of countless others: one would not realize this by reading the canon of Western realist fiction.

Such fiction is committed, as Woolf put it in a gender context, to producing mirrors that make the (male) subject look twice his size. Modernism corrects the visual error; it does so by puncturing the balloon of male project, reducing its sway. Made smaller thus, the subject shares a canvas with others whom he does not succeed in knowing and converting to dimensions of the same.

In her study of trauma as centering on belatedness and incapacitation, Cathy Caruth approaches a related point (though she is not talking about literature). She attends at length to one of Freud's dream analyses, that of a burning child. The context of the dream involves a father who has just lost his child and who is passing the night next to the candle-lighted bedside of the corpse, witnessing. Despite his vigilance, the father falls asleep; an old man engaged to be witnessing with him likewise falls asleep. The bedside candle, melting, touches the linen of the dead child's clothing; the clothing catches fire. The sleeping father dreams the following: that his dead child is no longer dead, but alive—yet burning, and begging the father to waken immediately and put out the flames. The father awakens and, seeing with horror his dead child in flames, extinguishes the fire. Caruth reads this dream as a fable of belatedness: "Waking up in order to see, the father discovers that he has once again *seen too late* to prevent the burning."[8] In life, we are always too late, despite the stories we tell ourselves about being cannily in time. In the dream the child is alive, but it is, so to speak, the actual dead child behind the fictive live one who awakens his sleeping father, so that the father himself not die in the flames: "It is precisely the dead child," Caruth writes, "the child in its irreducible inaccessibility and otherness, who says to the father: *wake up, leave me, survive; survive to tell the story of my burning*" (105; emphasis in the original).

Wake up, tell the story of my burning: in Caruth's reading of trauma, speech is always meant for others, it is too late for the traumatized one. He will not awaken. But his story—told properly—might awaken others in time. This vignette powerfully suggests the candor and the urgency of the modernist fiction I have been analyzing. Candor in that the damage is already done: there is no pretense here of plotting its redress, righting wrongs that have occurred, suffering that has taken place. The dead are dead. More, there is no illusion that beings as discrete as mere individual subjects are likely to change the world significantly—no corrective plot. Urgency because, although what has happened has happened, yet we who receive it are alive, in process, our journey uncompleted. This news is meant for us; in Benjamin's words, "our coming was expected" (*Illuminations,* 254).

Entered, we might even see ourselves (however briefly) as other, as in Rilke's "for there is no place / that does not see you." It is our penetrability itself that modernist fiction engages. Realism, by contrast, tells the story of gathered self-recovery. We are invoked as spectators of this renewal, perhaps as imitators, but nothing more intimate is asked. Space/time behaves normally within such fiction; the intentional ego remains projective, revising (in time) its projects according to what has been learned. Postmodernism suspends the identificatory process itself, delivers its materials to us, so to speak, in quotes—a conversation that is coming our way.[9] There is no arrest of the subject in a disordered space/time that can be neither accepted nor altered. Only modernism seeks to envelop its reader within a potentially self-altering structure of guilt, call, and responsibility. Something must be done; it has not been done in the plot. In Faulknerian terms, "it cant matter, you know that, or the Ones that set up the loom would have arranged things a little better, and yet it must matter . . ." (*Absalom,* 105).What must matter, finally, is my coming to acknowledge how much more is in my scene than I can know—in my scene and bearing upon me. Knowing enacts a fantasized possession of the other that undoes its otherness, erasing therein my contingency, my "discreteness." Knowing puts me at the center of the picture—as Descartes hoped it would—with others arranged around me, smaller and in the margins. Acknowledging involves a continuous subject-other traffic, registering that I am in the midst of— touched by—more than I know, and that this "more," in issuing its call, turns "I" into "me." The fiction of Proust, Kafka, and Faulkner—like the phenomenological practice of Freudian psychoanalysis—represents the unconvertible difference of others in our field (inside us, outside us, but not us) with all its subject-altering power. Unknowable, they must be acknowledged. Such acknowledging neither advances my project nor sharpens or empowers the contours of my identity. But it does extend them, even as it reconceives the dream of progress in terms of which, for over three hundred years, the singular, knowing subject of the West has understood its passage through space and time.

Reflecting on Paul Klee's painting titled *Angelus Novus,* Walter Benjamin describes the subject's movement through a space and time hauntingly figured otherwise: "But a storm is blowing from Paradise; it has got caught in his [the angel's] wings with such violence that the angel can no longer close them. This storm irresistibly propels him into the future to which his back is turned, while the pile of debris before him grows skyward. This storm is what we call progress" (*Illuminations,* 257–58). Paradise behind rather than ahead; being propelled into a future one is forced to enter backward, unknowing; the gathered history of the West a series of failures misnamed progress: these tropes—reversing, point for point, Enlightenment premises—are hardly unfamiliar in the literature we have been analyzing. The idea of progress is reconceived. "To believe in progress," as Kafka wrote, "is not to believe that progress has already taken place. That would be no belief."

All is still to be done, that is the bad news; no one to do it but us who are still alive, that is the challenge. As the far from optimistic Benjamin put it (he wrote these words on the eve of World War II): "Our coming was expected on earth. Like every generation that preceded us, we have been endowed with a *weak* Messianic power, a power to which the past has a claim" (*Illuminations,* 254; emphasis in the original). "Wake up, leave me, survive; survive to tell the story of my burning," these modernist texts seem to call out, for the dead do speak, even though dead. They speak to us—not clearly, as in a realism that remounts past time with confidence; nor illusorily, as in a postmodernism that accesses history only as fictional convention—but rather in a mode requiring that we unknow what we know if we would hear. Such hearing cannot bring them back to life. But Benjamin believed that it might incomplete the completeness of their death, putting us in a sudden and exigent contact with their still unresolved suffering. Whatever the content of their saying, it comes with an unchanging accusative charge: "And you are———?" To this address we are called somehow—with the mere, terminally weak Messianic powers we all possess—to respond.

Notes

INTRODUCTION

1. Although a case can be made for other writers, Proust, Kafka, and Faulkner are the supremely haunted modernists, the most resonantly Freudian. They are haunted, not by repressed sexuality, but more broadly and unpredictably—their texts intimating a sort of underweave of the socially *unworkable*. Among those writers missing from this book, James Joyce is of course the indispensable, indeed iconic, modernist, yet Joyce's texts are not revealingly haunted. The play of consciousness fills the pages of *Ulysses*. He has little interest in repressed psychic materials; Bloomian consciousness is amply "streamed" onto the page. When Joyce wants to access his characters' unacted desires, he invents in "Circe" less a discourse of subject repression than one of fantastic social carnival. Virginia Woolf, likewise, writes a modernist fiction centering on the dance of consciousnesses, not that which lies repressed beneath. She produces in Septimus Smith a breathtaking case study in psychosis, not a neurotic who reveals symptomatically the psychic disturbances he ignores. One would not align him with the duplicities of a Charlus or Legrandin, the obsessions of a Quentin or Joe Christmas, the blankness of an unreadable Joseph K. Thomas Mann might well have a claim on my argument—his great work is laden with the collapse of exhausted Western norms—yet Hans Castorp (to take a telling instance) has little unconscious. Mann distributes Castorp's possibilities into the array of surrounding characters atop the magic mountain, even as he plays out the implications of Aschenbach's collapse into the surrounding Venetian setting and imagery. D. H. Lawrence, no less than Mann, was creatively attentive to the collapse of the "knowing subject," but he is finally more interested, like André Gide and Hermann Hesse, in representing release than in dramatizing the kinds of arrest that are central here. I omit Robert Musil because his protagonists lack what Proust figures as "infrared"—an interior cathecting energy intimating that what lies beneath the surface is shaping unawares the surface itself. My point is less to disqualify all other modernist candidates than to shore up, briefly, the logic of my particular grouping.

2. The term "subject" is crucial to my argument. I tend to use it rather than "individual" or "self" or "protagonist" for the following reasons: (1) unlike the "individual," the "subject" is

not premised as centered, *undivided;* (2) unlike the "self," the "subject" implies a larger social realm within whose norms she or he is implicated (indeed, subjected: by contrast, "self" implies a realm of sovereignty, however restricted or illusory); (3) unlike the "protagonist" (who is always a literary figure), the "subject" can fluidly refer to writer, reader, or character, according to the context.

3. The pertinent Sartre passage is as follows: "This is what I thought: for the most banal even to become an adventure, you must (and this is enough) begin to recount it. This is what fools people: a man is always a teller of tales, he lives surrounded by his stories and the stories of others, he sees everything that happens to him through them; and he tries to live his own life as if he were living a story. But you have to choose: live or tell." *Nausea* (1938), trans. Lloyd Alexander (New York: Grove Press, 1964), 39.

4. Theodor Adorno, *Negative Dialectics* (1966), trans. E. B. Ashton (New York: Continuum, 1995), 148. Subsequent citation from *Negative Dialectics* refers to this edition and will be indicated in the body of my text, parenthetically, following the quote.

5. Inasmuch as my argument centers on modernist fictional practice, I sketch here a necessarily brief portrait of Enlightenment premises that modernist writers repudiate. Drawing on other seventeenth- and eighteenth-century thinkers, one could stress other Enlightenment norms and produce a picture with different emphases. I select Descartes, Newton, Locke, and Kant as certain ideal types of Enlightenment thinking—instances that, gathered together, economically permit a larger narrative to come into focus.

6. Theodor Adorno, "Notes on Kafka," in *Prisms* (1967), trans. Samuel Weber and Shierry Weber (Cambridge: MIT Press, 1983), 252. Subsequent citation from *Prisms* refers to this edition and will be indicated in the body of my text, parenthetically, after the quote.

7. The term comes from the contemporary philosopher Richard Rorty, and it designates a kind of writing that no longer strains to refer accurately—to "correspond"—to some set of nonverbal real-world conditions. A literature of "vocabularies" offers itself frankly for enjoyment and imaginative release.

8. This sentence points toward a project aligned with mine but not here actively pursued: the correlations between an Enlightenment model of liberal subjectivity and a larger Western history of capitalism and colonialism. Their correlations, I believe, are undeniable; but adequate analysis of the interplay of aesthetic forms, on the one hand, and the pertinent facts of Western capitalism and empire, on the other, would require a book different from this one. Undertaking to do justice to the imaginative projects of a range of Western writers over three centuries—and to link these, where appropriate, to the philosophic traditions out of which they arise—already taxes the limits of critical good sense; to try for more than this would risk jeopardizing all of it. Yet my own argument probes the problematic of the acquisitive Western subject—at home and abroad—in such ways as to invite the cognate study I cannot responsibly provide.

9. Difficult to categorize, Levinas's thought is marked fundamentally by his (Lithuanian/French-Jewish) prison experience during World War II. Increasingly in the 1950s and 1960s he developed an anti-Heideggerian philosophy in which selfhood is a necessarily secondary term in relation to the primacy of the *other.*

10. Benjamin's restless wandering through the thought systems of his time, in search of an encounter with the world that might escape the confines imposed by Enlightenment disenchantment, is well known. He speaks in his essay "Surrealism" of "*profane illumination*" (*Reflections: Essays, Aphorisms, Autobiographical Writings,* trans. Edmund Jethcott [New York: Schocken, 1978], 179; emphasis in the original), moments in which the profane city "exposes its Surrealist face" (182), thanks to "a dialectical optic that perceives the everyday as impenetrable, the impenetrable as everyday" (190). Elsewhere he talks of the need to "mortify" the works on which he

bears down—to make them reveal the unknown allegiances, the liberatory flash, they do not know they contain. The inimitable freshness of his essays on Baudelaire, Proust, and Kafka derives from his removing their work from familiar moorings, so as to insert it aggressively (by way of cryptic juxtapositions) into a "constellation" of meanings the work itself hardly premeditated. (Subsequent citation from Benjamin's *Reflections* refers to this edition and will be indicated in the body of my text, parenthetically, following the quote.)

11. Cited in Walter Benjamin, *Illuminations,* ed. Hannah Arendt, trans. Harry Zohn (New York: Schocken, 1969), 130. Subsequent citation from Benjamin's *Illuminations* refers to this edition and will be indicated in the body of my text, parenthetically, following the quote.

12. Cited in Jürgen Habermas, "Walter Benjamin: Consciousness-Raising or Rescuing Critique," in *On Walter Benjamin: Critical Essays and Recollections,* ed. Gary Smith (Cambridge: MIT Press, 1988), 100.

13. I approach here the dilemma of authorial pronouns. Works of contemporary scholarship typically proceed within a third-person-singular narrative frame, as does this book. But at recurrent moments I recur to the first person, and there I draw on both "I" and "we." My "I" is never mine alone, confessional, nor is my "we" a fatuous bid for universality. Between these two extremes lives the adventure of discourse: the launching of a set of statements at once one's own, marked by the communities to which one belongs, and in search of others who might genuinely entertain (if not adopt) one's argument.

14. Rainer Maria Rilke, "Archaic Torso of Apollo" (1908), in *The Selected Poetry of Rainer Maria Rilke,* trans. Stephen Mitchell (New York: Vintage, 1989), 61.

1. KIERKEGAARD'S *FEAR AND TREMBLING*

1. I owe this linguistic information to Jill Robbins's provocative reading of "the Abraham story" within a number of frames, from Genesis through Levinas. See her *Prodigal Son/Elder Brother: Interpretation and Alterity in Augustine, Petrarch, Kafka, Levinas* (Chicago: University of Chicago Press, 1991). Subsequent citation from Robbins refers to this edition and will be indicated in the body of my text, parenthetically, following the quote.

2. The implication that my presence is located—in advance of any intention on my part—in the field of the other can be seen to participate in a Levinasian frame of values. That is, the "I" is a priori preceded by and responsible to the other; such an "I," emptied of project, inverts and brings to a halt realism's fully funded "I." Jacques Derrida makes a related claim in his meditation on Kierkegaard's Abraham: "'Here I am': the first and only possible response to the call by the other" (*The Gift of Death,* trans. David Wills [Chicago: University of Chicago Press, 1995], 71). I argue later that Kafka, Proust, and Faulkner understand their narrative project less as the centering of subjectivity than as the awakening of subjectivity (that of the protagonist and reader) to the call of the other, often arising from within the precincts of (what seemed) the same.

3. For a preview of how a novel might register *my being at issue* as an insignificant (if not absurd) premise, consider the opening sentence of John Barth's *The End of the Road:* "In a sense, I am Jacob Horner." Individual identity thus disclaimed leaves no room for construing "here I am" as something that matters. There must be an undisclaimable "I" before that "I" can be at stake in space, time, and the presence of another. I return to Barth later, in my discussion of postmodern fiction.

4. Søren Kierkegaard, *Fear and Trembling* (1843), trans. Howard V. Hong and Edna H. Hong (Princeton: Princeton University Press, 1983), 63. Subsequent citation from *Fear and Trembling* refers to this edition and will be indicated in the body of my text, parenthetically, after the quote.

5. Derrida glosses this dynamic of an imminent future "apprehended precisely *as* unforeseeable, unpredictable; approached *as* unapproachable" (*Gift*, 54); and he goes on to ask: "What does *the body mean to say* by trembling or crying?" (*Gift*, 55). Emphasis in both citations is in the original.

6. But see, later, my discussion of Anna Karenina. Though she does not tremble, she ceases—and this becomes suicidal—to recognize herself as herself.

7. Of my three novelists, Proust is the one whose insertion into this paradigm may seem debatable. The narrator, after all, serves as a very fount of knowledge about others who remain permanently self-mystified! True indeed, but true on the premise (admitting of no exception) that the narrator (as opposed to the character we refer to as Marcel) operates outside the spatial/temporal frames that condition subjectivity itself. See, extensively, my treatment of Proust's fiction in part 2.

8. I claim that Freud "keeps their company"; I do not claim that a Freudian diagnosis would explain their malaise. This study proposes no Freudian "readings" of their works; I am not looking for repressed sexual motives. Rather, I explore the ways in which their fictional universes memorably deploy—at the level of narrative forms—concepts that Freud developed at the analytic level. Put otherwise, my argument is that Freud serves as a fruitful theorist of the postrealist subject moving within a postrealist framing of space and time. In the central portion of this study, "Unknowing," I analyze at length these Freudian tropes operating, reconfigured, as narrative procedures.

9. William Faulkner, *The Hamlet,* in *Faulkner's Novels: 1936–1940* (New York: Library of America, 1990), 1019.

10. Gregor to the chief clerk come to get him: "I'll put my clothes on at once, pack up my samples and start off. . . . You see, sir, I'm not obstinate, and I'm willing to work; traveling is a hard life. . . . Where are you going, sir? To the office? Yes? Will you give a true account of all this? One can be temporarily incapacitated, but that's just the moment for remembering former services and bearing in mind that later on, when the incapacity has been got over, one will certainly work with all the more industry and concentration. I'm loyally bound to serve the chief . . ." Kafka, *The Metamorphosis, In the Penal Colony, and Other Stories* (New York: Schocken, 1975), 82. Subsequent citation from Kafka's stories refers to this edition and will be indicated, parenthetically, following the quote.

11. Søren Kierkegaard, *Concluding Unscientific Postscript* (1846), trans. David F. Swenson and Walter Lowrie (Princeton: Princeton University Press, 1968), 107, as cited (and slightly revised) in Gabriel Josipovici, "Kierkegaard and the Novel," in *Kierkegaard: A Critical Reader,* ed. Jonathan Ree and Jane Chamberlin (Oxford: Blackwell, 1998), 121.

12. As Sylviane Agacinski has noted, Kant's Abraham differs wholly from Kierkegaard's:
It was precisely the *possibility* of this false and misleading voice that Kant invoked in connection with the command that Abraham should "slaughter his own son like a lamb." To Kant this command was not only monstrous but absurd, in view of God's promise concerning Abraham's descendants. To obey . . . such a "terrible injunction" would necessarily be to act without conscience. . . ."This is the case with respect to all historical and visionary faith; that is, the *possibility* ever remains that an error may be discovered in it. Hence it is unconscientious to follow such a faith with the possibility that perhaps what it commands . . . may be wrong, i.e. with the danger of disobedience to a human duty which is certain in and of itself." ("We Are Not Sublime: Love and Sacrifice, Abraham and Ourselves," in Ree and Chamberlin, 141, citing from Kant's *Religion within the Limits of Reason Alone*)

13. Marcel Proust, *Remembrance of Things Past* (1913–22), trans. C. K. Scott Moncrieff and Terence Kilmartin, 3 vols. (New York: Random House, 1981), 1:395. Subsequent citation from *Remembrance of Things Past* refers to this edition and will be indicated in the body of my text, parenthetically, after the quote.

14. Emmanuel Levinas, *Totality and Infinity: An Essay on Exteriority* (1961), trans. Alphonso Lingis (Pittsburgh: Duquesne University Press, 1969), 36. Subsequent citation from *Totality and Infinity* refers to this edition and will be indicated in the body of my text, parenthetically, after the quote.

15. Thus Kierkegaard (throughout his career) invents a range of fictional narrators for purposes other than to disguise his own authorial identity. (The limited group of readers in Copenhagen who cared about his work knew he was its author.) Rather, the invented personae keep the material fictive, subjunctive rather than pseudodeclarative, openly an affair of "swimming" rather than the pretense of swimming.

16. Freud and Proust seek, each in his own way, to turn expenditure into recovery, the blindness of experience into the preciousness of insight. One could even say that such a mission defines their project. Their inexhaustible interest, however, lies less in their proposed solutions than in the kinds of self-loss and self-opacity their work brings into visibility. The emergence of the labyrinth itself is what we prize in their work (a labyrinth foreign to the protocols of knowing that fuel Western realism).

2. GENEALOGY OF REALISM

1. The landmark study of the emergence of the novel in the eighteenth century, written almost a half century ago, is Ian Watt's *The Rise of the Novel: Studies in Defoe, Richardson, and Fielding* (Berkeley: University of California Press, 1957). My own argument takes Watt as its point of departure, in order to explore dimensions of the "realist contract" he never considered. Although Watt read realist fiction as reconfiguring the representation of individuals in time and space—aligning this reconfiguring with the Enlightenment premises of Cartesian individualism and Lockean empiricism—he failed to unearth the deepest implication of his own findings: the individual's newfound and radical confidence in a knowable, secular world. I later conceptualize this confidence as "anaclitic," a Freudian term that means "leaning on" and that indicates a primordially stable relation between mind and world. Watt's argument has not, of course, gone unquestioned: Michael McKeon's *Origins of the Novel, 1600–1740* (Baltimore: Johns Hopkins University Press, 1987) mounts perhaps the best-known revision of Watt, arguing both for the importance of aristocratic romance in seventeenth-century fictional practice and for a dialectical interplay between romance and the (middle-class) novel that was replacing it. See also J. Paul Hunter's *Before Novels: The Cultural Contexts of Eighteenth Century English Fiction* (New York: Norton, 1990). Inasmuch as these studies attend only peripherally to realism's emergence outside of England, more comprehensive analysis of realism in its European context can be found in J. P. Stern, *On Realism* (London: Routledge and Kegan Paul, 1973); F. W. J. Hemmings, *The Age of Realism* (Sussex: Harvester Press, 1978); and Lilian R. Furst, *All Is True: The Claims and Strategies of Realist Fiction* (Durham: Duke University Press, 1995). Finally, the most provocative challenge to the standard genealogy of the novel has come from Mikhail Bakhtin. His influential *Dialogic Imagination: Four Essays,* trans. Caryl Emerson and Michael Holquist (Austin: University of Texas Press, 1981), locates and analyzes Western novelistic practices as early as the Greek romances. It distinguishes as well among a variety of medieval and Renaissance fictional genres (attending especially to the work of Rabelais) before arriving at eighteenth-century novelistic practice. Despite Bakhtin's tendency to dehistoricize the novel by seeing it as an intrinsically dialogic form from its earliest appearance forward, he nevertheless grants that the most memorable dialogic practice arises in the early modern period: "The era of the Renaissance and Protestantism, which destroyed the verbal and ideological centralization of the Middle Ages, was an era of great astronomical, mathematical and geographical discoveries . . . such an era could find adequate expression only through a Galilean

language consciousness of the kind embodied in novelistic discourse of the Second Stylistic Line" (415). By "Second Stylistic Line," Bakhtin means a fictional form that puts into play "all the social and ideological voices of its era" (411). Thus Bakhtin significantly hedges his claim to have reoriented the chronology of the novel in the West. No less than Watt, he grants that the great age of dialogic fiction—realist in its representation of the conflicting "voices of its era"— emerges in the seventeenth and eighteenth centuries. Let me close this long note by acknowledging that, of course, fictional forms other than realism flourish in the eighteenth and nineteenth centuries. One has only to conjure the names of Jonathan Swift, Laurence Sterne, Ann Radcliffe, and the Brontës to assent to the unanswerability of this claim. Yet the *hegemonic* form of emergent fictional practice remains realism: countless eighteenth- and nineteenth-century practitioners of fiction were unlikely to miss the ways in which an adroit deployment of verisimilitude might appeal to a rapidly enlarging, nonuniversity-trained, middle-class readership. At the end of this chapter and throughout the next, I explore extensively the dimensions of realist practice that made it both new and compelling.

2. Stephen Toulmin, *Cosmopolis: The Hidden Agenda of Modernity* (New York: Free Press, 1990), 107–8.

3. Henri Lefebvre, *The Production of Space* (1974), trans. Donald Nicholson-Smith (Oxford: Blackwell, 1991), 25.

4. Timothy Reiss, *The Discourse of Modernism* (Ithaca: Cornell University Press, 1982), 225. Subsequent citation from Reiss refers to this edition and will be indicated in the body of my text, parenthetically, following the quote.

5. When Thomas S. Kuhn proposes that paradigmatic assumptions not only control scientists' stances toward the "data" but indeed shape the "data" themselves, he is careful to place this proposition against a three-hundred-year history of epistemological norms that assume otherwise: "But is sensory experience fixed and neutral? Are theories simply man-made interpretations of given data? The epistemological viewpoint that has most guided Western philosophers for three centuries dictates an immediate and unequivocal Yes!" *The Structure of Scientific Revolutions,* 2nd ed. (Chicago: University of Chicago Press, 1970), 126. That unequivocal Yes bespeaks concisely the commonsensical narrative that funds realist fiction. Subsequent citation from Kuhn's book refers to this edition and will be indicated in the body of my text, parenthetically, following the quote.

6. A cultural period as broad as the Enlightenment supports, of course, a huge number of conflicting claims as to its central tenets. I claim that norms of literary realism descend from tenets held by this subset of significant Enlightenment thinkers.

7. Cited in Peter Gay, *The Enlightenment: An Interpretation,* 2 vols. (New York: Knopf, 1969), 2:129. Subsequent citation from this book refers to this edition and will be indicated in the body of my text, parenthetically, following the quote.

8. Commentary on this epochal transformation (virtually inventing what we think of as the West) is endless. I have learned most from the following sources: Michel Foucault, *The Order of Things: An Archeology of the Human Sciences* (New York: Vintage, 1973); Alasdair MacIntyre, *After Virtue: A Study in Moral Theory* (Notre Dame, Ind.: University of Notre Dame Press, 1981); Richard Rorty, *Philosophy and the Mirror of Nature* (Princeton: Princeton University Press, 1980); Ernest Gellner, *Reason and Culture* (Oxford: Oxford University Press, 1992); Stephen Toulmin, *Cosmopolis;* Charles Taylor, *Sources of the Self: The Making of Modern Identity* (Cambridge: Harvard University Press, 1989); and Timothy Reiss's *Discourse of Modernism.* Subsequent citation from these books refers to these editions and will be indicated in the body of my text, parenthetically, after the quote.

9. For more on this linguistic phenomenon, see Reiss's chapter "Medieval Discursive Practice."

10. Yet the "subject" emerges undeniably in certain Renaissance discourses, represented perhaps most saliently in the protagonists of Shakespeare and the musing narrative voice of Montaigne. The pertinent difference to note, as David Riggs of Stanford has suggested to me in conversation, may be that the Baconian subject (and a fortiori those who follow him) has both a project to pursue and a model for pursuing it, whereas the intellectual and emotional thrust of Shakespeare's greatest subjects—Hamlet, Lear—dramatically exceeds the contours of any available cultural narratives for focusing their subjectivity.

11. John Cottingham, "Cartesian Dualism: Theology, Metaphysics, and Science," in *The Cambridge Companion to Descartes,* ed. Cottingham (New York: Cambridge University Press, 1992), 238.

12. Cf. MacIntyre: "In many pre-modern, traditional societies it is through his or her membership in a variety of social groups that the individual identifies himself or herself and is identified by others. I am brother, cousin and grandson, member of this household, that village, this tribe. These are not characteristics that belong to human beings accidentally, to be stripped away in order to discover 'the real me.' They are part of my substance. Individuals inhabit a particular space within an interlocking set of social relationships; lacking that space, they are nobody" (32).

13. Francis Bacon, "The New Science," cited in *The Portable Enlightenment Reader,* ed. Isaac Kramnick (New York: Penguin, 1995), 40. Subsequent citation from this book refers to this edition and will be indicated in the body of my text, parenthetically, following the quote.

14. Lorraine Daston, "Enlightenment Fears, Fears of Enlightenment," in *What's Left of Enlightenment? A Postmodern Question,* ed. Keith Baker and Peter Reill (Stanford: Stanford University Press, 2001), 116.

15. Cited in George Levine, *Dying to Know: Scientific Epistemology and Narrative in Victorian England* (Chicago: University of Chicago Press, 2002), 22. Subsequent citation from this book refers to this edition and will be indicated in the body of my text, parenthetically, following the quote.

16. Here and throughout, the term "man," and the masculine pronouns that go with it, are likely to appear as an appropriate way of denoting the subject invoked in the philosophic texts under discussion. I apologize in advance for the absence of female terminology, and I urge my reader to understand that absence as in keeping, so to speak, with the materials themselves, not as a sign of my own sexism.

17. Compare Levinas: "But in knowledge there also appears the notion of an intellectual activity . . . of seizing something and making it one's own . . . an activity which *appropriates* and *grasps* the otherness of the known." "Ethics as First Philosophy," in *The Levinas Reader,* ed. Seán Hand (Oxford: Blackwell, 1989), 76, emphasis in the original.

18. René Descartes, *Meditations on First Philosophy,* in vol. 2 of *The Philosophic Writings of Descartes,* trans. John Cottingham. Robert Stoothoff, and Dugald Murdoch (Cambridge: Cambridge University Press, 1984), 16. Subsequent citation from Descartes's *Meditations* refers to this edition and will be indicated in the body of my text, parenthetically, following the quote.

19. As Dalia Judovitz puts it in her *Subjectivity and Representation in Descartes* (Cambridge: Cambridge University Press, 1986), "the establishment of the philosophical subject, as the universal subject of truth, involves a negative procedure, one of emptying the subject of any content other than that of thought. This leads both to the disembodiment of the subject and to its isolation and autonomous constitution as an entity independent of historical or social context" (87, cited in Levine, *Dying,* 52).

20. René Descartes, *Discourse on the Method,* in vol. 1 of *The Philosophic Writings of Descartes,* trans. John Cottingham, Robert Stoothoff, and Dugald Murdoch (Cambridge: Cambridge

University Press, 1984), 134. Subsequent citation from Descartes's *Discourse* refers to this edition and will be indicated in the body of my text, parenthetically, following the quote.

21. Francis Barker, *The Tremulous Private Body: Essays on Subjection* (London: Methuen, 1984), 63.

22. John Yolton, *Perception and Reality: A History from Descartes to Kant* (Ithaca: Cornell University Press, 1996), 14. Subsequent citation from this book refers to this edition and will be indicated in the body of my text, parenthetically, following the quote.

23. It may be appropriate to state here that Richard Rorty's eloquent critique of Enlightenment foundationalist epistemology not only helped me conceive the argument of this book but seemed—until I learned more about the Enlightenment texts themselves—fundamentally unshakable. Thanks to Yolton and others, I understand better that the vexing gap between human vocabularies and the wordless external realities they sought to describe was widely acknowledged—and addressed—by Enlightenment thinkers. Such thinkers worked to reduce this gap by remaining scrupulously attentive to its bearing; this may be the greatest difference between their modifiable Enlightenment skepticism and Rorty's absolute postmodern skepticism. As Yolton puts it, "Rorty, of course, does not agree with Locke that we can escape the confusion of language and get at the things themselves, but it was just that program that motivated Locke and the Royal Society" (82).

24. Ernst Cassirer, *Philosophy of the Enlightenment* (1932), trans. Fritz Koelln and James Pettegrove (Boston: Beacon Press, 1964), 24. Subsequent citation from this book refers to this edition and will be indicated in the body of my text, parenthetically, following the quote. For a searchingly negative take on this reduction of knowing to the orderliness of quantification (a reduction that Cassirer seems to find benign), see Adorno and Horkheimer's *Dialectics of Enlightenment,* trans. John Cumming (New York: Continuum, 1995). The following passage is representative: "In advance, the Enlightenment recognizes as being and occurrence only what can be apprehended in its unity: its ideal is the system. . . . Bacon's postulate of *una scientia universalis* . . . is as inimical to the unassignable as Leibniz's *mathesis universalis* is to discontinuity. The multiplicity of forms is reduced to position and arrangement, history to fact, things to matter" (7).

25. Emmanuel Levinas, *Ethics and Infinity: Conversations with Philippe Nemo,* trans. Richard A. Cohen (Pittsburgh: Duquesne University Press, 1985), 60.

26. I. B. Cohen and Richard S. Westfall, in *Newton: Texts, Backgrounds, Commentaries,* ed. Cohen and Westfall (New York: Norton Press, 1995), 221. Subsequent citation from Newton refers to this edition and will be indicated in the body of my text, parenthetically, following the quote.

27. Here is Hume on Newton's scrupulousness: "Cautious in admitting no principle but such as were founded on experiment; but resolute to adopt every such principle, however new or unusual" (from *History of England,* cited in Gay, 130).

28. Here as elsewhere Newton was independent; his unconventional form of Christianity was nearer to Arianism than to Anglicanism. He considered that the dogma of the Trinity betrayed earlier Christian doctrine.

29. Ernst Mach, letter, cited in *Newton,* 67.

30. Kuhn notes that, despite the persistent doubts scientists maintained toward this key "component," the Newtonian paradigm retained (for over a century) such authority that skeptics simply had to put up with gravity's inexplicability: "Unable either to practice science without the *Principia* or to make that work conform to the corpuscular standards of the seventeenth century, scientists gradually accepted the view that gravity was indeed innate. . . . Innate attractions and repulsions joined size, shape, position, and motion as physically irreducible primary properties of matter" (106).

31. Alexander Koyré, "The Significance of the Newtonian Synthesis," in *Newton,* 65–66.

32. One is tempted, at this point, to speak of Darwin, for his theory of natural selection (published 170 years later, in 1859) makes explicit and extensive, in the realm of living creatures, the amorality implicit in Newton's universe of forces and counterforces. More broadly, Darwin could be seen as a missing figure in a study that moves from Descartes, Newton, Locke, and Kant (as bearing on realist protocols) to Freud (as bearing on modernist protocols). Indeed, no sustained reflection on the naturalist novel of the late nineteenth and early twentieth centuries can afford to ignore the influence of Darwinian thought on fictional practice. Nevertheless, the main premises of realist fiction arise within the developing Enlightenment paradigm sketched in this chapter. Darwin's impact on naturalism only moderately reconfigures a fictional form already effectively in place and operative since the eighteenth century. For superb commentary on Darwin's impact on nineteenth-century British fiction (more thematic than formal), see Gillian Beer's *Darwin's Plots: Evolutionary Narrative in Darwin, George Eliot, and Nineteenth-Century Fiction,* 2nd ed. (Cambridge: Cambridge University Press, 2000).

33. So claim I. Bernard Cohen and Richard S. Westfall, editors of the Norton Critical Edition of *Newton,* 253.

34. Cf. Bakhtin: "Such a thing as Newton's law of gravity, in addition to its direct significance in natural and philosophical sciences, made an exceptional contribution to the visual clarification of the world. It made the new unity of the real world and its new natural law almost graphically visible and perceptible." *Speech Genres and Other Late Essays,* trans. Vern W. McGee (Austin: University of Texas Press, 1986), 44. Subsequent citation from *Speech Genres* refers to this edition and will be indicated in the body of my text, parenthetically, following the quote.

35. Cited in Frederick Keener, *The Chain of Becoming: The Philosophic Tale, the Novel, and a Neglected Realism of the Enlightenment: Swift, Montesquieu, Voltaire, and Austen* (New York: Columbia University Press, 1983), 68; emphasis in the original. Lest this instance should seem unique, Keener also cites the following speech from Fielding's *Amelia:* "that fundamental principle so strongly laid down in the institutes of the learned Rochefoucault, by which the duty of self-love is so strongly enforced, and every man is taught to consider himself as the centre of gravity, and to attract all things thither" (55).

36. Adam Smith, *The Wealth of Nations* (1776), cited in Kramnick, 509.

37. It may be pertinent here to emphasize Thomas Kuhn's claim that scientific paradigms are remarkably resistant to replacement. They persevere not because they are actually in touch with nature as she is, but because, under their aegis, "normal science" proceeds with maximal efficiency. Paradigms prioritize, indeed authorize, questions scientists find it important to ask; and no Western paradigm has ever carried more prestige than Newton's *Principia.* In Kuhn's words, "No other work known to the history of science has simultaneously permitted so large an increase in both the scope and precision of research" (30).

38. From d'Alembert's introduction to the *Encyclopédie,* cited in Kramnick, 14.

39. John Locke, *Essay concerning Human Understanding,* ed. Peter N. Nidditch (Oxford: Oxford University Press, 1975), 1.1.2; emphasis in the original. Subsequent citation from the *Essay* refers to this edition and will be indicated in the body of my text, parenthetically, after the quote. All emphases in these citations are Locke's, not mine. As is standard in Lockean commentary, I provide not the page number but the pertinent book, chapter, and subsection of the *Essay.*

40. Rorty's charge against Locke is that, like others in the classic epistemological tradition, he "thought of knowledge as a relation between persons and objects rather than persons and propositions" (*Philosophy,* 142). It is true that Locke sought a finer and more responsible relation between persons and objects, but he knew as well as Rorty that words—propositions—are indispensable vehicles for this traffic.

41. Roger Woolhouse, "Locke's Theory of Knowledge," in *The Cambridge Companion to Locke,* ed. Vere Chappell (New York: Cambridge University Press, 1994), 156; Woolhouse is citing *Essay,* 3.3.15. Subsequent citation from the Chappell volume of essays on Locke will be indicated in the body of my text, parenthetically, following the quote.

42. Immanuel Kant, *Critique of Pure Reason* (1781), trans. Paul Guyer and Allen W. Wood (Cambridge: Cambridge University Press, 1998), A228. Citation from the *Critique* is given according to Kant's 1781 (A) or 1787 (B) versions of the text. Subsequent citation from Kant's *Critique* refers to this edition and will be indicated in the body of my text, parenthetically, following the quote. At times, however, I cite the *Critique* from discussions of it in Paul Guyer's *Cambridge Companion to Kant* (Cambridge: Cambridge University Press, 1992), further reference to which will also be indicated in the body of my text, parenthetically, following the quote.

43. As Roger Scruton summarizes Kant on this matter, inasmuch as "space is the 'form' of 'outer sense,' [and] time is the form of 'inner sense' . . . the idea of experience is inseparable from that of time, and the idea of an experienced *world* is inseparable from that of space." *From Descartes to Wittgenstein: A Short History of Modern Philosophy* (London: Routledge and Kegan Paul, 1981), 143, emphasis in the original.

44. I am indebted to Richard Eldridge of Swarthmore's Philosophy Department for a fuller understanding of the relation of Kant's epistemology to his theory of subjectivity.

45. J. B. Scheewind, "Autonomy, Obligation, and Virtue," in Guyer, 309.

46. I have emphasized, in this brief discussion, the nonnegotiable priority of the (single) subject in Kantian epistemology, but Richard Eldridge reminds me that, on the ethical plane, Kantian autonomy is everywhere doubled by (and weightless without) a larger social project of freedom for all, not just for the (single) subject. These two stances require each other even as, from the perspective governing my argument, the tensions between them are no less telling.

47. Immanuel Kant, *Metaphysical Foundations of Natural Science,* cited in Michael Friedman, "Causal Laws and the Foundations of Natural Science," in Guyer, 182.

48. Onora O'Neill, "Vindicating Reason," in Guyer, 299.

49. Peter Brooks, "Freud's Masterplot," in *Literature and Psychoanalysis: The Question of Reading: Otherwise,* ed. Shoshana Felman (Baltimore: Johns Hopkins University Press, 1982), 280–300.

50. Michel Foucault, *The Archeology of Knowledge,* trans. A. M. Sheridan Smith (New York: Harper and Row, 1972), 203. Subsequent citation from *The Archeology* refers to this edition and will be indicated in the body of my text, parenthetically, following the quote.

51. Emmanuel Levinas, *Otherwise Than Being, or, Beyond Essence* (1981), trans. Alphonso Lingis (Pittsburgh: Duquesne University Press, 1998), 99, emphasis in the original. Subsequent citation from *Otherwise Than Being* refers to this edition and will be indicated in the body of my text, parenthetically, following the quote.

52. From romantic writers such as Edgar Allan Poe and William Wordsworth to twentieth-century critics such as Watt and John Sutherland, Defoe's power to imbue his exotic scenes with true-seemingness has been a critical commonplace. As Poe put it, "All this is effected by the potent magic of verisimilitude" ("Defoe's Faculty of Identification," in Daniel Defoe, *Robinson Crusoe,* ed. Michael Shinagel [New York: Norton Critical Edition, 1975], 291). Subsequent citation from *Robinson Crusoe* refers to this edition and will be indicated in the body of my text, parenthetically, following the quote.

3. ANATOMY OF REALISM

1. Bakhtin distinguishes pertinently between a context and a code: "A context is potentially unfinalized; a code must be finalized. A code is only a technical means of transmitting information; it does not have cognitive, creative significance. A code is a deliberately established, killed

context" (*Speech,* 147). It would be difficult to improve on this as a gloss for Barthes's purposes in breaking down the "potentially unfinalized" language of realism into the deadness of *codes.*

2. Christopher Prendergast, *The Order of Mimesis: Balzac, Stendhal, Nerval, Flaubert* (Cambridge: Cambridge University Press, 1986), 39. Subsequent citation from Prendergast refers to this edition and will be indicated in the body of my text, parenthetically, after the quote.

3. Culler, *Flaubert: The Uses of Uncertainty* (Ithaca: Cornell University Press, 1974). George Levine's *The Realistic Imagination* (Chicago: University of Chicago Press, 1981) reveals the unease of an established Victorianist beleaguered by deconstructive tactics: "At the risk of ideological and metaphysical complicity with things as they are," he writes, "criticism must behave at times as though something is really out there after all" (4). He goes on to claim that realism always involves an attempt "to discover some nonverbal truth out there" (6). "Out there": the phrase recurs and misleads, inasmuch as realists (like most writers) do not so much propose as *assume* a world to exist outside the self. As I go on to argue, their interest is less in "discovering" anything (the verb belongs to a scientific lexicon) than in positing a fictional canvas full of value even as it remains, to the hilt, fictional. Furst and Prendergast are, like Levine, nervous about the viability of realist procedures, given deconstruction's vehement attack on mimesis.

4. My criticism of deconstruction bears only on its nihilist dimension, for deconstruction's vigilant scrutiny of the constructedness of all discourse is by no means, in theory or practice, merely negative. (Derrida has been careful to distinguish the dual charge of "deconstruct" from the single, negative one of "destruct/destroy.") Given that linguistic usage never is (nor can be) innocent, the value of deconstructive linguistic scrutiny is considerable—and undeniable. Too often in practice, though, and with reverberations outside the academy for which deconstructive theorists like Derrida and Paul de Man cannot, perhaps, be held responsible, the name of deconstruction has served to legitimate knee-jerk attacks upon the viable meaning of any linguistic usage whatsoever. This practice, I believe, has led—among many of the West's best and brightest students—to a lingering distrust of language itself. (As though there were somehow a superior alternative we might rely on . . .)

5. Jonathan Crary's well-received *Techniques of the Observer: On Vision and Modernity in the Nineteenth Century* (Cambridge: Harvard University Press, 1990)—a Foucauldian demystification of changing models of observation in the nineteenth century—is representatively invested in revealing discursive paradigms regulating apparently discrete technological inventions and emergent models of subjectivity that accompany them. On this schema, as Crary develops it, invention and the language in which it is interpreted are already coopted by social forces, presaturated in suspect power plays that it is the task of criticism to uncover: "A more adaptable, autonomous, and productive observer," Crary writes, "was needed in both discourse and practice—to conform to new functions of the body and to a vast proliferation of indifferent and convertible signs and images" (149). "Was needed" and therefore was produced: individual agency has disappeared from this explanatory mode.

6. Genevieve Lloyd closes her study of time in philosophy and literature by noting that the metaphoric "as if-ness" of these two modes of discourse may allow them to do their most bracing work. She speaks of "the 'heuristic' function of mood in poetic metaphor—something which can go unnoticed when representation becomes the sole route to knowledge and the model of every relation between subject and object." *Being in Time: Selves and Narrators in Philosophy and Literature* (London: Routledge, 1993), 172. Subsequent citation from Lloyd refers to this text and will be indicated in the body of my text, parenthetically, after the quote. Approaching the overflowing inclusiveness of fiction from another perspective, Hunter's *Before Novels* argues effectively against straitjacketing the novel within narrow and timeless formal definitions (3–58).

7. I say "may elude." Realist representation may well propose, naively, the recovery of nonverbal experience; or it may participate covertly in a dubious ideological project. My point is

that, although it may do either of these things, it is not constitutively devoted to them. Realism's representational project cannot be a priori deduced; one arrives at it only by attending responsibly to the behavior of the text in question.

8. Theodor Adorno, *Aesthetic Theory* (1970), trans. Robert Hullot-Kentor (Minneapolis: University of Minnesota Press), 5. Subsequent citation from *Aesthetic Theory* refers to this edition and will be indicated in the body of my text, parenthetically, following the quote.

9. Charles Altieri, *Painterly Abstraction in Modernist American Poetry* (Cambridge: Cambridge University Press, 1989), 391. Subsequent citation from *Painterly Abstraction* refers to this edition and will be indicated in the body of my text, parenthetically, following the quote.

10. John Bunyan, *Pilgrim's Progress* (1678), ed. F. R. Leavis (New York: Signet, 1964), 17. Subsequent citation from Bunyan refers to this edition and will be indicated in the body of my text, parenthetically, following the quote.

11. Franz Kafka, *The Trial* (1937), trans. Willa Muir and Edwin Muir (New York: Schocken, 1968), 1. I use throughout this study the Muirs' translations of Kafka's texts. Subsequent citation from *The Trial* refers to this edition and will be indicated in the body of my text, parenthetically, following the quote.

12. Hunter sees as essential to fictional procedure the drama of protagonistic orientation: "The relentless sense of sorting—finding the 'rules' that govern a particular social or cultural or political ritual or round—is characteristic of novels as we experience them" (44–45).

13. The novel that most notoriously challenges this claim is Flaubert's *Education sentimentale* (1867), in which Frédéric finishes his growing up without having grown up—a protagonist incapable, precisely, of sentimental education. Culler was the first to see this move as a larger repudiation of realism's investment in coming to know, and both Prendergast and Meili Steele have followed suit in their readings of the novel. It is true, of course, that Frédéric does not learn, but the sustained scrupulousness of Flaubert's fictional form draws attention (but not necessarily judgment) to just that fact. In other words, a *Bildungsroman* without *Bildung,* a sequence of trials that are educational for us, but not for him. Steele deconstructs the protagonist even further, turning him into a mere vehicle for language by claiming that "'Frédéric' becomes the locus where the cultural codes are played out, where language is not an instrument of the subject but a force that hurls the hero through space and time. . . . There is no opposition [in this novel] between self and other, for otherness has invaded the self." *Realism and the Drama of Reference: Strategies of Representation in Balzac, Flaubert, and James* (University Park: Pennsylvania State University Press, 1988), 55–56. I would revise this by suggesting that Frédéric (not "Frédéric") uses language even as it uses him (he is hurled nowhere by it), and that the classic opposition between self and other—which fills *Education sentimentale,* as it does most realist novels—always involves selves invaded by otherness. (How could selfhood be free of the other?) Flaubert arguably understood the implications of subjectivity as a reservoir of social cliché (otherness) better than any other nineteenth-century novelist. He changes thus the ratio but not the novelistic formula itself; he is better seen as Joyce's realist precursor rather than his modernist peer. Frédéric, unlike Joyce's Bloom, remains focused enough to be *plotted,* however he may fail that plotting. This said, Flaubert's last (unfinished) novel, *Bouvard et Pécuchet* (1880), is only a step away from Joyce's bypassing of plot altogether and his massive textual investment in the impersonal discourses of cliché.

14. Jane Austen, *Emma,* ed. Stephen M. Parrish (New York: Norton Critical Edition, 1972), 1.

15. Fyodor Dostoevsky, *Crime and Punishment* (1865), trans. Jessie Coulson, ed. George Gibian, 3rd ed. (New York: Norton, 1975), 1. Subsequent citation from this book refers to this edition and will be indicated in the body of my text, parenthetically, following the quote.

16. Henry James, *The Wings of the Dove* (Baltimore: Penguin, 1965), 5.

17. Michael Holquist, *Dialogism: Bakhtin and His World* (London: Routledge, 1990), 81.

18. Leo Tolstoy, *Anna Karenina* (1877), trans. Aylmer Maude, ed. George Gibian (New York: Norton, 1970), 172–73, emphasis in the original.

19. Salman Rushdie, *The Satanic Verses* (New York: Viking, 1988), 432. Subsequent citation from this book refers to this edition and will be indicated in the body of my text, parenthetically, after the quote.

20. Elizabeth Ermarth, *Realism and Consensus in the English Novel* (Princeton: Princeton University Press, 1983), 16. Subsequent citation from this book refers to this edition and will be indicated in the body of my text, parenthetically, after the quote.

21. Darwin is of course the thinker whose model supplements Newton's for mapping such reciprocal figure/ground relations. Newton had grasped the "system of the world" as a constellation of infinitely interrelated entities, each held in balance by the tension between centripetal self-attraction and centrifugal response to force exerted by others. Though Newton's world is immersed in time, and geared to map movement in space, its foundational atoms do not change. In Darwin's world, by contrast, everything changes, nothing remains inalterably itself. As Lilian Furst puts it, "Darwin's conviction that everything is interconnected, even if the connections may not be apparent, provides the basis for the constant imbrication of place, persona, and plot in realist fiction" (176). Seeking to model life processes themselves, Darwin's world is saturated in waxing and waning, birth and death: "Declension and outcropping, the enactment or withering of potentialities," in Gillian Beer's words, "all takes place in time, in the medium of history" (*Darwin's Plots*, 155).

22. Hunter notes that a reading public already primed on confessional and autobiographical narratives was well prepared to understand the subject's passage through time as a journey from blindness to insight: "The text's [readerly] expectations were, in fact, quite sophisticated, for built into them was the implicit need to evaluate the observation—not just take it at face value—and to distinguish between an immediate observation and the context it ultimately is placed in as time passes and related observations stack up" (45).

23. J. F. Lyotard praises postmodern practice as a refusal, precisely, of realism's pretense that representation might correspond in any reliable way to the real: "The postmodern would be that which . . . puts forward the unpresentable in the presentation itself; that which denies itself the solace of good forms, the consensus of a taste which would make it possible to share collectively the nostalgia for the unattainable." *The Postmodern Condition: A Report on Knowledge*, trans. Geoff Bennington and Brian Massumi (Minneapolis: University of Minnesota Press, 1984), 81.

24. Again, Lyotard: "[T]he rule of consensus between the sender and addressee of a statement with truth-value is deemed acceptable if it is cast in terms of a possible unanimity of rational minds: this is the Enlightenment narrative in which the hero of knowledge works toward a good ethico-political end" (xxiii–xxiv).

25. Charles Dickens, *Great Expectations* (Oxford: Oxford University Press, 1966), 307–8.

26. Ronald Schleifer, *Modernism and Time: The Logic of Abundance in Literature, Science, and Culture, 1880–1930* (Cambridge: Cambridge University Press, 2000), 42. Subsequent citation from Schleifer refers to this edition and will be indicated in the body of my text, parenthetically, following the quote.

27. I have stressed the problematic of remembering, now, what one did (who one was), then. As modernist practice amply reveals, however, the project of sustained identity can be more distressful than the mere failure to remember one's continuity over time. One can change utterly, and in a moment; time is no one's friend. Kierkegaard's Abraham trembles on the verge of . . . and is then rescued by divine guidance. Gregor Samsa becomes, overnight and unconsciously, a something that neither he nor anyone else will ever succeed in domesticating as himself.

28. Elizabeth Ermarth, *Sequel to History: Postmodernism and the Crisis of Representational Time* (Princeton: Princeton University Press, 1992), 28.

29. Foucault, *Archeology*, 12. The art historian Meyer Schapiro referred to this cultural assumption about "historical thinking" as "the immense, historically developed capacity to keep the world in mind" (cited in Ermarth, *Sequel*, 5).

4. PLOTTING MODERNISM

1. This is not the place to characterize the fortunes of psychoanalysis over the past century. Suffice to say that, following the destruction of its European bases during World War II, psychoanalysis decamped, so to speak, to America, where its post-Freudian developments increasingly centered on the project of strengthening ego structures. Feminist criticism of Freud, never absent, has been especially prominent since the 1960s. In France (where the earlier prominence of Jean-Martin Charcot and Pierre Janet retarded the institutional development of psychoanalysis), Jacques Lacan emerged, during the middle and later decades of this century, as the leading exponent of a *"retour à Freud"*—a tragic Freud, or at least a darker one invested more than American analysts could concede in the death instinct and the inhuman prehistory of human being. As H.D. recalled Freud telling her, "My discoveries are not primarily a heal-all. My discoveries are a basis for a very grave philosophy. There are very few who understand this, *there are very few who are capable of understanding it.*" Cited in Frank Sulloway, *Freud: Biologist of the Mind: Beyond the Psychoanalytic Legend* (New York: Basic Books, 1979), 439; emphasis in the original. Subsequent citation from Sulloway refers to this edition and will be indicated in the body of my text, parenthetically, following the quote. For further information about the vicissitudes of psychoanalysis, see John Forrester, *Dispatches from the Freud Wars: Psychoanalysis and its Passions* (Cambridge: Harvard University Press, 1997); Peter Gay, *The Bourgeois Experience: Victoria to Freud,* 5 vols. (New York: Oxford University Press, 1984–98); and Sulloway.

2. Frederick Crews, *The Memory Wars: Freud's Legacy in Dispute* (New York: New York Review of Books Press, 1995), 298. Subsequent citation from Crews refers to this edition and will be indicated in the body of my text, parenthetically, after the quote.

3. Bruno Bettelheim, *Freud and Man's Soul* (New York: Knopf, 1983), 42. Subsequent citation from Bettelheim refers to this edition and will be indicated in the body of my text, parenthetically, after the quote.

4. Bettelheim begins by distinguishing between the European traditions of *Geisteswissenschaften* (the human sciences) and *Naturwissenschaften* (the natural sciences), placing Freud's work in the former tradition. He then focuses on the ways in which James Strachey's authorized Standard Edition of Freud's work (1953–74) consistently mistranslated Freudian terms into "scientese" in order to reach an Anglo-American audience assumed to be looking for Freud-as-natural-scientist. Two examples will suffice. (1) Freud's recurrent use of the portentous term *"Seele"* (soul) to indicate the full range of "psyche" is almost invariably translated by Strachey as "mind" or "mental apparatus." (2) Freud's brilliant coinage *"Fehlleistung"*—joining two common terms, *Fehl* (fail) and *Leistung* (accomplishment), in order to convey the paradoxical effect of a self-sabotaged achievement (what we loosely call a "Freudian slip")—is translated by Strachey as "parapraxis," a Greek-derived term no reader could emotionally respond to except, as Bettelheim remarks, "with annoyance at being presented with a basically incomprehensible word" (87–88).

5. Michel de Certeau, *Heterologies: Discourse on the Other,* trans. Brian Massumi (Minneapolis: University of Minnesota Press, 1986), 26. Scholars of the humanities, like Malcolm Bowie, are in general more likely to read Freud's subversion of scientific protocols positively: "Who has done more than Freud, in this present century [twentieth]," Bowie asks, "to imagine the consequences for science of its admitting rather than repressing the elementary desiring impulses on which the quest for knowledge is based?" *Freud, Proust and Lacan* (Cambridge:

Cambridge University Press, 1987), 17. One understands Bowie's point yet still needs to keep in mind Freud's refrain—insistent throughout his career—that advances in biology would eventually ground the theory of psychoanalysis. (A refrain, moreover, cunningly couched in the terms of 'let us remain on psychological terrain until developments in biology permit such grounding to take place': Sulloway explores persuasively and at great length Freud's lifelong dependence on/denial of a contextual frame of biological assumptions and premises.) To the extent to which Freud reveals the play of desire in his own quest for knowledge, such revelation is unwanted. Subsequent citation from both de Certeau and Bowie refers to these editions and will be indicated in the body of my text, parenthetically, after the quote.

6. It might be more accurate to say that my use assumes a certain measure of both complicity and critique. If I found Freud to be the scandalous imposter proposed by Crews, he would not figure in this study. However, as Hegel might put it, Freud has emerged (despite his host of detractors) as a "world-historical" figure on the stage of twentieth-century Western thought. Psychoanalytic theory enters my argument therefore not as a truth-producing body of thought but as a broadly enjoined, early-twentieth-century frame for understanding the drama of embodied subjectivity—one that allows us most succinctly to distinguish protocols of modernist fiction from those of its realist precursors.

7. Cf. Adorno: "Art is related to its other as is a magnet to a field of iron filings. . . . The identity of the artwork with existing reality is also that of the work's gravitational force, which gathers around itself its *membra disjecta,* traces of the existing. The artwork is related to the world by the principle that contrasts it with the world, and that is the same principle by which spirit organizes the world" (*Aesthetic,* 7).

8. I suggest, in part 3 of this study, that postmodern and postcolonial fictional departures from modernist premises involve, no less insistently, a rejection of Freudian assumptions. Gilles Deleuze and Félix Guattari's *Anti-Oedipus* is but the most clamorous postmodern repudiation, among a chorus of others.

9. Freud, *Outline of Psycho-Analysis,* in *The Standard Edition of the Complete Psychological Works of Sigmund Freud,* 23 vols. (London: Hogarth Press, 1953–74), 23:199, emphasis in the original; cited in Jean Laplanche and J. B. Pontalis, *The Language of Psycho-Analysis,* trans. Donald Nicholson-Smith (New York: Norton, 1973), 382. All citations from Freud's work refer to the Standard Edition and will be indicated in the body of my text, parenthetically, following the quote. Likewise for citation from Laplanche and Pontalis's invaluable dictionary of Freudian terms.

10. To see better how that "something-else" alters the entire logic of representation, we might place, side by side, two representations of Rome—the first one Goethe's description of the city he has come to know, and the second one Freud's conceit of historic Rome as modeling the con-fusion of scenarios inhabiting a single subject's unconscious:

Here is an entity which has suffered so many drastic changes in the course of two thousand years, yet is still the same soil, the same hill, often even the same column or the same wall, and in its people one still finds traces of their ancient character. Contemplating this, the observer becomes, as it were, a contemporary of the great decrees of destiny, and this makes it difficult for him to follow the evolution of the city, to grasp not only how Modern Rome follows Ancient, but also how, within both, one epoch follows another. (Goethe, *Italian Journey,* cited in Bakhtin, *Speech,* 40–41)

Now let us, by a flight of imagination, suppose that Rome is not a human habitation but a psychical entity with a similarly long and copious past—an entity . . . in which nothing that has once come into existence will have passed away and all the earlier phases of development continue to exist alongside the latest one. . . . In the place occupied by the Palazzo Caffarelli would once more stand—without the Palazzo having to be removed—the Temple of Jupiter Capitolinus; and this not only in its latest shape, as the Romans of the Empire saw it, but also in its earliest one, when it still showed Etruscan forms and was ornamented with terra-cotta antefixes. . . . On the Piazza of the Pantheon we should find not only the Pantheon of to-day, as it was bequeathed to us by Hadrian, but, on the same site, the original edifice erected by Agrippa. . . . And the observer would perhaps only have to change the direction of his glance or his position in order to call up the one view or the other. (Freud, *Civilization,* in *SE,* 18:17)

Goethe's Rome secures its resonance by way of time's orderly passage. Rome maintains its essential identity, even after so much has happened and departed. The dramas of those who have passed are open to Goethe; the city's history, however subject to drastic alterations, emerges as continuous over time. Rome's cogency—its legibility to the subject imagining it—comes from its sequence of avatars inhabiting a single, invariant, identity-confirming space. Its centuries of time are imagined as on speaking terms with each other; its current inhabitants, descendants of original ones. Everything in this "portrait" is socialized, made familiar, because of Goethe's representing the city within commonsensical spatial/temporal coordinates. This is Rome as it might be represented in a realist narrative.

Freud's Rome, by contrast, is "not a human habitation." Its temporal phases each lack the grace of *passing;* it misses thus the decorum of discreteness—of cumulative singular identity—that linear time provides. This Rome is simultaneous, kaleidoscopic, almost (temporally) cubistic. No past gets clear because nothing can pass; no space gets clear because every new structure doubles previous structures now archaic yet still in place. Freud's Rome is both crowded and unsocialized. This is a space no one has ever seen, yet suffocatingly full of everyone who has been there, thanks to his representation of it within "uncivil" spatial/temporal coordinates. This is Rome as it might be represented in a modernist narrative.

11. See especially de Man's *Allegories of Reading: Figural Language in Rousseau, Nietzsche, Rilke, and Proust* (New Haven: Yale University Press, 1979), as well as Derrida's much reprinted essay, "Différance."

12. David Ellison, *Ethics and Aesthetics in European Modernist Literature* (Cambridge: Cambridge University Press, 2001), 53. Subsequent citation from Ellison refers to this edition and will be included in the body of my text, parenthetically, following the quote.

13. Ellison draws on a kindred extension of the concept in Robin Lydenberg's "Freud's Uncanny Narratives." After examining a good deal of previous commentary on the uncanny, Lydenberg notes "that perhaps the most essential quality of narratives is uncanniness, a notion that in turn illuminates the more general uncanniness of language and of the speaking subject" (in *PMLA* 112 (1997): 1073). As if the opening of Freud's category into the generic conditions of "language" and "the speaking subject" were not enough, Lydenberg concludes by proposing "that the writing and reading of any narrative is potentially an uncanny experience" (1081). At this level of generality, what *is not* uncanny?

14. See Neil Hertz ("Freud and the Sandman," in *The End of the Line: Essays on Psychoanalysis and the Sublime* [New York: Columbia University Press, 1985]) and Sarah Kofman (*Freud and Fiction* [1974], trans. Sarah Wykes [Boston: Northeastern University Press, 1991]) for brilliant readings of Hoffmann's tale along lines other than Freud's castration complex.

15. Realism, as part 1 of this study sought to clarify, is to be understood not as reality but as a set of conventions for representing it "commonsensically," as though it could be accessed free of illusion. Freud's lifelong respect for the difficulty of encountering reality free of distortion led him to doubt that any mental mechanism existed that might *guarantee* the accuracy of a subject's take upon the world. Sarah Kofman takes Freud's suspicion all the way, arguing in her essay on "The Uncanny" that "Fantasy and reality coincide because reality is always structured by fantasy, because it has never been present as such" (140). I think Freud's position on this issue

comes into better focus if we assume that he would grant Kofman's claim, yet see it as indicating the need for further work, rather than legitimating a poststructuralist agnosticism toward the real itself.

16. This may be the place to insist that earlier nonrealist forms of fiction differ revealingly from modernism in this regard. Never pretending to operate on a commonsensical basis, they do not produce *shock* the moment that basis is removed. From *The Monk* to *Alice in Wonderland,* representational departures from realism tend to operate as they do (to use Freud's own example) in fairy tales: another set of procedures for world engagement, permitting other effects. The distinction is key: *Gulliver's Travels,* for example, is full of surprise, but not of shock. Its nonrealist representation of subjects encountering objects in space and time is always conceptually negotiable. The mind games it seeks to set in motion have little to do with suddenly revoking a subject's primordial trust in the commonsensical unfolding of experience. The same can hardly be said for Kafka's Georg or Gregor or Joseph K.: protagonists grotesquely upended from a realist schema of procedures that continues happily to operate for everyone else. As I show later, Proust and Faulkner participate as well, though less obviously, in representational practices centering on the abrupt collapse of fundamental assumptions about identity in space and time. Producing shock and outrage, such collapse typically occurs in a single, unbearable moment.

17. As Laplanche has pointed out, Strachey's term "anaclisis" is unnecessarily erudite (derived from a Greek term that means "leaning"); Freud's *Anlehnung* is a familiar noun for "leaning" or "propping."

18. Since the term "anaclitic" is an important marker in the following discussion of modernist fiction, I need to emphasize two points. First, although the term is Freudian, my usage of it is not: the readings that follow have everything to do with the sudden experience of defamiliarized space, but little to do with scenarios of repressed desire. Second, although I apply the term to realist practice, the Enlightenment narrative prefers to imagine the questing subject as a free-standing agent immersed in lawful, objective space and time: no "leaning" conceded. The burden of much of my analysis of that narrative, therefore, was to unearth the "anaclitic" premises that—by making the spatial/temporal world amenable to subjective encounter and exploitation (safe to "lean on")—underwrite realism's progressive plot.

19. This claim especially raises Crews's ire against "Freud's stubborn faith, in defiance of explicit challenges on the point, that messages from the unconscious are by and large incorruptible" (14). I return to this vexed issue later, in my discussion of recovered memories.

20. Rachel Bowlby, *Shopping with Freud* (London: Routledge, 1993), 76.

21. Sulloway has argued persuasively that this early statement of Freud's (from the 1895 *Essays on Hysteria*) needs to be revised in light of later developments in the system. The focus on *remembering* still assumes, in the mid-1890s, the seduction theory (the patients remember being aggressed by others, typically by a parental figure). By 1897, however, Freud was to revise his understanding, substituting for passive remembering the infant's active fantasizing: infantile sexuality thus enters the explanatory schema, never to depart from it.

22. *Scientific Project,* cited in Jean Laplanche, *Life and Death in Psychoanalysis,* trans. Jeffrey Mehlman (Baltimore: Johns Hopkins University Press, 1976), 41, emphasis in the original. Subsequent citation from *Life and Death* refers to this edition and will be included in the body of the text, parenthetically, following the quote.

23. Ian Hacking (*Rewriting the Soul: Multiple Personality and the Sciences of Memory* [Princeton: Princeton University Press, 1995]) has written illuminatingly of the multiple personality movement and its necessary prior assumptions: childhood abuse and repressed unconscious memory (which can be recovered intact). Deeply suspicious of their "recovery" procedures being passed off as empirically responsible, Hacking is nevertheless not intent (as

Crews is) on simply attacking the movement. Rather, his focus is on the genesis of "memoro-politics," the conviction that "there is knowledge of memory to be had. . . . Memoro-politics is above all a politics of the secret, of the forgotten event that can be turned, if only by strange flashbacks, into something monumental. It is a forgotten event that, when it is brought to light, can be memorialized in a narrative of pain" (213–14). Hacking understands our obses-sion with the "forgotten" as a central tenet of "the modern sensibility" that is "dazzling in its implausibility: the idea that what has been forgotten is what forms our character, our person-ality, our soul" (209). It would be hard to remove Freud's idea of the unconscious from the set of assumptions here operating as normative, even as we need to remember Freud's sophisti-cated awareness of the vicissitudes of memory, the ways in which its narrative revises over time. Subsequent citation of Hacking refers to this book and will be indicated in the body of my text, parenthetically, following the quote.

24. The crucial issue here is what Hacking identifies as "intentional frames." *These* are what alter over time: "We do not reproduce in memory a sequence of events that we have experi-enced. Instead we rearrange and modify elements that we remember into something that makes sense" (247), i.e., that makes sense now. It is one thing (and a precious one) to mean—when I reinterpret events of my past—that, under current intentional frames, I see them differ-ently. It is another thing (and a dangerous one) to mean that I now see, clearly and as never before, the "intentional frame" that actually governed the event in the past. (More dubious yet: for recovered memory therapy, this is often the infantile past.) Where Proust comes out on this issue is maddeningly difficult to say.

25. Put otherwise, only modernist fiction reprises Kierkegaard's radical insight that experi-ence in the present moment—unharnessed within a larger ideological schema that binds pres-ent, past, and future—is sprung free from teleological confines, replete with menace. Yet, as my above term "illuminated" suggests, modernist practice—however dark the present, shocking moment it foregrounds—often remains invested in binding time, in dispelling the murkiness of the present by providing the clarifying light of the past, but providing it *later*. Providing it, that is, for the reader, rather than for the bewildered protagonist, and even for the reader, only sometimes—Kafka (unlike Proust and Faulkner) never enlightens his scene. In this he fore-shadows the more thoroughgoing distrust of recognition characteristic of much postmodern practice.

26. If there is pathos in such incompatibility, there is also comedy. The Freudian subject is often moment by moment compelling/perplexing as the realist subject rarely is. One cannot anticipate what strange move or utterance will erupt next, and how the subject will then seek artfully to recontain it within a plausible design. Sulloway notes (following Ernest Jones's biog-raphy) that "Freud kept the two manuscripts [of *Three Studies of the Theory of Sexuality* and *Jokes and Their Relation to the Unconscious*] on adjoining tables so that he might work alter-nately on each one as the mood struck him" (357). The "adjoining table" not only makes me think of Faulkner's exact reprisal of this strategy (by writing "Old Man" and "The Wild Palms" in side-by-side manner, moving from one to the other as imagination waxed or waned); but it also suggests the juxtapositional (rather than sequential) genius of much modernist imagina-tion. Finally, it intimates the disruptive drama at the heart of Freud's narrative of subjectivity, whether it be expressed in the polymorphous perversity of infancy or the better-dressed malice lurking in the dynamics of adult joking.

27. Identification with others and establishment of selfhood are, in Freudian thought, inseparable: "It is by means of a series of identifications that the personality is constituted and specified" (Laplanche and Pontalis, 205).

28. In contrast with the mode of mental functioning that Freud calls the primary processes, "the operations traditionally described by psychology—waking thought, attention, judgement,

reasoning, controlled action—may be referred to as *secondary* processes" (Laplanche and Pontalis, 340; emphasis in the original). This is of course the privileged territory of realist fiction.

5. UNCANNY SPACE

1. To remind my reader: I make this claim for a selective subset of modernist authors. In joining British, French, Czech, and American writers, my focus is on the overarching inheritance they share, as writers attentive to the pitfalls of instrumental, orientational Western reason itself, explorers of the fallout of Enlightenment. I cannot attend here to the local factors conditioning their emergence. For an impressive version of such work—examining the rise of modernism in England at sometimes the week-by-week level between 1908 and 1922—see Michael Levenson's *A Genealogy of Modernism: A Study of English Literary Doctrine, 1908–1922* (New York: Cambridge University Press, 1984).

2. One recalls the motif of the "blackened breast" that punctuates all four of Kierkegaard's speculative narratives of the Abraham crisis. In each case the ordeal of individuation itself is at issue: the painful departure of the infant from the somatic security of the mother's breast, a departure into unmastered time and space that launches the no-longer-familiar career of the individual. But this casting out of the child from the nest—however painful—remains normatively inscribed in a developmental program, whereas Abraham's dilemma, like the modernist ones I here analyze, is removed from any horizon of temporal expectations.

3. What was repressed in realist narratives' premise of free-standing subjectivity becomes more salient now. A model of subjectivity is inseparable from a set of assumptions about space/time; as the one alters, so does the other. The realist subject represented and analyzed above does not just do different things than the modernist subject. The former is a different construction, produced through a different set of assumptions. Adorno's analysis of the opacity of the Kafkan "subject" obtains much of its power by grasping—without ever precisely articulating—just this point.

4. As mentioned in the discussion of realism above, a number of critics—most notably Michael McKeon—have persuasively revised Ian Watt's canonical argument about the rise of realism. For McKeon, scrutiny of the "prefictional" documents of English culture written throughout the seventeenth century mandates an acknowledgment of the shaping power of romance: "the origins of the English novel entail the positing of a 'new' generic category as a dialectical negation of a 'traditional' dominance—the romance, the aristocracy—whose character still saturates, as an antithetical but formative force, the texture of the category by which it is being both constituted and replaced" (268). The dialectical nature of McKeon's argument permits a richer sense of reciprocal influences and competing values in the rise of the novel than Watt makes available, yet their accounts of the "verisimilar" do not greatly differ from each other. Moreover, the argument I make above—that "verisimilar" assumes a subject's trust-suffused moves upon a canvas of lawful space/time—operates outside the conceptual territory of either Watt or his revisers.

5. McKeon: "[W]hat is most important about this [scientific] revolution is that it entails a transformation from metaphysics and theology *to* epistemology" (83).

6. As my analyses in part 1 revealed, Cartesian procedures involved an "emptying" of space and time, a substituting of quantitative terms for qualitative ones. The implications for the legitimizing of Western colonialism are enormous: "Once time and space have become emptied and disentangled, they can be systematically reappropriated. . . . Modernity globalizes insofar as space is separated from place and reintegrated with the empty dimensions of time." Anthony Giddens, foreword to *NowHere: Space, Time, and Modernity* (Berkeley: University of California Press, 1994), 12. Subsequent citation from *NowHere* refers to this edition and will be indicated

in the body of my text, parenthetically, after the quote. I remind my reader that, here and elsewhere, the term "modernity" refers to a history of instrumental Western rationality that begins in the seventeenth century, whereas the term "modernism" refers to a set of artistic practices (both fueled by and hostile to "modernity") that emerge in the late nineteenth century and continue into the first half of the twentieth.

7. Ernest Gellner persuasively reads what I call "fiat" as "compulsions." He asks, what belief systems actually compel behavior at a given time? And he answers that, during the three centuries of post-Cartesian Western modernity, "reason" is given as an all-compelling justification for procedures, "reason" as the Enlightenment counterpart to any merely traditional (and therefore "irrational") models for belief and behavior proposed by "culture." See his *Reason and Culture.*

8. Since I propose above a more extensive "anatomy of realism," my treatment of the stakes of realist familiarity and lawfulness is compressed here. Unlike a number of modernist and postmodernist commentators, I am eager to do justice to the compendious range of effects that flow from realism's investment in verisimilitude (even though modernism is founded on the blind spots of that investment). Not only does realism enjoy a powerful hold on its readers thanks to its deployment of the verisimilar, but at our peril we dismiss the familiar as merely the domain of cliché and ideology. This is not to deny deconstruction's claim that the most exploitable resource of realism is the reader's trust in its familiarity. But it is to warn against throwing out the baby with the bath powder. As for what I am calling the "moralizing" of the realist scene of representation, this ethical disposition increases in intensity in the nineteenth-century Western novel, spurred in many European cultures by romanticism's creative break (in the name of spirit) with Cartesian instrumentality and material empowerment. This break is perhaps most succinctly identified in the writing (and influence) of Jean-Jacques Rousseau.

9. Gustave Flaubert, *Madame Bovary* (1857), ed. and trans. Paul de Man (New York: Norton, 1965), 47.

10. I do not here attend to naturalist revisions of realism's narrative of the developmental subject. Rather than reconceive the model for representing the subject in space/time—as modernist fiction does—naturalism makes its creative move otherwise. It maintains the realist contract, but ups the ante, putting all the nails into the coffin of spiritual defeat. The plot, though grimmer, remains the same, virtually crying out for a new story. But naturalism has no new story to tell; nor has it a more diagnostically revealing way to tell the old one.

11. Franz Kafka, letter, January 27, 1904, cited in Ernst Pawel, *The Nightmare of Reason: A Life of Franz Kafka* (New York: Farrar, Straus, and Giroux, 1984), 158.

12. Stephen Kern (*The Culture of Time and Space: 1880–1918* [Cambridge: Harvard University Press, 1983]) draws on Eugene Minkowski (an early-twentieth-century French psychiatrist) to identify the two most prominent subject stances toward the future in this period of technological explosion: "activity" and "expectation." Minkowski aligned "activity" with instrumental, Cartesian man, reshaping the social (and natural) world as never before possible. But, in his psychiatric practice, Minkowski more often encountered "expectation." Its terms are startlingly apt for Kafka: "it [expectation] englobes the whole living being, suspends his activity, and fixes him, anguished. . . . It contains a factor of brutal arrest and renders the individual breathless. One might say that the whole of becoming, concentrated outside the individual, swoops down on him in a powerful hostile mass, attempting to annihilate him" (cited in Kern, 90). Impotence to master future space and time: this emerges as both Kafka's narrative signature and a precise rebuke of Western technological man's unprecedented mastery over space and time in the early twentieth century. I return to this issue at greater length in the next chapter, on modernist time. Subsequent citation from Kern refers to this edition and will be indicated in the body of my text, parenthetically, after the quote.

13. When he wants to, Kafka is just as likely to speed up the time as to freeze it. In *The Castle* (trans. Willa and Edwin Muir [New York: Schocken, 1959]), shortly after having dismissed Jeremiah, K. sees him again and is amazed: "'But who are you?' asked K. suddenly, for this did not appear to be the assistant. He seemed older, wearier, more wrinkled, but fuller in the face; his walk too was quite different from the brisk walk of the assistants, which gave an impression as if their joints were charged with electricity; it was slow, a little halting, elegantly valetudinarian" (301).

14. Arthur Stanley Eddington, *The Nature of the Physical World* (New York: Macmillan, 1929), 342; cited in Benjamin, *Illuminations,* 141–42.

15. It is crucial to register the *literal* dimension of Kafkan uncanny: all of Gregor's little legs moving uncontrollably, the ordeal of his getting out of bed and opening a locked door. In this moment of uncanny, he does not shape his room in the sense that Freud's return of the repressed reconfigures what is outside. Rather, it is Gregor who transforms, while the room remains the same:

> Slowly Gregor pushed the chair towards the door, then let go of it, caught hold of the door for support—the soles at the end of his little legs were somewhat sticky—and rested against it for a moment after his efforts. Then he set himself to turning the key in the lock with his mouth. It seemed, unhappily, that he hadn't really any teeth—what could he grip the key with?—but on the other hand his jaws were certainly very strong; and with their help he did manage to set the key in motion, heedless of the fact that he was undoubtedly damaging them somewhere, since a brown fluid issued from his mouth, flowed over the key and dripped on the floor. (*Metamorphosis*, 80)

Bedroom becomes estranged, bed and door and key become major obstacles, body becomes unrecognizable (one's very blood becomes an unknown "brown fluid"): Kafka reveals with supreme economy that "normal" resides neither in subjects in themselves nor in things in themselves, but rather in the habitual pact that relates the one to the other. That pact is here rescinded; the room becomes "uncanny" because the creature in it no longer functions as Gregor. More generally, throughout Kafka and central to the Eddington scenario as well, arrest and disturbance register on the assaulted *body*. Later writers like Calvino, Borges, and García-Márquez pursue postmodern (and in many cases postcolonial) strategies by releasing the body in space/time from modernist arrest. As I go on to argue, these strategies for remobilizing the body succeed, so to speak, by de-Newtonizing it (emptying it of its gravity). On the other hand, Beckett—more inextricably an inheritor of the Cartesian tradition turned dysfunctional in the modernist practice here explored—writes a fiction not of release but (as it were) of postarrest. I attend briefly to Beckett at the end of this chapter.

16. Franz Kafka, *The Diaries of Franz Kafka,* ed. Max Brod, trans. Joseph Kresh, 2 vols. (New York: Schocken, 1948–49), 1:59–60. Kafka's German, in this passage, is even more suggestively oneiric. His adjective for the latch (*Schloss*) that "sprang open of itself" is *"freiwillige"*—a hatch that, almost demonically invested with agency, is eager to open.

17. Adorno explains as follows the objective need of the modernist work of art to distance itself from the norms—both representational and experiential—of the bureaucratic society within which it arises: "When artworks have nothing external to which they can cling without ideology, what they have lost cannot be restored by any subjective act" (*Aesthetic,* 153). I take this to mean that no impulse on the part of the artist can repair the empirical "untruth" (Adorno's term) of the work's surrounding social framework; such art has no choice other than a refusal of external "harmony."

18. As is well-known, *Remembrance of Things Past* is an unsuitable title for Proust's huge novel. His first translator, C. K. Scott Moncrieff, drawing on Shakespeare's sonnet 30, assigned this title in the 1920s (to Proust's considerable dismay). Ever since, commentators have noted

that the backwards-looking nostalgia featured in the Shakespearean phrase is foreign to the intellectual drive of Proust's work. *A la Recherche du temps perdu* translates better as *In Search of Lost Time;* the philosophical project becomes visible. It is therefore frustrating that Scott Moncrieff's first reviser, Terence Kilmartin, nevertheless agreed to retain Scott Moncrieff's misleading main title (as well as some misleading subnovel titles), despite altering so much else! D. J. Enright, "re-revising" Kilmartin in the 1990s, at least restored to the book its proper overarching title in English (*In Search of Lost Time*). Since then, an intrepid, collective translation of Proust has appeared (2002–2003), under the general editorship of Christopher Prendergast. More notable than any particular improvements in this latest translation is Prendergast's deployment of six different translators for the seven subnovels that make up Proust's novel (*The Captive* and *The Fugitive* are joined in one volume). Prendergast justifies his policy as follows: "One of the benefits of the division of labour entailed by a collective translation is that it arguably heightens the chances of bringing into focus the stylistic variety we encounter as we move from one volume to the next. . . . Multiple selves, multiple worlds, multiple styles: this, paradoxically, is the quintessence of Proust" (general editor's preface, *The Way by Swann's* [London: Penguin, 2003], xvii–xviii). Much as I admire Prendergast's critical acumen, I believe that a translation produced by six translators inflicts an irredeemable violence on this single-authored text: it fractures Proust's voice (however "multiple," always his). On pragmatic grounds—that no single translator is likely to rise to the Herculean task of all thirty-five hundred pages—Prendergast's policy could perhaps be justified, but not, I think, otherwise. For this reason, as well as because Kilmartin's revision of Scott Moncrieff has held sway since its appearance in 1981, I cite the Kilmartin Proust throughout. In keeping with scholarly usage, I refer to the text by way of its shortened French title, as the *Recherche.*

19. Freud's "The Uncanny," written quite near the time when Proust was composing *Within a Budding Grove,* at one point virtually echoes such Proustian interiors. Just after the Italian vignette discussed above, Freud speaks of further uncanny occasions when "[o]ne may wander about in a dark strange room, looking for the door or the electric switch, and collide time after time with the same piece of furniture" (*SE,* 17:237). In Freud this mis-take appears opaque, perhaps daemonic. Transposed into Proustian terms, such a mis-take yields the Balbec hotel room that stubbornly refuses to accommodate a former Parisian room, just as it recalls even more suggestively the landscape that launches the entire Proustian narrative: a man asleep in a room he mentally reconfigures, a man intermittently aware that until he awakens and finds out where he is, he does not know who he is.

20. Malcolm Bowie argues impressively for the scientific spirit as Marcel's spatial guide, nourishing even his most jealous suppositions: "Jealousy . . . is a comprehensive way of inhabiting time and space. When these things [stimulation, alertness, thought] are produced by pain and absence, they may be called jealousy. But the same things, rediscovered in joy, and by joy transformed, may as fittingly be called *knowledge*" (64). Though I respect Bowie's insights, I differ from him here. What knowledge is available in Proust is at least as darkened by "pain and absence" as it is "by joy transformed." As for jealousy's being a spatial guide, I think of the nocturnal Swann outside Odette's apartment, summoning his courage to knock, enter, and complete his "search for truth" (1:299). He knocks, they open—and it is the wrong house!

21. Sanford Schwartz, *The Matrix of Modernism: Pound, Eliot, and Early Twentieth-Century Thought* (Princeton: Princeton University Press, 1985), 22.

22. William Faulkner, *Light in August* (1932), in *William Faulkner: Novels 1930–1935* (New York: Library of America, 1985), 555–56. Subsequent citation from *Light in August* refers to this edition and will be indicated in the body of my text, parenthetically, following the quote.

23. In pressing home the degradation of such maturational norms (their dedication to material acquisition), Charles Altieri nevertheless recognizes the extent to which, no less than

realism, modernism arises out of these same bourgeois conditions—in order to rebuke them: "They [the modernists] had to use all of the freedoms of the bourgeois revolution to criticize the meanings that their society was giving to freedom" (*Painterly,* 491). Altieri sees the contamination lodged in the representation model itself (the meanness, as in Flaubert, of the normative behavior being represented) as motivating modernism's repudiation of mimesis. I largely share this view and yet dissent from it too; mimesis is an aesthetic resource greater (more precious) than all the abuses one may lay at its door. More, modern fiction (unlike modern poetry, Altieri's main focus) pays a considerable emotional price whenever it seeks radically to free itself from mimesis.

24. Michael Taussig, *Mimesis and Alterity: A Particular History of the Senses* (London: Routledge, 1993), 97.

25. It is worth reiterating, here, that the subject in any great text of realism is more complex and self-divided than the hasty critique of realism (fostered by both modernism and postmodernism) typically concedes. Put more accurately, the realist subject does not so much possess as seek unification: not as natural birthright but as provisional basis for any form of self- or social fulfillment worth the having. As Altieri writes (in his rebuke of postmodern nihilism), "For both Kant and [George] Eliot, the reason we need an ethical sense of the unitary ego is that otherwise the 'I' is deeply fragmented in its pursuit of heteronomous, imaginary goods; so unification is always provisional, and always a mode of resisting the pressure of precisely those modes of social subjection that postmodernism wants to see itself as inventing." *Canons and Consequences: Reflections on the Ethical Force of Imaginative Ideals* (Evanston: Northwestern University Press, 1990), 209.

26. As my sentence makes clear (by acknowledging the social provenance of subjectivity), the price paid for a "phenomenological" criticism is its poverty of recourse to any theoretical model beyond the sense of (individual) lived experience. Phenomenology privileges a discourse of the single subject; as such it minimizes analysis of the ways in which subjectivity is always (in advance) inserted into larger discursive and behavioral paradigms that allow it to come into focus. That said, my study remains (critically) invested in phenomenological categories for two reasons: (1) readers—however vigilant—experience fiction individually, phantasmatically, and by way of shifting identifications, as an unfolding of mental experiences (hence phenomenologically), and (2) the modernist fiction I attend to is creatively invested in protagonists' moment-by-moment mind-body interactions in space/time, interactions that differ significantly from realist and postmodern models of such interaction in space/time. Notwithstanding, as Adorno puts it, "[l]ived experiences are indispensable, but they are no final court of aesthetic knowledge" (*Aesthetic,* 353).

27. I return, in the conclusion of this book, to the notion—as precious as it is impossible to ground—of affinity between the subject and the object. Affinity, not mastery but a relation nearer to acknowledgment: such a notion drives Walter Benjamin's sustained effort to conceptualize language itself as nonsensuous correspondence, as the grasp (however brief or flashing) of the word upon its referent. See Benjamin's "On Language as Such and on the Language of Man," as well as "On the Mimetic Faculty," both in his *Reflections,* 314–37.

28. Not that the shock lasts forever or stays deterritorialized. Raymond Williams argues persuasively for the ways in which modernism's formal brilliance—its suppression of connectives, its genius for fragmentary effects—was recuperated by capitalist technologies: "The isolated, estranged images of alienation and loss, the narrative discontinuities, have become the easy iconography of the commercials." *The Politics of Modernism: Against the New Conformists,* ed. Tony Pinckney (London: Verso, 1989), 35. As I hope this note indicates, I do not wish to sentimentalize modernism. Postmodern revisions of its effects were inevitable, even though the cozy relation of advertising to much pop culture is no less distressing than capitalism's

increasing capacity (beginning in the 1950s) to coopt modernist techniques. Finally, we remain as much in need today as in Kafka's time of an art that would break through our intricate skein of mystifications and thaw the frozen deep within. It remains an irreplaceable ideal yet one that, in a postmodern and post-Utopian climate of surfaces without depths, is difficult even to conceptualize.

29. Robert Siegle, "Postmodernism ™," in *Modern Fiction Studies* 41:1 (spring 1995): 179.

30. W. V. O. Quine, *Ontological Relativity and Other Essays* (New York: Columbia University Press, 1969), 82–83; cited in Rorty, *Philosophy,* 221.

31. Richard Rorty, "The Contingency of Language," in *Contingency, Irony, and Solidarity* (New York: Cambridge University Press, 1989), 7. Subsequent citation from this book refers to this edition and will be indicated in the body of my text, parenthetically, following the quote.

32. In an essay that never fails to stimulate, Bruno Latour (*We Have Never Been Modern,* trans. Catherine Porter [Cambridge: Harvard University Press, 1993]), takes aim at what he sees as the mystique of believing we have ever been modern. His most caustic remarks are directed at the pretensions of postmodernist thinkers: "they invent speech, hermeneutics and meaning, and they let the world of things drift slowly in its void" (59). He reminds his reader that "it is hard to reduce the entire cosmos to a grand narrative, the physics of subatomic particles to a text, subway systems to rhetorical devices, all social structures to discourse" (64).

33. Henry Sussman, *After-Images of Modernity: Structure and Indifference in Twentieth-Century Literature* (Baltimore: Johns Hopkins University Press, 1990), 178.

34. Samuel Beckett, *Molloy,* in *Three Novels by Samuel Beckett: Molloy, Malone Dies, The Unnamable* (New York: Grove Press, 1965), 38–39.

6. UNBOUND TIME

1. The most celebrated passages devoted to the moment are the "privileged moments" (*"moments bienheureux"*), beginning with the madeleine and moving through the Martinville steeples, the "return" of the grandmother in the Balbec hotel room, and concluding with the swift sequence of sensations that befall Marcel at the Guermantes home, in *Time Regained.* Given that Proustian commentary has already richly and extensively discussed the thematics of these famous passages, I shall focus instead on the textual practice itself involved in *staging* them.

2. Vincent Descombes, *Proust: Philosophy of the Novel,* trans. Catherine Chance Macksey (Stanford: Stanford University Press, 1992), 199. Subsequent citation from Descombes refers to this edition and will be indicated in the body of my text, parenthetically, following the quote.

3. Legrandin does serve, of course, as an *analogy* for Marcel. In *Time Regained* Marcel realizes that his own admission into the society of the Guermantes—which felt at the time unique—shares the scene with other "men who, like Swann and Legrandin and myself and Bloch, could be found at a later stage in their lives flowing into the ocean of 'high society'" (3:1015). Descombes reads this casual analogy as something more deeply revealing, seeing in Legrandin's social aspirations the model for Marcel's own concealed snobbism. This is to assume that Marcel leads a significant plot-life in the *Recherche,* but, as I go on to show, his very mode of being—his ontological status—differs from that of the book's plotted characters.

4. One wonders if *"être de fuite"* is meant to contain a double meaning—not only a being in flight, but a being that leaks (as one says *"une fuite d'eau"* for a water leakage). The "lower" prosy meaning is no less apt, for the human being in all three of these writers exists in time, precisely, as a being continually leaking its being.

5. As the following passage makes even clearer: "And I realised the impossibility which love comes up against. We imagine that it has as its object a being that can be laid down in front

of us, enclosed within a body. Alas, it is the extension of that being to all the points in space and time that it has occupied and will occupy" (3:95).

6. Perhaps the best scenes for demonstrating this departure from Newtonian spatial/temporal norms would be the two famous kiss scenes: the first when Marcel, misled by all of Albertine's apparent signals, seeks to kiss her and is rebuffed; the second when, appearing out of nowhere in his Paris apartment, she enigmatically offers the kiss she earlier enigmatically refused. Both scenes are suffused with details inconceivable in realism—the suddenly whirling room and her enlarging irresistible body in the failed kiss scene, the no less sudden emergence of all the other (heretofore unseen) facets of Albertine's approaching face in the successful scene. No less pertinently, they are—for all their differences—two versions of the same scene: a subject radically incapable of dealing with desired objects in actual space and present time.

7. Gérard Genette's booklength study of Proustian form (first published in his *Situations III* [1972], translated later as *Narrative Discourse: An Essay in Method* [1980]) attends brilliantly to the aberrances of Proust's representational schemas for "doing narrative time"—his willingness to devote over one hundred pages to events transpiring in a two-hour soirée, or to telescope years of a character's lifetime into the straitjacket of a five-line paragraph.

8. If we wish to speak of repression here, it involves not a character's desires but an entire representational schema's will not to know. For realism will not "know" what modernism here grasps: that our compacts are ruptured by an immersion in time no longer domesticated but impersonally hostile to our project of renewed self-sameness.

9. Earlier, in the chapter on modernist space, we encountered the same dynamic: Marcel's anguish in an unfamiliar hotel room. There the sequence unfolded in reverse: first displacement, then the saving return of the maternal breast in the form of the grandmother's entry into the room.

10. Compare this vignette from Freud's "The Uncanny": "I was sitting alone in my *wagon-lit* compartment when a more than usually violent jolt of the train swung back the door of the adjoining washing-cabinet, and an elderly gentleman in a dressing-gown and a traveling cap came in. I assumed that . . . he had taken the wrong direction and come into my compartment by mistake. Jumping up with the intention of putting him right, I at once realized to my dismay that the intruder was nothing but my own reflection in the looking glass on the open door. I can still recollect that I thoroughly disliked his appearance" (*SE,* 17:248n).

11. There are ways of escaping from this dilemma, of which the most common is habit. By confining our moves in the present to the framework of moves established in the past, habit is our surest strategy for eluding the menace to our being (as well as the insult to our mastery) that undefensive passage through time actually risks. Proust is wonderfully tender toward habit, even as he recognizes the sterility it imposes. Beckett, in his study of Proust, is less generous: "Habit is the ballast that chains the dog to his vomit. Breathing is habit. Life is habit. Or rather life is a succession of habits, since the individual is a succession of individuals . . . the pact must be continually renewed, the letter of safe-conduct brought up to date." *Proust* (New York: Grove Press, 1931), 8.

12. "What we have not had to decipher, to elucidate by our own efforts, what was clear before we looked at it, is not ours" (3:914). Descombes has forcefully criticized the idealist premises underlying the assumption here of an authentic private realm wholly separate from social conventions. Yet I believe that the passage, and the stance that more broadly accompanies it, remain (at least in part) persuasive. Short of claiming any effectively private realm of secured individuality, can we not speak of a painfully achieved realm of partial self-enlightenment, no less precious for its partiality, no less personal for its taking place within a publicly available vocabulary?

13. Though not speaking of Proust, Levinas identifies the stubborn tension between lost time and recovered time: "The Critique of introspection . . . has always been suspicious of a

modification that a supposedly spontaneous consciousness might undergo beneath the scrutinizing thematizing, objectivizing and indiscreet gaze of reflection." "Ethics as First Philosophy," in Hand, 80.

14. I posit such suffering at the heart of the Proustian enterprise, without forgetting the lyrical beauty of the privileged moments. Nor (if we emphasize the term "quest") do I dissent from Walter Benjamin's reminder of what Jean Cocteau saw in Proust: his "blind, senseless, frenzied quest for happiness" (*Illuminations,* 203).

15. Kafka's word for what Gregor turns into is not the neutral *Insekt* but the noxious *Ungeziefer,* indicating something nearer to "vermin" than to "insect." However, vermin (in English) is plural, and the meaning here is clearly individual! Hence I have stayed with "insect." Kafka's adjective for this creature, *ungeheuer,* does mean "gigantic," but with strong overtones of "monstrous."

16. Sometimes, seemingly from pure malice, Kafka reverses the opening note of doom: "It was a Sunday morning in the very height of spring" (first sentence of "The Judgment"). "It was late in the evening when K. arrived" (first sentence of *The Castle*). Georg Bendemann will never advance one day further into this fine spring; K. will never arrive at the Castle he seems to have already (virtually) reached. I note as well that the opening of "A Country Doctor" emphasizes further the doctor's lack of agency: *"eine dringende Reise stand mir bevor"* translates less as "I had to start off on an urgent journey" than as "an urgent journey [the subject of the clause] was in store for me."

17. This response is not limited to philistines; the frustrated Einstein himself famously remarked, after reading *The Castle,* that God does not play dice thus with the world.

18. Nowhere does Proust differ more from Kafka than in his implicit promise to the reader—wrought throughout some thirty-five hundred pages of text—that genuine attention may transform one's sense of life. As the young Marcel reflects: "he [the novelist] sets free within us all the joys and sorrows in the world, a few of which only we should have to spend years of our actual life in getting to know, and the most intense of which would never be revealed to us because the slow course of their development prevents us from perceiving them" (1:92). On this model, the conversion of time—readerly time—into insight is fiction's raison d'être.

19. Kafka most deeply offends readerly assumptions not through any particularly abusive event in his narratives. Rather, he shows language itself in failure—fibrillating despite its apparently systolic/diastolic behavior. At a certain point in any reading of Kafka's longer fictions (the three novels), one realizes that all this seemingly purposive language (that already read, that still to read) is not going anywhere. It ceases to mediate; one is not going to arrive ("there is a goal but no way"). Thus the Kafka text most effectively reaches the frozen deep of his reader, raising the question of "where one is going" within the very medium itself (language) that we unthinkingly use to ground our sense of life as a meaningful temporal passage. Kafka's "flypaper" passage is even more gruesome than the Muirs' translation conveys: not a question of their struggling away "till their little legs were torn off," but rather, as they struggle away, "their little legs tear into pieces" (*zerreißenden Beinchen*): all in the implacable present tense.

20. To Block's cringing complaint Huld thunders: "What's the matter with you? You're still alive" (*Trial,* 196).

21. Seeking to gain control of the audience, K. engages here in his most lawyerlike peroration: "there can be no doubt," he proclaims, "that behind all the actions of this court of justice . . . there is a great organization at work" (45). He goes on confidently to lay out the structure of "servants, clerks, police, and other assistants, perhaps hangmen, I do not shrink from that word. And the significance of this great organization, gentlemen? It consists in . . ." (45–46). At this moment we are nearest to realist fiction's representation of law: a discrete courtroom, opposing speeches, pertinent descriptions, ascribed motives, sought-after effects. K.'s fulsome speech however, is greeted as follows: "Here K. was interrupted by a shriek from the end of the hall; he peered from beneath his

hand to see what was happening, for the reek of the room and the dim light together made a whitish dazzle of fog" (46). It would be hard to find a purer instance of modernist fiction as the subject's sudden incapacity to negotiate others and objects in space and time.

22. I make this claim without ignoring the brouhaha caused by Amalia's trouble-making refusal of Sortini's sexual advance. That vignette presents Castle-sponsored eroticism as damaging to others in its wake, and perhaps it pairs with Klamm's considerable sexual powers (lavishly remembered by the landlady and others). But these are both vignettes of the past. What we see in the present is a range of male bureaucratic labors so unremittingly file-obsessed as to reject not only sexual distraction but even the loss of time that would be occasioned by being bodily *seen*. Work-reinforcing modesty can go no further.

23. As instances of opaque scripture, one thinks of the unreadable newspaper in "The Judgment," the illegible scriptures Block pours over without decoding, the law books that have no text, the endlessly reinterpretable letters in *The Castle,* the indecipherable "guiding plans" for the "apparatus" in "The Penal Colony."

24. It remains true that Fraülein Bürstner is often mentioned, and perhaps seen once more, later in *The Trial.* Even more pertinent is that *The Trial* is an unfinished text and that we cannot be certain how Kafka might have later modified it. I take my cue, however, from the text that we actually have (including its unfinished and deleted passages). A brief comparison along these lines with Flaubert's *Sentimental Education* reinforces the point I made in the chapter on realism. The earlier novel's realist identity lodges—despite Frédéric's inability to grow up—in his persistent pursuit of a single and impossible love interest, Mme. Arnoux.

25. Much of the following discussion draws on essays published earlier in *Etudes Faulkneriennes I* (Rennes, 1996), and *Etudes Faulkneriennes II* (Rennes, 2000). I have considerably revised and extended the argument of both essays, in order to maintain the focus on a single problematic: the protocols at issue in a modernist representation of the subject in space/time.

26. William Faulkner, *The Town* (New York: Random House, 1957), 317–18.

27. I attend amply in the following pages to the stylistic dislocations that follow from this representational project. I want to emphasize here what might be otherwise merely implicit: that the modernist subject's incomprehension in the present is (at first, perhaps for quite a while) doubled by corresponding readerly incomprehension. For the sizable number of readers who cling stubbornly to the subject/space/time assumptions of realism, such sustained disorientation levied upon them—such *unknowing*—is an intolerable price, which they refuse to pay.

28. William Faulkner, *Flags in the Dust,* ed. Douglas Day (New York: Random House, 1974), 279. Subsequent citation from *Flags* refers to this edition and will be indicated in the body of my text, parenthetically, following the quote.

29. William Faulkner, *The Sound and the Fury* (1929), ed. David Minter, 2nd ed. (New York: Norton, 1994), 51; emphasis in the original. Subsequent citation from *The Sound and the Fury* refers to this edition and will be indicated in the body of my text, parenthetically, following the quote.

30. Compare Proustian "infrared" and Kafkan affective flatness, both as discussed above. There, as here, the modernist representational schema proceeds by way of an assault upon the Newtonian premise of the subject's orderly, and familiar, insertion in space/time.

31. William Faulkner, *Sanctuary,* in *William Faulkner: Novels 1930–1935* (New York: Library of America, 1985), 331. Subsequent citation from *Sanctuary* refers to this edition and will be indicated in the body of my text, parenthetically, following the quote.

32. William Faulkner, *As I Lay Dying,* in *William Faulkner: Novels 1930–1935* (New York: Library of America, 1985), 43–44. Subsequent citation from *As I Lay Dying* refers to this edition and will be indicated in the body of my text, parenthetically, following the quote.

33. Vardaman's anguish powerfully recalls Marcel's agonizing discovery of his grandmother's "real" death (years after her actual one). Yet, whereas Proust understands the deepest

stakes of this loss as Marcel's discovery of his own incurable intermittence in time, Faulkner focuses on the suddenly unfurnished Vardaman as a being in such pain that only a "deranged" use of language could articulate his emotional state. Proust remains, throughout, as accepting of classic syntax (his ruptures are elsewhere) as Faulkner remains suspicious of linguistic norms ("just a shape to fill a lack," he has Addie Bundren contemptuously declare of language itself).

34. William Faulkner, *Absalom, Absalom!* in *William Faulkner: Novels 1936–1940* (New York: Library of America, 1990),115; emphasis in the original. Subsequent citation from *Absalom* refers to this edition and will be indicated in the body of my text, parenthetically, after the quote.

35. "Confession" as an invasive, truth-producing exercise suggests, of course, the conceptual schema of Foucault, in which truth and power are no longer oppositional terms (truth as disinterested, power as the swerve occasioned by interest). Foucault writes: "We must cease once and for all to describe the effects of power in negative terms: it 'excludes,' it 'represses,' it 'censors,' it 'abstracts,' it 'masks,' it 'conceals.' In fact, power produces; it produces reality; it produces domains of knowledge and rituals of truth." *Discipline and Punish: The Birth of the Prison* (1975), trans. Alan Sheridan (New York, 1979), 194. I cite this dazzling assertion not to endorse it entirely—for how could we pursue intellectual work if we submitted fully to its claims?—but rather to suggest the ways in which a text produces its truth effects as a function of the sense-making alignments it works within. *Sanctuary* is shaped so as to produce "truth" as the destruction of sanctuaries, whereas, I argue in the paragraphs below, *Requiem* is shaped to produce "truth" as the cathartic effect of retrospection.

36. It would be difficult to exaggerate *Sanctuary*'s reputation as a modernist masterpiece. A poetics of disillusionment, an assault on traditional ceremonies, an undoing of the integument that enables a given social contract—these traits of modernist aesthetics have long been praised for their capacity to deliver modernist authenticity. I only gesture, here, toward the construct-edness of such a conviction of finally reaching unmediated bedrock, the thing itself. For extensive commentary on the politics of Faulkner's modernism, see Richard Moreland, *Faulkner and Modernism: Rereading and Rewriting* (Madison: University of Wisconsin Press, 1990).

37. William Faulkner, *Requiem for a Nun* (1951), in *William Faulkner: Novels 1942–1954* (New York: Library of America, 1994), 535. Subsequent citation from *Requiem* refers to this edition and will be indicated in the body of my text, parenthetically, following the quote.

38. Faulkner stubbornly defended the reappearance of earlier characters under later "guises." Armstid in *The Hamlet,* for instance, hardly resembles Armstid in *As I Lay Dying.* I have myself argued, in *Faulkner's Subject: A Cosmos No One Owns* (New York: Cambridge University Press, 1992), that Lucas Beauchamp undergoes significant alteration in his three avatars: the short stories (late 1930s), *Go Down, Moses* (1942), and *Intruder in the Dust* (1948). With respect to such alterations (especially noted in his introduction to *The Mansion* [1959]), Faulkner claimed that, over time, his people had changed, as had he. None of these other characterological changes is troublemaking like Temple's, however, because none of these characters is invested, as *Requiem*'s Temple is, in recovering the hidden truth of an earlier self. Put otherwise, the retrospective mission of *Requiem* mandates an accurate reprisal of first Temple—a project revealed as ultimately bankrupt.

39. André Bleikasten makes a related point: "A vrai dire, la jeune femme blessée et traquée ne ressemble guère à la petite garce du roman" ("L'Education de Temple Drake," in *RANAM* [Paris] 23 [1980]: 79). Noel Polk speculates as well (in *Faulkner's "Requiem for a Nun": A Critical Study* [Bloomington: University of Indiana Press, 1981]) that the standard indictment of *Requiem*'s Temple prejudges her according to the behavior of her avatar in *Sanctuary.* So far as I know, no one has seen that the failure of the later confessional—indeed the collapse of the retrospective project—derives from the gap between a realist model of the subject in space/time and a modernist one.

40. Polk reads the "tomorrow" passage as a stoic commitment to survival and engagement, rather than an expression of incapacity to shed light on one's earlier (and from a later perspective, incomprehensible) behavior.

41. See Zender ("Faulkner and the Power of Sound," *PMLA* 99 [1984]: 89–108) for a related inquiry into the pathos of the later Faulkner's rhetorical insistences.

42. Rainer Maria Rilke, *The Notebooks of Malte Laurids Brigge* (1910), trans. M. D. Herter Norton (New York: Norton, 1949), 80. Subsequent citation from the *Notebooks* refers to this edition and will be indicated in the body of my text, parenthetically, following the quote.

43. Friedrich Nietzsche, *Twilight of the Idols* (1888), in *The Portable Nietzsche,* ed. and trans. Walter Kaufmann (New York: Viking, 1954), 483.

7. SUBJECT AND/AS OTHER

1. Edmund Husserl, "Phenomenology" (1927), in *Phenomenology and Existentialism,* ed. Richard Zaner and Don Ihde (New York: Putnam, 1973), 50.

2. Maurice Merleau-Ponty, preface to *The Phenomenology of Perception* (1945), trans. Colin Smith, in Zaner and Ihde, 72.

3. The following passage from Kierkegaard, cited at the beginning of this study, reads as presciently phenomenological: "A system of existence cannot be given. Is there, then, not such a system? That is not at all the case. . . . Existence itself is a system—for God, but it cannot be a system for any existing spirit. System and conclusiveness correspond to each other, but existence is the very opposite. . . . In order to think existence, systematic thought must think it as annulled and consequently as not existing. Existence is the spacing that holds apart; the systematic is the conclusiveness that brings together" (from *Concluding Unscientific Postscript*). The world, for God, may be a system, but for us who exist in it, it can only be an unsystematic life-world. Our way of inhabiting space and time registers existence as a something "that holds apart," not a "conclusiveness that brings together."

4. Maurice Merleau-Ponty, from *The Phenomenology of Perception,* in *The Body: Classic and Contemporary Readings,* ed. Donn Welton (Oxford: Blackwell, 1999), 152, 155; emphasis in the original. Subsequent citation from Merleau-Ponty's *Phenomenology,* as well as from Welton's collection of essays on *The Body,* refer to these two editions and will be indicated in the body of my text, parenthetically, following the quote.

5. Though he was no phenomenologist, Bertrand Russell—in seeking to account for Einstein's work—was keenly attentive to the need to describe, not time-indifferent phenomena, but phenomena as constitutively spatial/temporal:

In the old view, a piece of matter was something which survived all through time, while never being at more than one place at any given time. This way of looking at things is obviously connected with the complete separation of space and time. . . . When we substitute space/time for space and time, we shall naturally expect to derive the physical world from constituents which are as limited in time as in space. Such constituents are what we call "events." An event does not persist and move . . . it merely exists for its little moment and then ceases. A piece of matter will thus be resolved into a series of events. . . . The whole series of these events makes up the whole history of the particle, and the particle is regarded as *being* its history, not some metaphysical entity to which events happen" (*An ABC of Relativity* [London, 1925], 208–9, cited in Schleifer, 162)

6. One could hardly be further from Descartes's dismissive relegation of bodiness to secondary status: "The first thought to come to mind," Descartes writes in his Second Meditation, "was that I had a face, hands, arms and the whole mechanical structure of limbs which can be seen in a corpse, and which I call the body" (17). Descartes associates movement, sense perception, and

thinking (dimensions of human resourcefulness) with the soul; body he associates with inert corpse-matter. Kant, we recall, echoes this alignment: "The inertia of matter is and signifies nothing else but its *lifelessness* as matter in itself. Life means the capacity of a substance to act on itself from an inner principle" (cited in Guyer, 182). This brief dismissal of the somatic realm as a space of alienation lets us glimpse realism's typical prioritizing of disembodied reason—the agency of *res cogitans*—in representing human being. Phenomenological thinking refuses this binary, envisaging human being as intrinsically somatic, temporal, and spatial: not essentializable as realism's timeless soul lodged in a time-affected body.

7. Martin Heidegger, "Building, Dwelling, Thinking" (1954), trans. Albert Hofstadter, in *Martin Heidegger: Basic Writings* (New York: Harper and Row, 1977), 334–35. Subsequent citation from Heidegger's essays refers to this edition and will be indicated in the body of my text, parenthetically, following the quote. In *Being and Time* Heidegger recurs to the human being's unceasing, preconscious extension into his/her spaces, making those spaces part of a larger human field of familiarity and capacitation: "Hearkening too has the kind of Being of the hearing which understands. What we 'first' hear is never noises or complexes of sounds, but the creaking waggon, the motor-cycle. We hear the column on the march, the north wind, the woodpecker tapping, the fire crackling. It requires a very artificial and complicated frame of mind to 'hear' a 'pure noise.' The fact that motor-cycles and waggons are what we proximally hear is the phenomenal evidence that in every case Dasein, as Being-in-the-world, already dwells *alongside* what is ready-to-hand within-the-world" (as cited in Welton, 110; emphasis in the original).

8. Emmanuel Levinas, *Totality and Infinity* (1961), trans. Alphonso Lingis (Pittsburgh: Duquesne University Press, 1969), 37–38; emphasis in the original. As indicated earlier, subsequent citation from *Totality and Infinity* refers to this edition and will be indicated in the body of my text, parenthetically, following the quote. For the temporal counterpart to such spatial bolstering—the ways in which time joins space in a configuration that orients human being as unifyingly *projective*—consider, again, this passage from Foucault's *Archeology of Knowledge:* "continuous history is the indispensable correlative of the founding function of the subject: the guarantee that everything that has eluded him may be restored to him; the certainty that time will disperse nothing without restoring it in a reconstituted unity; the promise that one day the subject—in the form of a historical consciousness—will once again be able to appropriate . . . all those things that are kept at a distance by difference, and find in them what might be called his abode" (12; cited in Schleifer, 43). The passage echoes both Proust (the project of recovery in time) and Heidegger (our relation to space as homeland, dwelling) in salient ways.

9. Schleifer explores extensively this model of Enlightenment temporality: "For the Newtonian tradition of the Enlightenment, the homogeneity of time allowed for secular simplicity: every moment is 'original'; every moment presents the subject of experience with a new beginning, a clean slate" (38).

10. Elizabeth Ermarth's *Realism and Consensus* remains the most capacious study of realism's array of assumptions and strategies for managing experience in space/time.

11. Martin Heidegger, "What Is Metaphysics?" (1949), trans. David Farrell Krell, in *Martin Heidegger: Basic Writings,* 103.

12. Rollo May, *Love and Will* (New York: Dell, 1973), 243.

13. See Levinas: "The passivity of the self precedes the voluntary act that ventures toward a project, and even the certainty which in truth is coinciding with itself. The oneself is prior to self-coinciding" (*Otherwise,* 195 n. 17).

14. The dynamic of Kafkan interpellation echoes—by way of the absurd—the celebrated Althusserian argument for "interpellation" as the identity-bestowing activity of Ideological State Apparatuses. Within Althusser's model, attainment of individual subjectivity just is the process of heeding voluntarily an ideological call to participate in a combination of beliefs, rituals, and

practices. It is the empowering entry into group-bestowed, group-shared identity. In Kafka, by contrast, K.'s heeding the priest's call is tantamount to the erasure of both group-bestowed identity and life itself.

15. Although "capital charge" fits my reading perfectly, Kafka's phrase is actually less uncanny: *"die Hauptverhandlung"* means something closer to "capital hearing" than "capital charge."

16. As my German colleague Hansjakob Werlen confirms, the structure of Kafka's actual sentence is revealingly more contorted than the Muirs' translation suggests: "In diesem Augenblicke ging über die Brücke ein geradezu unendlicher Verkehr" bends itself out of shape to emphasize the intensity, resonance, and finality of all that "traffic." Normal German usage would more typically end the sentence, as the Muirs' translation does, with the bridge rather than the traffic.

17. In a different register, one might compare K.'s unexpectedly receiving from Bürgel a virtual offer of the keys to the Castle and then . . . falling asleep.

18. Malcolm Bowie cites the Proustian passage that perhaps most echoes the Freudian symptomatology of *The Psychopathology of Everyday Life:* "the words themselves [of others] did not enlighten me unless they were interpreted in the same way as a rush of blood to the cheeks of a person who is embarrassed, or a sudden silence. Such and such an adverb . . . bursting into flames through the involuntary, sometimes perilous contact of two ideas which the speaker has not expressed but which . . . I was able to extract from it, told me more than a long speech" (3:83).

19. Descombes is rare among critics in his alertness to Proust's ways of distinguishing Marcel's mode of being from that of other characters in *la Recherche.* Of Albertine sequestered he writes: "Albertine has been caught up in a tragic drama: She is a subject of action. Marcel, like a tourist, has recorded his memories: he is a subject of experience" (210). Notwithstanding this insight into Marcel's different ontological status, Descombes's insistence on characterizing the novel as, after all, a novel rather than a treatise leads him to claims like the following: "Marcel takes a great step forward on the long path toward final illumination when, in the atelier of Elstir, he receives instruction from painting" (253). As I argued above, Marcel *as character* learns nothing from Elstir, hardly even hears him. Descombes is thinking in the inappropriately teleological terms of realist fiction.

20. Elias Canetti, *Crowds and Power,* trans. Carol Stewart (New York: Viking, 1962), 297. See also Freud's pithy remarks about judgment in his essay titled "Negation": "Judging is a continuation . . . of the original process by which the ego took things into itself or expelled them from itself, according to the pleasure principle" (in *The Freud Reader*, ed. Peter Gay [New York: Norton, 1989], 669).

21. Adorno's *Aesthetic Theory* hammers home art's essential incapacity to change the real: "It is self-evident that nothing concerning art is self-evident any more, not its inner life, not its relation to the world, not even its right to exist" (1). Art's famous *"promesse de bonheur"* (Stendhal's phrase for the larger spiritual life the artwork harbors) is a Utopian promise only: "Art is the ever-broken promise of happiness" (*Aesthetic,* 136).

22. To put this more accurately, in Faulkner's earlier masterpieces centered on outrage, there is little interest in canniness. By contrast, the Snopes trilogy (conceived in the 1920s but written from the late 1930s forward) revolves around the machinations of a figure of supreme canniness, Flem Snopes. I think it is fair to say that, for Faulkner the modernist, canniness is a secondary stance (though never negligible: see Jason in *The Sound and the Fury* and Cash in *As I Lay Dying*).

8. ADVENTURES IN HYPERSPACE

1. Two days later, the *Herald Tribune* reported: "After five days of investigation, U.S. energy and utility officials are still no closer to a definitive explanation of what triggered last

week's power failures across large sections of the United States and Canada. But they insist that this is no indication that the U.S. power grid is incomprehensible or uncontrollable. Rather, the blackout shows how complex the grid has become, with events in Cleveland and Detroit able to set off a chain reaction as far away as New York City and Toronto" (5). No magic here, just scientifically orchestrated technology, developed not only past the capacity of my New York daughter to envisage what happened, but also past the capacity (despite five days of unremitting analysis) of the best experts in the field to locate the exact problem: subject, space, and time in a new configuration indeed. I close this note by acknowledging that the August 2003 blackout will, of course, be past history by the time these words are read. The point is not that something so technologically new as to seem inexplicable took place—even as it occurred, commentators were noting the outdated U.S. model for distributing electricity on a continental scale—but rather that no individual "inserted in" this contemporary power grid can readily conceptualize its spatial/temporal dynamic. The larger rubric for the collapse of subjects' orientational boundaries is "globalization."

2. Thomas Nagel, *The View from Nowhere* (Oxford: Oxford University Press, 1986), 85.

3. In pursuing his critique of the Western epistemological tradition from Descartes through Kant, Rorty posits that "real-world claims" are still *sayable* (elements of our "conversation"), but not *demonstrable,* despite that older tradition's unceasing quest: "Philosophy as epistemology will be the search for the inimitable structures within which knowledge, life, and culture must be contained—structures set by the privileged representations which it studies. The neo-Kantian consensus thus appears as the end-product of an original wish to substitute *confrontation* for *conversation* as the determinant of our belief" (*Philosophy,* 163; emphasis in the original).

4. Fredric Jameson, *The Jameson Reader,* edited by Michael Hardt and Kathi Weeks (Oxford: Blackwell, 2000), 278. Subsequent citation from this collection of Jameson's essays will be indicated in the body of my text, parenthetically, following the quote.

5. Jameson draws heavily on Ernest Mandel's *Late Capitalism* (trans. Joris De Bres [London: Verso, 1978]) for his linkage of representational strategies in the domain of culture with technological inventions in the domain of economics. Mandel, Jameson writes (in "Postmodernism, or the Cultural Logic of Late Capitalism"), "outlines three . . . fundamental breaks or quantum leaps in the evolution of machinery of capital: . . . 'Machine production of steam-driven motors since 1848; machine production of electric and combustion motors since the 90s of the 19th century; machine production of electronic and nuclear-powered apparatuses since the 40s of the 20th century—these are the three general revolutions in technology engendered by the capitalist mode of production since the "original" industrial revolution of the later 18th century'" (18; cited in *Reader,* 216). Jameson thus aligns three salient "moments" of capitalism's increasingly sophisticated power systems with three sustained "moments" of Western representational norms: realism (coherent development of mid-nineteenth-century narratives), modernism (speed and shock of early-twentieth-century narratives), and postmodernism (vertigo and incomprehension of mid-twentieth-century narratives).

6. As Stephen Kern argues, early-twentieth-century discoveries in physics "wiped out the classical distinction between the plenum of matter and the void of space" (153) and laid the foundation for the "weightlessness" of objects that a later technology would render a daily (though still counterintuitive) experience. At about the same time Einstein was announcing the irrelevance of the very notion of "space": "We entirely shun the vague word 'space,' of which, we must honestly acknowledge, we cannot form the slightest conception," Einstein writes, "and we replace it by 'motion relative to a practically rigid body of reference'" (*Relativity,* cited in Kern, 136). Space here loses its Newtonian absoluteness, becoming "relative" to bodies in differential motion.

7. Perry Anderson, *In the Tracks of Historical Materialism* (Chicago: University of Chicago Press, 1984), 48.

8. He cannot die but others can. Barth's novel operates an increasingly moralized pressure upon Horner, as we watch the impregnated Rennie Morgan suffer from his irremediable "absence," arrange to be aborted, die on the table. Yet the text never suggests, as Camus's *Stranger* seems to at the end, that some stance other than inhuman detachment might be more appropriate.

9. John Barth, *The End of the Road* (New York: Grosset and Dunlap, 1969), 67. Subsequent citation from Barth's novel refers to this edition and will be indicated in the body of my text, parenthetically, after the quote.

10. This is not to say that Sutpen does not harbor socially conflicting body schemas. His ritual of fighting with his own black slaves, as I have myself argued (*What Else But Love* [New York: Columbia University Press, 49–50), at once scandalizes Southern racial proprieties (where the ritual occurs) and recalls, nostalgically, the mountain culture of his childhood, where demonstrated physical strength betokened identity still intact, outside the reach of any racial codes. My point is that a somatically *single* Sutpen takes into himself these opposed cultural orientations.

11. I do not propose modernist rhetorics of stream of consciousness as accurate representations of human consciousness. They proceed by convention, just as postmodern pastiche proceeds by convention; but in the former case the convention seeks to *conceal* itself, so that the representation of consciousness might seem to be *real* and therefore (as only what seems to be real can) elicit from other subjects (including the reader) an identificatory response. Such seemingly real subjectivity is open, in modernist representation, to unpremeditated change in time. (Not change signaled in advance of its arrival—as in realism—but more startling change: the consequence of an untamed encounter with others in time and space.) In closing this note, let me be clear about postmodern fiction's typical refusal to deliver such a narrative. It is not that Pynchon cannot write a discourse that feigns the unmediated real, but that the readerly identification (investment in another's seemingly real subjectivity) invited by such writing is foreign to his project of demystification. One would be looking for his signature, so to speak, in the wrong place.

12. An extreme but astute articulation of this point is Gianni Vattino's: "The consumption of Being in exchange-value, that is, the transformation of the real world into a fable, is nihilistic even insofar as it leads to a weakening of the cogent force of 'reality.' In the world of generalized exchange-value all is given . . . as a narration or *récit*. Essentially, this narration is articulated by the mass media." *The End of Modernity: Nihilism and Hermeneutics in Post-modern Culture,* trans. Jon R. Snyder (Cambridge: Polity Press, 1988), 27. A more neutral characterization of postmodern narrative voice is the following from Jean Baudrillard: "An air of nondeliberate parody clings to everything . . . like an undecidable game to which is attached a specifically aesthetic pleasure, the pleasure in reading and in the rules of the game." *Baudrillard Reader,* trans. Mark Poster (Stanford: Stanford University Press, 1988),146–47.

9. URBAN NIGHTMARE AND CITY DREAMS

1. One wonders whether the insistent name "Malte" invites the reader to read the protagonist as already superannuated, a member of a long-exhausted medieval sect—the Knights of Malta—and thus upholder of a set of values wholly at odds with the urban ones of twentieth-century Paris.

2. Richard Swinburne, *Space and Time* (London: Macmillan, 1968), 17.

3. Malte experiences, in nightmarish fashion, the phenomenological configuration of subject-bodies-in-space that Umberto Boccioni's "Technical Manifesto" gleefully celebrated the same year (1910): "our bodies penetrate the sofas upon which we sit, and the sofas penetrate our bodies. The motor bus rushes into the houses which it passes . . ." (cited in Kern, 197).

4. Italo Calvino, *Invisible Cities,* trans. William Weaver (New York: Harcourt, Brace, Jovanovich, 1974), 32. Subsequent citation from Calvino's novel refers to this edition and will be indicated in the body of my text, parenthetically, after the quote.

5. The study my sentence references is of course Edward Said's magisterial *Orientalism* (1978).

6. This is perhaps the time to concede that, though less emphatically than Calvino's text, canonical modernism is all too often a male affair as well (though not an Orientalist one). Nietzsche's centrality to modernist thought—his emphasis on isolation, authenticity, creative self-overcoming, heroic confrontation with the real in all its disorder—suggests, in microcosm, many of the male tropes fueling modernist experimentation. (As is well known, Nietzsche was a major influence on Rilke's thought.) That said, much fascinating work has recently begun to map out modernism's other affiliations: with women writers, with the Harlem Renaissance, with the technologies and commodities of mass culture, to name a few. See, for example, Crary, Sheri Benstock, *Women of the Left Bank: Paris, 1900–1940* (Austin: University of Texas Press, 1986); Michael North, *The Dialect of Modernism: Race, Language, and Twentieth-Century Literature* (New York: Oxford University Press, 1994); Rita Felski, *The Gender of Modernity* (Cambridge: Harvard University Press, 1995); and *The Cambridge Companion to Modernism,* ed. Michael Levenson (New York: Cambridge University Press, 1999).

7. One should acknowledge modernism's sometimes knee-jerk penchant for the lexicon of crisis. Raymond Williams has reflected trenchantly on the ease with which postmodern advertising has recuperated and exploited the sensationalism of modernist tropes. At a more wholesale level, Bruno Latour derides the melodramatic stance itself: "Why do we get so much pleasure out of being so different not only from others but from our own past? What psychologist will be subtle enough to explain our morose delight in being in perpetual crisis and in putting an end to history?" (114). Latour goes on to note: "A Kafkaesque society cannot be renegotiated. . . . A West radically cut off from other cultures and natures is not open to discussion. . . . A past from which we are forever separated by radical epistemological breaks cannot be sorted out again by anyone" (125).

8. The phrase is Rushdie's, and he uses it in one of his most powerful essays—"Outside the Whale"—to characterize the zone of turbulence that literature must enter if it would engage the ceaselessly transformative real world outside the text.

10. PASSAGE AND PASSING

1. The tension I speak of—between a postcolonial project of subject emancipation and a postmodern critique of subjectivity—is widely known in postcolonial discourse. Both Edward Said ("East Isn't East") and Kwame Anthony Appiah ("The Postcolonial and the Postmodern," *In My Father's House: Africa in the Philosophy of Culture* [New York: Oxford University Press, 1992], 137–57) explore, to my mind persuasively, the different vectors of postmodern and postcolonial discourse. Here is Said:

> whereas post-modernism, in one of its famous programmatic statements (by Jean-François Lyotard), stresses the disappearance of the grand narratives of emancipation and enlightenment, the emphasis behind much of the work done by the first generation of post-colonial artists and scholars is exactly the opposite: the grand narratives remain, even though their implementation and realization are at present in abeyance, deferred or circumvented. This crucial difference between the urgent historical and political imperatives of post-colonialism and post-modernism's relative detachments makes for altogether different approaches and results. (Cited in Neal Lazarus, *Nationalism and Cultural Practice* [Cambridge: Cambridge University Press, 1999], 22)

2. I realize that these terms are troublesome, ever since the fall of Soviet empire in the early 1990s and the disappearance of a second-world problematic. I retain them in order to emphasize

the differences between a cultural dilemma of the contemporary West—how, in the wake of post-structuralist criticism and the rampant commodification of human behavior, continue to speak seriously of the individual subject at all?—and the plight of non-Western cultures whose distinctively different voices and traditions have yet to be adequately recognized abroad. As has been widely remarked, it is passing ironic that first-world cultures are busy eradicating the idea of the subject just when third-world subjects are seeking to find their voice. A first-world/third-world binary is under increasing pressure for other reasons as well, given the impact of global capitalism upon the native character of what were once "other" cultures—a claim that the most cursory comparison between Forster's Chandrapore and Rushdie's Bombay would sustain. Finally, "other" cultures were never simply "other," nor did the noninnocent project of pretending that they were so begin only recently. For fascinating analysis of this last, see *The Invention of Tradition,* ed. Eric Hobsbaum and Terence Ranger (New York: Cambridge University Press, 1983).

3. Jameson speaks of such a Utopian dimension as "whatever collective structures seem to resist the anomie of the modern industrial state and to offer some negative and critical power over against the larger and more diffuse demographies in which the group's current oppression is practiced" (*Reader,* 392). The contrast between a third-world imaginary of the collective and our notions of the modern industrial state is powerfully present in García-Márquez's Macondo. In a more refracted manner it operates as well, I believe, in the kinds of pressure Rushdie's visionary mode brings to bear on realist specular assumptions, as in the hallucinatory images of London—"a city visible but unseen"—that recur in *The Satanic Verses.*

4. E. M. Forster, *A Passage to India* (New York: Harcourt Brace, 1965), 38. Subsequent citation from Forster's novel refers to this edition and will be indicated in the body of my text, parenthetically, after the quote.

5. Pierre Macherey, *A Theory of Literary Production* (1966), trans. Geoffrey Wall (London: Routledge and Kegan Paul, 1978), 132.

6. The Fielding-Aziz bond (which I do not here analyze) is central to the book's intricate investment in gender norms. For provocative commentary on the implications and limitations of their bond, see Sara Suleri (*The Rhetoric of English India* [Chicago: University of Chicago Press, 1992]) and Ian Baucom (*Out of Place: Englishness, Empire, and the Locations of Identity* [Princeton: Princeton University Press, 1999]).

7. The exception, of course, is *The Longest Journey,* Forster's only novel (before *Maurice*) centered on the desire for homosexual release, and therefore doomed (within a realist scenario) before it begins.

8. Baucom sheds great light on the ideological stance guiding early-twentieth-century British tours to India (the standard "passage")—what guidebooks, hotels, and sites the tourist organizations made use of, and to what memorial ends they were used.

9. Salman Rushdie, *The Satanic Verses* (New York: Viking, 1988), 44. As indicated earlier, subsequent citation from the novel refers to this edition and will be indicated in the body of my text, parenthetically, after the quote.

10. Homi Bhabha, "How Newness Enters the World," in *The Location of Culture* (London: Routledge, 1994), 218.

11. The quoted passage is from Rushdie's essay "Outside the Whale," in his *Imaginary Homelands: Essays and Criticism, 1981–1991* (New York: Viking, 1991), 100.

11. ARREST AND RELEASE

1. This extensive final comparison, though originally conceived and written as the conclusion to my book, has appeared in altered form in *Look Away: The U.S. South in New World Studies,* ed. Jon Smith and Deborah Cohn (Durham: Duke University Press, 2004), 355–82.

2. That the subject is conceived as "committed to life, liberty, and the pursuit of happiness" does not mean that these goals are always represented as achievable. Late-nineteenth-century "naturalism" attends no less insistently than modernism to the failure of subject quests. It envisages these quests, however, within the same narrative conventions as the realism it follows. It tells kindred stories, but this time they finish badly. Modernist fiction tells its stories differently—crafts the subject trajectory through space/time differently—without, however, dismantling an inherited loom of Enlightenment assumptions. Modernism is, after all, a Western cultural phenomenon; even as it targets norms of Western thinking, it also works within the problematics of those norms. By contrast, the freshness of much postcolonial fiction—which is nourished by an encounter with third-world cultural traditions—lies in its Utopian refiguring, at the representational level, of the procedural loom itself.

3. The phrase, cited so frequently as to have taken on a life of its own, appears at the end of the first chapter of Jameson's *The Political Unconscious* (Ithaca: Cornell University Press, 1981), 102. Jameson's larger argument—that ideology functions as selective discourses about a history that exceeds discourses—underlies my own claims about ideology as a noninnocent repertory of discursively proposed pathways through social time and space. Jameson serves, throughout this chapter, as an illuminating guide for thinking about postmodern and postcolonial protocols.

4. The essay alluded to is, of course, "The Mirror Stage" (in *Ecrits* [1966], trans. Alan Sheridan [New York: Norton, 1977]). One of the most provocative readings of Lacan's argument is Jane Gallop's in *The Daughter's Seduction* (Ithaca: Cornell University Press, 1982).

5. For further discussion of this moment of body coding in *Absalom,* see my *Faulkner's Subject* (New York: Cambridge University Press, 1992), 131–35. Such subjective vertigo registers precisely in Bon's son's incoherent passage through space and time: from New Orleans to Jefferson, from Jefferson to "frowsy stinking rooms in places–towns and cities–which likewise had no names . . . broken by other periods, intervals, of furious and incomprehensible and apparently reasonless moving . . ." (*Absalom,* 170–71). In him "existence" ceases to be "experience" and—spatially and temporally uncoordinated—becomes absurd.

6. Benjamin makes this remark in "The Storyteller" (87), the essay on Leskov in which, drawing on Lukács's *Theory of the Novel,* he speculates most directly upon the kinds of alienation wrought into the very institution of the novel as an Enlightenment print genre. Benjamin analyzes the notion of "experience" as split between two distinct categories: *Erfahrung,* a communal and reflective subject trajectory through space/time, and *Erlebnis,* events that have been brutely lived but not turned into subjective value. He sees the increasing polarizing of "experience" as an inevitable byproduct of Western capitalism's deforming mark upon individual behavior—promoting work rhythms reduced to unthinking, instrumental repetition, and reaching its alienating extremes in the habit/shock binary characteristic of modernist narratives. Benjamin's essays on Proust, Kafka, and above all Baudelaire (all three in *Illuminations*) explore this phenomenon in detail.

7. This said, the supreme realist instance of an absurd ending is surely Flaubert's *Sentimental Education* (1867), as Lukács recognized over a half century ago. See my brief commentary on this novel in chapter 3, n. 13.

8. The archive for exploring Faulkner's relation to the Boom writers is considerable. Salient texts include Patricia Tobin's *Time and the Novel: The Genealogical Imperative* (Princeton: Princeton University Press, 1978), José Saldívar's *The Dialectics of Our America: Genealogy, Cultural Critique, and Literary History* (Durham: Duke University Press, 1991), Lois Zamora's *Writing the Apocalypse: Contemporary U.S. and Latin American Fiction* (New York: Cambridge University Press, 1989), Deborah Cohn's *History and Memory in the Two Souths: Recent Southern and Spanish American Fiction* (Nashville: Vanderbilt University Press, 1999), and Cohn and Smith's collection of essays in *Look Away.*

9. As Amaryll Chanady claims, "It is against this complex background of the colonized subject's rebellion against imposed models [among these, read: realism], the resistance of the newly independent Latin American countries to neocolonial domination and the European philosophical delegitimation of metaphysical and epistemological paradigms that we must situate certain twentieth-century literary practices." "Territorialization," in *Magical Realism: Theory, History, Community,* ed. Lois Parker Zamora and Wendy Faris (Durham: Duke University Press, 1995), 136. A key dimension of these imposed models is the hegemonic authority of a linear/mimetic vision of things—such as realism (and its philosophic counterpart, positivism) so adroitly puts in place. The contestatory "practices" Chanady speaks of share an investment in magic realism.

10. Carlos Fuentes and Mario Vargas Llosa have been equally laudatory in their tribute to Faulkner's germinal practice, but since García Márquez is my figure for comparison, his words are most pertinent. Faulkner, he says, is "a writer from the Caribbean," for the Caribbean "extends from northern Brazil to the U.S. South. Including, of course, Yoknapatawpha County" (cited in Cohn, *History,* 44).

11. For useful analyses of the crisis in epistemology (and, relatedly, in representation) that characterizes so much modernist work, see William R. Everdell, *The First Moderns: Profiles in the Origins of Twentieth-Century Thought* (Chicago: University of Chicago Press, 1997), Astrádur Eysteinsson, *The Concept of Modernism* (Ithaca: Cornell University Press, 1990), Kern, Rorty (*Philosophy*), and Williams (*Politics of Modernism*), among others. See as well the above discussion of Forster's *A Passage to India.*

12. Only in the last two pages of the text do "sighs of disappointment" (447) briefly take over the narrative voice, impose a retrospective judgment laden with disapproval, and—for a moment—make this book look like a gathered Faulknerian indictment. While it would be a mistake to overlook this souring of narrative tone, it would be a greater mistake to generalize it as the disillusioned keynote of the entire novel's structure of feeling—a greater mistake because an imposition of teleological means/end thinking upon a text whose way of inserting the subject in space/time has so magnanimously operated otherwise during the previous 445 pages.

13. *One Hundred Years of Solitude* is, of all of García Márquez's works, the one that aligns best with my reading. Indeed, I would claim that this breakthrough text rivals Faulkner's greatest novels—precisely by escaping from Faulknerian procedures. *As I Lay Dying* hovers too closely over *Leaf Storm,* and the brooding paralysis of *Sartoris* suffocatingly recurs in *No One Writes to the Colonel.* These early texts are modernist-inspired: portentous, immobile, heavy with an atmosphere of stifled aspirations, ghosts waiting in the wings. The scene they narrate is one of dysfunction, stasis. In the terms of my argument, they are still attached to the realist loom of performance, yet they access it in modernist terms, as purely disabling. It may follow that—compelling as these early fictions are—García Márquez comes into his own only when he conceives another way of setting up the loom: magic realism. Magic realism frees his work from oppressive mimesis and gives it, for the first time, *motion and scope*—the freedom to move everywhere in space and time. (As Wendy Faris puts it, "These fictions [of magic realism] question received ideas about time, space, and identity" ["Scheherezade's Children: Magical Realism and Postmodern Fiction," in Zamora and Faris, 173].) The immobilized psychological Colonel transforms into the released archetypal Colonel of thirty-two uprisings. The latter figure, equally tragic in his implications, has become available to a new kind of narration. Put otherwise, his very emptiness attains gigantic resonance; the writer has figured out how to *activate* his cast of characters, how to choreograph their being rather than lament their failed-being.

14. It is pertinent to cite again MacIntyre's distinction between Western and non-Western conceptions of the individual: "In many pre-modern, traditional societies it is through his or her membership of a variety of social groups that the individual identifies himself or herself and is identified by others. I am brother, cousin and grandson, member of this household, that village,

this tribe. These are not characteristics that belong to human beings accidentally, to be stripped away in order to discover 'the real me.' They are part of my substance. . . . Individuals inherit a particular space within an interlocking set of social relationships; lacking that space, they are nobody, or at best a stranger or an outcast" (32). In part 1 of this study I explored in some detail the destructive potential, in the Enlightenment narrative and later in realist fiction, of a simultaneous commitment to individual flourishing and to social constraint.

15. Gabriel Garcia Marquez, *One Hundred Years of Solitude* (1967), trans. Gregory Rabassa (New York: Harper and Row, 1970), 275. Subsequent citation from the novel refers to this edition and will be indicated in the body of my text, parenthetically, following the quote.

16. It is widely acknowledged that, from early days with his grandparents through his cub reporting and into his own mature research, García Márquez has remained fascinated with Colombian folk materials. The artistic use of such materials allows him to escape "the limitations that rationalists and Stalinists from all eras have attempted to impose" upon a reality bursting with difference, as he put it in *The Fragrance of Guava* (London: Faber and Faber, 1983), 59–60. The freshness such materials bring to *One Hundred Years of Solitude* is attested to by such vignettes as the rising from the earth of Remedios the Beauty and Father Nicanor (in such different yet appropriate ways); Petra Cotes's feeding her last mule on her remaining sheets, rugs, and velvet drapes; the poor girl who—to recompense her grandmother for accidentally allowing her house to burn down—must sleep with customers every night for the next ten years (at a rate of seventy men per night). For related commentary on the folkloric dimension of García-Márquez's work, see Clive Griffin, "The Humor of *One Hundred Years of Solitude,*" in *Gabriel García Márquez: New Readings,* ed. Bernard McGuirk and Richard Cardwell (Cambridge: Cambridge University Press, 1987), 81–94; Vera M. Kutzinski, "The Logic of Wings: García Márquez and Afro-American Literature," in *Modern Critical Views: Gabriel García Márquez,* ed. Harold Bloom (New York: Chelsea House, 1989), 169–82; and Gene H. Bell-Villada, *García Márquez: The Man and the Work* (Chapel Hill: University of North Carolina Press, 1990).

17. Rey Chow, *Ethics after Idealism: Theory, Culture, Ethnicity, Reading* (Bloomington: Indiana University Press, 1998), xx. Chow effectively exposes the limitation of binary structures by speculating on Hong Kong, a city at present situated uneasily between two colonial powers. See her "Between Colonizers," in *Ethics,* 149–67, for the problematic of Hong Kong's culture as not accurately mappable onto either British or Chinese models. J. Michael Dash's *The Other America: Caribbean Literature in a New World Context* (Charlottesville: University of Virginia Press, 1998) is devoted to the importance of this argument. Recognizing that postcolonial and postmodern discourses are repeatedly tempted by "the current intellectual zeitgeist of the romance of otherness" (x), Dash seeks to offer a flexible and still-developing regional paradigm for Caribbean literature that might avoid both the myopia of nationalist thinking and the systematization of global thinking.

18. Again Jameson: Utopian imagination "must be based fully as much on solidarity as on alienation or repression, and it necessarily feeds on . . . images of primitive or tribal cohesion . . . [as it feeds on] whatever collective structures seem to resist the anomie of the modern industrial state" ("Utopianism and Anti-Utopianism," in *Reader,* 391–92).

19. By "no Western plotting" I do not mean that Western plotting is absent from *One Hundred Years of Solitude.* I mean, rather, that such plotting is figured negatively, as colonial incursion (indeed, the plot of the West), rather than positively, as enacted and *subjectified* within Buendía trajectories. A host of Western myths (as opposed to a structure of Western plot) shape the doings deployed in the novel, along with the array of folk materials already discussed.

20. Alejo Carpentier, "Baroque," in Zamora and Faris, 98–100.

21. "The nature of things, their coexistence, the way in which they are linked together and communicate is nothing other than their resemblance. And that resemblance is visible only in the network of signs that cross the world from one end to the other" (Foucault, *Order,* 29).

22. A chapter in the human drama because that non-Western drama is constitutively social before it can become individual. By contrast, death tends to be the end of the book in Western narrative inasmuch as, when the Enlightenment chips are down, we "desocialize" into solitary individuals who aspire, achieve or fail, and die. The folk culture nourishing García-Márquez understands the contours and trajectory of individual being otherwise—as involuntarily cradled within the larger resources of social being. Thus Prudencio comes back to talk with someone who knew him, Amaranta goes forward carrying letters to the dead . . .

23. Lest my remarks about magic realism sound naively laudatory, I acknowledge that no artistic form, however emancipatory, is free from becoming commodified and "mass-produced" by later writers. The signature moves of magic realism, like those of experimental modernism and surrealism earlier, are open to later cliché and exploitation. As early as 1949 Carpentier saw that "[t]he result of willing the marvelous or any other trance is that the dream technicians become bureaucrats. . . . Poverty of the imagination, Unamuno said, is learning codes by heart" ("America," in Zamora and Faris, 85). See, in related fashion, Raymond Williams's *The Politics of Modernism* for incisive commentary on mid-twentieth-century cooptation, by corporate power, of the tonic tropes of an earlier modernism: "The originally precarious and often desperate images—typically of fragmentation, loss of identity, loss of the very grounds of human communication—have been transferred from the dynamic compositions of artists who had been, in majority, literally exiles . . . to become . . . a 'modernist' and 'post-modernist' establishment" (130).

24. Kumkum Sangari, "The Politics of the Possible," *Cultural Critique* 7 (1987): 164; emphasis in the original. Subsequent citation from Sangari refers to this article and will be indicated in the body of my text, parenthetically, following the quote.

25. Chanady, "Territorialization," in Zamora and Faris, 130. Cortázar makes a kindred point when he speaks of *Hopscotch* as a narrative "where everything has value as a sign and not as a theme of description" (cited by Chanady, 139). Put this extremely, the representational model of magic realism becomes indistinguishable from an aesthetics of postmodernism, both of them refusing an arid and played-out mimetic model. Ever since Carpentier's earliest comments about magic realism, however, many critics have mounted a vigorous counterargument, claiming a mimetic *cultural* resonance for these nonmimetic procedures that realism itself could never deliver. For my purposes, this is both a precious distinction and a necessary undertaking, given the degree to which realism has systemically denatured the complexities of non-Western history by representing it within unified (linear-progressive-instrumental) forms of narrative. Postmodern practice, as I argue above in the commentary on Pynchon and Calvino, tends to differ from postcolonial practice on just this issue: the former's verbal texture is often composed of nonreferential, historically "unremembering" signs, whereas García-Márquez's "Elephant" (not to mention Morrison's Beloved) comes to the reader inexhaustibly saturated in extratextual folk custom and racial/ethnic memory.

26. I cannot leave *One Hundred Years of Solitude* without speculating (somewhat along the lines of Chow's and Dash's critiques) upon the complex noninnocence of García-Márquez's representational strategies. As Dash might say, this novel insinuates in its own manner a story of "between colonizers": the Buendías as both descendants of Hispanic colonizers and victims of American-capitalist incursions. Superior to indigenous Indians, they suffer at the hands of foreigners. The text's center-periphery imaginary (Macondo as authenticity, elsewhere—the highlands, the United States—as colorless bureaucracy and power) seems oddly colonial in its

own right. Finally, how better to endorse "native" Buendía vitality than to silhouette it against the unbearable Fernanda of the highlands, a character that the text keeps extensively available for narrative abuse? This text so suspicious of "othering" does its own share of just this activity, and perhaps García-Márquez's shrewdest move is to conclude his novel in a way that intimates interior malaise even as it shows the full destructive measure of external Western incursions.

27. To call Morrison "postcolonial" is not a self-evident claim, nor is it to deny her identity as a Western and an American writer. Yet the crucial phrase in my sentence—"the damage her people suffer from patriarchal paradigms"—may explain my use of the term. As an African American, she knows—in her memories and the stories passed on to her, if not by personal experience—a history of disenfranchisement different from, but deeply related to, that of colonization. In like manner, she can access, as Faulkner cannot, a store of marginalized non-Western forms of thinking and feeling that will be crucial for her own creative practice.

28. Toni Morrison, *Beloved* (New York: Knopf, 1987), 88. Subsequent citation from *Beloved* refers to this edition and will be indicated in the body of my text, parenthetically, after the quote.

29. Toni Morrison, *Paradise* (New York: Knopf, 1998), 73. Subsequent citation from *Paradise* refers to this edition and will be indicated in the body of my text, parenthetically, following the quote.

30. As I explored in fuller detail above, it took Faulkner three prior novels to find his way into the speechless dispossession that is Benjy. Donald Mahan and Bayard Sartoris are trial figures en route to Benjy. Their wounds are as decisive as his, but Faulkner has not yet learned how to make his own language "speak the wound." Once he achieves such speech in Benjy, he brilliantly redeploys it in several of his most memorably afflicted characters (Darl and Vardaman in *As I Lay Dying,* Joe Christmas in *Light in August*).

31. The best study of Faulkner's will to tragedy is Wadlington's *Reading Faulknerian Tragedy* (Ithaca: Cornell University Press, 1987). See also Bleikasten's *Ink of Melancholy* (Bloomington: Indiana University Press, 1990), as well as my *Faulkner's Subject.*

32. Frost, "For Once, Then, Something," in *Robert Frost: Collected Poems, Prose, and Plays,* ed. Edward Connery Latham (New York: Holt, Rinehart, Winston, 1995), 208.

33. I first developed, in *What Else But Love,* this general schema for the creative arc of Morrison's career.

34. Toni Morrison, "Rootedness," in *Toni Morrison: Critical Perspective, Past and Present,* ed. Henry Louis Gates and Kwame Anthony Appiah (New York: Amistad, 1993), 342. Subsequent citation from Morrison's essays and interviews refers to this edition and will be indicated in the body of my text, parenthetically, following the quote. Morrison returns in her essays to the folkloric dimension of her practice: "If my work is to confront a reality unlike that received reality of the West, it must centralize and animate information discredited by the West—discredited not because it is not true or useful or even of some racial value, but because it is information described as 'lore' or 'gossip' or 'sentiment.'" "Memory, Creation, and Writing," cited in Terry Otten, *The Crime of Innocence in the Fiction of Toni Morrison* (Columbia: University of Missouri Press, 1989), 2.

35. *Beloved's* African origin takes the novel—geographically and generically—beyond the familiar territory and procedures of Western realism. Crossing the death barrier is linked, in Morrison's work, to crossing the Newtonian gravity barrier. In both instances the human figure is launched onto a spatial-temporal trajectory incompatible with the limits and powers of individualism. Sula's strange moment of post-death consciousness leads to *Song of Solomon's* "flying Africans"—Morrison is seeking ways to figure life even in the midst of death—and these non-Newtonian tropes coalesce memorably in Beloved. For a suggestive meditation on the use of African American motifs in García Márquez's work (more specifically, the motif of the "flying

Africans" in his story "A Very Old Man with Enormous Wings"), see Kutzinski ("Logic"). Caribbean and slave trade motifs play a telling role in Morrison's *Paradise* as well, surfacing in the Convent women's death-eluding practice of the African-Brazilian religion of Candomblé. See Bouson (*Quiet As It's Kept: Shame, Trauma, and Race in the Novels of Toni Morrison* [Albany: State University of New York, 2000], 238–41) for discussion of how Morrison draws on such folk religion to access ways of thinking and feeling outside the range of Western instrumental reason.

36. Toni Morrison, *Jazz* (New York: Knopf, 1992), 133. Subsequent citation from *Jazz* refers to this edition and will be cited in the body of my text, parenthetically, following the quote.

37. One might compare Joe Trace's fallen Adam with Derek Walcott's "second Eden": "The myth of the noble savage could not be revived, for that myth . . . has all along been the nostalgia of the old world, its longing for innocence. The great poetry of the New World does not pretend to such innocence, its vision is not naïve. Rather, like its fruits, its savor is a mixture of the acid and the sweet, the apples of its second Eden have the tartness of experience. In such poetry there is a bitter memory and it is the bitterness that dies last on the tongue. It is the acidulous that supplies its energy" ("The Muse of History," in Zamora and Faris, 372). It would be hard to better Walcott's sentences in their capacity to gesture toward the post-tragic territory shared by García-Márquez and Morrison. For telling differences between Faulkner's and Morrison's critiques of innocence, see my *What Else But Love?* (115–20).

38. The "rogue" element in *Jazz*—its refusal to proceed "lawfully"—has been noted by Eusebio Rodrigues: "The text, vibrant with sound and rhythm, invites us, we slowly realize, to set aside Cartesian logic in order to enter a magic world that cries out for deeper modes of knowing." "Experiencing Jazz," *Modern Fiction Studies* 39 (1993): 734.

39. Western readers sufficiently inured to realism may fail to note how many lights must be turned off for it to function. Meditation on its procedures allows one to glimpse how cautious and conservative realism is, how taut with epistemological worries—is this real? or merely appearance?—its vigilance requires it to be. Writing about magic realism, Rawdon Wilson speculates on the intrinsic propensity of narrative to exceed the austerity of realist discipline: "The magicalness of magic realism lies in the way it makes explicit (that is, unfolds) what seems always to have been present. Thus the world interpenetration, the dual worldhood [acknowledging both the real and the fabulous] . . . of magic realism . . . are an explicit foregrounding of a kind of fictional space that is perhaps more difficult to suppress than to express. . . . Realism's typical limpidity arises from the muscular suppression of narrative potential" ("Metamorphosis," in Zamora and Faris, 226).

CONCLUSION

1. Adorno: "The being-in-itself to which artworks are devoted is not the imitation of something real but rather the anticipation of a being-in-itself that does not yet exist" (*Aesthetic,* 77).

2. The great text harboring Benjamin's decade-long quest to find liberatory significance within modernity's "phantasmagoric" (his term) production and discarding of commodities is, of course, his posthumous *Arcades Project*. For useful commentary on Benjamin's struggle to find redemptive possibilities within the urban settings—both intellectual and material—of nineteenth- and twentieth-century Europe, see see Terry Eagleton (*Walter Benjamin, or Toward a Revolutionary Criticism* [London: Verso, 1981]; Richard Wolin (*Walter Benjamin: An Aesthetic of Redemption* [New York: Columbia University Press, 1982]; Michael Jennings (*Dialectical Images: Walter Benjamin's Theory of Literary Criticism* [Ithaca: Cornell University Press, 1987]; Margaret Cohen (*Profane Illumination: Walter Benjamin and the Paris of Surrealist Revolution* [Berkeley: University of California Press, 1993]; and the incomparable work of Susan Buck-Morss (*The Dialectic of Seeing: Walter Benjamin and the Arcades Project* [Cambridge: MIT Press, 1991]).

3. For searching commentary on Benjamin's understanding of critique as rescue, see Rolf Tiedemann ("Dialectics at a Standstill," in *Walter Benjamin, The Arcades Project*, trans. Howard Eilen and Kevin McLaughlin [Cambridge: Harvard University Press, 1999], 929—45); Jürgen Habermas ("Walter Benjamin: Consciousness-Raising or Rescuing Critique," in *On Walter Benjamin: Critical Essays and Recollections* [Cambridge: MIT Press, 1988], 90—128), and Jennings.

4. Paul Ricoeur, *Time and Narrative,* trans. Kathleen McLaughlin and David Pellauer (Chicago: University of Chicago Press, 1984–88), 3:118. Subsequent citation from *Time and Narrative* refers to this edition and will be indicated in the body of my text, parenthetically, after the quote.

5. The last piece of the puzzle, that is, unless one considers the earlier discovered but now released and unlocatable Jim Bond as the last piece, the "one nigger left" that—as Shreve says on the book's penultimate page—"[y]ou still hear . . . at night some times" (310).

6. Adorno speaks of our commerce with modern art as necessarily time-laden, requiring a second level of reflection: "The knowledge of art means to render objectified spirit [that which has wrought upon—and now inheres within—the work's form] once again fluid through the medium of reflection" (*Aesthetic* 357). Such spirit remains otherwise, so to speak, congealed—reified and unrecognizable.

7. Keynes's letter is cited in Ann Banfield, *The Phantom Table: Woolf, Fry, Russell, and the Epistemology of Modernism* (Cambridge: Cambridge University Press, 2000), 112.

8. Cathy Caruth, *Unclaimed Experience: Trauma, Narrative, and History* (Baltimore: Johns Hopkins University Press, 1996), 100. Subsequent citation from Caruth refers to this edition and will be indicated in the body of my text, parenthetically, following the quote.

9. I realize that this generalization about postmodern novelistic tendencies cannot account for a good deal of postcolonial fictional practice. As my commentary on García Márquez, Morrison, and Rushdie has suggested, postcolonial fiction is capable of engaging human possibility—as well as human deformity—in ways unavailable to postmodern fiction. It remains true that none of these writers (or others who draw on and revise the resources of magic realism) can ignore the juggernaut of global capitalism and its denaturing of the drama of the subject in space and time. Yet, as hybrid writers, they access their scene by way of opposing cultural traditions whose incompatibility is as fertilizing as it is frustrating. By contrast, Pynchon, Barth, DeLillo, and Calvino (as well as others whom we would designate as postmodern rather than postcolonial) appear to be nourished—and limited—by a more purely Western set of problematics. Enlightenment thought and the realist practice it underwrote loom larger, I believe, in their cultural inheritance, affecting their normative allegiances as well as their experimental departures. Such a claim—especially so briefly and baldly put as in this note—is of course debatable, and in twenty-five years may well seem quaint or wrongheaded. But late-twentieth-century postcolonial and postmodern fictional practices remain sufficiently different, I submit, to justify my argument. Even so, though I do not forget the power of postcolonial procedures, I do not wish to conclude this study of Western fiction in such a way—unavoidably dialectical—as to propose that practice as the answer to questions posed (or avoided) by realism, modernism, and postmodernism. Not least among reasons for refusing to do so is the pell-mell Westernizing of the globe: a process that seems unstoppable (for now), and whose influence on future fictional practice is, so far as I can tell, unknowable.

Index

Aarsleff, Hans, 39

Abraham: as conceived by Kierkegaard, 12, 18–19; as rewritten by Kafka, 15

Absalom, Absalom! (Faulkner), 191–93, 202–5, 231–36; habit versus shock in, 234–36; "here I am" in, 256; patriarchy in, 231–33

"acknowledging," 252–60; as other than knowing, 119–20. *See also* "beyond knowing"; "knowing"; "unknowing"

Adorno, Theodor, 5–6, 106, 111, 115–17, 129, 216; on art and external world, 275n7, 291n21; on art and spirit, 256–57, 302n6; on form as decisive, 191; on identity as ideology, 3; on Kafka, 159; on mimesis, 53; on modernist art as a self-shattering, 175; on subject affinity with object, 116, 216; on Utopian dimension of art, 301n1

Agacinski, Sylviane, 264n12

Altieri, Charles, 53, 282–83nn23–25

"anaclisis": in Freudian thought, 85–86; as fundamental to realist space, 277n18; as subverted in modernism, 96, 165–69. *See also* Freud

Anderson, Perry, 200

Angelus Novus (Klee), 259–60

Anna Karenina (Tolstoy), 60–62

As I Lay Dying (Faulkner), 149–50

Bacon, Francis, 25–26

Bakhtin, Mikhail, 76, 253, 255, 265–66n1, 269n34, 270–71n1

Barker, Francis, 28

Barth, John, 200–201

Baudrillard, Jean, 293n12

Beckett, 118–19; on Proust, 285n11

Beer, Gillian, 273n21

Beloved (Morrison), 247–48

Benjamin, Walter, 5, 7, 136, 258; on Arcades Project, 301–2n2; on Kafka, 136, 159; on Klee's *Angelus Novus*, 259–60; as resisting Enlightenment worldview, 254–55, 258–60, 262–63n10; on tradition, 234–35, 241, 296n6

Bettelheim, Bruno, 80, 274n4

"beyond knowing": in postcolonial and post-modern narratives, 4–5, 117–20, 197–202. *See also* "acknowledging"; "knowing"; "unknowing"

Beyond the Pleasure Principle (Freud), 84, 86–89

Bhabha, Homi, 228

Bleikasten, André, 288–89n39

Bluest Eye, The (Morrison), 245–6

Boccioni, Umberto, 108, 293n3

Bouvard et Pécuchet (Flaubert), 100, 272n13

Bowie, Malcolm, 274–75n5, 282n20

Bowlby, Rachel, 87

Calvino, Italo, 210–16; and Proust, 214–15;
  and Rilke, 206–16
Canetti, Elias, 188
Carpentier, Alejo, 241, 299n23
Caruth, Cathy, 258
Cassirer, Ernst, 29
Castle, The (Kafka), 104, 140–41, 281n13
Certeau, Michel de, 93, 190–91
Chanady, Amaryll, 242, 297n9
Chow, Rey, 298n17
Civilization and Its Discontents (Freud), 89, 91,
  275–76n10
Clarissa (Richardson), 56–57; Diderot on, 56
Cottingham, John, 25
Crary, Jonathan, 271n5
Crews, Frederick, 79–80, 277n19
Crime and Punishment (Dostoevsky), 70–76;
  as ego-logy, 75–76; Nietzschean versus
  Christian motives in, 75–76; as protomod-
  ernism, 73–76; as realism, 70–72
Critique of Pure Reason (Kant), 40–42; iden-
  tity as ground of representations in, 41;
  phenomenal and noumenal in, 42; space
  and time in, 41
Culler, Jonathan, 50

Darwin, Charles, 269n32, 273n21
Dash, J. Michael, 298n17
Daston, Lorraine, 25–26
David Copperfield (Dickens), 12–13, 92–93
death: in postcolonialism, 300–301n35; in
  Proust, 130–35; in realism, 14
Derrida, Jacques, 50, 263n2, 264n5
Descartes, René, 26–31; alienation in, 27–28;
  on dismissal of body, 289–90n6; doubt in,
  26–28; knowing in, 28–30
Descombes, Vincent, 121–22, 291n19
Dialectics of Enlightenment (Adorno and
  Horkheimer), 268n24
Dickens, Charles, 12
Discourse on the Method (Descartes), 28
Doctorow, E. L., 205
Don Quixote (Cervantes), 25

Eddington, Arthur, 103

"ego-logy," 30, 45; of realism, 46–48, 70–76
Eliot, T. S., 135, 155–56
Ellison, David, 83–84, 140
Emma (Austen), 57–58
Encyclopédie (Diderot and d'Alembert), 44
End of the Road, The (Barth), 200–201
Enlightenment narrative of coming to know,
  2–3, 23–25, 45–46; alienation in, 44–45;
  representation in, 46–47; subject/space/
  time in, 44–48. *See also* "knowing"; realism
Ermarth, Elizabeth, 63–64, 69
Essay concerning Human Understanding
  (Locke), 36–39; epistemology in, 38–39;
  experience in, 36–40; selfhood in, 38–39,
  68

Faulkner, William, 1, 4, 14, 154–57, 231–35;
  and García Márquez, 231–43; and Morrison, 243–51; and Pynchon, 202–5; the
  subject as not-I in, 186–93, 255–56; time
  as trauma in, 143–53; uncanny space in,
  111–14
Fear and Trembling (Kierkegaard), 10–19; as
  anti-system, 16–17; as protomodern, 3,
  12–15; suspension of the ethical, the universal, the linguistic in, 16; swimming
  and "swimming" in, 18–19
figure/ground: in modernism, 9–10, 161, 200,
  257–58; in realism, 9, 44
Flags in the Dust (Faulkner), 145–46
Flaubert, Gustave, 99–100; critics on, 50–51,
  272n13
Forster, E. M., 217–22, 225–26; and Rushdie,
  217–30
Foucault, Michel, 69–70, 288n35, 290n8
Freud, Sigmund, 1, 3–4, 6, 79–94, 170,
  291n20; conscious and unconscious
  memory in, 90–91; Freudian space, as
  uncanny, 4, 83–86; Freudian subjectivity, self and/as other, 91–94, 278n26;
  Freudian time, as traumatic/modernist,
  4, 86–91; intersubjectivity in, 92–94; letter to Fliess, 136; limitations as critical
  model, 81–82; as modernist thinker, 1,
  3–4, 79–80; ongoing pertinence of,
  80–81; plotting modernism, 82–83; reality principle and realism, 82–83; and

recovered memory syndrome, 90–91. *See also* "anaclisis"

Frost, Robert, 246

Furst, Lillian, 273n21

García Márquez, Gabriel, 120, 236–43; and Faulkner, 231–43; on Faulkner, 297n9

Gellner, Ernest, 280n7

Giddens, Anthony, 279–80n6

Go Down, Moses (Faulkner), 113–14

Gravity's Rainbow (Pynchon), 202–5

Great Expectations (Dickens), 67

Hacking, Ian, 277–78nn23–24

Heidegger, Martin, 165, 168, 290n7

"here I am": as drama of subject/space/time, 11–12; in Genesis, 11; in Kierkegaard, 11–13; in modernism, 163–69, 256; in postmodernism, 96, 201, 263n3

Holquist, Michael, 60

Hunter, J. Paul, 273n22

Husserl, Edmund, 164

identity. *See* "subject"

Invisible Cities (Calvino), 210–16; "Orientalism" in, 212–13; as postmodern literature of "vocabularies," 210–16

Italian Journey (Goethe), 275n10

Jameson, Fredric, 198–99, 205, 224, 232, 295n3, 298n18

Jazz (Morrison), 248–49

Joyce, James, 261n1

"Judgment, The" (Kafka): subject as other in, 173–74; uncanny space in, 103–4

Judovitz, Dalia, 267n19

Kafka, Franz, 1, 4, 6, 15; meanings of arrest in, 21, 286n19, 286–87n21; subjectivity as accused in, 169–75; time as arrest in, 135–43; uncanny space in, 101–6, 281n15

Kant, Immanuel, 40–44; autonomy in, 43; and God, 42; Kantian ethics, as categorical imperative, 16, 42–43; and Newton, 40–41

Kern, Stephen, 280n12, 292–93n6

Keynes, John Maynard, 257

Kierkegaard, Søren, 3, 11–19; and fictional narrators, 265n15

"knowing": as central to Enlightenment and realism, 2–3, 44–48; as enabled by scientific project of Bacon, Descartes, and Newton, 25–36; as plotted and moralized by Locke and Kant, 36–44. *See also* "acknowledging"; "beyond knowing"; Enlightenment narrative of coming to know; "subject"; "unknowing"

Kofman, Sarah, 276–77n15

Koyré, Alexander, 33

Kramnick, Isaac, 30

Kuhn, Thomas, 266n5, 268n30, 269n37

Lacan, Jacques, 93–94, 233–34

Language of Psycho-Analysis, The (Laplanche and Pontalis), 79, 278–79nn27–28

Laplanche, Jean, 86, 92–94

Latour, Bruno, 284n32, 294n7

Levinas, Emmanuel: biographical context, 262n9; on erasure of time in representation, 46–47, 166–68; on "I" as "here I am," 163; on identity as self-recovery in time, 166–68, 188; on knowing as grasping, 267n17; on narratives of return and of departure, 19; on space/time pact and its rupture, 165–68; on subjectivity as accused, 170, 174–75; as thinker of self-loss, 5, 168–69, 257, 290n13

Levine, George, 28, 63, 99, 271n3

Light in August (Faulkner): subjectivity as not-I in, 189; uncanny space in, 111–13

Lloyd, Genevieve, 69, 271n6

Locke, John, 9, 36–40; Lockean narrative and fictional plot, 40; and Rilke, 208–10; Voltaire on, 36;

Lyotard, J. F., 252, 273nn23–24

Macbeth (Shakespeare), 156

MacIntyre, Alasdair, 43, 97–98, 267n12

Madame Bovary (Flaubert), 99–100

magic realism: as non-Newtonian genre, 5; in *One Hundred Years of Solitude*, 240–43; and postmodern refusal of mimesis, 299n25; in *The Satanic Verses*, 229–30

Mann, Thomas, 261n1

Mathematical Principles of Natural Philosophy (Newton), 31–36; atoms in, 32–33; gravity in, 5, 33–35; laws of motion in, 33–36; space and time in, 33; system of the world in, 34–36

McKeon, Michael, 265n1, 279nn4–5

Meditations (Descartes), 25–27

Merleau-Ponty, Maurice, 164

"Metamorphosis, The" (Kafka), 135–36, 281n15

Mill on the Floss, The (Eliot), 60–62

Minkowski, Eugene, 280n12

misrecognition. *See* recognition and misrecognition

modernism: "acknowledging" in, 252–60; difference from modernity, 24; hopefulness of, 6–7; as identificatory, 7, 203–5; and judgment, 187–89; masculine bias of, 294n6; and postmodernism, 4–5, 202–5, 214–15, 223–26, 236–51; and realism, 1–3; as shock, 114–17, 165–69; as style rather than plot, 190–92; as trouble, 160–62, 287n27. *See also* "unknowing"

modernist space, as uncanny: in Faulkner, 111–13; in Kafka, 101–6; in Proust, 106–111; in Rilke, 206–10. *See also* modernism; "space"

modernist subjectivity: as accused in Kafka, 169–75; as not-I in Faulkner, 186–93; as self-and-other in Proust, 175–85. *See also* modernism; "subject"; "unknowing"

modernist time: as arrest in Kafka, 135–43; as trauma in Faulkner, 143–53; as unbound in Proust, 121–35. *See also* modernism; "time"

Molloy (Beckett), 118–19

Morrison, Toni, 243–51; interviews, 246, 300n34

Nagel, Thomas, 198

narrative and time, 44–48, 68–69; in St. Augustine's *Confessions*, 69

naturalism, as revision of realism, 280n10, 296n2

nature, as construed in Enlightenment, 25–26

Nausea (Sartre), 3, 160, 262n3

Newton, Isaac, 30–36; and God, 31–32, 35; letter to Bentley, 31–32; and Adam Smith, 35; Voltaire on, 24–25

Nietzsche, Friedrich, 159

Notebooks of Malte Laurids Brigge, The (Rilke), 157; modernist disorientation in, 206–210

One Hundred Years of Solitude (García Márquez), 120, 236–43; beyond patriarchy, 240–41; community as orientation, 238–39; and Faulkner's fiction, 297n12; folklore in, 239, 298n16; magic realism in, 240–43; postcolonial release in, 237–43; privileged binaries in, 299–300n26

Paradise (Morrison), postcolonial release from Newtonian constraints, 248–51

Parsons, Charles, 41

Passage to India, A (Forster), 217–22; crisis of knowing in, 220–21; failure of subject-passage in, 217–20; ideology in, 218–20, 235–36

phenomenology, 163–69; as philosophical model for modernism, 283n26

Pilgrim's Progress (Bunyan), 54–55

Polk, Noel, 288–89nn39–40

postcolonialism: and community, 238–39; and modernism, 236–51; and postmodernism, 217–18, 229–30, 294–95n1, 299n25; release from patriarchal norms, 240–41, 250–51

postmodernism: as "beyond knowing," 117–20; and hyperspace, 197–202, 210–16, 224–30; as literature of "vocabularies," 7; and modernism, 202–5, 214–15, 223–26; and postcolonialism, 217–18, 229–30, 294–95n1, 299n25

Prendergast, Christopher, 50–53, 57, 64

Proust, Marcel, 1, 4; subject and/as other in, 175–85; unbound time in, 121–35; uncanny space in, 106–111

Pynchon, Thomas: and Faulkner, 202–5

Quine, W. V. O., 117

realism: canny space of, 97–100; contradictions in, 44, 62–63; and credibility, 53–54;

and deconstruction, 49–51; and its discontents, 49–54; ethics and temporality of, 47–48; familiarizing the subject in, 59–63; family in, 60–63; introducing the subject in, 54–59; as judgment-centered, 187–89; Kantian morality of, 60–62; memory in, 67–70; misrecognition as recognition in, 70–76; and readerly versus writerly texts, 49–50; as not reality, 276–77n15; and "really," 66–67; recognition in, 64–70; representation in, 52–53; space and time travel in, 63–66; verisimilitude in, 52–53. *See also* Enlightenment narrative of coming to know

la Recherche (Proust). See *Remembrance of Things Past* (Proust)

recognition and misrecognition, 64–70; in Dostoevsky, 70–76; in Eliot (T. S.), 155–56; in Faulkner, 154–57, 162; in Freud, 89–91; in Proust, 131–35

Remembrance of Things Past (Proust): dynamic of narratorial authority in, 179–85; embodiment and disembodiment in, 180–83; neurosis in, 107–9; the present as defective in, 126–27; subject and/as other in, 175–85; time as photographic in, 129–33; time as trauma in, 127–31; translations of, 281–82n18; unbound time in, 121–35; uncanny space in, 106–11; unplottedness in, 123–26

Reiss, Timothy, 24–26, 36, 47, 51

Requiem for a Nun (Faulkner), time as recovery in, 154–57

Ricoeur, Paul, 255

Riggs, David, 267n10

Rilke, Rainer Maria, 7, 206–10; and Calvino, 206–16; and Locke, 208–9

Robbins, Jill, 17, 263n1

Robinson Crusoe (Defoe), 46–48, 57

Rodrigues, Eusebio, 301n38

Rorty, Richard, 37, 117–18, 262n7, 269n40

Rushdie, Salman, 63, 223–30

Russell, Bertrand, 289n5

Sanctuary (Faulkner), time as trauma in, 148–53

Sangari, Kumkum, 241–42

Sartre, Jean-Paul, 3, 160, 253, 262n3

Satanic Verses, The (Rushdie), 63, 223–30; hybridity in, 223–25; non-Newtonian representation in, 223–24; as postmodern and postcolonial, 229–30; shattering of subjectivity in, 226–28

Saussurean linguistics, as deconstructive model, 50–51

Scheewind, J. B., 42

Schleifer, Ronald, 290n9

Sentimental Education (Flaubert), 272n13

Siegel, Robert, 117

Sound and the Fury, The (Faulkner), 18; not-I in, 186; time as trauma in, 146–48; tragic insistence in, 244–45

"space," 2–10, 25–36; as hyperspace in postmodernism, 114–20, 197–202; as lawful in realism, 54–59, 63–66, 97–100; as uncanny in modernism, 101–14. *See also* "subject"; "time"

"subject," 2–10, 261–62n2; as birthed in Descartes, 26–31; as dependent on conventions of space and time, 2–4; as moralized by Kant, 40–44; as operative in Enlightenment narrative and realism, 44–48, 97–100; as plotted by Locke, 36–40. *See also* Enlightenment narrative of coming to know; "knowing"; "space"; "time"; "unknowing"

subjectivity, modernist: in Faulkner, as not-I, 186–93; in Freud, as self-deluded, 91–94; in Kafka, as accused, 169–75; in Proust, as self-and-other, 175–85

subjectivity, postmodern: as "assumptions" (in Calvino), 210–16; as fictive (in Beckett, Barth, and Pynchon), 118–19, 197–205; as hybrid and incommensurable (in Rushdie), 223–30; as undermined, 114–20

Steinmetz, Horst, 138

Sula (Morrison), 246–47

Sulloway, Frank, 277n21

Sussman, Henry, 216

Swinburne, Richard, 206–7

S/Z (Barthes), 49–50

Taussig, Michael, 114

Taylor, Charles, 97

"time," 2–10; in Faulkner, 143–57; in Kafka; 135–43; in modernism, 157–62; in post-modernism, 197–202; in Proust, 121–35; in realism, 47–48, 63–70. *See also* "space"; "subject"

Toulmin, Stephen, 23–24

Town, The (Faulkner), 143

Trial, The (Kafka): nonprogressive time in, 136–39, 141–43; and postmodernist proto-cols, 200–201; subject as other in, 171–72; uncanny space in, 101–3

trauma: Faulkner's rhetoric of, 88, 145–51

Ulysses (Joyce), 261n1

"unknowing": as central in Kafka, Proust, and Faulkner, 1–2, 9; as interrelation of subject, space, and time, 1–5, 8–10, 157–62. *See also* "acknowledging"; "beyond knowing"; "knowing"

"Uncanny, The" (Freud), 84–85, 95–96, 282n19, 285n10. *See also* Faulkner: uncanny space in; Kafka: uncanny space in; Proust: uncanny space in

Vattino, Gianni, 293n12

Walcott, Derek, 301n37

War and Peace (Tolstoy), 67, 126

Watt, Ian, 55, 64–65, 265n1

Weinstein, Philip, 293n10

"What is Enlightenment?" (Kant), 43, 93

Williams, Raymond, 283–84n28, 299n23

Wilson, Rawdon, 301n39

Wings of the Dove, The (James), 58–59

Woolf, Virginia, 261n1

Woolhouse, Roger, 37–38

Yolton, John, 28, 37, 50–51, 268n23

Zamora, Lois, 237